Lecture Notes in Computer Science

Edited by G. Goos, J. Hartmanis and J. van Leeuwen

Advisory Board: W. Brauer   D. Gries   J. Stoer

Springer

Berlin
Heidelberg
New York
Barcelona
Budapest
Hong Kong
London
Milan
Paris
Tokyo

Juhani Iivari Kalle Lyytinen
Matti Rossi (Eds.)

Advanced Information Systems Engineering

7th International Conference, CAiSE '95
Jyväskylä, Finland, June 12-16, 1995
Proceedings

Springer

Series Editors

Gerhard Goos
Universität Karlsruhe
Vincenz-Priessnitz-Straße 3, D-76128 Karlsruhe, Germany

Juris Hartmanis
Department of Computer Science, Cornell University
4130 Upson Hall, Ithaca, NY 14853, USA

Jan van Leeuwen
Department of Computer Science, Utrecht University
Padualaan 14, 3584 CH Utrecht, The Netherlands

Volume Editors

Juhani Iivari
Kalle Lyytinen
Matti Rossi
Department of Computer Science and Information Systems
University of Jyväskylä
P.O. Box 35, FIN-40351 Jyväskylä, Finland

CR Subject Classification (1991): H.2, D.2, H.5.2-3, H.1, K.6.3-4

ISBN 3-540-59498-1 Springer-Verlag Berlin Heidelberg New York

CIP data applied for

© Springer-Verlag Berlin Heidelberg 1995
Printed in Germany

Typesetting: Camera-ready by author
SPIN: 10486266   06/3142 - 543210 - Printed on acid-free paper

Preface

CAiSE•95 was the seventh International Conference on Information Systems Engineering. It was held in Jyväskylä, Finland, 12-16 June 1995. The conference continued the tradition of the previous years, when CAiSE was held in Stockholm, Trondheim, Manchester, Paris, and Utrecht. These conferences have established a reputation of providing a lively meeting point for researchers and practioners. People from academia and industry come in growing numbers to these events to exchange ideas and experiences in methods, tools and techniques and thereby improve the way we manage, design and implement advanced information systems.

The general theme of CAiSE•95 was Information Systems Engineering: Current Practice and Future Prospects. Concerning current practice, CAiSE•95 aimed at soliciting empirical contributions describing and evaluating the current adoption and diffusion of information systems engineering (ISE) technologies (methods and tools) in practice. Concerning the future, CAiSE•95 invited contributions introducing new emerging ISE technologies, methods and tools. The international Programme Committee, with representatives from 20 countries, received 101 papers. Each paper was reviewed by three referees using a double-blind process. These conference proceedings include the outcome of the process: 26 papers selected by the Program Committee and the contributions of the three invited speakers.

A conspicious feature of the submissions was the paucity of empirical papers on the current practice of ISE. Consequently, the accepted papers predominantly address the future prospects of ISE. The accepted papers are of high academic quality and treat a broad variety of topics including requirements engineering, conceptual modelling, behaviour modelling, metamodelling, process modelling, object orientation, reuse, CASE integration, user interface issues and software engineering issues. The research approaches followed in these papers range from conceptual analysis to formal modelling, experimental studies and constructive prototypes. The keynote speeches address the future prospects of process improvement, the impact of new information architectures on industry and government redesign, and industry experiences in large-scale development of object-oriented applications.

CAiSE•95 comprised a two-day programme of workshops and tutorials before the beginning of the conference itself. Workshops were organized on topics including requirements engineering, next generation CASE tools, end-user development with visual programming and object-orientation. Also included among the workshops was a doctoral consortium for Ph.D. students in the area of information systems engineering. Tutorials formed the backbone of the industrial programme and addressed object-orientation, database reverse engineering, workflow automation and method integration. The conference programme was further supplemented with panels, poster sessions and product presentations. As a result, the programme of CAiSE•95 continued the tradition of offering an excellent arena for practitioners and researchers to exchange and share ideas on advanced information systems engineering.

Finally, we wish to express our gratitude to all those individuals and institutions who have made this conference and these proceedings possible: to the authors for making significant contributions to the field of Information Systems Engineering; to the members of the Programme Committee and the additional referees for carefully reviewing the papers; to the publisher for the pleasant co-operation; to the local organizers for sharing the workload involved; to the participants without whom there would be no conference; and to the sponsors for helping to make this possible.

March 1995

Juhani Iivari
Kalle Lyytinen
Matti Rossi

General Conference Chair

Kalle Lyytinen

Programme Committee Chair

Juhani Iivari

Organising Chair

Anna-Liisa Takkinen

Programme Committee

Rudolf Andersen
Richard Baskerville
Sjaak Brinkkemper
Janis Bubenko
Sue Conger
Panos
Constantopoulos
Valeria De Antonellis
Jan Dietz
Eric Dubois
Eckhard Falkenberg
Anthony Finkelstein
Göran Goldkuhl
Hele-Mai Haav
Terry Halpin
Igor Hawryszkiewycz
Matthias Jarke
Keith Jeffery

Paul Johannesson
Hannu Kangassalo
Pentti Kerola
Rob Kusters
Eva Lindecrona
Frederick Lochovsky
Pericles Loucopoulos
Pertti Marttiin
Lars Mathiassen
Robert Meersman
David Monarchi
John Mylopoulos
Ron Norman
Antoni Olive
Andreas L. Opdahl
Terttu Orci
Barbara Pernici
Naveen Prakash

Colette Rolland
Gunter Saake
Amilcar Sernadas
Henk Sol
Arne Sølvberg
Stefano Spaccapietra
Bernhard Thalheim
Costantino Thanos
Babis Theodoulidis
Juha Pekka Tolvanen
Aimo Törn
Yair Wand
Benkt Wangler
Roel Wieringa
Gerard Wijers
Stanislaw Wrycza
Roberto Zicari

Additional Referees

Meike Albrecht
Margita Altus
Esa Auramäki
Herman Balsters
Philippe Brèche
Silvana Castano
Corine Cauvet
Rolf Engmann
Fabrizio Ferrandina
Massimo Gentile
Paul Grefen

Georges Grosz
Remigijus Gustavs
Sari Hakkarainen
Frank Harmsen
Peter Hartel
Peter Holm
Stef Joosten
Steven Kelly
Kari Kuutti
Sven E. Lautemann
Erkki Lehtinen

Han Oei
Harri Oinas-Kukkonen
Stefano Paraboschi
Erik Proper
Matti Rossi
Michael Rüger
Markku Sakkinen
Ingo Schmitt
Carine Souveyet
William Song
Can Tüerker

Organising Committee

Taru-Maija Heilala
Juhani Iivari
Erkki Lehtinen

Kalle Lyytinen
Risto Nevalainen
Seppo Puuronen

Matti Rossi
Anna-Liisa   Takkinen

Contents

Keynote Speech

Process Improvement: The Way Forward   1
M. M. Lehman

Behaviour Modelling

A Method for Explaining the Behaviour of Conceptual Models   12
A. Olivé, M.-R. Sancho
COLOR-X: Linguistically-based Event Modeling: A General Approach to   26
Dynamic Modeling
J. F. M. Burg, R. P. van de Riet
Supporting Transaction Design in Conceptual Modelling of Information   40
Systems
J. A. Pastor-Collado, A. Olivé

Requirements Engineering

Facet Models for Problem Analysis   54
A. L. Opdahl, G. Sindre
A Framework for Requirements Analysis Using Automated Reasoning   68
D. Duffy, C. MacNish, J. McDermid, P. Morris
Towards a Deeper Understanding of Quality in Requirements Engineering   82
J. Krogstie, O. I. Lindland, G. Sindre

OO Concepts and Applications

Modelling inheritance, composition and relationship links between objects,   96
object versions and class versions
E. Andonoff, G. Hubert, A. Le Parc, G. Zurfluh
Hypertext Version Management in an Actor-based Framework   112
A. Dattolo, V. Loia

Work and Communication Modelling

Modelling Ways-of-Working   126
V. Plihon, C. Rolland
Modelling Communication between Cooperative Systems   140
F. Dignum, H. Weigand

Invited Speech

Challenges in Applying Objects Large Systems   154
J.-M. Aalto

Metamodelling

Feasibility of Flexible Information Modelling Support   168
T. F. Verhoef, A.H.M. ter Hofstede
A Meta-Model for Business Rules in Systems Analysis   186
H. Herbst
Metrics in Method Engineering   200
M. Rossi, S. Brinkkemper

User Interface Issues

InfoHarness: Use of Automatically Generated Metadata for Search and   217
Retrieval of Heterogeneous Information
L. Shklar, A. Sheth, V. Kashyap, K. Shah
Designing the User Interface on Top of a Conceptual Model   231
M. Pettersson
Graphical Representation and Manipulation of Complex Structures Based   243
on a Formal Model
G. Viehstaedt, M. Minas

CASE Integration

Providing Integrated Support for Multiple Development Notations   255
J. C. Grundy, J. R. Venable
A Federated Approach to Tool Integration   269
M. Bounab, C. Godart

Reuse

Domain Knowledge Reuse During Requirements Engineering   283
M. D. Gibson, K. Conheeney
Strategies and Techniques: Reusable Artifacts for the Construction of   297
Database Management Systems
A. Geppert, K. R. Dittrich

Keynote Speech

The Impact of New Information Architectures on Industry and Government   311
Transformation
G. Bracchi

Conceptual Modelling Issues

Standard Transformations for the Normalization of ER Schemata 313
O. Rauh, E. Stickel
The Rapid Application and Database Development (RADD) Workbench -- 327
A Comfortable Database Design Tool
M. Albrecht, E. Buchholz, A. Düsterhöft, M. Altus, B. Thalheim
A Psychological Study on the Use of Relationship Concept -- 341
Some Preliminary Findings
K. Siau, Y. Wand, I. Benbasat

Software Development Issues

Alignment of Software Quality and Service Quality 355
P. Parmakson
A Guide for Software Maintenance Evaluation: Experience Report 366
V. Narat, A. Vila
Natural Naming in Software Development: Feedback from Practitioners 375
K. Laitinen

Process Improvement - The Way Forward

M M Lehman
Department of Computing
Imperial College of Science, Technology and Medicine
London SW7 2BZ
tel.:+44 (0)171 594 8214
fax: +44 (0)171 594 8215
email: mml@doc.ic.ac.uk

1   Introduction

Means for evolving, that is, developing, adapting and enhancing E-type[1] [LEH80] software have been significantly advanced over the years. Continuing efforts to improve the process of software evolution have produced numerous concepts, methods, techniques and tools. High level languages, structured programming, abstract data types, formal methods, non-procedural programming, CASE environments and object orientation exemplify innovations expected to overcome problems that have for so long [NAU69] frustrated consistent, cost effective, on-time development of functionally satisfactory and reliable software. Such innovation did indeed yield process-local benefit. Introduction of structured programming and high level languages, for example, greatly improved program design and coding. The study of programming methodology [GRI78] led to major advances in computer science and to the development of formal methods. These, in turn, provided opportunities for increasing individual and small group effectiveness by facilitating CASE based process mechanisation. Continuing technical innovation has played a significant role in major growth in size and functional complexity of computing applications and systems.

It has, however, not yielded a panacea, neither a silver bullet [BRO86] nor a philosophers' stone [TUR86]. Many problems still haunt industrial software development [GIB94]. Introduction of improved methods, techniques and tools into practice has not yielded a consistent capability for planned, on time, controlled-cost development of quality software. Nor has it resulted in major productivity growth, cost reduction or faster response to user needs. It has proven equally difficult to achieve major improvement in maintaining systems satisfactory as user needs and expectations change in evolving application and operational domains. Software evolution from concept to first installation and from release to release relies on processes still far from satisfactory [GIB94].

Despite the belief of major industrial organisations to the contrary [MAJ93] it may, of course, be unreasonable to expect order of magnitude improvement from individual innovations or in the overall process. Anticipation of benefit is, after all, not a proof that it is attainable. Software development is a creative, intellectual activity requiring human involvement, learning, judgment, decision and revision. It can be supported but not replaced by mechanisation. This by itself limits increases in global process quality, productivity and responsiveness. Moreover, since the operational

---

[1] *E*-type software is informally defined as software that implements an application or addresses a problem in the real world [LEH78]

environment undergoes continual change software products cannot, for long, remain fault free [LEH91]. The consequent need for continual change and evolution presents a further major obstacle to overall process effectiveness. There may well be others. Software development is intrinsically and will always remain a challenging and hazardous enterprise.

Nevertheless, the consistent failure of innovative ideas to yield major improvement in E-type processes despite their apparent effectiveness in S-type[2] [LEH80,95] programming suggests that there may be some common *cause* or *causes* constraining the former. If that is so, its identification should provide clues as to how more effective software processes might be achieved.

One possible cause is immediately apparent. Technical development is only one of many software process activities. Project management, user support, application analysis, marketing and enterprise management, for example, all contribute to system evolution, absorbing resources and impacting progress. All influence software process and product attributes. Individual innovations impact directly only a fraction of the total activity. Global impact of any single innovation must, therefore, be limited.

The slow rate of progress may also relate to the number or diversity of people and organisations involved in E-type application development, the complexity of the organisations and the processes executed and controlled or specific characteristics of E-type systems [LEH94B]. Each of these factors could explain the continuing difficulty in achieving major improvement.

2   Feedback and the Software Process

Recently a more basic constraint on process improvement has been suggested [LEH94]. It relates to the role of feedback in S-type and E-type processes respectively. By definition, the specification of an S-type program completely defines what is to be implemented. Its operational domain is bounded by a specification which is sacrosanct. Conformance to the specification completely determines, in a mathematical sense, *correctness* of the program and its parts. If, at any time and for whatever reason, the specification is considered unsatisfactory, if for example it does not fully address client needs, a *new* one must be generated and a *new* program to satisfy it developed. Each may be derivable from its predecessor. But technically both are new since specification *changes* are ruled out by definition. Validation of the specification and, when necessary, its revision is entirely separated from the process transforming the specification into its program implementation. Feedback, iteration, backtracking over process steps may be used to achieve convergence to a solution, to rectify errors or to escape from *blind alleys* but not to increase fitness for purpose by change of the specification. The global S-type process is, by definition, open-loop. In so far as changing perceptions, opportunities and needs require adaptation, enhancement or extension of an S-type system it evolves as a succession of new systems rather than by changes to its parts.

In strong contrast, the applications and operational domains realised by E-type programs are unbounded [LEH94B]. Knowledge about them cannot be absolute or complete. As a model of the application in its domain the bounded E-type system is an

---

[2] *S*-type software is required to be *correct* in the full mathematical sense with respect to a fixed specification [LEH78]

abstraction of *reality*. Behavioural judgments and pragmatic inputs about implementation resources and technology play a major role in setting the properties of the model. The gap between the reality of the application in its operational domain and the system model is bridged by assumptions [LEH91]. This gap must be maintained sufficiently narrow to ensure that, in usage, program behaves as required, that the system as a model reflects reality to the extent needed. The concept of *correctness* determining the acceptability of *S*-type programs is replaced by user *satisfaction* with the domain covered, system behaviour, program functionality and program execution [LEH91]. But experience, insight and understanding acquired during system evolution and usage generate new perceptions, needs and opportunities, changing expectations and criteria of satisfaction; and the external world also changes independently. Constant observation and a stream of information drive, guide and control system evolution to maintain user satisfaction as the application, its operational domain and user perception of both change. Bounds are continually redrawn during development and usage as feedback provides information and impetus for controlled change. The very nature [TUR81,LEH91,95] of real world applications and of the *E*-type software that models and implements them sets up continuing pressure for change and evolution based on observation, experience, learning, judgment and decision. Some of the information communicated serves to enlighten recipients. Other is used to control future execution of the activity that generated the information. It constitutes genuine feedback control [OXF81]. In contrast to *S*-type development the *E*-type process is inherently closed loop with iteration and backtracking guided and controlled by feedback from users, developers, managers and many others [LEH69,85]. The regular system dynamics that results determines many of the characteristics of the evolution process [BEL72, LEH85].

The significance of feedback in the software process and its role in determining the dynamics of that process has long been recognised. It was referred to in passing by several speakers at the Garmisch Conference [NAU69]. At about the same time it was briefly discussed in the 1969 *Programming Process* [LEH69] report. The first tangible evidence of an identifiable dynamics of evolution followed some years later [BEL72]. More detailed studies were reported in subsequent papers [BEL72, LEH85]. As an example brief mention may be made of the early identification of the feedback stabilised and controlled growth characteristics of OS/360 and other systems [LEH80] as illustrated in the growth plot reproduced in the figure below.

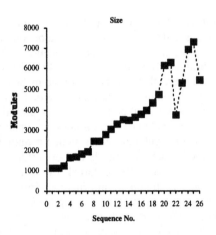

Fig. 1 The growth of OS/360

The cyclic pattern discernible in this plot is characteristic of feedback systems. As observed at the time [LEH72] "… the ripple is typical of a self stabilising process with positive and negative feedback loops. From a long-range point of view the rate of system growth is self-regulatory, despite the fact that many different causes control the selection of work implemented in each release, with budgets varying, increasing numbers of users reporting faults or desiring new capability, varying management attitudes towards system enhancement, changing release intervals and improving methods.…". The period of instability beyond release twenty representing OS/360 fission some months after the '72 paper was published is equally indicative of the feedback nature of the software release process. The oscillatory behaviour indicates a loss of control over system evolution. It is consistent with all known facts that this chaotic behaviour was triggered by over ambitious growth targets, that is, excessive positive feedback.

Further analysis of these and observations on a number of other systems [LEH80] led to identification of five laws of program evolution [LEH74,78,85]. These reflect human and organisational attributes and behaviour rather then software technology. From within the technology they must, therefore, be accepted as laws. More recent studies of organisational and managerial aspects of software process dynamics have developed techniques for the exploitation of that dynamics [ABD91]. Taken together the results of this work provide the basis for an emerging theory of software evolution [LEH85,91, ABD91].

3   A Consequence of Feedback Control

The 1969 - 72 studies from which the feedback nature of the software process was first inferred were restricted to release level evolution. But information generation and feedback play a major role at all levels of the process. Processes of *E*-type evolution constitute multi-level, multi-loop feedback systems. Loop characteristics and those of their mechanisms determine process dynamics. Such processes may therefore be expected to display the stable behaviour which is the hallmark of feedback systems in general [LEH94]. Despite changes in the characteristics of forward path elements and in the operational environment externally observable system properties are held relatively constant by negative feedback within specified limits over the operational range until, as a consequence of excessive positive feedback, instability sets in.

The above observations may have been interpreted in the context of the transformation processes applied to refine computer application concepts into solution systems. After all, the 1970s investigation concentrated on technical development. Their relevance is, however, much wider. Management, customer support, quality assurance, process engineering and so on all apply feedback controls derived from monitoring and reporting mechanisms, checks and balances. More feedback and control comes from the organisational (business) environment. Technical developers and their management seek to meet project goals. The software process is changed as participants and software process engineers observe the effectiveness and appropriateness of the current process, as technology advances. Organisational processes use feedback procedures to ensure steady business and organisational growth with disciplined product evolution as, for example, user experience and changing client needs are reported and economic circumstances change.

There can be no doubt that feedback based control plays a significant role in software development processes and in the improvement of such processes. In accordance with the stability property of feedback controlled systems, changes to forward path elements of such processes cannot, therefore, be expected to produce major global improvement unless accompanied by commensurate changes to related feedback mechanisms [LEH94]. Software process improvement must be pursued in the context of the total process domain and the feedback controls that regulate its behaviour. That domain includes, amongst others, users of all types, corporate management, marketing, customer and user support, project, process and information management, technical development, quality assurance, process engineering, interaction with related processes, process improvement and monitoring of all these. Such a broad focus provides a realistic framework for the study of process effectiveness, process dynamics and changes in both.

The innovations listed in the opening paragraph were all forward path mechanisms. Yet their introduction into practice did not, in general, include a comprehensive review of total process-domain and its feedback controls. Thus though their adoption may have changed local process properties it should not come as a surprise that the wider impact was far less than expected. It is suggested that a common factor constraining major software process improvement has been a lack of attention to the impact of feedback on forward path innovation. Support for this conclusion is provided by the positive contributions arising from the introduction of innovative techniques such as *inspection, reviews, prototyping, incremental* and *evolutionary development* and the emerging *metrics technology*. These techniques all include a strong negative feedback control component. Their potential for major impact on global process effectiveness provides further support for the feedback hypothesis.

4 The FEAST Conjecture

The above above observations have been formalised in the following conjecture:

As a multi loop feedback system the E-type software process will display global invariance characteristics

This conjecture includes three separate and distinct assertions

I   The *software evolution process* for *E*-type systems constitutes a complex feedback system

II Process feedback is likely to limit the benefit derived from individual forward path changes

III Major process improvement requires that changes to individual steps are accompanied by adjustment of feedback paths and/or mechanisms

The first assertion is undeniable. The others follow from the global stability characteristic property of other feedback systems. If, as seems likely, the software process as a feedback system also possesses this property, improvement resulting from changes to one of its forward path mechanisms will be constrained by pre-existing negative feedback. To remove such constaints requires examination, probable modification, possible removal of at least some of the feedback controls that are almost certain to be in place. But can examination and adjustment of process feedback can be systematised? Can software process feedback design be disciplined? The general theory and practice of analysis, control and design of feedback systems is advanced and well understood. A question arises in the case of the software process because of the major, independent and creative role of the many individuals involved in the process, the varied roles they fullfill, the unpredictable nature of their influence on feedback information. Humans observe and participate in the process and in the operation of its product. They manipulate and control information fed over paths that link organisations, activities, *spaces* [BEN93] and people involved in system and process evolution. They *observe, interpret, verbalise, transform, communicate, assess, decide, control* and *apply* both forward and feedback information. They feed back their interpretation to other units involved in the evolution. Each of these acts imposes a personal stamp on the information. One must, therefore, ask whether human involvement is so extensive, so ingrained, so individual, so judgmental, so creative that meaningful and exploitable formalisation and modelling with optimised design and integration of the feedback mechanisms is, at least for the moment, beyond reach, cannot be disciplined? The issue is not the validity of the assertions but their practical implications.

5   Exploiting Process Feedback

To exploit feedback one must be able to model the process and its dynamics. Techniques currently employed in process modelling do not, in general, provide the necessary facilities since they have not sought to reflect detailed feedback properties. But relevant formalisms and methods have been developed in other areas. Comprehensive techniques for feedback design and control of continuous and of stochastic systems is embodied, for example, in control theeory and in dynamic systems theory. Both have been extended and applied, though admittedly with limited success, to systems involving humans; economic systems, organisational dynamics and the application of control theory to software development [WOO79, LEH85, ABD91], for example. There exists, therefore, a *prima facie* case suggesting that models reflecting feedback mechanisms may be successfully developed and applied to the design and improvement of software processes at least at levels of detail where statistical abstraction of people activity has meaning. Such models are an essential tool if the above conjecture is to be exploitable for the process of process improvement. Modelling techniques that will permit the representation and evaluation of *all* aspects of the process are an urgent necessity.

In the many spaces in which the process operates and at the many levels of detail at which it occurs feedback may take one of two forms. *Control feedback* describes the situation in which information derived from information originating at an output of some process elemen is injected, after some delay, to an input of that or an earlier element to effect some form of control. It is this meaning of feedback that is studied in, for example, control theory where it refers to a control signal derived directly from a mechanism, from the change in value of some output variable relative to a previously observed value, from the rate of change of a variable and so on. But the term *feedback* is also used colloquially to refer to information flow without any indication as to how, where or when, if at all, that information is to be used. It provides *enlightenment*, advances human *understanding*, facilitates *learning*. Since no control information is derived, such feedback can have no analysable impact on the processes from which it stems or which it reaches.

In the context of the software process both usages are relevant. At levels, where interest and concern focus on the work of individuals, isolated, and in some sense spontaneous and unpredictable, items of information are fed for use as seen fit by the recipient. That recipient may choose not to act directly in response to the information though it may, nevertheless, effect further action as a consequence of its impact on *understanding*, *viewpoint*, *attitude* and so on. But any changes in the latter are all internal to the individual or individuals concerned. As such, they cannot be reflected in process models or formal descriptions of the system dynamic, at most, as noise or randomised variations on unit inputs. Decision to take action (or to take no action), on the other hand, leads to a control action. This situation is an instance of the first, the normal, engineering usage of feedback. Whether these low level aspects of feedback loops and mechanisms in the software process and their impact can be modelled and exploited, requires further investigation .

At higher levels of the process there will be many continuing streams of (discrete) information. The same distinction must, nevertheless be made. Where information is simply absorbed its receipt will not directly impact the process. Where the information is assessed for possible action a control signal is derived, though if the decision is not to act (for the moment) that control signal may be a null signal. Here too the term *feedback* is being used in its normal engineering connotation. Nevertheless, because of the non determinacy of human involvement its modelling and management poses difficult technical and managerial problems.

The belief that systematic techniques for the observation, measurement, modelling and management of feedback can be developed stems from the fact that the total information flow in the process generally involves many decisions. The information fed back and, more significantly, the resultant action is a composite of many inputs. These, whilst not absolutely predictable or independent, are amenable to meaningful statistical representation and analysis [LEH80]. Consequent system behaviour has been shown to display statistically *normal* properties [CHO81]. It is therefore reasonable to expect that at these levels of the software process, control theoretic and statistical process models reflecting the system dynamics can be developed for use on their own or in conjunction with modelling techniques currently in vogue. When statistical representation is not meaningful new formalisms will have to supplement current process modelling techniques. At this level simulation techniques would likely constitute an important element of the design and evaluation process.

6   Feedback as the Constraint on Process Improvement

Reasoning as outlined above has suggested that the *common cause* referred to in section 1 is related to the feedback nature of the evolution process. Whether it *explains* the failure of process innovations such as those identified in the opening paragraph to produce impact of the order of magnitude anticipated at the global level remains to be determined. In truth many, if not all, of the innovations yielded significant benefit at the local level, improving the effectiveness of individual process steps or activities significantly. As an example consider the conception and introduction of high level languages. This certainly increased the quality, productivity and predictability of program code development and its changeability by an order of magnitude. What is now suggested is that the constraining effect of feedback has prevented the full potential of such languages from being experienced at the global level. And so for other innovations.

The feedback hypothesis provides an explanation that is consistent with an established property of other feedback systems. But that observation by itself does not *prove* that the lack of major advances in process improvement is due to this common cause. It could still be primarily due to reasons specific to each innovation. In view of the number of such failures a common cause must, however, be suspected. It is, therefore, of interest to examine innovations individually in the context of processes within which they have been employed to determine whether their limited impact at the global level can be attributed to the constraining effect of feedback control. If it can, it can be overcome by modifying the feedback structure. Failure would not prove the conjecture invalid. It *would* cast doubt on its practical relevance.

In summary, from the facts that feedback systems, in general, display global stability and resistance to change to a degree dependent on the detailed characteristics of their feedback mechanisms and that the software evolution process constitutes a feedback system, one must suspect that the benefits obtained from innovative changes to forward path methods techniques or tools in the software evolution process will be limited. The extent and degree of the constraining effect will depend on the characteristics of the many individual feedback paths and on the interactions between them. It may equally be anticipated that the global benefit obtained from improvements in forward path technology can, in general, be increased by attention to (adjustment of) the characteristics of relevant feedback mechanisms. It is thus tempting to suggest that the feedback phenomenon explains why, despite the many innovative concepts that have been introduced into forward path technology, it has proven so difficult to achieve major improvement in the global software process. Whether this is indeed so remains to be explored as does the question whether, if true, it can be systematically exploited.

An aside is appropriate at this point. In papers at IFIP Congress '86 Brooks [BRO86] and Turski [TUR86], respectively, pointed out that one must expect neither a silver bullet nor a philosophers' stone to solve the software engineering problem once and for all. The FEAST conjecture is not an exception. If it can be exploited, it may make a significant contribution to improvement of the software evolution process. It must be seen just as that, no more.

7 The FEAST Project- (Feedback, Evolution And Software Technology)

Feedback control and its role in software evolution, the software process and process evolution (improvement) are now being investigated with international collaboration, in a project, FEAST, supported for its first year by a grant from the UK Department of Trade and Industry. If successful, the project may be expected to have a profound impact on the software development and maintenance processes and on the process of process improvement The investigation will seek to verify the feedback conjecture and search for ways in which the feedback phenomenon may be exploited.

As already observed, the basic fact that the software evolution process constitutes a feedback system is self evident. But has feedback really constrained the benefit derived from the introduction of innovative concepts, methods, tools and techniques in forward path mechanisms? How may feedback control be exploited? Ideally one should be able to identify feedback paths that inhibited or damped the benefit obtained from individual innovations in current industrial processes and to explore beneficial changes to the feedback structure and mechanisms. This will require the development of methods, techniques and tools whereby the process, including its feedback mechanisms, may be modelled, evaluated and implemented or changed to maximise the global benefit, however defined in any circumstance, obtained from each innovation. Given success it this activity, exploitation means will follow.

As a first step it is intended to model the process and its properties using appropriate techniques and representations to expose the role and impact of feedback in software evolution. A preliminary model has already been derived from process theory. Models derived from observation, measurement and analysis of industrial processes will follow once the process is in full swing with industrial collaboration. Detailed examination of the role and contribution of people in such mechanisms must be included. A necessary precursor to extended modelling activity is the adoption of formalism that permits adequate representation, at various levels of detail, of software processes with their feedback loops and mechanisms. Exploration of suitable techniques and representations must also include control theoretic and system dynamics approaches as well as formal languages such as those currently used in process modelling. Nevertheless, the proposed modelling activity will differ radically from the process modelling currently in vogue. The latter tends to divert attention from, even hide, feedback and global process properties in general. Project FEAST will focus on them.

The insight and understanding developed in the early stages of this integrated analysis of current software process technology will lead to process evaluation and improvement in terms of both forward and loop properties. Exploitation of existing and emerging development and support technology must be enhanced to address and exploit feedback properties and thereby yield improved process attributes. Methods, techniques and tools for the design and evaluation of feedback control mechanisms must be developed. New and improved mechanisms exploiting the potential of feedback must be developed. Finally, lessons learned must be applied to the extension of process theory and the generation of principles and guidelines that will facilitate the transfer of results of the study to software engineers responsible for design, support and improvement of the software process, to software developers and to their managements in industry and elsewhere.

FEAST studies have now (March 1995) been underway for some nine months. During that time three workshops involving participants from industrial, academic and research organisations in Canada, Finland, France, Norway, Poland, Portugal, UK and USA have been held. The main focus so far has been on the identification and definition of basic concepts, the adoption of outline definitions, preliminary examination of project issues and objectives and consideration of how best and most profitably the investigation should proceed. Funding by the UK Department of Trade and Industry is about to end. The rate of progress from now (April 1995) will depend on the further funding obtained. Success in the the project will ensure, sustain and extend future advances in the software evolution (development *ab initio*, enhancement, extension) process, yielding methods, tools and metrics for the systemisation of process technology, effective evaluation techniques, support tools, further improvement of the process. By its very nature the study will also make a significant contribution to process theory and the development of a scientific base and framework for software process technology.

The project is challenging but feasible. First practical results should be available within two years from the availability of adequate support. But in view of the difficulty of the issues under study and the spectrum of disciplines involved the main body of results is likely to require 3 to 5 years to achieve. The degree of success and the rate at which it is achieved will clearly depend, in part, on the funding obtained. The calibre of people attracted to and participating in FEAST suggests that significant progress can be anticipated.

References

[ABD91]   Abdel-Hamid T and Madnick S E, Software Project Dynamics - An Integrated Approach, Prentice Hall, Englewood Cliffs, NJ 07632, 263 p.

[BEL72]   Belady L A and Lehman M M., An Introduction to Program Growth Dynamics, in Statistical Computer Performance Evaluation, W Freiburger (ed), Academic Press, New York, 1972, pp. 503 - 511

[BEN93]   Benford S and Fahlen L, A Spatial Model of Interaction in Large Virtual Environments, Proc. Third European Conf. on Comp. Supported Cooperative Work - ECSCW '93, Milan, 1993, Michelis, Simona and Schmidt (eds), Kluwer Acad. Publishers, pp. 109 - 124

[BRO86]   Brooks F P, No Silver Bullet - Essence and Accidents of Software Engineering, Information Processing 86, Proc. IFIP Congress 1986, Dublin, Sept. 1-5, Elsevier Science Publishers (BV), (North Holland), pp. 1069 - 1076

[CHO81]   Chong Hok Yuen C K S, Phenomenology of Program Maintenance and Evolution, PhD Thesis, Dept. of Comp., Imp. Col. 1981

[GIB94]   Gibbs W W, Software's Chronic Crisis, Scientific American, Sept. 2994, pps. 72 - 80

[GRI78]   Gries D, Programming Methodology - A Collection of Articles by Members of IFIP WG2.3, Springer Verlag, New York, 1978, 437 p.

[LEH69]   Lehman M M, The Programming Process, IBM Research Report RC xxxx, also in [leh85]

[LEH74]   Lehman M M, Programs, Cities, Students - Limits to Growth, Imperial College. Inaugural Lect. Series, vol. 9, 1970 - 1974, also. in [gri78], pp. 42 - 69 and [leh85], pp. 133 - 163

[LEH78]   Laws of Program Evolution - Rules and Tools for Programming Management, Proc. Infotech State of the Art Conf., Why Software Projects Fail, - Apr. 9 - 11 1978, pp. 11/1 - 25

[LEH80]   Lehman M M, Programs, Life Cycles and Laws of Software Evolution, Proc. IEEE Special Issue on Software Engineering, vol. 68, no. 9, Sept. 1980, pp. 1060 - 1076

[LEH84]   Lehman M M, Stenning V and Turski W M, (1984). Another Look at Software Design Methodology, ICST DoC Res. Rep. 83/13, June 1983. Also, Software Engineering Notes, v. 9, no 2, April 1984, pp. 38 - 53

[LEH85]   Lehman M M and Belady L A, Program Evolution, - Processes of Software Change, Academic Press, London, 1985, 538 p.

[LEH91]   Lehman M M, Software Engineering, the Software Process and Their Support, IEE Softw. Eng. J. Spec. Iss. on Software Environments and Factories, Sept. 1991, vol. 6, no. 5, pp. 243 - 258

[LEH94]   Lehman M M, Feedback, Evolution and Software Technology, Preprints of the First FEAST Workshop, Imperial Col., June. 1994

[LEH94B]   Lehman M M, The Characteristics of S- and E-Type Systems, Preprints of the Second FEAST Workshop, Imperial Col., Nov. 1994

[LEH95]   Lehman M M, Feadback, Evolution and Software Technology, Software Process Newsletter, IEEE, Apr. 1995

[MAJ93]   Major J, Keynote Address, ICSE15, Baltimore, 17 - 21 May 1993

[NAU69]   Naur P and Randell B, Software Engineering - Report on a Conference, Sponsored by the NATO Science Committee, Garmisch, 1968, Scientific Affairs Division, NATO, Brussels 39, 1969

[OXF81]   See, for example, The Concise Oxford Dictionary, Seventh Edition, Apr. 1981, p. 355

[TUR81]   Turski W M., Specification as a Theory with Models in the Computer World and in the Real World, Infotech State of the Art Report, se. 9, no. 6, 1981, pp. 363 - 377

[TUR86]   Turski W M And No Philosophers Stone Either, Information Processing 86, Proc. IFIP Congr., Dublin, Sept. 1 - 5, 1986, Elsevier Sci. Pubs, London, pp. 1077 - 1080

[WOO79]   Woodside C M, A Mathematical Model for the Evolution of Software, ICST CCD Res. Rep. 79/55. Also in J. of Sys. and Softw. vol. 1, no. 4, Oct. 1980, pp. 337 - 345 and in [leh85], pp. 339 - 354

A Method for Explaining the Behaviour of Conceptual Models

Antoni Olivé
Maria-Ribera Sancho

Facultat d'Informàtica, Universitat Politècnica de Catalunya
Pau Gargallo 5, 08028 Barcelona - Catalonia
e-mail:{olivelribera}@lsi.upc.es

Abstract. Traditional information modelling methods have been concerned with the important task of checking whether a model correctly and adequately describes a piece of reality and/or the users' intended requirements, that is, with model validation. In this paper, we present a new method for model validation which can be applied to conceptual models based on the concept of transaction. It provides explanations of the results of model execution. We extend the facilities of methods developed so far in this context by providing answers to questions about the value of derived information, to questions about how an information can be made true or false, and to hypothetical questions.

1 Introduction

This paper describes a new method for explaining the behaviour of conceptual models of information systems. The method aims at improving the validation of conceptual models. By validation we mean the process of checking whether a model correctly and adequately describes a piece of reality and/or the users' intended requirements [Gul93]. It is widely recognised that validating a conceptual model is an important task in Information Systems Engineering, and a broad variety of techniques and tools have been developed over recent years to support designers in that task. Among the support capabilities that are used (or have been investigated) there are [Bub88]: paraphrasing specifications in natural language [RoP92,Dal92], generation of abstractions and abstracts of specifications [JeC92], animation and symbolic execution [LaL93], explanation generation [Gul93,GuW93], infological simulation and semantic prototyping [LTP91,LiK93].

Our method contributes to model validation by providing explanations of the results of model execution. Specifically, we can explain, in several complementary ways, why some facts hold (or do not hold) in the information base (IB), why some facts have been inserted to (or deleted from) the IB, how some intended effect on the IB can be achieved, and what would have happened if some other input had been given (hypothetical explanation).

This paper extends our previous work on model execution explanations, which focused on deductive conceptual models. In [CoO92] we presented a method, based on plan generation techniques, which explains how some intended effect on the information base can be achieved. In [San93,San94] we described a method for explaining the temporal behaviour, through execution, of a model. Both methods were implemented.

We now present the result of extending our previous work to usual conceptual models of information systems, based on the concept of transaction rather than on deductive rules. The new method is limited by the fact that we do not consider the internal structure of transactions, while in our previous methods we know the full details of the effect of each external event (roughly, transactions) on the information base. Even so, we believe that the method provides helpful explanations in a rather simple and precise way.

For the sake of presentation, we describe the system in terms of four levels of explanations, from the simplest to the most complex level. For each level, we describe the explanations that can be obtained, the requirements for an explanation system able to give them, and the techniques and procedures that can be used. In Section 2 we deal with explaining the current contents of the information base. Section 3 deals with explaining the reasons for changes in a single transition of the information base. We will see that we need to record the transactions that are executed, and their effect. Section 4 moves a step forward and considers explanations taking into account the full history of changes. Finally, in Section 5 we describe the hypothetical explanations we can provide. The paper ends with the conclusions.

2 Explaining the Contents of the Information Base

The most elementary level of explanation in our method is that of explaining the current contents of the IB. At this level, we can only provide limited answers to the questions about why a fact is true and why a fact is false in the current IB state. In this section, we describe the requirements for a system to provide such explanations, and the procedures that may be used.

2.1 Requirements

Answering the above questions requires knowing the structure of the IB. This knowledge is, of course, available in all conceptual models. In general, we may assume that the IB consists of two parts: Base and Derived. The *Base* part includes all facts that are inserted, modified and deleted directly by the transactions, while the *Derived* part includes all facts that are derived from base and/or derived facts, by means of deduction rules.

Each conceptual modelling language provides a set of concepts and syntactic features to define the structure of the IB. Our method can be adapted to most languages. We will assume the IB contains facts of a given set of *fact types*. Each fact type consists of a name and a set of arguments. Base facts are updated by transactions, while derived facts are defined by *deduction rules* and, thus, their extension is defined declaratively. We will use the clausal form of logic, augmented with negation, to define deduction rules.

```
companies(company, name)
engaged_in(company, project) derived
    engaged_in(C,P) ← consortium(P,C), belongs_to(E,C), works_on(E,P)
employees(employee, name)
belongs_to(employee, company)
works_on(employee, project)
projects(project, name)
consortium(project, company)
active(project) derived
    active(P) ← projects(P,N), engaged_in(C,P)
inactive(project) derived
    inactive(P) ← projects(P,N), not active(P)
integrity constraints
ic1 ← works_on(E,P), not projects(P,N)
ic2 ← companies(C,N), not engaged_in(C,P)
```

Figure 1. Example of IB structure

We will also take into account, on the next levels of explanation, the integrity constraints on the IB. For the sake of uniformity, we define the constraints in denial form by means of integrity rules, which have the same form as the deduction rules.

Figure 1 is an example of the structure of an IB that we will use throughout this paper. The example has been adapted from [JMS92]. Note that we include two integrity rules. The first states that employees can only work in projects, while the second states that all companies must be engaged in some project.

It can be seen that there is a straightforward correspondence between our IB structure and that of ER [Che76], SDM [HaM81], NIAM [NH89] and many others. Note that not all of them include a derived part in the IB. Our method is even adaptable to languages based on the relational data model. In such case, views are derived fact types and their definition is a deduction rule.

2.2 Procedures

We now describe how answers to the questions given above can be obtained. Our approach to the problem is based on the solutions explaining the success of queries in the field of deductive databases [Llo87]. In fact, we can view the IB modelled by a conceptual model as a deductive database D. At any given state, the extensional part of D consists of all base facts that are true at this state, while the intensional part of D will be defined by the deduction rules of the conceptual model. Now, the problem of explaining the value of a derived fact is equivalent to the problem of explaining the success of a query in a deductive database, as we explain below.

why *f*? Assuming that fact *f* holds in the IB, the explanation depends on whether its fact type is base or derived. If it is base, we cannot provide any explanation at this level. If it is derived, we can give an explanation based on its deduction rules.

Intuitively, an explanation of why a derived fact *f* is true in the current state of the IB is supposed to detail the reasoning involved in proving that *f* is true. We will adopt here the most common approach for explaining the success of queries in the field of deductive databases [Llo87]. This approach considers that exhibiting an interpretation (or a trace) of the SLDNF proof tree is adequate for that kind of reasoning.

We will show this approach using the specifications of Figure 1. Assume that in the current state the following base facts are true:

companies(comp, name)	projects(proj, name)	consortium(proj, comp)
upc un_polit_cat	p1 odissea	p1 upc
employees(emp, name)	belongs_to(emp, comp)	works_on(emp, proj)
toni toni mayol	toni upc	toni p1
joan joan sistac	joan upc	joan p1

At this state, if the user queries the system about the value of derived fact *active(p1)* the answer will be "active(p1) is true". Now, the user can ask *why* this derived fact is true. The explanation given by the system consists of the deduction rule used to prove the desired fact (CM rule) and the corresponding set of instantiated literals. Then, the user can require more explanations for those literals representing derived information, as can be seen in the following.

```
why(active(p1))?
    active(p1) because:
    projects(p1,odissea) and engaged_in(upc,p1).
    CM rule: active(P) ← projects(P,N), engaged_in(C,P)
    engaged_in(upc,p1) can be further explained
```

---

why(engaged_in(upc,p1))?
  engaged_in(upc,p1) because:
  consortium(p1,upc) and belongs_to(joan,upc) and works_on(joan,p1).
  CM rule: engaged_in(C,P) ← consortium(P,C), belongs_to(E,C), works_on(E,P)

Sometimes, the truth value of a derived fact has several explanations, each one corresponding to a successful branch of the proof tree. In our the example case engaged_in(upc,p1) has the following alternative explanation:

---

alternative_explanation(engaged_in(upc,p1))?
  engaged_in(upc,p1) because:
  consortium(p1,upc) and belongs_to(toni,upc) and works_on(toni,p1).
  CM rule: engaged_in(C,P) ← consortium(P,C), belongs_to(E,C), works_on(E,P)

---

why_not *f*? A second capability consists in explaining why an information is false at the current state. See [OlS95] for the details and examples of how we answer this kind of question. Our approach is based on the work described in [DeT89,Dec91].

3 Explaining the Changes to the Information Base

The second level of explanation in our method is that of explaining the changes (transitions), induced by a transaction, from the previous to the current state of the IB. At this level, we improve the reasoning capabilities described in the previous level by giving explanations about why a fact has been inserted or deleted in the last transition, and providing the set of possible updates to make a given fact true or false at the next state.

3.1 Requirements

Answering the above kind of question requires knowing the transactions that have been executed, and their effect on the IB. Our method does not require knowing the internal details of the transactions. We will see that many helpful explanations can be given using only the knowledge of which updates have been performed by the transaction.

For each execution of a transaction, we record a fact of type *trans_log(name,parameters,time)*, with the name of the transaction, the list of its parameters (which may be empty) and the execution time. Without loss of generality, we assume that only one transaction is executed at a given time. We will use, in the next section, the execution time of transactions as identifiers for the states of the IB.

A transaction performs, among other things, several updates to the IB. An update may be an insertion or a deletion of a base fact. For each insertion of a fact of type p(x), where x is a set of arguments, we need to record a fact of type ιp(x,time), where time is the transaction time. We assume that inserted facts do not hold at the previous state.

Similarly, for each deletion of a fact of type p(x) we need to record a fact of type δp(x,time). We assume that deleted facts hold at the previous state.

For example, suppose that transaction *change_assignment* removes an employee from a given project and assigns him/her to another. Assume that, at time 10, the transaction is executed, changing employee *maria* from project *odissea* to project *folre*. We would record the following facts:

  trans_log (change_assignment,[maria,odissea,folre],10),
  δworks_on (maria,odissea,10), and ιworks_on (maria,folre,10)

Note that these facts may be obtained easily in most specification execution environments, and, in fact, some of them already capture traces of the transaction execution [LiK93].

3.2 The Internal Events Model

A transaction performs updates to only base facts of the information base. If we want to be able to give explanations of derived facts, we need to know how updates to base facts propagate to derived facts. This knowledge is given by the *Internal Events Model* (IEM), which is a model that can be obtained automatically from deduction rules. The model has been described in [Oli91,Urp93] and it is briefly reviewed below.

The key concept of an IEM is that of *internal event*. Let IB be an information base, U an update and IB' the updated information base. We say that U induces a transition from IB (the previous state) to IB' (the new state). We assume, for the moment, that U consists of an unspecified set of base facts to be inserted and/or deleted. Due to the deduction rules, U may induce other updates on some derived facts. Let p be one of such fact types, and let p' denote the same fact type evaluated in IB'. We associate with p an *insertion event predicate* ιp, and a *deletion event predicate* δp, defined as:

(1) $\forall X \ (\iota p(X) \leftrightarrow p'(X) \wedge \neg p(X))$

(2) $\forall X \ (\delta p(X) \leftrightarrow p(X) \wedge \neg p'(X))$

where X is a vector of variables. From the above we have the equivalences [Urp93]:

(3) $\forall X \ (p(X) \leftrightarrow (p(X) \wedge \neg \delta p(X)) \vee \iota p(X))$

(4) $\forall X \ (\neg p(X) \leftrightarrow (\neg p(X) \wedge \neg \iota p(X)) \vee \delta p(X))$

Let us consider a derived predicate p. Assume that the definition of p consists of m rules, $m \geq 1$. For our purposes, we rename predicate symbols at the head of the rules as $p_1,...,p_n$ and we add the set of clauses:

(5) $p(X) \leftarrow p_i(X)$ $i = 1..m$

Consider now one of the rules $p_i(X) \leftarrow L_{i,1} \wedge ... \wedge L_{i,n}$. When this rule is to be evaluated in the new state, its form is $p'_i(X) \leftarrow L'_{i,1} \wedge ... \wedge L'_{i,n}$, where $L'_{i,r}$ ($r = 1..n$) is obtained by replacing the predicate q of $L_{i,r}$ by q'. Then, if we replace each literal in the body by its equivalent expression given in (3) or (4) we get a new rule, called *transition rule*, which defines the new state predicate p'_i in terms of old state predicates and events.

For example, the transition rule corresponding to *inactive'1* in Figure 1 is given by:

inactive'1(P) ← ((projects(P,N) ∧ ¬ δprojects(P,N)) ∨ ιprojects(P,N)) ∧
            ((¬active(P) ∧ ¬ ιactive(P)) ∨ δactive(P))

which, after distributing ∧ over ∨ , is equivalent to the four transition rules:

inactive'1,1(P) ← projects(P,N) ∧ ¬ δprojects(P,N) ∧ ¬active(P) ∧ ¬ ιactive(P)
inactive'1,2(P) ← projects(P,N) ∧ ¬ δprojects(P,N) ∧ δactive(P)
inactive'1,3(P) ← ιprojects(P,N) ∧ ¬active(P) ∧ ¬ ιactive(P)
inactive'1,4(P) ← ιprojects(P,N) ∧ δactive(P)

with:

inactive'1(P) ← inactive'1,j(P)   j = 1..4

The transition rules for predicates *engaged_in* , *active* , *ic1* and *ic2* would be obtained similarly.

Insertion predicates ιp were defined in (1) as: $\forall X \ (\iota p(X) \leftrightarrow p'(X) \wedge \neg p(X))$

If there are *m* rules for predicate p, then $p'(X) \leftrightarrow p'_1(X) \vee ... \vee p'_m(X)$. Replacing p'(X) in (1) we obtain:

$\iota p(X) \leftarrow p'_i(X) \wedge \neg p(X)$ $i = 1..m$

which are called the *insertion internal events rules* of predicate p. In the example above, there would be only one rule (since m = 1):

ιinactive(P) ← inactive'$_1$(P) ∧ ¬inactive(P)

Similarly, deletion predicates δp were defined in (2): ∀X (δp(X) ↔ p(X) ∧ ¬p'(X))

If there are *m* rules for predicate p, we then have:

δp(X) ← p$_i$(X) ∧ ¬p'(X)   i = 1..m

and replacing p'(X) by its equivalent definition p'(X) ↔ p'$_1$(X) ∨...∨ p'$_m$(X) we obtain:

δp(X) ← p$_i$(X) ∧ ¬p'$_1$(X) ∧...∧ ¬p'$_m$(X)   i = 1..m

This set of rules is called the *deletion internal events rules* for predicate p. In our example, there would be only one rule (since m = 1):

δinactive(P) ← inactive(P) ∧ ¬inactive'$_1$(P)

The set of transition, insertion internal event and deletion internal event rules is called the *Internal Events Model* (IEM). These rules allow us to deduce which induced insertions and deletions happen in a transition, in terms of old state facts and events. In most cases, these rules can be substantially simplified, using the procedure described in [Oli91,Urp93]. Note that the Internal Events Model will be relevant even if our method is used in a language that does not consider derived facts. Recall that integrity constraints can be seen as rules defining when an inconsistency fact (ic1, ic2 in our example) holds. The insertion internal events rules for inconsistency predicates give the conditions upon which consistency is violated.

From the IEM, we compute the induced updates on derived facts, and store the result in a way similar to the base updates. For example, assume that, at the current state, the information base contains the following base facts:

companies(comp,	name)	projects(proj,	name)	consortium(proj,	comp)
upc	un_polit_cat	p1	odissea	p1	upc
		p2	folre	p2	upc
		p3	dream	p3	upc

employees(emp,	name)	belongs_to(emp,	comp)	works_on(emp,	proj)
toni	toni mayol	toni	upc	toni	p3
joan	joan sistac	joan	upc	joan	p3
maria	maria costal	maria	upc	maria	p1

which, implicitly, induce the derived facts:

engaged_in(company,	project)	active(project)	inactive(project)
upc	p1	p1	p2
upc	p3	p3	

Assume now that transaction:

trans_log (change_assignment,[maria,odissea,folre],10),
δworks_on (maria,p1,10), ιworks_on (maria,p2,10)

is executed at time 10. The computed induced updates would be recorded as:

δengaged_in (upc,p1,10), ιengaged_in (upc,p2,10), δactive (p1,10), ιactive (p2,10),
δinactive (p2,10), ιinactive (p1,10)

3.3 Procedures

Figure 2 depicts the architecture of our explanation system. There must be some kind of tracing system that traces the transactions executed (and adds a trans-log fact to 'Updates'), captures the insertions to (and deletions from) the Information Base (and adds an ιp or δp fact to 'Updates') and computes the induced insertions and deletions (adding also the corresponding ιp or δp facts to 'Updates'). Such a tracing system may be implemented in several ways, depending on the execution environment. The figure also shows all the sources used in giving explanations.

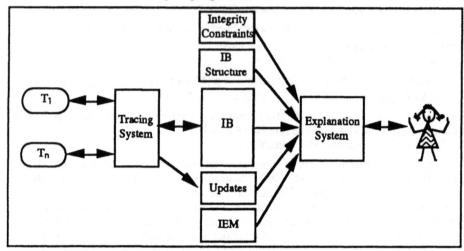

Figure 2. System architecture

We will now describe how answers to the questions described above can be obtained.

why *f*? Assuming that fact *f* holds in the IB, the explanation depends on whether its fact type is base or derived. If it is base, there are two possible explanations for fact *f* being true:

- *f* has been inserted by last transaction, or
- *f* was already true at previous state (and it has not been deleted).

Let us resume the execution of our example case at the point it was left in the previous subsection. Now, assume that at time 13, a transaction *change_project*(dream,odissea) moves all employees working on project dream to project odissea. The resulting set of base facts will be:

companies(comp,	name)		projects(proj,	name)	consortium(proj,	comp)
upc	un_polit_cat		p1	odissea	p1	upc
			p2	folre	p2	upc
			p3	dream	p3	upc

employees(emp,	name)	belongs_to(emp,	comp)	works_on(emp,	proj)
toni	toni mayol	toni	upc	toni	p1
joan	joan sistac	joan	upc	joan	p1
maria	maria costal	maria	upc	maria	p2

and the set of derived facts:

engaged_in(company,	project)	active(project)	inactive(project)
upc	p1	p1	p3
upc	p2	p2	

At this time, if the user queries the system about the value of base fact works_on(toni,p1) the answer will be "works_on(toni,p1) is true", and the explanation will be as follows:

why(works_on(toni,p1))?
  works_on(toni,p1) has been inserted by last transaction *change_project*(dream,odissea)

If fact *f* is derived, the explanation of *why* this fact *f* is true given on the first level can be substantially improved using the IEM. In particular, the use of the IEM allows us to reason in terms of the change induced in the transition from previous to current state. Reasoning in this way, there are two possible explanations for fact *f* being true:
- An insertion of *f* has been induced, or
- *f* was already true at previous state (and its deletion has not been induced).

In the first case, the user may be interested in the reasons for the change from the previous to the current state, that is, in explanations of why the insertion of a fact *f* has been induced. This is catered for the *why_inserted* explanations.

why_inserted *f*? The answer gives the reasons why derived fact *f* was inserted in the last transition. The desired explanations can be obtained from the internal events rules. From an analysis of the SLDNF proof tree of the corresponding insertion internal event fact (ι*f*) we can obtain the set of updates on base facts, performed by the last transaction, that induced the insertion of *f*.

Assume that the current IB state is the result of the execution of transaction *change_project*(dream,odissea) at time 13. At this state, if the designer wants to know why engaged_in (upc,p1) holds, the explanation will be as follows:

---

why(engaged_in (upc,p1))?
  engaged_in (upc,p1) because:
  consortium(p1,upc) and belongs_to(toni,upc) and works_on(toni,p1).
  CM rule: engaged_in(C,P) ← consortium(P,C), belongs_to(E,C), works_on(E,P).
  engaged_in(upc,p1) has been induced by last transaction: *change_project*(dream,odissea)

why_inserted(engaged_in(upc,p1))?
  inserted(engaged_in(upc,p1)) because:
  works_on (toni,p1) has been inserted.

alternative_explanation(inserted(engaged_in(upc,p1)))?
  inserted(engaged_in(upc,p1)) because:
  works_on (joan,p1) has been inserted.

---

why_not *f*? Assuming that fact *f* does not hold in the IB, the explanation depends on whether its fact type is base or derived. If it is base, there are two possible explanations for fact *f* being false:
- *f* has been deleted by last transaction, or
- *f* was already false at previous state (and it has not been inserted).

If *f* is derived, we can provide explanations of why it is false at the current state in terms of the change induced in the transition from the previous state. Now, the use of the IEM allows us to give two possible explanations for fact *f* being false:
- A deletion of *f* has been induced), or
- *f* was already false at previous state (and its insertion has not been induced).

As before, the reasons for the induced deletion can be obtained using the *why_deleted* explanations.

why_deleted *f*? The answer gives the reasons why derived fact *f* was deleted in the last transition. As in the case of *why_inserted*, the desired explanations can be obtained from the internal events rules. From an analysis of the SLDNF proof tree of the corresponding deletion internal event fact (δ*f*) we can obtain the set of updates on base facts, performed by the last transaction, that induced the deletion of *f*.

In our example case, if at time 13 the designer wants to know why active(p3) does not hold, the explanation will be as follows:

```
why_not(active(p3))?
  active(p3) is false because:
  [engaged_in(p3,C)] is false
  active(p3) has been implicitly deleted by last transaction: change_project(dream,odissea)
why_deleted(active(p3))?
  deleted(active(p3)) because:
  works_on (toni,p3) has been deleted and works_on (joan,p3) has been deleted.
```

how *f*? Assuming that fact *f* is currently false, the answer to this question consists in a set of base updates to the current state such that *f* will hold in the next state, and the information base will mantain its consistency. Note that we cannot provide here a simple solution for base facts (like "insert *f* into the IB"), because some integrity constraint could be violated.

Providing answers to this question is equivalent to view updating in deductive databases. The information base can be seen as a deductive database, and the request to make a fact *f* true can be seen as an insertion request of *f* in a view updating method.

Several methods for the solution of the view update problem do exist. We use the Events Method presented in [TeO92,Ten92]. The method is based on the Internal Events Model described above.

For example, if we assume that the current IB state is the result of the execution of transaction *change_project*(dream,odissea) at time 13, derived fact engaged_in(upc,p3) is false. If the designer wants to know how to make it true, the system answers in the following way:

```
how(engaged_in(upc,p3))?
  possible translations:
  [insert works_on(maria,p3)]
  [insert works_on(toni,p3)]
  [insert works_on(joan,p3)]
  [insert belongs_to(E,upc) and insert works_on(E,p3)]
```

In order to apply the desired update, the designer should choose and execute a transaction that modifies the IB in the way shown by one of the proposed translations. Note that the proposed translations maintain the information base consistency. Our method takes into account the integrity constraints, and translations that would leave the information base inconsistent are not generated.

In our example case, the designer could choose a transaction *assign(joan, dream)* to assign employee *joan* to project *p3*. This would imply the engagement of company *upc* to project *p3*.

how_not *f*? Assuming that fact *f* currently holds, the answer to this question consists in a set of base updates to the current state, such that *f* will be false in the next state, and the information base will maintain its consistency. We solve this problem as in the previous question, but now considering a delete request.

4 Explaining the Historical Evolution of the Information Base

The third level of explanation in our method shows the temporal evolution of the IB. At this level we can explain why a fact was true or false at a past state, what was known about a fact type at a given state, the intervals during which a fact has been true, and the set of states when a fact has been updated. In this section, we describe the procedures that may be used to obtain this kind of explanation. The knowledge needed to provide such explanations is exactly the same as on the previous level.

4.1 Procedures

If we want to be able to give explanations about the historical evolution of the IB, we need to know the value of base and derived facts at each state, from the initial to the current one. We will show that this knowledge can be obtained from the requirements established at the previous level.

The first requirement was to store all transactions executed from the initial state, and the corresponding updates. With this information we can 'reconstruct' the IB contents at any state. With respect to base predicates, it is easy to define the value of a base predicate p(X) at a given state s in terms of the insertion and deletion events occurred until s, as follows:

$$\forall X \ (p(X,S) \leftrightarrow \iota p(X,S1) \land S1 \leq S \land \neg \exists S2 \ (\delta p(X,S2) \land S1 < S2 \leq S)$$

meaning that a fact p(x) is true at state s if it has been inserted in a state $s1$ before s and has not been deleted between $s1$ and s. Recall that we identify states by the execution time of the transaction.

With respect to derived predicates, we only have to apply a minor transformation to deduction rules to take the state into account. For example, the deduction rule for predicate engaged_in would be transformed as:

engaged_in(C,P,S) ← consortium(P,C,S), belongs_to(E,C,S), works_on(E,P,S)

why f at s? Assuming that fact f was true at state s, the explanation depends on whether its fact type is base or derived. If it is base, there is only one possible explanation for fact f being true at s, which consists in identifying the transaction that inserted it. Then, if $f=p(k)$ we have to look for a transaction such that:

trans_log(name,parameters,S1) $\land$ S1≤s $\land$ ιp(k,S1) $\land$ ¬ ∃S2 (δp(k,S2) $\land$ S1<S2≤s)

Assume, for example, that the current IB state is the result of the execution of transaction *assign(joan, dream)* at time 16. At this time, if the user queries the system about the value of base fact works_on(maria,p2) at state 13 the answer will be "works_on(maria,p2) was true at state 13", and the explanation is as follows:

> why(works_on(maria,p2)) **at** 13?
> works_on(maria,p2) was true at 13 because:
> transaction*change_assignment*(maria,odissea,folre) executed at time 10 has inserted it, and no transaction between 10 and 13 has deleted it.

If fact f is derived, the explanation of *why f* was true in a given state s is exactly the same as that provided on previous levels for the current state. It can be obtained with the same technique, but taking into account the set of facts that were true at s.

why_not f at s? Assuming that fact f was false at state s, the explanation depends on whether its fact type is base or derived. If it is base, there are two possible explanations for fact f being false at s:
- fact f was never inserted in the IB before s.
- fact f was deleted by a transaction before s.

If $f = p(k)$, we identify the first case when the following condition holds:
$$\neg \exists S1 \ (\iota p(k,S1) \land S1 \leq s)$$

In the second case, we have to look for a transaction such that:

trans_log(name,parameters,S1) $\wedge$ S1$\leq$s $\wedge$ δp(k,S1) $\wedge$ $\neg$ $\exists$S2 (ιp(k,S2) $\wedge$ S1<S2$\leq$s)

For example, if at state 16 the user queries the system about the value of base fact works_on(toni,p3) at state 13, the answer will be "works_on(toni,p3) was false at state 13", and the explanation is:

> why_not(works_on(toni,p3)) at 13?
>   works_on(toni,p3) was false at 13 because:
>   transaction *change_project*(dream,folre) executed at time 13 has deleted it.

If fact f is derived, the explanation of *why* f was false in a given state s is exactly the same as that provided on previous levels for the current state. It can be obtained with the same technique, but taking into account the set of facts that were true at s.

what_known_about fact type **at** s? To obtain a list of all facts of the given type that were true at state s we have only to evaluate the extension of the corresponding predicate at this state, as explained at the beginning of this section.

when f? The answer to the question about *when* a fact f holds in the IB can be obtained from the stored updates. It does not depend on whether the corresponding fact type is base or derived. Basically, we have to look for all the pairs of consecutive insertion-deletion events of the required fact.

There are two possible answers to the question *when f*:
- fact f has never been true.
- the set of intervals during which fact f has been true.

If $f = p(k)$, we identify the first case when the condition $\neg$ $\exists$S (ιp(k,S)) holds. If this condition does not hold, we have to look for all the intervals [S1,S2] such that:

ιp(k,S1) $\wedge$ δp(k,S2) $\wedge$ S2 > S1 $\wedge$ $\neg$ $\exists$S3 (δp(k,S3) $\wedge$ S1 < S3 $\leq$ S2)   or
ιp(k,S1) $\wedge$ $\neg$ $\exists$S3 (δp(k,S3) $\wedge$ S3 > S1) $\wedge$ S2 = current_state

In our example case, the following explanations could be obtained at state 16.

> when(employees(enric, enric pastor))?
>   employees(enric, enric pastor) has never been true
> when(works_on(joan,p3))?
>   works_on(joan,p3) has been true **from state 1 to state 13 and at** current state

In the case of derived facts there is an alternative solution to answer this query, which does not require the use of the internal events. It consists in the evaluation of fact f, using the deduction rules, for each state from the initial to the current one.

when [ι|δ]f? The answer to the question about *when* an update [ι|δ]f occurred can be obtained from the stored updates. It does not depend on whether the corresponding fact type of f is base or derived. We have to look for all the events updating fact f which have occurred from the initial to the current state.

There are two possible answers to the question *when* [ι|δ]f:
- the update has never occurred.
- the set of states in which the update has occurred.

If $f = p(k)$, we identify the first case when the condition $\neg$ $\exists$S ([ι|δ]p(k,S)) holds. If this condition does not hold, we have to look for all the states S such that [ι|δ]p(k,S).

We can also consider the case in which f is not fully instantiated. That is, f has the form p(k,Y), Y being a set of variables. Then, the system will answer giving the set of tuples (y,s) such that [ι|δ]p(k,y,s) holds, if any.

5 Explaining the Effect of Hypothetical Past Updates

The last level of explanation in our method is that of explaining the effect of a potential update in the past. In this section, we describe the procedures that may be used. The knowledge needed to provide such explanations is exactly the same as on the third level.

5.1 Procedures

what_if $[\iota|\delta]p(k)$ **at** s **on** f? The system has to evaluate the impact that a potential update $[\iota|\delta]p(k)$ performed at state s would have on fact f at the current state. Given that a transaction performs updates on only base facts of the IB, the fact type of $p(k)$ is always base. The fact type of f can be base or derived. The answer consists in the difference between the current value of f and its hypothetical value if the update had been performed at state s.

As already mentioned, our explanation method does not consider the internal structure of transactions. In particular, we ignore the conditions under which each transaction performs updates to base facts. Then, the only way to evaluate the impact of a hypothetical update on a past state is to simulate a new execution of all transactions occurring since that state. This simulation can be done using the information about the transactions and their corresponding updates stored at execution time.

Also, we have to ensure that the IB consistency will be mantained from state s to the current state. Our method guarantees this condition by checking that the update does not violate any integrity constraint at the state in which it is performed, and by checking that transactions executed after s preserve this consistency. In addition, we may also ensure that, at every state, some implicit assumptions are preserved. Namely, that insertions and deletions are effective (insertions add non-existing information and deletions remove existing information). Such conditions are treated as constraints.

As a consequence, the procedure to obtain explanations regarding what_if $[\iota|\delta]p(k)$ at s on f is as follows:
- Make the hypothesis that the update $[\iota|\delta]p(k)$ is performed at state s.
- Ensure that the update does not violate any integrity constraint at s, by evaluating the inconsistency rules at this state.
- For each transaction occurring from s to the current state, check if the state resulting from the application of its updates is consistent, by evaluating the inconsistency rules. Then, two cases are possible:
    (1) The transaction violates some integrity constraints. In this case, the explanation will be: "This update leads the IB to an inconsistent state when transaction *name(parameters)* is simulated at time t."
    (2) No integrity constraint is violated. In this case, the system evaluates fact f at the resulting state, and gives the difference with respect to the real value of f at the current state.

Note that to evaluate the integrity constraints at each state, our method does not have to rebuild each state from s to the current one. We can obtain the value of base and derived facts at any state from the stored events, as explained in Subsection 4.1. Therefore, the inconsistency rules can be evaluated at each state like any deduction rule. In our example case, the integrity constraints would be transformed to take the state into account as:

ic1(S) ← works_on(E,P,S), not projects(P,N,S)
ic2(S) ← companies(C,N,S), not engaged_in(C,P,S)

Assume, for example, that the current IB state is the result of the execution of transaction *new_project(p4,bloom)* at time 20. The following explanations could be obtained at this state.

> what_if δworks_on(maria,p2) at 13 on active(p2)?
> active(p2) is currently true, but it would be false if the update was performed.
>
> what_if ιcompanies(uab,univ_autòn_de_barna) at 16 on engaged_in?
> This update would violate integrity constraint ic1 at state 16.
>
> what_if δprojects(p3) at 13 on active?
> This update leads the IB to an inconsistent state when transaction assign(joan, dream)
> is simulated at time 16. Integrity constraint ic2 would be violated.

what_if_not [ι|δ]p(k) at s on f? Assuming that an update [ι|δ]p(k) was performed by
a transaction at state s, the system has to evaluate the impact that the absence of this
update would have on fact f at the current state. Given that a transaction performs
updates on only base facts of the IB, the fact type of p(k) is always base. The fact type
of f can be base or derived. The answer consists on the difference between the current
value of f and its hypothetical value if the update was not performed at state s. The
procedure to obtain explanations about what_if_not [ι|δ]p(k) at s on f is similar to the
previous case. Both kinds of hypothetical explanations can also be combined.

6 Conclusions

We have presented a method for explaining the behaviour of conceptual models of
information systems. The method assumes a conceptual model in terms of information
base structure (with base and, optionally, derived facts), integrity constraints and
transactions. Therefore, the method may be adapted in most current methodologies.

Our method contributes to model validation by providing explanations about the
results of model execution. It provides, with a simple architecture, useful answers to
questions about why (or why not) a fact holds in the current state, why a fact has been
inserted (or deleted) in a transition, how a fact can be made true (or false), why (and
when) a fact has been true in the past and what would have happened if past updates had
been different.

Answers to some of the above questions are given by some existing explanation
systems. We extend them by providing answers to questions about derived facts, to
questions about how a fact can be made true or false, and to hypothetical questions.

Our method is based mainly on results obtained in the field of deductive databases.
We have seen how the procedures developed in that field for explaining the results of
queries, or their failure, and for updating consistent knowledge bases may be useful for
behaviour explanation of conceptual models. In this sense, our method links these two
fields.

Acknowledgements

The authors wish to thank the ODISSEA group for their comments and suggestions.
This work has been supported by the CICYT PRONTIC program, project TIC 680.

References

[Bub88] Bubenko,J.A. "Selecting a Strategy For Computer-aided Software
Engineering (CASE)", SYSLAB Rep. 59, University of Stockholm, 1988.

[Che76] Chen.P.P. "The Entity-Relational model. Towards a unified view of data".
ACM Trans. on Database Systems, vol. 1, no. 1, March 1976, pp. 9-36.

[CoO92] Costal,D.; Olivé,A. "A method for reasoning about deductive conceptual
models", Proc. of CAiSE 92, Manchester, May 1992, pp. 612-631.

[Dal92]   Dalianis,H. "A method for validating a conceptual model by natural language discourse generation", Proc. of CAiSE 92, Manchester, 1992, pp. 425-444.

[Dec91]   Decker,H. "On Explanations in Deductive Databases", Proc. Third Workshop on Foundations of Models and Languages for Data and Objects, Aigen, September 1991, pp. 173-186.

[DeT89]   Decker,H.; Tomasic,A. "Towards a foundation of explanations in deductive databases", Internal report ECRC, Munich 1989.

[Gul93]   Gulla,J.A. "Explanation generation in information systems engineering", PhD. Thesis. Norwegian Institute of Technology, Trondheim, 1993.

[GuW93] Gulla,J.A.;Willumsen,G. "Using Explanations to Improve the Validation of Executable Models", Proc. CAiSE 93, Paris, June 1993, pp. 118-142.

[HaM81]   Hammer,M.;McLeod,D. "Database description with SDM: A semantic database model". ACM TODS, vol. 6, no. 3, 1981, pp. 351-386.

[JeC92]   Jesus,L.;Carapuça,R. "Automatic Generation of Documentation for Information Systems",Proc. CAiSE 92, Manchester, May 1992, pp. 48-64.

[JMS92]   Jarke,M.; Mylopoulos,J.W.;Schmidt,J.W.;Vassiliou,Y. "DAIDA: An Environment for Evolving Information Systems". ACM Trans. on Information Systems, vol. 10, no. 1, January 1992, pp. 1-50.

[LaL93]   Lalioti,V.; Loucopoulos,P. "Visualisation for Validation", Proc. CAiSE 93, Paris, June 1993, pp. 143-164.

[LiK93]   Lindland,O.I.;Krogstie,J."Validating Conceptual Models by Transformational Prototyping", Proc. CAiSE 93, Paris, June 1993, pp. 165-183.

[Llo87]   Lloyd, J.W. "Foundations of logic programming". Springer-Verlag, 1987.

[LTP91]   Loucopoulos,P.;Theodoulidis,B.;Pantazis,D. "Business Rules Modelling: Conceptual Modelling and Object-Oriented Specifications". In Van Assche, F., Moulin,B.; Rolland,C. (eds.) "Object Oriented Approach in Information Systems", North-Holland, 1991, pp. 322-342.

[NH89]   Nijssen, G.M.; Halpin, T.A. "Conceptual Schema and Relational Database Design. A fact oriented approach". Prentice Hall, 1989.

[Oli91]   Olivé, A. "Integrity constraints checking in deductive databases", Proc. of the 17th. VLDB, Barcelona, 1991, pp. 513-523.

[OlS95]   Olivé, A.; Sancho,M.R. "A Method for Explaining the Behaviour of Conceptual Models - Extended version" Tech. Report LSI/95-R

[RoP92]   Rolland,C.;Proix,C. "A Natural Language Approach for Requirements Engineering", Proc. CAiSE 92, Manchester, May 1992, pp. 257-277.

[Ten92]   Teniente, E. "El mètode dels esdeveniments interns per actualització de vistes en bases de dades deductives" (in catalan), PhD. Thesis, Universitat Politècnica de Catalunya, Barcelona, 1992.

[TeO92]   Teniente, E; Olivé, A. "The Events Method for View Updating in Deductive Databases", Proc. EDBT'92, Vienna, 1992, pp. 245-260.

[San93]   Sancho,M.R. "Explaining the behaviour of a deductive conceptual model", Proc. Fourth Intl. DAISD Workshop, Tech. Report LSI/93-25-R, Universitat Politècnica de Catalunya, 1993, pp. 27-50.

[San94]   Sancho,M.R. "Disseny de transaccions a partir de models conceptuals deductius" (in catalan). PhD. Thesis, Universitat Politècnica de Catalunya, Barcelona, 1994.

[Urp93]   Urpi, A. "El mètode dels esdeveniments interns per al càlcul de canvis en bases de dades deductives" (in catalan). PhD. Thesis, Universitat Politècnica de Catalunya, Barcelona, 1993.

COLOR-$\mathcal{X}$: Linguistically-based Event Modeling: A General Approach to Dynamic Modeling

J.F.M. Burg* and R.P. van de Riet

Department of Computer Science
Vrije Universiteit
Amsterdam, The Netherlands
{jfmburg,vdriet}@cs.vu.nl

Abstract. This paper introduces a way of modeling the dynamic aspects of an Information and Communication System in which all the occurring events are listed and ordered in time. These graphical Event Models are based on formal (logical) specifications. Event Models are very close to the specifications in the informal requirements document, which describes the Universe of Discourse. By means of the underlying formal specifications Natural Language sentences are generated automatically, in order to give some feedback to the designer and user. By combining this feedback feature and the power of the logical foundation, the Event Models can be verified and validated. We will also present an algorithm and its implementation to generate State Transition Diagrams from Event Models automatically. This is especially useful in our environment in which programming code-generation is the key objective.

1 Introduction

The name of our current project, **COLOR-X**, is an acronym for the **CO**nceptual **L**inguistically based **O**bject oriented **R**epresentation Language for Information and **C**ommunication **S**ystems (**ICS** abbreviated to **X**). In the COLOR-X project we are using the logical conceptual modeling technique CPL (Conceptual Prototyping Language) [8], which is linguistically based, as a formal foundation for graphical modeling techniques. This approach is chosen to facilitate the process of conceptual modeling and which leads to more consistent and complete models that are linguistically correct. COLOR-X is the first phase of a larger project which has as objective the generation of object-oriented programming code from a natural language based modeling technique, which brings, as a side-effect, the conceptual models closer to programming code. In addition, by using a modeling technique based on linguistic notions, we are narrowing the gap between requirements documents, written in natural language, and conceptual models as well. The COLOR-X project is divided into several parts, analog to existing conceptual modeling methods, like OMT [20]). This paper contains the dynamic part,

---

* Supported by the Foundation for Computer Science in the Netherlands (SION) with financial support from the Dutch Organization for Scientific Research (NWO), project 612-123-309

whereas [4] describes the COLOR-X Static Object Model (CSOM), in which the static aspects of the Universe of Discourse (UoD) (i.e. objects, classes and the relations, like generalization and aggregation, between them) are contained. The graphical CSOMs are linguistically-based, and logically founded by underlying CPL-specifications. The CSOM-model contains the overall structure of the UoD for the programming code generator.

COLOR-X is part of the LIKE-project (Linguistic Instruments in Knowledge Engineering) which is a consortium of researchers of three disciplines: Linguistics, Business Administrators and Computer Science. The LIKE-project is focusing research around the theme: how linguistic instruments can be used profitably in the area of Knowledge Engineering, e.g. to build Information and Communication Systems (ICSs).

One of the main reasons to use linguistic knowledge is to make the use of words appearing in the models consistent, and thus making the models as a whole more meaningful. Earlier projects conducted in our group have shown the profitability of this approach, [3], [2], [4] and [5]. Another reason to use linguistic knowledge in modeling techniques is to give more expressive power to them. For example, it is now possible to express which events *should* and which *could* occur in a certain UoD. An additional nice feature of a linguistically based modeling technique is that it is relatively easy to generate natural language sentences from it, in order to give some feedback to the system designers and to the end-users as well, see also [7]. This feedback consists of generated sentences during the modeling phase, in order to check if the model is consistent with the requirements and on the other hand this feedback consists of explanation facilities, like [11]. The first kind of feedback is already incorporated into COLOR-X.

Now that we know *why* to use linguistic knowledge, we need to know *how* to use it. We will use a lexicon as a source containing this knowledge. Such a lexicon contains information about taxonomies, verb frames, synonym sets, etcetera. We are using (an extension of) WordNet [17], which is the result of an ongoing research program at Princeton University in the representation of lexical information.

The remainder of this paper is organized as follows: First we will give an overview of and remarks about the traditional way of dynamic modeling. After that we will offer an alternative by introducing COLOR-X Event Models (CEMs). The generality of this approach will be shown in section 5 and section 4.1 by generating State Transition Diagrams and formal CPL Specifications out of CEMs. We will conclude this paper by giving some conclusions and by listing work and research that is still to do.

2 Dynamic Modeling

The purpose of Dynamic Modeling is to show the time-dependent behaviour of the system as a whole or a particular part of the system. In general, there are three ways of modeling this information:

1. Dynamic and Deontic Logic, [8], interested in the states between actions

2. Process Algebra, [22] and [13], concentrating on the actions themselves
3. Petri Nets, which are useful in environments where simulation plays an important role [12], but which will not be discussed in this paper.

A popular example of a process algebra-based modeling technique is the graphical State Transition Diagramming (STD) technique, [20]. The use of STDs, however, causes some problems:

- It is not clear whether you should model one STD per object, one STD for the system as a whole or a mixture of these two approaches. Because of the lack of consensus concerning this point, it is very hard to parse or interpret STDs in computerized tools.
- The words used as transitions- and state-labels are not constrained by rules. The models would be more comprehensible if the *kind of words* used for actions, events and states would be pre-defined (like controlled verbs, non-controlled verbs and nouns, respectively). Another rule could constrain the *form of the words*, like infinitive verbs and singular nouns. Both kind of rules would facilitate the interpretation of the models and thus the generation of programming code out of them, but it is very hard to identify them and to establish some agreement about them.
- By adding different modalities (like necessary and possible) to actions and events, the resulting STD models would have more expressive power. In traditional STD techniques, just one modality (factual) is used.
- A state is not only defined by the attribute values of some object or (sub-) system, but also by common sense knowledge which is hard to capture in attributes (e.g. *"a person is ill"*).

An example of a dynamic and deontic logic-based modeling technique is the Conceptual Prototyping Language (CPL) [8]. The main problem with this approach is the awkward formal syntax, and the difficult underlying linguistic theory. To overcome these problems, we will propose Event Models in the next chapter. These models have CPL-specifications as an underlying formal representation. To understand these models properly we will first give a short introduction to CPL.

2.1 An Introduction to CPL

The Conceptual Prototyping Language (CPL) has been developed as a specification language as close as possible to natural language, by basing it on *Functional Grammar* [9], but formal enough to specify the requirements of an ICS in a precise and unambiguous way. The formal semantics, as defined in [8], is based on predicate, modal, deontic and temporal logic. Each CPL construct is translated into some combination of these logics. The general form of a CPL specification language is as follows:

Mode : Tense : Predication $T_1 \cdots T_n$ (**id:** $\cdots$) (**sit:** $\cdots$)

Mode   = **FACTUAL|MUST|NEC|PERMIT**
Tense   = **ACTION|DONE|PROSP|PERF|PRET**
Predication = a relation between n terms $T_1 \cdots T_n$,
T_i = a term denotes a (set, with cardinality c, of) object(s).
              Each object occurs in a specific role.
id   = identification of the objects
sit   = situation in which this CPL specification is supposed to hold

For example, the following specification says that
When a company has sold a car to a customer, it has to send a bill to this customer within a week.:

MUST: ACTION:
send(**ag**=C in company) (**pat**=bill) (**dest**=C2 in customer) (**temp**=T2 in time)
    (**id:** T2 = T1 + 1*week)
    (**sit: PERF:** sell(**ag**=C in company) (**pat**=car) (**dest**=C2 in customer)
    (**temp**=T1 in time))
The meaning of the used modalities (**MUST** means 'should'), tenses (**ACTION** means 'present tense' and **PERF** means 'perfect tense') and semantic functions (**ag, go, pat, dest** are the agent, goal, patient and destination of the event and **temp** is the time at which the event takes place) can be found in [8].

3 COLOR-X Event Modeling

The COLOR-X Event Model (CEM) is merely a trace of the events that could and should be performed in the Universe of Discourse (UoD). This way of modeling the dynamic aspects of the UoD links up very well with the way these aspects are described in the requirements document. There is however no automatic acquisition of conceptual models out of these natural language sentences provided yet, as [1] and [19] propose. The following example will illustrate this correspondence:

Requirements Document: *A user can borrow a book from a library. If a user has borrowed a book he has to return it within three weeks, before he is allowed to borrow a book again.*

COLOR-X Event Model (CEM): Figure 1 shows the corresponding CEM. It is fairly easy to read and corresponds very closely to the natural language sentences.

Informally, a box represents an event that could, should or has to take place (depending on the modality), a straight arrow represents the actual occurrence of that event and a 'lightning'-arrow represents the fact that the specific event did not take place.

A strong point of CEMs is the possibility to express the modality of the sentences. The occurrences of the words *'can'* and *'is allowed to'* in the requirements document trigger a **PERMIT**-box. The **MUST**-box is caused by the words *'has to'*. As will be shown further on in section 3.1 when we will treat the

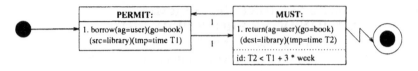

Fig. 1. Example of a COLOR-X Event Model

syntax and semantics of CEMs, a **MUST**-event requires two outgoing arrows to succeeding events: the obligatory event has taken place (as it should be) or the obligation is violated. Because of the fact that in our simple example there is no event specified that has to be done when the book is not returned within three weeks, the outgoing ('lightning'-) arrow ends in an end-node.

3.1 Syntax and Semantics of CEMs

The graphical notations of CEMS can be found in Figure 2. An event box, Figure 2(a), consists of a modality, one ore more event descriptions and zero or more constraint descriptions. An event description consists of a verb denoting an event, which is either an action (an event controlled by some agent) or a (not controlled) process, and one or more terms. The (CPL-) syntax of these terms is: *[<cardinality>] role = [variable in] noun* [2]. The components of a term were already mentioned in section 2.1. An example clarifies this abstract formulation:

one user borrows four books $\Leftrightarrow$ borrow(<1> ag = user) (<4> go = book)

This formal event representation expresses exactly what the modeler wants, which is not always true when using ambiguous natural language sentences. Another advantage of this approach is that it is now possible to use automatic tools to support the modeling process. It is always possible to generate natural language sentences automatically out of the CPL constructs.

A constraint description constrains the value of one or more terms (through the use of variables) absolutely (*age > 21*) or relatively (*age father > age son*). The syntax used to express these constraints is the same as the one used in CPL: (**id:** $V_1 > 21$) and (**id:** $V_1 > V_2$).

Besides the event-nodes there are two special nodes that denote start and final points (Figure 2(b) and (c), respectively).

Because of the fact that there are three modalities to use (permit, necessary and must), there are three different kinds of event-boxes (Figure 2(d) - (f)). In this way a certain degree of completeness is accomplished. When a **MUST**-box is used there are always two succeeding events to be specified. After finishing the model the remark "the model does not specify what has to be done when event X has not taken place" will not occur! One has always to specify a relative or absolute *expiration-time*, which may be infinite, when using a **MUST**-box, in order to verify whether the obligation has been violated or not. The event-boxes

---

[2] everything between square brackets ([..]) is optional

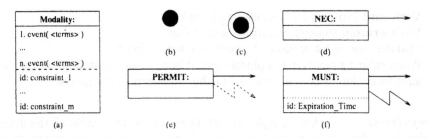

Fig. 2. CEM Notation, (a) general event, (b) start node, (c) final node, (d) necessary, (e) permitted, (f) obligatory

are connected with arrows which denote the fact that one or more events are performed (depicted by a straight arrow with one or more event-numbers) or are not performed at all (depicted by a lightning-arrow).

Creating CEMs: Almost every current conceptual modeling method contains some step in which the events occurring in the UoD are listed, see for example OMTs *event traces* [20]. CEMs do not only contain this kind of information, but also formalize it. The process of creating CEMs is supported with a lexicon. Although the initial step, listing the events and ordering them in time in an informal way, should be done manually by the modeler, the creation of the CEM itself is embedded, and thus supported, by a CASE-environment. The availability of standard building blocks, the reusable event specifications from a lexicon and the complementary information, like *antonym-events* that will be treated later on, generated out of the lexicon, will help the modeler very much in creating correct and complete CEMs.

4   Correct and Complete CEMs

In this section we will give an overview of the advantages yielded by our approach in which a lexicon plays an important role. After modeling a certain UoD, regardless the method used, there remain always two questions:

Correctness, i.e. Is this model right? Is the model constructed according to the syntax and semantics of the method used? By offering standard building blocks, see Figure 2, the resulting model could not be offending the graphical syntax rules. By checking if there exists exactly one start and final state, and that every arrow goes from one block into another, we can verify if the model is syntactically correct. The *kind* and *form* of the words used in the model are constrained by the use of a lexicon. The following information is retrieved from the lexicon in order to get the kind and the form of the words right, respectively.

1. An *event* is identified by a verb, and one or more nouns, that play certain roles. We retrieve the *verb frame* corresponding to the verb from the lexicon and check if the entered role-playing nouns fit into this frame. For example:

Verb and Nouns: borrow, user and book
Verb Frame: somebody borrows something [3]
Match: user *is a* somebody [3] , book *is a* something [3]

2. When entering nouns in the plural form, it is very easy to obtain the singular form from the lexicon, in order to further standardize the model.

Completeness, i.e. Is this the right model? Does the model contain all the information from the requirements document? To verify if the model corresponds to the text from the requirements document it is very helpful to generate a verbalized form of the model, see also [3], [18] and [7]. This is made possible in CEMs because the underlying CPL specification can be verbalized. Another heuristic to verify if a CEM contains all the information from the requirements document is to generate the *antonym-events*, which can be found in the lexicon, of all the events occurring in the CEM and to check if they appear in this CEM already. In the library-example, section 6, the *free*-event was generated as antonym of the *block*-event and added to the CEM. The antonym-event of *borrow* (i.e. *return*), however, is already appearing in the model. The next two sections will show the CPL- and Natural Language generators.

4.1 Generating CPL Specifications

The generation of CPL-specifications from CEMs is fairly easy, because CPL is used as a foundation for CEM. We will review all the concepts used in CEMs and give their CPL counterparts, as our demo-tool CEM2CPL generates:

1. CEMs start- and end-node and their in- and outgoing arrows have no CPL equivalent
2. **CEM:** general event box with modality *Modality*, events $event_1 \cdots event_l$ and corresponding terms $term_{i_1} \cdots term_{i_{p_i}}, 1 \leq i \leq l$, constraints $c_1 \cdots c_k$ and outgoing arrows $a_1 \cdots a_h, 1 \leq h \leq l$
   CPL: for each arrow $a_j, 1 \leq j \leq h$, with label $n\& \cdots \&m, 1 \leq n, m \leq l$:
       Modality: $event_n(\; term_n \cdots term_{n_{p_n}} \;)$
       and $\cdots$ **and**
       Modality: $event_m(\; term_m \cdots term_{m_{p_m}} \;)$
   All the CPL-blocks belonging to a certain arrow are OR-ed together (disjunctive normal form).
   All the constraints $c_1 \cdots c_k$ are AND-ed together (disjunctions between constraints should be expressed as one constraint).
       (id: c_1**) and** $\cdots$ **and (id:** c_k**)**
   If a 'lightning'-arrow is appearing in the model, the negation of the event(s) will appear in the CPL-specification.
3. **CEM:** a certain event box EB_i with all its predecessors ($EB_1 \cdots EB_{i-1}$, without their modalities and tenses). Each $EB_j, 1 \leq j \leq i$ contains events $E_{j_1} \cdots E_{j_l}$

---

[3] Retrieved from WordNet

CPL: Each $EB_j, 1 \leq j \leq i$, is translated into a CPL-disjunction CPL_j according to step 2. Combining each CPL_j will result in:
CPL_i
(**sit: DONE:** CPL_{i-1})
(**sit: PERF:** CPL_{i-2}) $\cdots$ (**sit: PERF:** CPL_1)
For $i = 2$ the CPL specification looks like: CPL_2 (**sit: DONE:** CPL_1)

There are four reasons why we would like to generate CPL-specifications:

1. It is possible to generate Natural Language (NL) sentences out of CPL specifications. Because CPL exists for several years now, we have got some CPL-parsing and NL-generation tools already (section 4.2).
2. Because CPL is logically founded, see [8], it is possible to formally derive new specifications out of existing ones and to check if the specifications are correct. We will not treat the logical foundation of CPL in this paper.
3. CPL supplies formal semantics for the dynamic, as well as the static, aspects of a UoD and its related database, which restricts the behaviour of the *generated* computer programs exactly to the behaviour modeled.
4. By using CPL as the underlying specification language for all kinds of COLOR-X models, we have a uniform way of representing different kinds of information. This uniform format facilitates the integration of the different views on a UoD and makes updates and queries on the integrated information more manageable.

4.2 Generating Natural Language

Our Prolog-translator CPL2NL translates any form of CPL-specifications into correct Natural Language sentences. In this translation process the lexicon plays a very important role, because it contains (information about) verb derivations, plural and singular form of nouns, numerals, adjectives, determiners, etc. We will list some aspects of the CPL specifications that have their impact on the generated sentences. First, the modality determines the auxiliary verb of the sentence as follows: **NEC**, **MUST** and **PERMIT** trigger *obliged to*, *should* and *permitted to* respectively. Secondly, the cardinality of the subject (agent or zero) of the relationship determines the singular or plural form of the related verb. The identification of the objects is added as a subordinate clause, starting with *where....* Finally, the satellites of the CPL specification are translated into adjuncts of place or time.

There are three basic forms of CPL-specifications: [4]

1. *Unconditional:*
   PERMIT:ACTION: borrow(ag=user)(<+>go=book)(<1>src=library)

   [an,user,is,permitted to,borrow,one or more,books,from,a,library]

---

[4] The consonant sound of *user* is not noticed because we do not use a phonetical analyzer. Therefore, the article *an* is generated instead of *a*.

2. *Conditional:*
   MUST:PROSP: return(ag=user)(<+>go=book)(<1>dest=library)
   (sit: **PERF:** borrow(ag=user)(<+>go=book)(<1>src=library))

   ```
   [if,an,user,borrowed,one or more,books,from,a,library,
     then,an,user,will have to,return,one or more,books,to,a,library]
   ```

3. *Identified:*
   PERF: borrow(ag=user)(go=book)(tmp=V1 in time)(id: V1 = yesterday)

   ```
   [an,user,borrowed,a,book,at,a,time,V1,where,V1,is,yesterday]
   ```

5 Generating STDs

There are mainly two reasons to generate State Transitions Diagrams (STDs) out of COLOR-X Event Models:

1. STDs have become a standard (to a certain degree) in modeling the dynamic aspects of an ICS. Although we have had some difficulties and problems using STDs, see section 2, we have shown that our CEMs contain also the information normally found in STDs by generating STDs out of CEMs. The reverse process is only possible if the STD is not violating the STD-rules that are mentioned below.
2. A lot of research in the field of programming code generation from STDs is already done, and most of the existing CASE-tools support such a generation facility, see for example [21]. We can gain from this knowledge and experience by generating STDs as intermediate results.

The generated STDs satisfy the following rules:

- Every STD belongs to exactly *one* active object occurring in the UoD. Active objects are nouns that play the *agent*-role in one or more CEM-events.
- A state is represented by a box, identified by a unique number. A verbal label can be added manually, but has no semantic meaning in the model. This decision is made because it is really hard to find meaningful labels for every state, and to maintain a certain degree of conformity among the labels.
- A transition is represented by a uni-directional arrow labeled with a verbal phrase, describing the event that causes the state-transition. Constraints can be attached to a transition as an optional component of it.
- There exist two special states: the *start*-state and the *final*-state, that are connected with the first 'real' state (i.e. the state before the first event) and the last state, respectively, by empty transitions. These states correspond to the creation and destructions, respectively, of the object.

The next section will describe the algorithm that generates STDs for each active object out of CEMs.

5.1 Algorithm

The following steps describe roughly the STD-generation process, which has as an input a COLOR-X Event Model, consults a lexicon, and has as an output STDs for each active object of the CEM:

1. create the start-node (N_s), the first node (N_1) and an empty transition (T_ϵ) between them
2. for each event box (EB_i) with events $E_{i_1} \cdots E_{i_l}$: create for each outgoing arrow (with label $n\& \cdots \&m$, $1 \leq n, m \leq l$) a state transition to a new or an existing node (depending on whether the succeeding event box (EB_j) is already traversed ($j < i$) or not ($j > i$)). The label attached to this transition is a conjunction of the *verbalized* event descriptions of each E_{i_k}, $1 \leq k \leq l$. The verbal phrase describing event E_{i_k} are adjusted as follows: it is stripped from its modality and tense, and
   - if the object, described by the STD, is the agent of the CEM-event, the CEM-event is copied into the transition-label
   - otherwise, the sentence is transformed into a new one in which the object is the linguistic subject of it. To achieve this the perspective antonym of the verb describing the event is retrieved from the lexicon. This new sentence becomes the transition-label. E.g. the transition label in the library-STD corresponding to the CEM-event *"a user borrows a book from a library"* will become *"a library lends a book to a user"*.
   If the CEM-arrow is a 'lightning'-arrow the negation of the verbal phrase is attached to the STD-transition.
   The (optional) constraint descriptions of event box EB_i is attached to the constraint part of the transition.
3. create the final node (N_f), and an empty transition (T_ϵ) from the last state (N_n) to it

Implementation We have implemented the algorithm as described in the previous section. The resulting Prolog-translator CEM2STD reads in a CEM and generates for each active object occurring in the CEM a corresponding STD-description. These STD-descriptions are translatable into internal representations of several tools. One of these tools is the CASE-tool *Software through Pictures (StP)*, another one is of course the code-generator of our overall project.

5.2 Related Work

In [15] the inference of state machines out of OMT trace diagrams [20] is described. The main difference between their approach and ours is the fact that we use a formalized input, whereas their OMT trace diagrams are informal. The advantages we gain out of this difference are the natural language generation facility, the possibility to use other kinds of (logical) inferences (also using the static information, which has the same logical foundation [4]) and the syntactical and semantical verification of the models. Another difference is that we are generating STDs as an intermediate result to generate programming code, and [15] are incorporating their method into an environment which supports the conceptual modeling process using the OMT methodology.

6 Example

To visualize the techniques, algorithms and tools described in this paper, we will present an example. This example consists of the simplified library book circulation system.

Library: Requirements Document: *The library gives passes to persons that want to become users of the library. If a person does not want to be a user any more, he returns his pass. A user can borrow a book for three weeks. At the end of the allowed lending period, the user should return the book. If a user does not return a book action is taken, by sending him a reminder. If one week after the reminder is sent there is no message from the user, he must pay a fine of Dfl 70 and is blocked for borrowing any more books until the book is returned and the fine is paid.*

Library: COLOR-X Event Model: Figure 3 shows the COLOR-X Event Model corresponding to the requirements stated in the previous chapter, which is *syntactically correct*, i.e. the model is right, and it is semantically correct, i.e. the right model, according to the rules, stated in section 4.

Library: CPL and NL: The CEM2CPL tool has generated all the CPL-specifications, which we will not show here. Some corresponding NL-sentences (generated by CPL2NL) are listed below:

1. [a,library,is,permitted to,give,a,pass,to,an,user]
2. [if,a,library,gave,a,pass,to,an,user,
    then,an,user,is,permitted to,borrow,a,book,from,a,library]
4. [if,a,library,blocked,an,user,
    and,an,user,did not return,a,book,to,a,library,
    and,a,library,sent,a,reminder,to,an,user,
    then,an,user,should,return,a,book,to,a,library,at,time,T4,
    and,an,user,should,pay,a,fine,F,to,a,library,at,time,T4,
    where,F,is,70,and,where,T4,is,infinite]

Library: State Transition Diagram: We haven chosen to let the CEM2STD-tool generate a State Transition Diagram for the active object *Library*. This has led to sentences at the transition-labels in which the library is the subject, see Figure 3 (e.g. *borrow* has become *lend*).

7 Conclusions and Further Research

This paper shows an approach to dynamic modeling (COLOR-X Event Modeling, CEM), the result of which is very close to the original natural language sentences that describe the Universe of Discourse. By facilitating the modeling

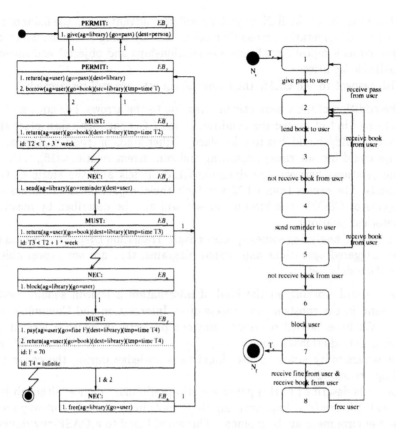

Fig. 3. The CEM and library-STD of a Library Book Circulation System

process itself, by means of a lexicon and offering standard building blocks, the resulting models will tend to be correct and complete. By generating natural language sentences out of CEMs the correspondence with the requirements document can be verified. A nice feature of CEMs is the fact that for each object a State Transition Diagram can be generated, which gives in turn very useful information (object states, state transitions and causes for those transitions) for a programming code generator. A similar project which focuses on Jacksons Entity Structure Diagrams [14] is currently carried out. We are also comparing CEMs with process graphs [10]. All these steps are meant to narrowing the gap between problem specification and implementation.

The resulting dynamic event model is one way of viewing the Universe of Discourse. To get a complete view of the UoD, we have already defined the COLOR-X Static Object Model (CSOM), [4], that describes the static aspects of the UoD in a linguistically-based graphical way, that links up closely with the object model of the OMT-method, [20]. We have also defined a logical foundation of CSOM by giving a translation to CPL-facts. The CSOM-model contains the overall structure of the UoD for the programming code generator.

After finishing the COLOR-X project we will gain advantages in the fields of programming code generation, reusable models (also by using a lexicon, which can be regarded as a repository of reusable relationships and objects) and software and feedback facilities.

With respect to the CEMs the following aspects are still researched:

- The addition of more semantic information to the arrows. For now, we have just one kind of arrow: the conditional one (if $event_i$ has taken place then $event_j$ could/should/has to take place). Other kinds of (rhetorical) relationships could include causal, resulting and concurrent relations [16], [11].
- The relations between the dynamic CEM-models and the static CSOM-models. The events from CEM will have their impact on the relations and objects of CSOM. The kind of impact will also be described by means of rhetorical relations.
- We are still analyzing some aspects of State Transition Diagram- Techniques, like triggered operations and nested diagrams, that are not expressable in CEM-models, yet.

We are still working on the kind of information a lexicon should contain to be useful in the construction process of an Information and Communication System. We have carried out some previous projects, in which a lexicon was used in a data-dictionary environment [6], to interpret ER-diagrams [3], and a general feasibility study to use linguistic knowledge during the conceptual modeling process [2].

The tools described in this paper are still preliminary demos, although fully functional. We are (re-) implementing these tools in a more efficient way into a coherent environment at the moment. This should lead to a CASE-environment in which a Lexicon Management System plays an important role. The overall idea is to support the modeling process, according to the COLOR-X method, with linguistic knowledge and tools in order to generate correct programming code easily.

References

1. W.J. Black. Acquisition of conceptual data models from natural language descriptions. In *Proceedings of the 2nd Conference of the European Chapter of the ACL*, Copenhagen, 1987.
2. P. Buitelaar and R.P. van de Riet. A feasibility study in linguistically motivated object-oriented conceptual design of information systems. Technical Report IR-293, Vrije Universiteit, Amsterdam, 1992.
3. P. Buitelaar and R.P. van de Riet. The use of a lexicon to interpret er diagrams: a like project. In *Proceedings of the ER Conference*, Karlsruhe, 1992.
4. J.F.M. Burg and R.P. van de Riet. Color-x: Object modeling profits from linguistics. Technical Report IR-365, Vrije Universiteit, Amsterdam, 1994.
5. J.F.M. Burg and R.P. van de Riet. Color-x: Object modeling profits from linguistics. 1995. To appear in the Proceedings of the KB&KS'95, the Second International Conference on Building and Sharing of Very Large-Scale Knowledge Bases, Enschede, The Netherlands.

6. J.F.M. Burg, R.P. van de Riet, and S.C. Chang. A data-dictionary as a lexicon: An applicication of linguistics in information systems. In B.Bhargava, T.Finin, and Y.Yesha, editors, *Proceedings of the 2nd International Conference on Information and Knowledge Management*, pages 114–123, 1993.

7. H. Dalianis. A method for validating a conceptual model by natural language discourse generation. *Proceedings of the 4th International Conference on Advanced Information Systems Engineering*, 1992.

8. F.P.M. Dignum. *A Language for Modelling Knowledge Bases. Based on Linguistics, Founded in Logic*. PhD thesis, Vrije Universiteit, Amsterdam, 1989.

9. S.C. Dik. *The Theory of Functional Grammar. Part I: The Structure of the Clause*. Floris Publications, Dordrecht, 1989.

10. R.B. Feenstra and R.J. Wieringa. Lcm 3.0: A language for describing conceptual models – syntax definition. Technical Report IR-344, Vrije Universiteit, Amsterdam, 1993.

11. J.A. Gulla. *Deep Explanation Generation in Conceptual Modeling Environments*. PhD thesis, University of Trondheim, Trondheim, 1993.

12. K.M van Hee, L.J. Somers, and M. Voorhoeve. Executable specifications for distributed information systems. In E.D. Falkenberg and P. Lindgreen, editors, *Information System Concepts: An In-depth Analysis*, pages 139–156. North-Holland/IFIP, Amsterdam, 1989.

13. A.H.M. ter Hofstede. *Information Modelling in Data Intensive Domains*. PhD thesis, Katholieke Universiteit Nijmegen, Nijmegen, 1993.

14. M Jackson. *System Development*. Prentice-Hall, 1983.

15. K. Koskimies and E. Makinen. Inferring state machines from trace diagrams. Technical Report A-1993-3, University of Tampere, 1993.

16. W.C. Mann and S.A. Thompson. Rhetorical structure theory: Description and construction of text structures. In G. Kempen, editor, *Natural Language Generation: New Results in Artificial Intelligence, Psychology and Linguistics*, pages 85–95. Martinus Nijhoff Publishers, 1987.

17. G.A. Miller, R. Beckwith, C. Fellbaum, D. Gross, K. Miller, and R. Tengi. Five papers on wordnet. Technical report, Cognitive Science Laboratory, Princeton University, 1993.

18. G.M. Nijssen and T.A. Halpin. *Conceptual Schema and Relational Database Design : A Fact Oriented Approach*. Prentice Hall, 1989.

19. C. Rolland and C. Proix. A natural language approach for requirements engineering. In P. Loucopoulos, editor, *Proceedings of the 4th International Conference on Advanced Information Systems Engineering*. Springer-Verlag, Manchester, 1992.

20. J. Rumbaugh, M. Blaha, W. Premerlani, F. Eddy, and W. Lorensen. *Object-Oriented Modeling and Design*. Prentice-Hall International, Inc., Englewood Cliffs, New Yersey, 1991.

21. A.I. Wasserman and P.A. Pirchner. A graphical extensible integrated environment for software development. In P. Henderson, editor, *Proceedings of the ACM SIGSOFT/SIGPLAN Software Engineering Symposium on Practical Software Development Environments*, pages 131–142. ACM, ACM Press, March 1986.

22. R.J. Wieringa. *Algebraic Foundations for Dynamic Conceptual Models*. PhD thesis, Vrije Universiteit, Amsterdam, 1990.

Supporting Transaction Design in Conceptual Modelling of Information Systems

Joan A. Pastor-Collado, Antoni Olivé

Dept. de LSI - Facultat d'Informàtica
Universitat Politècnica de Catalunya
Pau Gargallo, 5, 08028 Barcelona, Catalonia
{pastor I olive}@lsi.upc.es

Abstract. A method and a tool for supporting transaction design in conceptual modelling of information systems is presented. The method derives automatically a transaction specification that integrates in a uniform manner the updating of base and derived information and the checking and maintenance of integrity within an information base conceptual schema. Transaction specifications thus obtained achieve their intended purpose and guarantee that information base consistency will be preserved. When there are several possible solutions, the method derives all of them. The designer may then intervene in various ways in order to select the most appropriate ones. From this choice on, the transaction processing system and the end-user can also play a role in the final application of the transaction specification, for this one can be directly executable. Using a declarative, logic-based approach, the method is general, and can be adapted easily to most conceptual modelling methodologies.

1. Introduction and Previous Work

We present here a method and a tool that we have developed for supporting transaction design in conceptual modelling of information systems.

Transaction design is one of the key activities in most current information systems development methodologies. In essence, transaction design has as input the conceptual schema of the information base, including a set of integrity constraints (ICs) that must be satisfied, and the expected result (or intended effect) of a given transaction. From this input, the designer's job consists in specifying, in some language, a set of preconditions and a sequence of operations such that, if the preconditions are satisfied, the sequence of operations will produce the expected result, while leaving the information base consistent [CA+94].

It is not difficult to see that in presence of a complex conceptual schema, possibly considering derived as well as base information, and a large set of ICs, transaction design may be an error-prone activity. On the other hand, transaction specifications are very sensitive with regard to schema changes in deductive laws and integrity constraints: addition, removal or modification of a deductive law or a constraint may invalidate a given transaction specification.

Despite its importance and difficulty, transaction design support has not received the same level of attention as other activities in conceptual modelling. In most methodologies, the task of deriving the preconditions from the ICs is entirely manual, without a supporting tool. The same happens to the task of deriving the appropriate sequence of operations. As an example, [CFT91] presents an information system design expert tool that enforces a modularisation methodology where the designer is confronted with questions relevant to the preservation of consistency when defining update operations, but the designer must somehow ensure manually that transaction execution preserves consistency. In [SO94] we presented, in the context of temporal deductive conceptual models, a method for deriving transactions that included consistency checking preconditions. These were derived from a single base ground update, integrity maintenance was not addressed, and updating derived information did not make sense in such context. There has also been some related work in the database field [CW90,Qia93,SS89,Wal91]. See [PO94,PO95] for more comparative details.

In this paper, we describe a method that can be used to derive automatically a transaction specification, or *Trek* (Transaction enforcing -view and integrity-knowledge), that integrates in a uniform manner the updating of base and derived information and the checking and maintenance of integrity within an information base conceptual schema. The method is an extension and an adaptation of our previous work in the context of transaction synthesis for relational and deductive databases [PO94]. We now regard the output of our synthesis more as transaction specifications to be further refined by a transaction designer. The method is general, and can be adapted easily to most conceptual modelling methodologies. We use a declarative, logic-based language for the definition of conceptual schemas, in the manner of [CHF92]. Transaction specifications obtained with our method achieve their intended purpose and guarantee that information base consistency will be preserved. Often, there are several possible solutions and the method derives all of them. However, the designer may intervene in various ways in order to select the most appropriate ones.

The paper (see [PO95] for an extended version) is organised as follows. Next section defines our accepted information base schemes and introduces the example that will be used throughout the paper. Section 3 reviews the components of the augmented information base schema, a key concept for the method. Section 4 illustrates our synthesis method through a detailed example. In section 5 we comment on how the method can be used to furtherly support transaction design with some additional examples. Finally, in section 6 we present our conclusions.

2. Information Base Conceptual Schemes

We define here the kind of information base schemes treated in this paper. We want to be general, and therefore we use a simple formalism, easily adaptable to any conceptual modelling language. An information base (conceptual) schema IBS consists of three finite sets: a set B of base predicates, a set D of derived predicates with their deductive rules, and a set I of integrity constraints (ICs). Base predicates are the schemes of the facts explicitly stored in the information base, which form the so called extensional information base. Derived predicates are schemes representing information that is not stored in the information base but can be derived using deductive rules. ICs are used to specify unwanted information base states and forbidden state transitions.

Before providing more formal definitions for some of the previous concepts, let us introduce the base predicate schemes corresponding to the information base example that we will be using throughout the paper. They are shown in Fig. 2-1 on next page, together with their intended meaning. Our example, inspired upon the one in [Qia93], is an information base for an "Employment Office" that arranges labour interviews between its registered job applicants and some employer companies collaborating with it. For the people administered by the office, it also keeps track of those already employed.

Fig. 2-1

Base predicate	Base predicate meaning
App(x)	'x' is a job applicant
Eco(y)	'y' is an employer company
Int(x,y)	'x' has an interview with 'y'
Emp(x)	'x' is an employee

Fig. 2-2

Derived predicate with rule	Derived predicate meaning
Cand(x) ← Int(x,y) ∧ Eco(y)	'x' is considered a job candidate when s/he has an interview with an employer

Fig. 2-3

Integrity rule	Integrity constraint meaning
Ic1 ← Emp(x) ∧ App(x)	Nobody can be both employee and applicant
Ic2 ← Cand(x) ∧ ¬ App(x)	Candidates must be applicants

Formally, a deductive rule is a formula of the form: $A \leftarrow L_1 \wedge ... \wedge L_n$ with $n \geq 1$ where A is an atom denoting the conclusion or derived predicate, and the $L_1,...,L_n$ are literals representing the conditions, which can be base, derived or evaluable predicates, possibly negated. Evaluable predicates are system predicates, such as the comparison or arithmetic predicates, that can be evaluated without accessing the information base. Any variables in $A, L_1,..., L_n$ are assumed to be universally quantified over the whole formula. The terms in the conclusion must be distinct variables, and the terms in the conditions must be variables or constants. Variables in the body of a rule not appearing in its head are called the "local variables" of such rule. As usual, we require that the schema is allowed. Fig. 2-2 has our single derived predicate for defining job candidates.

Integrity constraints (ICs) are conditions that the information base is required to satisfy at all times. Formally, an IC is a closed first-order formula that the information base is required to satisfy. We deal with constraints that have the form of a denial: $\leftarrow L_1 \wedge ... \wedge L_n$ with $n \geq 1$ where the L_i are literals (i.e. positive or negative base, derived or evaluable predicates) and variables are assumed to be universally quantified over the whole formula. For the sake of uniformity, we associate to each IC an inconsistency predicate Icn , thus taking the same form as deductive rules. We call them integrity rules. We will use in our example the two ICs shown in Fig. 2-3 above. The set of employees is disjoint with the set of applicants (Ic1), which is a superset of candidates (Ic2). Note that Ic2 is furtherly defined in terms of the derived predicate Cand.

3. The Augmented Information Base Schema

In this section we shortly present and define the concepts and terminology of internal events, transition and internal events rules, key concepts in our method. Conceptually, internal events, transition rules and internal events rules are meta-level constructs describing the dynamic behaviour of an information base when confronted with updates. These rules depend only on the information base schema. They are independent from the base facts stored, and from any particular update. In section 4, we will discuss the use of transition and internal events rules for transaction specification synthesis. The following presentation is an overview of theory explained elsewhere [for ex. PO94], where the reader will find the full details on their formal derivation.

Let IB be a information base, U an update and IB^n the "new" updated information base. We say that U induces a transition from IB (current state) to IB^n (new, updated state). We assume that U consists of a set of base facts to be inserted and/or deleted.

Due to the deductive rules, U may induce other updates on some derived predicates. Let P be a (derived) predicate in D, and let P^n denote the same predicate evaluated in IB^n. Formally, we associate to each predicate P an *insertion internal events* predicate ιP and a *deletion internal events* predicate δP, defined as:

(1) $\quad \forall x(\iota P(x) \leftrightarrow P^n(x) \wedge \neg P(x))$

(2) $\quad \forall x(\delta P(x) \leftrightarrow P(x) \wedge \neg P^n(x))$

where x is a vector of variables. From (1) and (2) we have:

(3) $\quad \forall x(P^n(x) \leftrightarrow (P(x) \wedge \neg \delta P(x)) \vee \iota P(x))$

(4) $\quad \forall x(\neg P^n(x) \leftrightarrow (\neg P(x) \wedge \neg \iota P(x)) \vee \delta P(x))$

If P is a base predicate, then ιP facts and δP facts respectively represent insertions and deletions of base facts, i.e. base updates. They will represent derived updates if P is a derived predicate. If P is an inconsistency predicate (i.e. Ic), then ιIc facts that occur during the transition will correspond to violations of its corresponding IC and δIc facts cannot happen in any transition. Two special-purpose system events are also used, 'ιAbort' and 'ιExit'; their meaning will be clear with the examples of sections 4 and 5.

Let us take a base, derived or inconsistency predicate P of the database. The definition of P consists of the rules in the database schema having P in the conclusion. Consider now one of such rules, say rule 'i': $P_i(x) \leftrightarrow L_1 \wedge ... \wedge L_q$. When the rule is to be evaluated in the updated state its form is $P^n_i(x) \leftrightarrow L^n_1 \wedge ... \wedge L^n_q$. Now if we replace each literal in the body by its equivalent definition, given in (3) and (4), we get a new rule, which defines predicate P^n_i (new state) in terms of current state predicates and of internal events. When this is done for all deductive rules defining predicate P, we obtain a whole new rule set, where it is convenient to distinguish between two types of rules:

1) Rules 'nO': They explain when P remains true in the new state because it has not been changed during the transition, thus remaining as in the Old state. They are headed with $P^{nO}_i(x)$ when they apply to a single definition 'i' of P, and with $P^{nO}(x)$ when applying to P as a whole.

2) Rules 'nT': They indicate all possible ways for P to become true in the new state due to some internal events occurred within the Transition. They are headed with $P^{nT}_i(x)$ when they apply to a single definition 'i' of P, and with $P^{nT}(x)$ when applying to P as a whole.

Finally, we may now refer to both P^{nO} and P^{nT} through: $P^n(x) \leftarrow P^{nO}(x)$ and $P^n(x) \leftarrow P^{nT}(x)$. We call these rules, i.e. with (possibly subindexed) conclusions P^n, P^{nT} and P^{nO}, *transition rules* for predicate P. The transition rules corresponding to the information base example are shown in Fig. 3-1 with a clear intuitive meaning. Thus, for example, TR.6 states that 'x' is a candidate in the new state, if s/he had a programmed interview with 'y' in the old state that has not been cancelled in the transition, and 'y' has been inserted as employer company during the transition.

Fig. 3-1

Code	Transition rule
TR.1	$Cand^n(x) \leftarrow Cand^{nO}(x)$
TR.2	$Cand^n(x) \leftarrow Cand^{nT}(x)$
TR.3	$Cand^{nT}(x) \leftarrow Cand^{nT}_1(x)$
TR.4	$Cand^{nO}(x) \leftarrow Cand^{nO}_1(x)$
TR.5	$Cand^{nO}_1(x) \leftarrow Int(x,y) \wedge \neg\, \delta Int(x,y) \wedge Eco(y) \wedge \neg\, \delta Eco(y)$
TR.6	$Cand^{nT}_1(x) \leftarrow Int(x,y) \wedge \neg\, \delta Int(x,y) \wedge \iota Eco(y)$
TR.7	$Cand^{nT}_1(x) \leftarrow \iota Int(x,y) \wedge Eco(y) \wedge \neg\, \delta Eco(y)$
TR.8	$Cand^{nT}_1(x) \leftarrow \iota Int(x,y) \wedge \iota Eco(y)$
TR.9	$Ic1^{nO} \leftarrow Emp(x) \wedge \neg\, \delta Emp(x) \wedge App(x) \wedge \neg\, \delta App(x)$
TR.10	$Ic1^{nT} \leftarrow Emp(x) \wedge \neg\, \delta Emp(x) \wedge \iota App(x)$
TR.11	$Ic1^{nT} \leftarrow \iota Emp(x) \wedge App(x) \wedge \neg\, \delta App(x)$
TR.12	$Ic1^{nT} \leftarrow \iota Emp(x) \wedge \iota App(x)$
TR.13	$Ic2^{nO} \leftarrow Cand(x) \wedge \neg\, \delta Cand(x) \wedge \neg App(x) \wedge \neg\, \iota App(x)$
TR.14	$Ic2^{nT} \leftarrow Cand(x) \wedge \neg\, \delta Cand(x) \wedge \delta App(x)$
TR.15	$Ic2^{nT} \leftarrow \iota Cand(x) \wedge \neg\, App(x) \wedge \neg\, \iota App(x)$
TR.16	$Ic2^{nT} \leftarrow \iota Cand(x) \wedge \delta App(x)$
TR.17	$App^n(x) \leftarrow App^{nO}(x)$
TR.18	$App^n(x) \leftarrow App^{nT}(x)$
TR.19	$App^{nO}(x) \leftarrow App(x) \wedge \neg\, \delta App(x)$
TR.20	$App^{nT}(x) \leftarrow \iota App(x)$
TR....	$Eco^n(y) \leftarrow ...;\ Int^n(x,y) \leftarrow ...;\ Emp^n(x)$

Let P be a derived or inconsistency predicate. Once P^{nT} has been stated, from formula (1) we get: $\iota P(x) \leftarrow P^{nT}(x) \wedge \neg P(x)$ which is called the *insertion internal events rule* of predicate P, and allows us to deduce which ιP facts (induced insertions) happen in a transition. If P is an inconsistency predicate we can remove the literal $\neg P(x)$ since we will assume that $P(x)$ is false, for all x, in the old state. For this case we further define general database inconsistency with the standard auxiliary rules: $\iota Ic \leftarrow \iota Ick$ with $k = 1..r$, where r is the number of ICs in the database. Fig. 3-2 shows the insertion internal events rules for the example.

If P is a derived predicate, we can use definition (2) for a deletion internal event to generate its corresponding *deletion internal events rule* of predicate P: $\delta P(x) \leftarrow P(x) \wedge \neg P^n(x)$. Last row in Fig. 3-2 includes the deletion internal events rule for our example.

Fig. 3-2

Code	Insertion internal events rule
IR.1	$\iota Cand(x) \leftarrow Cand^{nT}(x) \wedge \neg Cand(x)$
IR.2	$\iota Ic1 \leftarrow Ic1^{nT}$
IR.3	$\iota Ic2 \leftarrow Ic2^{nT}$
IR.4	$\iota Ic \leftarrow \iota Ic1$
IR.5	$\iota Ic \leftarrow \iota Ic2$
	Deletion internal events rule
DR.1	$\delta Cand(x) \leftarrow Cand(x) \wedge \neg Cand^n(x)$

Let IBS be a information base schema. We call *augmented information base schema*, or A(IBS), the schema consisting of IBS, its transition rules and its internal events rules. In the next section we will discuss the important role of A(IBS) in our method for transaction specificacion synthesis. The augmented information base schema for our example would be the union of the contents of Figs. 2-1, 2-2, 2-3, 3-1 and 3-2. It is easy to show that, because IBS is allowed, then A(IBS) is also allowed.

4. Synthesis of Transaction Specifications

4.1 Transaction Requests

We envision a transaction-design-support-system that builds transactions specifications from the corresponding design-time parameterised *transaction requests*. A transaction (specification) request (Tr) basically includes those transaction "postconditions requirements" posed by the designer, i.e. his/her intents about the effect of the expected transaction. Formally, a parameterised update transaction request Tr consists of either $[P^n(p)]$ or $[\neg P^n(p)]$ at least, where P can be a base, a derived or an auxiliar predicate, and p is a vector of terms. Usually, terms will mostly be parameters (i.e. 'Per', 'Comp') but some could also be constants ('joan','UPC').

The simplest case is that of Tr being a postcondition expressed in terms of one of the base or derived predicates of the information base schema. As examples, two of the transaction requests that we will later elaborate on are $[App^n(Per)]$ and $[\neg Cand^n(Per)]$. With the first one the designer wants a transaction specification to insert the person 'Per' as applicant. In the case of $[\neg Cand^n(Per)]$, our method will synthesise a transaction specification for removing the job candidate status of a particular person if s/he had it. Note that this means a deletion from a derived predicate.

More complex is the case where Tr represents a compound postcondition affecting more than one base and/or derived predicate. For doing so, the designer must temporarily use an auxiliar (derived) predicate (i.e. P), different from any other in the information base schema, whose definition expresses the intended postcondition. The (auxiliar) augmented schema corresponding to the rules of such predicate is generated on the fly, to be used in the synthesis of the pursued transaction specification. For example, $[Aux1^n(Per)]$ with $Aux1(x) \leftarrow Emp(x) \wedge \neg App(x)$ can be used to synthesise a transaction specification for doing whatever is needed so that 'Per' is a non-applicant employee.

4.2 Our Approach

We now focus on the problem of the automatic generation at design-time of consistency-preserving transaction specifications from transaction requests. Stated more precisely, the problem is: Given an initial transaction request, which reflects the transaction designer's updating intents, and considering the information base schema, obtain a transaction capable of performing those intents without violating consistency. In order to realise this purpose, we have designed and implemented a method that can be briefly described and exemplified as follows. See [PO95] for a detailed formalisation of the method.

4.2.1 Synthesis Output from [App^n(Per)]

Assume that a designer poses the request [App^n(Per)] in search of a transaction specification for adding someone as a job applicant. From this request and our example (augmented) information base schema, our method ultimately generates the corresponding transaction text (i.e *trek_text*) contained in Fig. 4-1. Note the slightly different syntax used for the various predicate types, which comes directly from our implementation of the method in Prolog. The only differences are that base and derived predicates must begin with a lower-case letter, that the super-index 'n' qualifying new predicates is implemented with prefix 'n_', and that meta-level update operators 'ι' and 'δ' are also handled as prefixes 'i_' and 'd_', respectively. Horizontal and vertical lines have been added for ease of reading. This layout format will be also followed for the other example outputs in section 5.

Fig. 4-1

	trek_text([n_app(Per)],
1	-------- if app(Per) then
2	----------|--- i_exit
3	----------|- else
4	----------|--- i_app(Per) ,
5	----------|---- if emp(Per) then
6	----------|-----|- either
7	----------|-----|--|--- d_emp(Per)
8	----------|-----|--|- or
9	----------|-----|--|--- i_abort
10	----------|-----|- end_either
11	----------|---- end_if
12	-------- end_if
	). % end of trek text

With regard to our assumed run-time environment in this and any other examples, we consider delayed-update semantics for transaction-processing-time.

Within Fig. 4-1, line 1 controls if the person is already an applicant, in which case line 2 proposes to exit the transaction without any updating. In general, the special event 'i_exit' is used to exit its nesting compound instruction but keeping any update so far proposed. If the person under consideration is not an applicant, line 4 proposes to insert him/her as such. However, in this case, our integrity constraint Ic1 is directly affected by such base update, and a checking/maintenance preventive repair can be offered. The repair notices that, if we want to insert as applicant (line 4) some employee (line 5), then there are only two alternatives not to violate database consistency: either to delete the person as employee (line 7) or to abort the whole transaction (line 9).

4.2.2 Synthesis process from [App^n(Per)]

The above used transaction request [App^n(Per)], together with the implicit consistency requirement [¬Ic] and the A(IBS), implicitly configure a generic search space that we conveniently explore through two types of design-time derivations: *Translate* and *Repair* derivations. From the interleaving of those derivations we draw an interim tree, the *trek_tree*. The process is independent of any particular value that parameter 'Per' could take. For the case of our example, Fig. 4-2 on next page shows the generic search space of interest, together with the resulting trek_tree.

A *translate derivation* is used to obtain a "translation" from the original transaction request. Box T_1 in Fig. 4-2 includes the starting translate derivation rooted at the original request. Single translate steps explore and resolve their input goals until none is left. Intuitively, $App^n(Per)$ will succeed if it was already true in the old state (step 1, left branch), that is if App(Per) holds (step 3, left) and is not deleted during the transition (to be controlled in box R_1). Alternatively, it will also succeed if added in the transition (step 1, right branch), i.e. if App(Per) is inserted (step 3, right). On their way, translate steps add new nodes to the trek_tree under construction, depending upon the semantics of their input goal and selected literal within such goal. Note how various new predicates in the example have resulted in different node types in the trek_tree (steps 1, 2 left, 2 right). Their concrete semantics can be found in [PO95].

However, for the translation above to be consistency-preserving, consistency needs to be enforced with regard to some conditions, such as the schema ICs and other particular transaction requirements either initially given by the designer or drawn from the A(IBS) while doing the translate derivation. *Repair derivations* are in charge of enforcing such external and internal consistency conditions. A repair derivation represents a subsidiary derivation spawning from a Translate derivation. Repair derivations maintain, check and use the "Consistency conditions set" C, an internally maintained set of conditions representing situations that we want any transaction to avoid. C is the source of all possible repairs or branch invalidations in our interim tree. For efficiency considerations, C is initially filled with all consistency conditions implied by the special consistency request [¬Ic], which is implicitly appended to every other transaction request. For our current example, only one such condition is used, which coincides with the body of rule TR.10 from Fig. 3-1. For this and other consistency conditions there is always an implicit preserving action, i.e. that of aborting whatever updates had been proposed so far, as shown in Fig. 4-2.

Back to our example, box R_1 in Fig. 4-2 includes the appropriate repair derivation for ensuring that App(Per) has not been deleted and, more important, that it will not be deleted later on; this is accomplished by including such internal consistency condition in set C. On the other hand, repair derivation in box R_2 follows the right branch in T_1, where the insertion of App(Per) was considered. This insertion affects one of our ICs, i.e. Ic1, in the way shown in R_2. There, the above mentioned consistency condition is relevant to the proposed insertion (step 1), particularly if 'Per' was already employee in the old state (step 2). Since we do not want such potential inconsistency to succeed, we may force its failure in either two ways (step 3): by deleting 'Per' as employee, or by aborting the whole transaction. Both alternatives are respectively considered by the two translate derivations in boxes T_2 and T_3. This ends the derivation process, for ICs are not further affected.

In this way, repair derivations call other translate derivations in order to obtain the translations for their found redressing actions. These actions may include base updates, such as $\delta Emp(Per)$ in T_2, or the special 'abort' event, like in T_3, cases where the translation is straightforward. But they may also include derived events, for which an appropriate translation in terms of base events must be found through the further exploration of the search space implied by their internal events rules from A(IBS).

Fig. 4-2

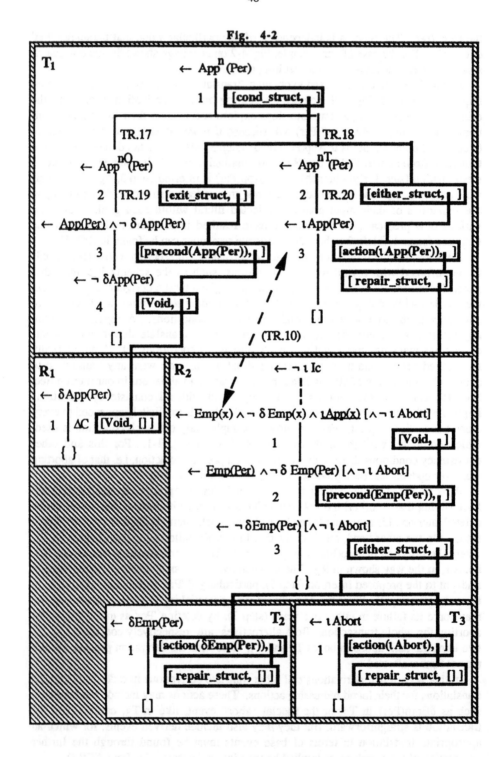

Trek_trees such as the one in Fig. 4-2 usually need to be optimised in various ways: redundant and empty nodes as well as useless or unsuccessful branches must be pruned away. Finally, a simple in-order search of the remaining tree is the base for the layout of the final transaction specification text, or *trek_text*, in whatever appropriate transaction language syntax we choose. The labels in the nodes of the trimmed trek_tree are interpreted and treated according to their implied semantics and the language chosen; this guides the inclusion of the appropriate keywords in the text, as well as the correct composition of condition conjunctions and disjunctions. Fig. 4-1 portraits the trek_text resulting from the above tree, once trimmed, using an English pseudo-code language.

5. Supporting Transaction Design

In general, a transaction specification synthesised with our method may include every possible way in which its request could be accomplished. This may embrace several alternative ways for preserving consistency, translating an update to a derived predicate, or selecting relevant tuples for any of those. In our transaction specifications, all such alternative options may be presented under the premises of special ad-hoc control instructions, such as 'either' in Fig. 4-1. However, there are cases where a designer is not necessarily interested in the fullblown transaction specification but in a (still consistency-preserving) version of it. Such refinement may result from specialising the synthesis to particular design requirements, and/or from the appropriate handling of the synthesis (interim) outputs.

For a simple example, recall from Fig. 4-1 the two alternative ways of preserving consistency included within the 'either' control instruction. That was our first example of non-determinism within a transaction specification. In our transaction specifications, non-determinism may appear within consistency repairs, and in the context of translating updates to derived predicates. Since, in general, translate and repair transaction pieces may interleave, the resulting transaction specifications can be highly non-deterministic. However, we regard such non-determinism both as a good specification knowledge source for further transaction design, as well as the basis for an advanced transaction processing system and a sophisticated user-interaction system.

The trek_tree in Fig. 4-2 includes all consistency-preserving alternatives relevant to its original request. We used them all in the trek_text of Fig. 4-1. However, we could have searched such trek_tree in a more specialised way in order to come up with different (customised) trek_texts. For example, a designer could be interested in considering just consistency checking for a particular transaction, thus only aborting any potential integrity violation. This would leave our example trek_text without lines 6, 7, 8 and 10. For some other transaction, s/he could be after integrity maintenance alone, i.e. not to consider aborts as long as there are possible compensating actions. There are also interesting intermediate situations, where consistency checking might be used for some constraints while for some other constraints integrity maintenance is preferred.

From a trimmed trek_tree, a designer could further choose, out of all the valid updating alternatives considered in it, those options most interesting for his/her application. This would not require to undo every non-deterministic situation within the tree. On the other hand, s/he can also rely on the run-time transaction processing system or the end-user to take some or all of the (remaining) decisions. The next two examples show more complex non-deterministic situations amenable to further design refinement and advanced use.

5.1 Synthesis output from $[\neg App^n(Per)]$

If the designer issues the $[\neg App^n(Per)]$ request to our system, the method will generate the trek_text contained in Fig. 5-1. Within this figure, line 1 controls if the person to be employed is already an applicant, in which case line 2 proposes to delete him/her as such. Such deletion of applicant directly affects Ic2, so a checking/maintenance preventive repair is drawn from a consistency condition that coincides with the body of rule TR.14 in Fig. 3-1. That is, in case that such not-to-be-applicant were also a candidate (line 3) either it should be deleted as such (lines 5 to 12) or an abort should be proposed (line 14).

For the alternative of deleting the person as candidate, we initially draw the proposal that $\delta Cand(Per)$ should be pursued, shown in line 5 as a commented action preceding its unfolding. Later on, our method translates such derived-update request into the needed base update instructions (lines 5 to 12).

Line 3 together with lines 5 to 12 in fact correspond to the main body of the transaction that would be synthesised from the $[\neg Cand^n(Per)]$ request. This is a request for deleting an instance of a derived predicate defined using a local variable. To accomplish such objective, we should eliminate any existing way in which the contents of the information base support the fact Cand(Per), for which we will now need to take into account the values taken by the local variable(s) in the definition(s) of the view predicate. In our example, this is obtained with the 'foreach' instruction of lines 6 to 12. For this instruction we automatically synthesise the needed meaningful Skolem variable names (i.e. '_Comp'). Line 6 walks through the set of all employer companies with whom the person in 'Per' has an arranged job interview, thus setting the cursor variable '_Comp' appropriately.

Fig. 5-1

	trek_text([not n_app(Per)],
1	--------- if app(Per) then
2	----------l- d_app(Per) ,
3	----------l--- if cand(Per) then
4	----------l----l-- either
5	----------l----l----l- { d_cand(Per) }
6	----------l----l----l- foreach [_Comp] in int(Per, _Comp) and eco(_Comp) do
7	----------l----l----l----l--- either
8	----------l----l----l----l--- l--- d_int(Per, _Comp)
9	----------l----l----l----l--- l- or
10	----------l----l----l----l--- l--- d_eco(_Comp)
11	----------l----l----l----l--- end_either
12	----------l----l----l-- end_foreach
13	----------l----l----l- or
14	----------l----l----l--- i_abort
15	----------l----l-- end_either
16	----------l--- end_if
17	--------- end_if
	). % end of trek text

For each such company, lines 7 to 11 offer to either delete the pending interview or delete the employer status for the company. In this way, 'Per' will no longer remain a job candidate since s/he will not have any more interviews with employer companies, although s/he could still keep some interviews with non-employers.

This example shows how we address in an integrative way the problems of base and derived updating, integrity checking and integrity maintenance within our transaction specification synthesis approach.

Again, Fig. 5-1 includes the transaction obtained directly from a trek_tree that includes all possible consistency-preserving and derived-update alternatives. But, as was said before, the designer could intervene in order to customise the resulting transaction to particular application-domain semantics or to personal requirements. Integrity checking alone, or integrity maintenance alone, or both adequately mixed would result in various versions of the above transaction in Fig. 5-1.

5.2 Synthesis output from [Cand^n(Per)]

This example deals with a derived-update request for a transaction specification to make some person 'Per' candidate. For space limitations, we only show in Fig. 5-2 the synthesis output for [Cand^n(Per)] without considering ICs.

Fig. 5-2

	trek_text([n_cand(Per)], % without ICs
1	-------- if int(Per, _Comp) and eco(_Comp) then
2	----------|--- i_exit
3	----------|- else
4	----------|--- either
5	----------|---|--- forsome [_Comp] in int(Per, _Comp) do
6	----------|---|----|- i_eco(_Comp)
7	----------|---|--- end_forsome
8	----------|---|- or
9	----------|---|--- forsome [_Comp] in eco(_Comp) do
10	----------|---|----|- i_int(Per,_Comp)
11	----------|---|--- end_forsome
12	----------|---|- or
13	----------|---|--- forsome new [_Comp] such that
14	----------|---|----|---- not int(Per, _Comp) and not eco(_Comp)
15	----------|---|----|- do
16	----------|---|----|---- i_int(Per, _Comp) ,
17	----------|---|----|---- i_eco(_Comp)
18	----------|---|--- end_forsome
19	----------|--- end_either
20	-------- end_if
	). % end of trek text

Fig. 5-2 above contains the trek_text for this request. When 'Per' already has some interview with some employer (line 1), i.e. s/he is already a job candidate, line 2 exits the transaction. Otherwise, three alternatives exist: namely, to consider as employers some (at least one) of the companies with whom 'Per' has interviews, if any (lines 5 to

7); or to arrange an interview between 'Per' and some (one or more) of our already considered employer companies, if any (lines 9 to 11); or to ask the user for some (one at least) yet unknown companies in order to make them employers with interviews with 'Per' (lines 13 to 18).

The condition within line 14 can be used to help the user look for the right companies, or to help the system check for wrong user elections. Similarly, the conditions in lines 5 and 9 could be used to present the respectively satisfying companies to the user for him/her to select some.

The above combination of 'either' with 'forsomes' is highly non-deterministic. Of course, the designer could purge some 'either' options. S/he could also restrict some 'forsome' instructions to their "forone" counterpart, which asks the user (resp. system) for just one (resp. the first found) Skolem-variable value satisfying the condition. Out of the remaining alternatives, at run-time the user should choose one or more relevant 'either' options and guide the selection of (or provide) 'forsome' values. While the last 'either' option may always be relevant, the other two depend on the existence of values in the nformation base satisfying their conditions. Note that the (three) relevant alternatives could be freely combined within one transaction execution, thus making 'Per' a candidate through various non-conflicting ways. A run-time update solution involving these multiple ways might not be minimal, but it could be meaningful, and thus useful. The lack of conflicts is given by the delayed-update semantics; recall that it guarantees that 'forsome' and 'forsome-new' conditions are only affected by the old database state, and not by the proposed base updates, to be applied at transaction-finish.

The flexibility implied by the above instructions will require a sophisticated run-time user interaction system that we have not yet developed. Such flexible user-interaction framework could sometimes prove too demanding for some types of user, or even inadequate for some types of applications (i.e. user-less applications, with update requests issued programmatically). It is for situations like these that our transactions should better be synthesised under the selective guidance of a designer. In this case, s/he could also use application-domain knowledge to purge alternatives and/or assign them priorities to be used by the transaction processing system. Evaluation cost-estimates could be used at design-time, such as the length or complexity of 'either' options, or types of 'forsome' conditions (i.e. base vs. derived, simple vs. compound); as well as at run-time, such as database population statistics. The transaction processing system, on its side, could also incorporate mechanisms to automatically select or invent variable values. Other additional features of our method are explained in [PO95].

6. Conclusions and Further Work

Transaction design is one of the key activities in conceptual modelling of information systems but its support has not received enough attention by the research community.

In this paper we have presented a new method for the generation of consistency-preserving transaction specifications in the context of conceptual modelling of information systems. The method is based on the transition and internal events rules, which explicitly define the dynamic behaviour of the information base when updated. Using these rules, a formal method allows us to automatically synthesise a legal transaction specification from an initial update transaction request. The integrative way in which the method deals with the problems of base and derived updating, integrity checking and integrity maintenance can be considered as its most important asset. However, the results are also useful as the basis for more advanced transaction design support and more sophisticated transaction processing and user-interaction systems.

At its current stage, the synthesis part of the method has been fully prototyped using meta-programming techniques in Prolog. We can also generate directly executable transaction specifications in Prolog in order to simulate information base updating within the dynamic main-memory Prolog database.

We plan to extend this work along several lines: formalisation and implementation of the case of schemes with recursive rules and rules with aggregate functions; explicit treatment of the modification operation; consideration of more complex initial transaction requests. Last, there is plenty of further implementation work along the advanced transaction design support, processing and utilisation introduced in this paper.

Acknowledgements

The authors would like to thank H. Decker and the rest of the Odissea Group (T.Urpí, E.Teniente, J.Sistac, M.R.Sancho, C.Quer, C.Martin, E.Mayol, D.Costal) for many useful comments and discussions on the theme of this paper. We also appreciate the valuable comments from the unknown referees.

This work has been partially supported by the CICYT PRONTIC project TIC 680.

References

[CA+94]   Coleman,D.;Arnold,P.;Bodoff,S;Dollin,C;Gilchrist,H.;Hayes,F.;Jeremes,P.
          "Object-oriented Development. The Fusion Method". Prentice Hall Intl.,
          1994.

[CFT91]   Casanova,M.A.;Furtado,A.L.;Tucherman,L. "A Software Tool for Modular
          Database Design". ACM TODS, Vol. 16, No. 2, June 1991, pp. 209-234.

[CHF92]   Casanova,M.A.;Hemerly,A.S.;Furtado,A.L. "A Declarative Conceptual
          Modelling Language: Description and Example Application". Proc. of the 4th
          Int. Conf. CAiSE'92, Manchester, 1992, pp. 589-611.

[CW90]   Ceri, S.; Widom,J. "Deriving Production Rules for Constraint Maintenance".
          Proc. of 16th VLDB, Brisbane, Australia, 1990, pp. 566-577.

[PO94]   Pastor,J.A.; Olivé,A. "An Approach to the Synthesis of Update Transactions
          in Deductive Databases", Proc. of the 5th. Int. Conference on Information
          Systems and Management of Data (CISMOD'94), Madras, India, 1994.

[PO95]   Pastor,J.A.; Olivé,A. "Supporting Transaction Design in Conceptual
          Modelling of Information Systems (Extended Version)", Internal research
          report LSI-95-11-R, Dept. LSI, UPC, Barcelona, 1995.

[Qia93]   Quian,X. "The Deductive Synthesis of Database Transactions".ACM TODS,
          Vol. 18, No. 4, December 1993, pp. 626-677.

[SO94]   Sancho,M.R.; Olivé,A. "Deriving Transaction Specifications from Deductive
          Conceptual Models of Information Systems". Proc. of the 6th Int. Conf.
          CAiSE'94, Utrech, The Netherlands, 1994, pp. 311-324.

[SS89]   Sheard,T.;Stemple,D. "Automatic Verification of Database Transaction
          Safety", ACM TODS, Vol. 14, No. 3, September 1989, pp. 322-368.

[Wal91]   Wallace,M. "Compiling Integrity Checking into Update Procedures", 12th
          Int. Conf. on Artificial Intelligence, Sydney, Australia, 1991, Vol. 2, pp. 24-
          30.

Facet Models for Problem Analysis

Andreas. L. Opdahl[1] and Guttorm Sindre[2]

[1] Dept. of Information Science, University of Bergen, N-5020 Bergen, Norway
[2] Fac. of El. Eng. and Comp. Sci., Norwegian Institute of Technology, N-7034 Trondheim, Norway

Abstract. The paper points to weaknesses of modelling approaches which are *orientated* towards certain aspects of the problem analysis domain (e.g., process orientation, object orientation.) It is concluded that modelling approaches are needed that allow the modeller to 1) choose to represent a wide range of aspects of real-world phenomena depending on the problem at hand, and 2) simultaneously represent several aspects of the same real-world phenomenon whenever needed. A framework for *facet modelling* of real-world problem domains is therefore outlined. It is discussed how facet models can be defined and visualised to deal with the complexity of contemporary problem domains, and with the complexity inherent from the ambition of the facet-modelling framework itself.

1 Introduction

In problem analysis, models of the problem are established, assessed, improved and used as a starting point for IS design. Different paradigms have emerged for this purpose, corresponding to various classes of modelling approaches. Each of the approaches are *orientated* towards certain aspects of the phenomena in the real-world problem domain. Some of the most prominent types are: 1) function or process orientation (i.e., structured analysis, SA), emphasising the activities performed in the real-world system, e.g. [6, 8]; 2) information orientation (i.e., entity-relationship (ER) modelling), emphasising the information resources of the system and their relationships, e.g. [4, 24]; 3) object orientation, emphasising the objects manipulated by the system, e.g. [22, 5], and 4) subject orientation (or agent orientation), emphasising the roles, units etc. performing the activities in the system, e.g. [7].

Each of these orientations has its pros and cons. Criticism of structured analysis can be found in, e.g., [18, 3, 16]; of purely information-oriented approaches in, e.g., [10], and of object-orientation in, e.g., [15, 12, 13, 2]. The more recent, subject-oriented approaches have been less criticised in literature so far.

This paper is written from the viewpoint that clearly orientated models are not to be striven for in the early phases of problem analysis, but rather a source of problems on their own. The rest of the paper will explore this hypothesis. First, Section 2 will discuss what orientation really means, before Section 3 presents the facet-modelling framework which attempts to limit orientation problems to the extent possible. Afterwards, Section 4 will go on to outline important facet types, and Section 5 will discuss how to visualise the resulting models. Finally, section 6 will conclude the paper and suggest some paths for further work.

2 Orientation

2.1 What is It?

Four examples of possible orientations for modelling a problem domain were given above. One might think that the difference between them is that they capture different aspects of the real world, i.e., that process-orientated models capture information about processes, information-oriented ones about data structures, object-orientated ones about encapsulated data types, and so on. However, this is only half the truth. The point is rather that they capture real-world aspects *differently*. The final IS, if it is built, will have to deal with both processes and data in a manner satisfactory to human agents. Hence, all the aspects mentioned in Section 1 must be captured one way or the other at some stage of development. The difference between the modelling approaches therefore becomes one of priority:

- Some aspects are captured explicitly, others only implicitly
- Some aspects are captured earlier than others.
- Some aspects are shown in diagrams, others only textually.

Also, orientated approaches tend to promote a single aspect (e.g., functional transformations in dataflow diagrams) as fundamental to modelling. The corresponding modelling construct is therefore equipped with the most powerful abstraction mechanisms, and the other kinds of constructs are grouped around it. For instance, SA explicitly captures the processes performed, their composition to higher level processes, their sequence, and how the output of one process is passed as input to the next. This is not given as high a priority in object-oriented analysis (OOA) approaches, in which it is not easy to grasp overall dynamics without elaborate model assessment. On the other hand, OOA does easily capture that a number of processes are working on objects of the same class. This is not shown explicitly in SA and can only be established through tedious inspection of the model.

2.2 Why Avoid It?

Obviously, the priorities set by choosing one particular orientation will mean that the aspects not promoted by that orientation will be more difficult to account for during analysis. For instance,

- In SA, it is not easy to see which processes are dealing with the same objects. This makes it difficult, e.g., to ensure change-locality.
- In OOA, it is not easy to comprehend sequences of low-level processes, and since low-level processes are not aggregated to higher level processes, it is also difficult to see exactly how end-to-end services are delivered to the system's users [1]. This makes dynamic analyses more difficult.

- In both SA and OOA, the human actors in the information system and their interrelationships are usually not described in detail (e.g., persons and units, their competence and the roles they can play, the responsibility of each role etc.). This makes it difficult for future users to relate to the model and to evaluate organisational changes caused by the system.
- Most traditional modelling methods are weak on requirements traceability [9]. Since for wicked problems the solution itself is likely to later become part of new problems [19], traceability (i.e., of the requirements that led to the current state of the problem domain) should be an integrated part of the problem analysis model, just as representations of processes performed in sequence or of processes and the objects they work on.

The above points explain why it might be a good idea to reduce the importance of orientation in analysis:

Avoiding representational bias: Orientation means that some aspects of phenomena in the problem domain will be difficult to capture and/or easy to forget because the modelling constructs which represent them are less important in (or even missing from) the modelling approach used.

Avoiding perspective bias: Orientation means that the problem domain will be looked at from one particular perspective the whole time, thus hiding weaknesses that would be more apparent from other perspectives.

Avoiding communication bias: Orientation means that it will be difficult to communicate a model to people to whom the particular orientation is unnatural, although easy to others.

Avoiding interest bias: Orientation means that the problem-domain models may inherently support the participation and interests of some of the individuals and groups affected by development, but not those of others.

Another problem with orientation is that it will force you to see any phenomenon — or any aspect of a phenomenon — as represented by one particular construct of the modelling approach. However, in reality several aspects of the same phenomenon may be simultaneously important for the problem at hand. It may be important for a single modeller to be able to represent several of these aspects at the same time, and it may be important to be able to co-represent aspects emphasised by several of the individuals or groups involved or affected. Capturing several different aspects at the same time is difficult in a strictly orientated approach, where it is often necessary to select a single modelling construct to cover a phenomenon, or at least to use several independent modelling constructs for each of its aspects. A particularly interesting remark in this direction is made in [12]: With the increasing distribution and interoperability among applications, the same or overlapping information is likely to be used for many different purposes, i.e., by different applications with different perspectives. This is used as an argument against pure objects, which focus on the information itself as opposed to the different perspectives on the information.

Example 1. Consider the development of an information system for managing the production and administration equipment of a beverage production company, which produces both beers and soft drinks. The new equipment administration system (EAS) is to keep an inventory of each of the production tools (robots, computers, etc.) owned by the company, together with information about, e.g., its current state, application, and placement.

An assembly line in the beverage company can be perceived from several perspectives, e.g., as an entity (information about the assembly line), as a relationship between two entities (the start and stop area), as a transportation or functional transformation of workpieces, as a process in which workpieces are crafted, as a store (since it introduces production delays), and as an agent transporting or processing items. Furthermore, the appropriate perspective will depend on the subjects perceiving the assembly line, e.g., inventory managers (who see it as an entity), the workers labouring along it (who see it as a process or a flow), and process managers (who see it as a store or delay). □

3   The Facet-Modelling Framework

Having discussed the weaknesses of orientation, the high-level goals for a modelling approach which attempts to avoid orientation can be identified:

- It should enable the modeller to capture any aspect of a problem-domain phenomenon, and any kind of relation between phenomena and between aspects. The choice of what to represent should be left to the modeller on basis of the problem at hand.
- If several aspects of the same phenomenon are relevant for the problem at hand, it should be possible to capture them simultaneously, instead of having to use several separate modelling constructs.

These are the two main properties of what is now to be introduced as the *facet-modelling framework*. The framework has the power to embed many of the oriented approaches. Hence it implicitly covers problem domains where these approaches are already sufficient. The facet-modelling framework is therefore not "yet another modelling approach," but an offer to generalise, integrate and extend contemporary approaches to make orientation problems less dominating in the early phases of IS development. Also, it is *not* in any fundamental sense "orientation free": Modelling is always about selecting certain aspects of the real world at the expense of ignoring others. What the facet-modelling approach contributes is a simple and intuitive, yet powerful and formalisable way of extending the set of aspects available, thus alleviating many orientation problems.

3.1   Items and Facet Types

A *facet model* represents concrete and abstract phenomena in the analysis domain as *items*. The term "item" has been chosen deliberately to avoid connotations to other analysis approaches such as ER-diagrams ("entities") or OOA ("objects"). Items do, however, share with objects the possession of an *identity*. The modeller's perception of a real-world phenomenon is represented in the facet

The real-world	The facet model
Phenomena	Items
Aspects	Facets
Relations	Referencing facets ("links")

Table 1. The relation between the real-world problem domain and basic facet-modelling concepts.

model as one or more typed *facets* belonging to the item, as shown in Table 1. This means that any number of aspects of the phenomenon that are relevant for the problem at hand can become facets of the corresponding item. Apart from its identity, an item encompasses nothing more than a set of facets.

A *facet-modelling language* is defined as a non-empty set of *facet types*. A *facet model* is correspondingly a non-empty set of *items*. All the items in a facet model have the same type, which is implicitly defined by the facet types in the language.

Hence, the facet types available to the modeller will depend on the particular facet-modelling language being applied. Examples of facet types are *methodological facets* such as the purpose of and requirements put on an item; *existential facets* such as the lifetime, physical location and movement of an item, and its material substance; *organisational facets* such as the actor of an item, the responsibilities assigned to an item, its capabilities and the roles it may assume; *informational facets* such as the material properties and data contents of an item; *structural facets* such as the parts, members, instances and refinements of an item; and finally *behavioural facets* such as the transformations, transportations and preservations effectuated by an item. This particular set of facet types is by no means the only one possible, and the authors do not attempt to argue that it is in any sense "better" than other alternatives. Hence this paper simultaneously deals with two problem-levels:

1. The idea of facet modelling in general.
2. An example of a particular facet-modelling language.

The second level serves to exemplify the first.

Example 2. Consider a facet-modelling language which integrates some of the modelling orientations commonly applied in structured analysis: dataflow diagrams, ER-diagrams, and agent models. The following facet types are needed:

- Dataflow diagram types for: external entity node, process node, store node and flow edge.
- ER-diagram facet types for: entity node, relationship node and subset edge.
- Agent model facet types for: agent node, role node, agent-role edge, and subagent edge.

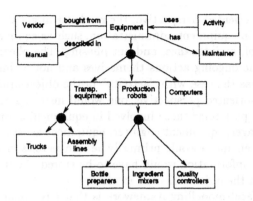

Fig. 1. Some perceived objects in the EAS.

- Inter-model facet types for: entity-flow edge (which entities move on which flows) and role-process edge (which roles perform which processes).

Hence the facet-modelling language has one facet type for each node type supported by the orientated modelling approaches it embeds, as well as additional types used for inter-model connections. An advantage with the facet based approach is that these important inter-model connections become part of the facet-modelling language, at the same level as other statements. □

3.2 Facets and Links

As already mentioned, each relevant aspect of a real-world phenomenon is represented as a facet of the corresponding item. Each item in a facet model therefore has a non-empty set of *facets*. Every facet has one and only one facet type.

Example 3. The arbitrariness of choosing which real-world aspects to represent can now be demonstrated in terms of the equipment administration system (EAS) example:

Choosing an information- or object-oriented approach, one might decide to explore what different kinds of equipment there are (i.e., build a classification hierarchy with relations.) In an object-oriented model, it would also be interesting to specify which possible operations have to be supported for each of these, as well as identifying other objects relevant for the equipment administration. A small example is shown in Figure 1, where every piece of equipment has a vendor, a manual, and a responsible maintainer within the company. It is also considered interesting to have information about what activities are using the various forms of equipment. Notice, however, that the "maintainer" and "activity" nodes represent only *information* about the phenomena, rather than the "maintainer" itself as an agent or the "activity" itself as a process.

From a process-oriented perspective, the modeller might start capturing the activities involved in equipment administration, such as equipment purchasing, registration, control, maintenance, and out-phasing. The phenomena modelled here are seen as the ongoing actions themselves and not as information about the processes, as was the case with "activity" in the object-oriented case.

From an agent-oriented perspective, one would instead start with the roles of the company, in particular those involved in equipment administration, such as equipment manager, equipment engineer, equipment assistant, operator, and secretary. These phenomena would primarily be seen as roles in the organisation, not as objects that information would have to be stored about, as was the case for "maintainer" in the object-oriented model.

The idea of a facet-modelling framework is that any orientation (function-, information-, object-, subject-, or other) may be useful, and the framework should be able to capture them explicitly whenever needed. Hence, e.g., an "equipment maintenance" phenomenon will have several facets:

- A process facet, the activity, which will have links to other activities done in connection with maintenance (at the same level of abstraction), and to activities above or below it in the decomposition hierarchy.
- An entity (or object) facet, the information about maintenance, which will have links to other information objects, again both to the same level of abstraction and to the levels below and above.
- A role facet, the maintainer, which may be linked to other roles that it communicates with and to agents able to fill this role. □

A facet is specified according to its facet type. Facet type outlines will be presented in Section 4. In general, a facet is either a single (typed) *value*, or a set or tuple of *subfacets*. Examples of value types are conventional types, such as integers and free text, as well as *references* which link facets to other items. Subfacets are themselves facets which may in turn have subfacets on their own. Links are directional in that they always go from the facet being specified to the item which is referenced. Hence the concept of "link" is not basic in the facet-modelling approach. It is just another (referencing) type of facet value. It is nevertheless a useful term when discussing and presenting facet models, and it will therefore be used in the sequel.

Example 4. In *Example 2* some of the facet types could be conveniently defined as links:

- For DFD diagrams: (external entity node, flow edge), (process node, flow edge), and (store node, flow edge).
- For ER-diagrams: (entity node, relationship node) and (entity node, subset edge).
- For agent diagrams: (agent node, subagent edge), (agent node, agent-role edge), and (role node, agent-role edge).

In addition, the inter-model facet types would probably also be represented as link facet types. □

4 Outlining Facet Types

Section 3 mentioned a large number of facet types for a particular facet-modelling language. Although it is not the purpose of this paper to define each of these proposals in detail, it is nevertheless clarifying to discuss some of them more elaborately.

4.1 Facet Type Outlines

Methodological facets such as the purpose of and the requirements placed on items might easily be specified as free text associated with the item. As the facet model becomes more detailed, it should also be possible specify requirements in 1. order predicate calculus. Furthermore, it should be possible to *link* a requirement facet to other items to represent how requirements trickle through the model. In this way, traceability is incorporated as part of the facet model itself. The structural facet types outlined below will provide such links.

Existential facets of an item are represented as simple, valued facets: Its lifetime is defined by birth and death times, while physical location and item movement are represented as a location facet. The presence of material substance of an item in the model is represented as a truth valued facet.

Organisational facets such as actors, responsibilities, capabilities and roles may again best be represented textually. Actor and role facets should of course have links to represent actor-subactor and actor-role relationships.

Informational facets such as the material properties and the data contents of an item are represented as sets of typed values.

Structural facets are represented as links to other items. Hence, the parts of an item are a set of references to items. Similarly, the members, instances and refinements of an item are also represented as links. Links can be traversed in both directions, so the inverse structural relations are also covered.

Behavioural facets are unsurprisingly the most complex facet types to define. The authors have previously considered this problem in [16, 17], and the facet-modelling framework has been designed to incorporate the ideas presented there. More specifically, a transportation (or flow) is an (instantaneous or gradual) modification of another item's position facet leaving its other facets unchanged, while a preservation (or storage) is a conservation of position. In its most primitive form, a transformation is a modification of an informational facet.

Example 5. Section 3.1 presented a simple first example which integrated some of the modelling orientations of structured analysis. It turns out that some of the facets introduced for that purpose correspond to those presented here:

- Dataflow diagrams facet types for processes, stores and flows correspond to transformation, preservation and transportation facets, as discussed in [16]. As for the external entity facet type, the actor or role facet of this section seems appropriate.

- ER-diagram facet types for entities are represented through the data contents (and possibly material properties) facets of this section. The relationship facet can be represented as a part facet comprising references to items with related entity facets.
- Agent model facet types for agents are best represented as actor facets, while roles of course remain roles. Subagents are again best represented through the part facet type. □

4.2 Facet Type Dependencies

The facets defined for an item are obviously not independent. Instead, the value of one facet — or the fact that it is specified or unspecified — has consequences for facets of the same or of other items.

Most fundamental is the lifetime facets of an item, which restrict the specification of facets such as position, as well as the item's participation in transportation, preservation, and transformation. Along the same lines, an item can only have material properties if it has material substance.

Rather than adding complexity to the framework, these and other dependency rules aid the modelling process by 1) making inconsistencies easy to detect by inspection or by formal verification; 2) making changes made to one facet immediately apparent in terms of another facet also; 3) implicitly specifying facets as consequences of other explicitly specified ones, and 4) designing versatile and friendly user interfaces.

5   Visualisation

Visual representation has many advantages over textual representation, both when it comes to comprehension (e.g., in providing at a glimpse overviews) and expressive economy [11, 23]. Therefore, many modelling languages have been designed with a particular visual representation in mind.

Large facet models will have many items, and even more interconnections among these along various dimensions. Hence they will be impossible to display nicely in two dimensions and possibly hard also in three. This is not really a new problem — all realistic models of detailed material- and information-processing systems will be too complex to visualise all at once. Therefore, abstractions and filtering techniques are needed [20, 21]. However, the inherent complexity of the facet-modelling framework makes such visualisation and filtering techniques all the more important.

No visualisation tool has yet been built for the approach presented in the previous sections. Still, it is found important to discuss visualisation here to indicate the feasibility of the facet approach for visual presentation. Actually, this section attempts to demonstrate that the facet-modelling framework may have an advantage in providing *greater flexibility for views*, since no particular view is promoted by the modelling framework as such. The ideas presented here are partly inspired by [21].

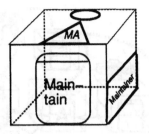

Fig. 2. An item-cube

Visualisation may be addressed according to two different principles: 1) browsing and 2) associatively selected views. In both cases, useful views will have to rely on filtering, i.e., not showing the entire model at once. The difference is that for browsing, filtering will be implicit: the nodes which are far away from the current viewpoint, will be vaguely or not at all visible. For associatively selected views, on the other hand, the user will describe through some suitable interface what should be included in the view.

Looking at browsing first, although the screen is two-dimensional, the user can easily be provided with 6 working directions: up, down, left, right, in, out, providing a three-dimensional feeling. As long as items have a fairly limited number of facets, this can be utilised to create a versatile interface for browsing. Imagine one item presented as a cube where different sides correspond to different facets. In the example in Figure 2 we see the front side being used for a process facet, the right side for an object (or entity) facet, and the top side for an agent (or role) facet. The three remaining sides are still vacant for other facets of interest. Turning the cube around, the user can focus on the facet of most interest, whose relations to other nodes will then also be shown. Moreover, zooming into a particular side, the decomposition of the corresponding facet will emerge (e.g., the decomposition of "Maintain" into lower lever activities), and zooming away from it, the composition will emerge (e.g., the higher level business function that "Maintain" is part of).

With such an approach, one could browse around more complex structures such as the one indicated in the upper part of Figure 3. However, browsing may not be suitable for all situations. For rapid exploration into a complex model, it is probably a good idea, but for detailed discussions of the model among a large group of people, it will probably be necessary to generate more persistent views. Filtering for such views may be done by

- facet (i.e., stating what facets should be included and/or excluded)
- item (i.e., stating what items should be included and/or excluded)

Of course, it should be possible to combine facet and item filtering, and also filtering statements of the inclusive (what should be *in* the view) and exclusive (what should be hidden) kind. In the example of Figure 3, a messy model —

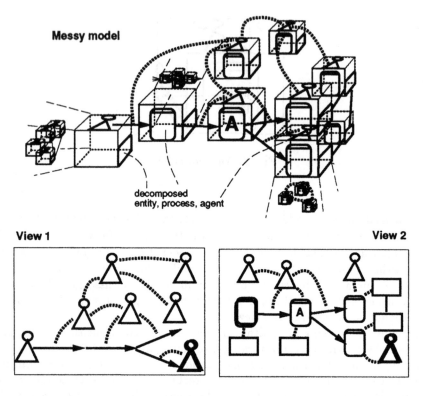

Fig. 3. Filtering

which is still only a small fraction of what would be the total facet model for a large system — has been filtered to two different views. In View 1, only flows, agents, flow-agent, and agent-agent edges are shown. Assuming that the diagram has been sensibly annotated, this could be a useful view for seeing what is moving around in the system and who is responsible for the transportation. View 2 displays only the node whose process facet is marked **A** in the messy picture, the edges directly connected to this node, and the nodes connected to these edges (i.e., filtering by item.) Both the resulting views have become so simple that they can be displayed nicely in two dimensions. For larger models, the first filtering operation might not be sufficient to yield a good looking view, so that several iterations of filtering will be required. Combining filtering and browsing might also be a good idea in many cases.

6   Conclusion

The paper has explained why clearly orientated models is not anything to strive for in the early phases of problem analysis, but rather a source of problems on their own. To alleviate this situation, a facet-modelling framework was introduced, and a simple facet-modelling language was outlined. The paper also outlined important facet types, as well as visualisation.

Facet models represent the dynamics, processing, functions, structure and purpose of items using natural and dedicated concepts, while maintaining an internal representation of the item per se, as a sum of its defined facets. Hence, the facet approach is a departure from conventional problem analysis approaches in several ways:

- From visual models to *visualisable structures.*
  Instead of designing modelling approaches with visualisations in mind, the facet modelling approach encourages selection of important aspects of the real-world problem domain as a distinct activity from visualisation.
- From diagrams on paper to *diagramming tools.*
  A diagrammatic modelling language as of 1995 must fully utilise contemporary technology. The facet-modelling framework has been designed with powerful visualisation mechanisms in mind.
- From items as objects to *items with aspects.*
  While the object-oriented modelling approaches focus on the real-world phenomena per se, the facet-modelling approach focusses on representing important aspects of the phenomena. Furthermore, a rich set of concepts is provided for specifying relevant facets. Hence facet modelling is a departure from claims made by OOA-proponents that a single concept (the object) — or at least a small set of core concepts (e.g. objects, states, classes, inheritance, instances, operations and messages) — is sufficient to create rich and intuitive models of real-world problems.
- From description-driven to *problem domain-driven methodology.*
  Available SA and OOA approaches are description-driven in that the description techniques themselves set the agenda for which pieces of knowledge about the problem domain to collect at any given time of analysis. A facet model can be extended at any time with any type of problem-domain knowledge that may become relevant. This is in line with recent methodology frameworks, e.g., [14], which emphasise IS development as inquiry processes driven by the analysis problem itself, rather than by assumptions inherent in some fixed modelling language.
- From repositories of separate models to *a single integrated model.*
  Instead of distributing the specification of a real-world system between several (visual) models and then maintaining the references between model components, the facet-modelling approach maintains a single model only. The simplifications implied by this are obvious.

Facets can also be added for non-functional aspects of the problem domain, such as performance and reliability, and for representing developers and the development process itself as part of the model. It may be possible to regard the final implementation itself as a set of linked facets of items.

Of course, the facet-modelling framework is more ambitious than the traditional approaches. Thus, if a traditional approach is able to deliver a satisfactory model for a certain problem, the facet framework might not be needed. However, there are several reasons to believe that there is a need for an ambitious approach covering many aspects of the problem area in one comprehensive model:

First, real-world problem domains are becoming ever more complex, partly because the easier problems are being solved and turned into shelfware, frameworks, or reusable libraries, leaving only the difficult problems for analysis.

Second, problem domain models are becoming assets in themselves, because of the drastically increased turbulence in organisations and society. The trend towards virtual organisations, organising on demand to do a particular job, means that organisations will end up being more short-lived than the ISs they use. If a company is supposed to live only for a year or two, not to speak of a month or two, it is no longer feasible to take up a traditional development project, making a detailed analysis model for business processes and the IS support needed. Instead, it will be necessary to reuse, modify and combine existing models for similar businesses, so that the IS support for the organisation can be up and running from day one, with just some customisation afterwards. When the organisation phases itself out, the models of IS support that it has generated, will be useful input to new organisations popping up. Hence, models will be a commodity in their own right, to a much larger extent than today (when many regard them mostly as a necessary step towards a running software system). Then it will also make sense to invest more resources in the construction of high quality models, and to have an ambitious approach to allow flexible customisation of these models.

References

1. S. C. Bailin. An object-oriented requirements specification method. *Communications of the ACM*, 32(5):608–623, May 1989.
2. T. Bryant and A. Evans. OO oversold. *Information and Software Technology*, 36(1):35–42, January 1994.
3. J. A. Bubenko jr. Problems and unclear issues with hierarchical business activity and data flow modelling. Technical Report 134, SYSLAB, Stockholm, June 1988.
4. P. P. S. Chen. The entity-relationship model: Toward a unified view of data. *ACM Transactions on Database Systems*, 1(1):9–36, March 1976.
5. P. Coad and E. Yourdon. *Object-Oriented Analysis*. Prentice-Hall, Englewood Cliffs, 1990.
6. T. DeMarco. *Structured Analysis and System Specification*. Yourdon Inc., New York, 1978.
7. E. Dubois et al. ALBERT: an agent-oriented language for building and eliciting requirements for real-time systems. In *Proc. of HICSS'27, vol.IV, Information Systems: Collaboration Technology, Organizational Systems and Technology*, pages 713–722. IEEE Computer Society Press, 1994.
8. C. Gane and T. Sarson. *Structured Systems Analysis: tools and techniques*. Prentice-Hall International, 1979.
9. O. C. Z. Gotel and A. C. W. Finkelstein. Modelling the contribution structure underlying requirements. In K. Pohl et al., editor, *Proc. 1st International Work-*

shop on Requirements Engineering: Foundation of Software Quality (REFSQ'94), *Utrecht*, June 1994.

10. J. A. Gulla, O. I. Lindland, and G. Willumsen. PPP — an integrated CASE environment. In R. Andersen, J. A. Bubenko jr., and A. Sølvberg, editors, *Advanced Information Systems Engineering, Proc. CAiSE'91, Trondheim*, pages 194–221, Heidelberg, 1991. Springer Verlag (LNCS 498).

11. D. Harel. On visual formalisms. *Communications of the ACM*, 31(5):514–530, May 1988.

12. W. Harrison and H. Ossher. Subject-oriented programming (a critique of pure objects). In A. Paepcke, editor, *OOPSLA'93 Conference Proceedings*, pages 411–428. ACM Press, 26 Sep–1 Oct 1993. (Also as ACM SIGPLAN Notices 28(10), Oct 1993).

13. G. M. Høydalsvik and G. Sindre. On the purpose of object-oriented analysis. In A. Paepcke, editor, *OOPSLA'93 Conference Proceedings*, pages 240–255. ACM Press, 26 Sep–1 Oct 1993. (Also as ACM SIGPLAN Notices 28(10), Oct 1993).

14. J. Iivari and E. Koskela. The pioco model for information systems design. *MIS Quarterly*, pages 401–419, September 1987.

15. S. McGinnes. How objective is object-oriented analysis? In *Proc. CAiSE'92: The Fourth Conference on Advanced information Systems Engineering, Manchester, UK*, Heidelberg, 1992. Springer Verlag (LNCS 593).

16. A. L. Opdahl and G. Sindre. Concepts for real-world modelling. In C. Rolland et al., editor, *Advanced Information Systems Engineering, Proc. CAiSE'93, Paris*, pages 309–327. Springer Verlag (LNCS 685), 1993.

17. A. L. Opdahl and G. Sindre. Representing real-world processes. In J. F. Nunamaker and R. H. Sprague, editors, *Proc. of the 28th Annual Hawaii International Conference on System Sciences (HICSS'28)*, volume IV, pages 821–830. IEEE CS Press, 1995.

18. C. A. Richter. An assessment of structured analysis and structured design. *SIG-SOFT Software Engineering Notes*, 11(4), 1986.

19. H. Rittel. On the planning crisis: Systems analysis of the first and second generations. *Bedriftsøkonomen*, (8), 1972.

20. A. H. Seltveit. An abstraction-based rule approach to large-scale information systems development. In C. Rolland et al., editor, *Advanced Information Systems Engineering, Proc. CAiSE'93, Paris*, pages 328–351. Springer Verlag (LNCS 685), 1993.

21. A. H. Seltveit. *Complexity Reduction in Information Systems Modelling*. PhD thesis, DCST, NTH, University of Trondheim, 1994. NTH 1994:121.

22. S. Shlaer and S. J. Mellor. *Object-Oriented System Analysis: Modeling the World in Data*. Prentice-Hall, Englewood Cliffs, NJ, 1988.

23. G. Sindre. *HICONS: A General Diagrammatic Framework for Hierarchical Modelling*. PhD thesis, Faculty of Electrical Engineering and Computer Science, University of Trondheim, 1990. NTH 1990:44, IDT 1990:31.

24. G. Verheijen and J. van Bekkum. NIAM: an information analysis method. In T. W. Olle et al., editor, *Information Systems Design Methodologies: A Comparative Review*, Amsterdam, 1982. North-Holland.

A Framework for Requirements Analysis Using Automated Reasoning

David Duffy*, Craig MacNish, John McDermid, Philip Morris*
Department of Computer Science
University of York,
York YO1 5DD, UK
{dad,craig,jam,philipm}@minster.york.ac.uk

Abstract. The problem of analysing the effects of changing requirements imposes strict demands on system representations, particularly in safety-critical domains. We argue that solving this problem will require structured representations that highlight the interaction between requirements, and record the rationale for decisions made during the development process.

As a means of providing and analysing this information, we propose the use of a goal-oriented model for structuring requirements and the use of formal reasoning techniques to aid in the analysis of changes and their consequences.

1 Introduction

The need to analyse the effects of changing requirements adds to the demands on system representations. In addition to verifying the integrity of the initial system, we would like to have the capability to trace the implications of changes through the system, and also to reason back from desired outcomes to determine what changes could bring them about. These capabilities rely upon a representation that focuses on both the interactions between system requirements and the interactions between the system and the context in which it operates. For this analysis to be productive, we also need some way of assessing the susceptibility of individual requirements to change, and therefore some way of recording the rationale for the design decisions that led to those requirements. All of these issues are particularly important in saftey-critical domains where maintaining the integrity of the system is paramount.

In this paper we propose a framework, called *goal-structured analysis* (GSA), which addresses these needs. The framework is based on goal decomposition supported by automated reasoning. A distinguishing feature of our approach from previous goal-based approaches (see for example [1, 3, 10]) is that we link the evolution of the requirements and design through the development of goals and system models, reflecting the fact that, for embedded systems, requirements and

* Supported by the DTI/SERC "PROTEUS" PROJECT IED4/1/9304 under the Safety-Critical Systems Initiative.

design must evolve in concert. We also place a strong emphasis on formal properties, such as non-circularity of justifications. The reasoning aspect is achieved through a logical representation which avoids many of the complexities of previous proposals (see for example [4, 9]) by operating in tandem with informal descriptions.

The main benefits of our approach include:

- Informal descriptions of requirements and design decisions, along with supporting evidence, are recorded in a structured way.

- Formal (logical) statements are coupled with the informal descriptions, facilitating formal and mechanised analyses. This allows us to make guarantees about the integrity of the specifications. For example, we can ensure that system models are consistent and that all goals are satisfiable under appropriate conditions.

- Conditions are provided for incremental development of requirements which, if followed during the development process, guarantee the above properties in the final structure.

In the following section we provide an overview of the framework and describe the intuitions behind the components. This is followed in Section 3 by a simple example of (informal) system development, which is used throughout the remainder of the paper. Section 4 discusses the addition of formal statements to the system description, while Section 5 defines some of the properties we would like to attain, and the conditions for incremental development which will bring these about. In Section 6 we give a very brief illustration of the way in which the framework allows us to predict system behaviour under different scenarios and examine changes to the system to improve its behaviour. Finally in Section 7 we summarise the work presented and discuss some future research directions.

2 Overview of the Framework

The fundamental components of our approach are goals, effects, facts and conditions, each containing both informal and formal information. In this section we briefly describe each of these components and their relationships, the types of information they contain, and the way in which this information is stored. In later sections we give a more rigorous account of the formal relationships between these components.

2.1 Goals and Effects

A *goal* contains a statement, or assertion, identifying a desired property of a (proposed) system. Goals are intended to be more flexible than (the traditional view of) requirements, which are often used to set contractual boundaries between customer and designer. The statements may express requirements that the system should fulfil, derived requirements which emerge because of higher-level design decisions, or constraints (for example to do with cost or power consumption).

We associate with each goal *strategies* describing how that goal may be achieved. Alongside the strategies we record information that might be significant if changes are to be made at a later stage, such as the reason that the strategies are believed to be successful, criteria for choosing amongst strategies, and a justification for the selection of a particular strategy. A strategy will generally introduce further goals (along with effects, facts and conditions) leading to a hierarchy or, more generally, a network which we call a *goal structure*.

An *effect* is similar to a goal in that it makes a statement that requires further decomposition or explanation. The difference is that effects describe properties of the system which we might not necessarily *want* to achieve. From a decompositional point of view goals and effects are treated in a similar manner, and we will simply refer to goals where no confusion arises.

2.2 Facts and Conditions, Models and Scenarios

Whereas goals contain statements about the system that we wish to decompose further, *facts* are statements that we take to be true. For example, they may be statements about properties of the system that are known to hold, or design commitments (such as a choice of technology).

Conditions, like facts, contain statements that we do not wish to decompose any further. Unlike facts, conditions may not always hold. As the name suggests, we use conditions to analyse the behaviour of the system under different operating conditions. We call a (consistent) set of conditions a *scenario*.

We will see that all goals are eventually decomposed in such a way as to be supported or satisfied by the facts in some scenario. In this way, the set of facts can be regarded as a *model* of the system being developed, a scenario represents the input to that model, and the goals represent requirements on the output, or behaviour, of that system. This relationship is illustrated in Figure 1. The model will be developed or expanded in parallel with decomposition of the goals.

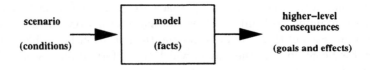

Fig. 1. Relationship between facts, conditions and goals.

2.3 Systems and Contexts

A new system is rarely developed in isolation, but rather is developed in the context of available components, subsystems, and the environment in which it operates. This might include the "physical" world, a commercial environment such as the stockmarket, or a previously developed software system such as an operating system. In safety-critical systems constraints will also typically be imposed by regulatory bodies.

It is often convenient to separate the statements referring to different systems under consideration. For this reason we allow system labels. Furthermore any particular system under consideration may involve relationships with only a subset of the other systems being modelled. We call these other systems the *context* of the system under consideration. This modular view of systems and their associated contexts helps to address problems of scale.

2.4 Frame Representation

A natural representation for goals, effects, facts, conditions and their associated information is a *frame*, a data structure commonly used for representing hierarchical information in AI (see for example [7]). The following table shows some of the slots needed in a goal frame and the information envisaged for each slot.[2]

Slot	Information
Label	*identifier for the frame*
System	*system identifier*
Context	*identifier of directly related systems*
Assertion	*goal to be achieved or explained*
Alternatives	*list of alternative strategies*
Rationale	*reasons for belief in each alternative strategy*
Selection	*the chosen strategy*
Justification	*reason for selection of chosen strategy*

We concentrate our attention on these slots for the remainder of the paper. Examples are given in the following section.

Fact, effect, and condition frames are essentially cut down versions of goal frames. The selection slot in an effect frame will contain will contain an explication of the effect, and no alternatives slot will generally be needed. Since facts and conditions are not decomposed no strategy information is needed. However, the Rationale slot may be used to store the reason for believing in the fact or condition.

For brevity we have shown only one slot for each type of information, but in general many entries will involve two slots, one for an informal description and one for a formal description. The informal component allows the developers to describe the system in natural or semi-structured language. The formal component is used to guarantee properties of the system and to permit automated analysis. Note that both components need not necessarily be filled by the same engineer — for example the first may be the responsibility of the system designer while the second may contain a formalisation of this information by a specialist in formal languages.

---

[2] In practice a strategy will need to provide a solution to multiple goals (including making trade-offs between those goals) and may be shared between frames. For ease of exposition, however, we only associate strategies with single goals.

3 Buiding Goal Structures — An Example

In order to illustrate the construction and use of goal structures we will consider a simplified landing control system for an aircraft. The motivation for this example comes from various accounts concerning an landing incident (see for example [6]), but the details given here are contrived purely for the purposes of the example.

Briefly, the example involves the development of an automated system for applying wheel brakes and reverse thrusters with the aim of stopping an aircraft within 1000m of landing. The controller will make decisions about applying the brakes and reverse thrusters on the basis of measurements of wheel speed, load and altitude. These in turn will depend on environmental conditions when the aircraft touches down and the procedures followed by the pilot. We wish to analyse the behaviour of the aircraft under different scenarios involving these conditions.

There are four different 'systems' involved in the development: the landing control system itself, the dynamics of the aircraft, the operating procedures, and the environment in which the landing takes place. In this case, the latter three systems will provide the context in which the landing control system operates, and will mainly provide facts and conditions, since we are less concerned with interactions within those systems.

3.1 Developing the Landing Control System

We now run briefly through the development of the goal structure and system models. This allows us to illustrate how strategies may be derived from, or generate, facts and goals. For clarity we will consider only informal information at this stage, and show only those slots in the frames that are of principal interest. The corresponding formal information is detailed in the following section.

Deriving Strategies from Facts (or Goals) In the first step we give an example of the generation of a strategy from known information. We take our top-level goal to be to stop the aircraft within 1000m. (Note that in practice there will be other top-level goals such as those relating to safety.) The options available for the control system involve invoking wheel brakes and reverse thrusters, and an appropriate strategy must be developed with reference to the physical properties of the aircraft. We will assume that these physical properties have already been assessed in the process of designing, prototyping and/or testing the aircraft, and that this is reflected by the following facts:

Fact	
Label	F1
System	Aircraft dynamics
Assertion	The aircraft will stop within 1000m if wheel brakes are applied when speed $\leq$ 154km/h.
Rationale	Engineering tests

Fact	
Label	F2
System	Aircraft dynamics
Assertion	The aircraft will stop within 1000m if wheel brakes and reverse thrusters are applied when speed $>$ 154km/h and $\leq$ 170km/h.
Rationale	Engineering tests

These facts clearly suggest a strategy for satisfying our high-level goal. Since we wish to satisfy the goal for both ranges of speed, the facts are combined into a single strategy:

Goal	
Label	G1
System	Landing control
Context	Environment, Aircraft dynamics, Operating procedures
Assertion	Stop aircraft within 1000m
Selection	Apply wheel brakes when speed $\leq$ 154 knots, apply wheel brakes and reverse thrusters when speed $>$ 154 knots and $\leq$ 170 knots
Rationale	Based on F1, F2

The rationale for this strategy provides a pointer to the facts upon which it was based, thus recording the reason that the strategy is expected to be successful. Note that the assertions in the above facts may themselves appear as goals in the process of designing the dynamics of the aircraft. In future we will omit the Context slot as this will be inherited by other frames in the same system.

The strategy for G1 refers to four pieces of information. The application of the wheel brakes and reverse thrusters will be treated as new goals, while the statements concerning landing speeds (which result from the landing procedures and environmental conditions) will be treated as effects. Each of these can be decomposed further. In the next step we provide an example in which there are no predetermined strategies, and a design decision is made which in turn leads to a system description.

Generating Facts or Goals from Design Decisions In satisfying the goal of applying the reverse thrusters during landing, we will assume the designer has a choice of two strategies used in previous models, and makes a decision based on a safety constraint:

Goal	
Label	G2
System	Landing control
Assertion	Apply reverse thrust
Alternatives	Wheels loads $>$ 12 tonnes; altitude $<$ 10m and wheel speed $>$ 72km/h
Rationale	Both strategies have been used in previous models
Selection	Wheel loads $>$ 12 tonnes
Justification	Wheel loads considered more reliable in preventing premature application of reverse thrusters

For completeness of the goal structure, the causal relationship between the selected strategy and the goal must now be treated as a new goal or, in the case where we do not wish to decompose this any further, as a fact. For example:

Fact	
Label	F3
System	Landing control
Assertion	If wheel loads $>$ 12 tonnes then reverse thrust is applied
Rationale	Design decision from G2

Again the rationale contains a reference, this time from the fact to the goal, thus linking this "requirement" to the design decision upon which it is based.

The goal and fact frames for the application of the wheel brakes can be generated in a similar manner. For the sake of brevity we assume there is only one (disjunctive) alternative for the wheel brakes, leading to the following frames:

Goal	
Label	G3
System	Landing control
Assertion	Apply wheel brakes
Selection	Wheel loads > 12 tonnes or
	altitude < 10m and wheel speed > 72 km/h

Fact	
Label	F4
System	Landing control
Assertion	If wheel loads > 12 tonnes, or
	altitude < 10m and wheel speed > 72 km/h,
	then wheel brakes are applied

The above strategies introduce three new subgoals concerning the wheel load, wheel speed, and aircraft altitude, in addition to the two describing approach speed from G1. Apart from the altitude these subgoals can all be decomposed further by considering the dynamic properties of the aircraft.

Further Goals and Facts We will assume that the loading on both wheels depends on the way in which the aircraft is brought down. For simplicity we will say that the wheels are adequately loaded if there is a cross wind and the aircraft is banked, or if there is a tail wind and the aircraft is brought in level:

Fact	
Label	F5
System	Aircraft dynamics
Assertion	Wheel loads > 12 tonnes if the aircraft is
	banked when there is a cross wind or the
	aircraft is level when there is a tail wind

Goal	
Label	G4
System	Operating procedures
Assertion	Wheel loads > 12 tons
Selection	Bring the aircraft in banked in a
	cross wind and level in a tail wind

For simplicity we will assume the wheel speed is always greater than 72 km/h after touch down (a more sophisticated model might take account of conditions such as aquaplaning) and represent this with a fact F6.

The approach speed of the aircraft depends similarly on environmental conditions and the operating procedures. For example:

Fact	
Label	F7
System	Aircraft dynamics
Assertion	In a cross wind high throttle leads
	to a speed ≤ 154 km/h

Fact	
Label	F8
System	Aircraft dynamics
Assertion	In a tail wind high throttle leads to a
	speed > 154 km/h and ≤ 170 km/h

These facts provide explanations for the following effects:

Effect	
Label	E5
System	Operating procedures
Assertion	speed ≤ 154 km/h
Selection	Results from high throttle in a cross wind
Rationale	F7

Effect	
Label	E6
System	Operating procedures
Assertion	154 km/h < speed ≤ 170 km/h
Selection	Results from high throttle in a tail wind
Rationale	F8

Finally, we will assume that we are only interested in landing and therefore the altitude will necessarily be less than 10m, which is represented by a fact F9.

Conditions Describing a Scenario We are now left with subgoals referring to the operating procedures and weather conditions which will vary with different scenarios. For example, under normal landing conditions we might have:

Condition	
Label	C1
System	Environment
Assertion	Cross wind

Condition	
Label	C2
System	Operating procedures
Assertion	Bank aircraft and use high throttle

We leave the reader to verify informally that the aircraft lands successfully under these conditions, and return to this example in the following section.

3.2 Models and Support for Goals

During the construction of a goal structure we make use of existing descriptions of how components of the systems work, as well as generating new requirements for components. These are reflected in the facts, which form our model of the systems, and the conditions which describe the scenario in which they operate.

In each case where we specified a strategy for a goal (or explication for an effect) we "satisfied" ourselves that the strategy, along with other goals and facts expressed in the model, meant that the goal would be satisfied. We refer to this as *local support* for the goal, "local" because there is an assumption at this stage that any other goals referred to can be achieved through further decomposition. In some cases, where a fact directly expressed an implication from the subgoals in the strategy to the goal, it follows in a straightforward way that satisfying the subgoals would, in turn, satisfy the goal. In other cases a number of facts may have been required to ensure that the strategy led to the goal being satisfied.

As the development of a goal structure continues, any subgoals in the strategy that are not themselves facts are decomposed further. If this process is continued, with each decomposition being locally supported, until there are no further subgoals to be reduced, *every goal in the structure will be supported by the model alone*. In this case we say that all the goals are *globally supported*. It can be seen, therefore, that the strategies provide a means of developing, through a series of incremental steps, a model in which all the goals are satisfied.

Finally, we can investigate the response of the systems under various scenarios, as well as various changes to the systems, by following the implications of the changes through these "paths" of support.

In the remainder of the paper we formalise all of the above ideas by attaching logical descriptions of goals, facts and strategies to frames, and using formal proof methods to investigate and confirm local and global support for goals.

4 Formal Information in Goal Structures

In order to ensure properties such as consistency of our model and support for our goals, we need to have unambiguous representations of the assertions in goals, effects, facts and conditions, in a language that supports formal reasoning. We achieve this by adding logical information to our frames.

4.1 Examples of Logical Assertions

In this paper we will make use of only ground first-order sentences of a classical logic to describe assertions. (In general we may wish to use languages in which we can represent different kinds of causal relationships, numerical constraints, precedence of requirements and so on.)

As an example, the fact F1 might be expanded as follows:

Fact	
Label	F1
System	Aircraft dynamics
Assertion	The aircraft will stop within 1000m if wheel brakes are applied when speed $\leq$ 154km/h.
Assertion*	speed $\leq$ 154 $\rightarrow$ (applied(wheel.brakes) $\rightarrow$ stop.length $<$ 1000)
Rationale	Engineering tests

Assertion* contains the formal description of the contents of Assertion. We will sometimes use the notation $assert(F1)$ to refer to this slot directly. Similarly, if S is a set of frames we will write $assert(S)$ for the set of assertions therein.

In the case of a goal, as well as formalising the assertion made, we require a logical expression of the selected strategy. The reason for this is that, in the construction of a goal structure, the strategy temporarily takes the place of subsequent goals, effects, facts and conditions. This strategy also forms a semantic link between a goal and its "children". Thus G1 may be expanded to include:

Goal	
Label	G1
Assertion*	stop.length $<$ 1000
Selection*	[speed $\leq$ 154 $\wedge$ applied(wheel.brakes)] $\vee$ [154 $<$ speed $\leq$ 170 $\wedge$ applied(wheel.brakes) $\wedge$ applied(rev.thrust)]

Logical expressions can be similarly added to the other frames. Full lists for our example are shown in Table 1 and the two scenarios in Table 2.

As indicated earlier, whereas the informal descriptions will be provided by an engineer who has intimate knowledge of the design, the translation into logical form may be passed to someone with specific skills in logical representation and theorem proving. This is one of the motivations for combining formal and informal descriptions in this way.

5 Formal Properties of Goal Structures

Now that we have a formal description of the assertions and strategies in goal structures we are in a position to prove properties of the goal structure and the model. To simplify the exposition we will, where appropriate, refer to frames and their assertions interchangeably. For example, if G is a goal and M a set of facts, we will write $M \models G$ as shorthand for

$$\{assert(F) \mid F \in M\} \models assert(G).$$

Goals and Effects
G1 stop.length < 1000
G2 applied(reverse.thrust)
G3 applied(wheel.brakes)
G4 wheel.loads > 12
E5 speed ≤ 154
E6 154 < speed ≤ 170

Model M1
F1 speed ≤ 154 → (applied(wheel.brakes) → stop.length < 1000)
F2 154 < speed ≤ 170 →
    (applied(wheel.brakes) ∧ applied(reverse.thrust) → stop.length < 1000)
F3 wheel.loads > 12 → applied(reverse.thrust)
F4 wheel.loads > 12 ∨ altitude < 10 ∧ wheel.speed > 72 → applied(wheel.brakes)
F5 (cross.wind → (banked → wheel.loads > 12)) ∧ (tail.wind → (level → wheel.loads > 12))
F6 wheel.speed > 72
F7 cross.wind → (throttle(high) → speed ≤ 154)
F8 tail.wind → (throttle(high) → 154 < speed ≤ 170)
F9 altitude < 10

Table 1. Logical assertions corresponding to goals and facts.

Scenario W1	Scenario W2
C1 cross.wind	C3 tail.wind
C2 banked ∧ throttle(high)	C2 banked ∧ throttle(high)

Table 2. Logical descriptions of two scenarios.

5.1 Consistency and Global Support

First, we would like to ensure that our model is consistent, any scenario we apply the model in is consistent, and also that the union of any such scenario and the model is consistent (otherwise *any* goal assertion will be a consequence). These can all be tested using a standard theorem prover.

Secondly, we would like all goals (and effects) to be satisfiable in some scenario. This is the condition of global support introduced in Section 3.2, and ensures that the goals have been adequately (at least from a logical point of view) decomposed. We achieve this by ensuring that all goals are logical consequences of the union of the model and some scenario consistent with the model, as illustrated in Figure 2.

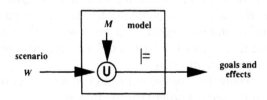

Fig. 2. Formal relationship between facts, conditions, goals and effects.

Definition 1 *Let G be a goal or effect in some context with model M. Then G is* (globally) supported *in a scenario W iff*

$$W \cup M \models G.$$

We say that a goal or effect is *supportable* if and only if it is supported in some scenario W such that $W \cup M$ is consistent.

In our example we can see that goals G1,...,G4 and effect E5 are consequences of M1 and W1, while E6 is a consequence of M1 and W2. Thus all goals and effects are supportable.

Like the consistency properties, global support can be established using a standard theorem prover once the goal structure has been completely decomposed. A more difficult task is to specify checks that can be made during the decomposition process to ensure that the final goal structure will be globally supported. That is, we wish to specify the formal conditions for local support.

5.2 Local Support

Recall that we would like a goal (or effect) to be locally supported if it is satisfied by other goals (intuitively those at the next level of decomposition) as well as facts and conditions. This includes subgoals mentioned in the strategy for which new frames have not yet been added. Thus if a context C includes model M, goals and effects H, and a scenario W such that $W \cup M \cup H$ is consistent, then for any particular goal (or effect) G with selection S, we would like to have:

$$assert(M \cup (H - \{G\}) \cup W) \cup \{S\} \models assert(G).$$

Note that we are assuming here that C and its components may not be completely decomposed. Providing we are dealing with a monotonic logic (as in this case) the above relationship will still hold as any further assertions are added to the left of the consequence relation.

This relationship would not, however, be sufficient to guarantee global support. The reason is that it allows circular paths of support. Consider, for example, a goal G_1 with assertion A and strategy B. This would be locally supported by another goal G_2 with assertion $B \rightarrow A$. However G_2 is also locally supported by G_1. In this case neither goal need be globally supported.

To overcome this problem we impose a partial order $\preceq$ (and corresponding quasi-order $\prec$) on assertions, and hence on the goals (effects) containing them. We then insist that the local support for a goal from other goals comes only from those that are strictly lower in the partial order. We also require that the goal's strategy is eventually entailed by goals that are lower in the partial order, along with facts and conditions. Since the partial order is transitive and antisymmetric this prevents the occurrence of loops.

If G is a goal in context C we use $\prec_G C$ to denote the set of goals in C that are strictly lower in the partial order than G; that is

$$\prec_G C = \{A \mid A \in C \text{ and } A \prec G\}.$$

We can then define local support recursively as follows:

Definition 2 *Let G be a goal or effect with strategy S and context C. Let M be the model in C and W a scenario in C such that $M \cup \prec_G C \cup \{S\} \cup W$ is consistent. Then G is locally supported in W iff there exists*

$$T \subseteq \prec_G C$$

such that

$$assert(M \cup T \cup W) \cup \{S\} \models assert(G) \tag{1}$$

and

$$assert(M \cup T \cup W) \models S \tag{2}$$

and the goals and effects in T are locally supported in W.[3]

The partial order will be constructed along with the goal structure. The general idea is that the assertions of any goals, facts or conditions that the developer makes use of to satisfy a goal must precede the goal in the partial order. Note that the strategy is provided for convenience and may be empty.

Theorem 3. *In a finite goal structure, any goal that is locally supported in some scenario is globally supported in that scenario. Hence any locally supportable goal is globally supportable.*

Proof. Let G, S, C, M, W and T be defined as in Definition 2. If T is empty, then G is trivially globally supported in W. Suppose then that T is non-empty. Since the goal structure is assumed finite and $\prec$ is an irreflexive partial order, $\prec$ is well-founded on the goal structure. Hence it may be assumed as an inductive hypothesis that the goals in T are globally supported in W. Thus, for any goal $J \in T$, we have $M \cup W \models J$; but then by equation (2) $assert(M \cup W) \models S$ and by equation (1) $assert(M \cup W) \cup \{S\} \models assert(G)$. It follows that $M \cup W \models G$ and thus G is globally supported in W. $\square$

As an example, in Scenario W1, goal G1 is locally supported by G3 and E5 along with the model. G3 is supported directly by the model in W1, as is E5. Therefore by Theorem 3 G1 is globally supported in W1. E6, on the other hand, is locally (and globally) supported in W2.

6 Simple Analysis of Changes

Just as the logic-based framework allows us to reason about consistency and support, it allows us to assess the implications of various changes to the system. While we do not have space in this paper to address this issue in depth, the simple

---

[3] Note that from equations (1) and (2) it follows that $assert(M \cup T \cup W) \models assert(G)$. This is what we would expect — the strategy simply provides a convenient intermediate stage.

example we have set up allows us to give a flavour of how the system might be used.

In the incident described, it is assumed that the pilot is informed of a cross wind, and adopts the standard landing procedure of increasing the thrust and banking the aircraft — Scenario W1. Applying this to our model provides G1 (that is, the aircraft stops within 1000m) as a logical consequence as expected.

Just prior to the landing, however, the wind swings around to a tail wind — Scenario W2. As can be seen from the model, this causes a coincidence of two effects: first, the landing speed is increased so that both the reverse thrusters and the wheel brakes are required; and second, the banking of the aircraft means that the wheels are not both adequately weighted, so the reverse thrusters do not fire. Taken together these effects mean that the aircraft no longer stops within the required distance. Using a theorem prover we see that G1 is no longer a logical consequence of the model in this scenario.

While in this case it is not difficult to trace the implications of scenario W2 by hand (at least once the exercise of formalising the relationships has been performed) in a complex system this will not always be the case, increasing the benefits of automated impact analysis.

Finally, we would like to see what changes can be made to our system in order to prevent this incident occurring. Here the logical model can be used for "what if" analysis. In this example there is a simple change which prevents the accident — the alternative strategy is chosen for goal G2. Modifying fact F3 accordingly and resubmitting the second scenario to the proof system verifies that the problem no longer occurs.

7 Conclusions and Future Work

Goal-structured analysis provides a methodology for structuring system requirements, underpinning these with logical representations, and conducting automated analyses of the resulting systems.

The framework we have presented here is restrictive and further work is needed from both theoretical and pragmatic points of view. This work is continuing with reference to case-studies, carried out with industrial partners on the project, to ascertain what information it is most important to represent and what functionality is required for analysing this information. At present we are investigating adding the following facilities:

- A *suggestion* facility, based on abductive reasoning (e.g. [2]), that proposes ways of developing the goal structure to support goals which do not hold.

- A *sensitivity* facility that uses labelled deduction [5] to partition out goals which cannot be affected by changes to specific parts of the system, avoiding reprocessing.

- A *selection* facility, based on prioritized logics (see for example [11]), that allows requirements to be ranked in terms of the difficulty of change, and enables the reasoning system to select candidates accordingly.

- An *information extraction* system that assists the user in extracting logical information from the informal descriptions expressed in controlled natural langauge [8].

- An *explanation* facility that conveys to the user the line of reasoning used in deductions.

While more research needs to be carried out to ascertain the feasibility of these facilities, we believe that the framework described in this paper provides a useful platform for investigating these areas.

Acknowledgements

We would like to thank the academic and industrial partners on the Proteus project for valuable discussions.

References

1. BARBER, G. Supporting organizational problem solving with a workstation. *ACM Trans. on Office Information Systems 1*, 1 (1983), 45–67.
2. BONDARENKO, A. G. Abductive systems for non-monotonic reasoning. In *Logic Programming: First and Second Russian Conferences on Logic Programming, LNAI 592* (Berlin, 1992), A. Voronkov, Ed., Springer-Verlag, pp. 55–66.
3. DARDENNE, A., VAN LAMSWEERDE, A., AND FICKAS, S. Goal directed requirements acquisition. *Science of Computer Programming 20* (1993), 3–50.
4. DUBOIS, E. A logic of action for supporting goal-oriented elaborations of requirements. *5th International Workshop on Software Specification and Design, ACM Sigsoft Engineering Notes 14* (1989), 160–168.
5. GABBAY, D. Abduction in labelled deductive systems — a conceptual abstract. In *Symbolic and Quantitative Approaches to Uncertainty: Proc. European Conference ECSQAU. LNCS 548*, R. Kruse and P. Siegel, Eds. Springer-Verlag, 1991, pp. 3–11.
6. LADKIN, P. Analysis of a technical description of the Airbus A320 braking system. CRIN-CNRS & INRIA Lorraine, BP 239, Vandoeuvre-Lès-Nancy, France.
7. LUGER, G. F., AND STUBBLEFIELD, W. A. *Artificial Intellegence: Structures and Strategies for Complex Problem Solving.* Benjamin Cummings, 1993.
8. MACIAS, B., AND PULMAN, S. Natural language processing for requirements specifications. In *Safety-critical Systems*, F. Redmill and T. Anderson, Eds. Chapman and Hall, 1993, pp. 67–89.
9. MAIBAUM, T. A logic for the formal requirements specification of real-time embedded systems. Tech. rep., Dept. of Computing, Imperial College, London, 1987. Forest Deliverable R3.
10. MYLOPOULOS, J., CHUNG, L., AND NIXON, B. Representing and using nonfunctional requirements: A process-oriented approach. *IEEE Trans. on Software Engineering 18*, 6 (1992), 483–497.
11. RYAN, M. *Ordered Presentations of Theories — Default Reasoning and Belief Revision.* PhD thesis, Dept. of Computing, Imperial College, London, 1992.

Towards a Deeper Understanding of Quality in Requirements Engineering

John Krogstie   Odd Ivar Lindland   Guttorm Sindre

Faculty of Electrical Engineering and Computer Science
University of Trondheim, Norway

Abstract. The notion of quality in requirements specifications is poorly understood, and in most literature only bread and butter lists of useful properties have been provided. However, the recent frameworks of Lindland et al. and Pohl have tried to take a more systematic approach. In this paper, these two frameworks are reviewed and compared. Although they have different outlook, their deeper structures are not contradictory.

The paper also discusses shortcomings of the two frameworks and proposes extensions to the framework of Lindland et al. The extensions build on social construction theory and the resulting framework should contribute to understanding quality in requirements engineering and conceptual modelling.

Keywords: **Requirements engineering, conceptual modelling, quality, social construction**

1 Introduction

The notion of quality in requirements specifications is so far poorly understood. Software metrics [7] have mostly concentrated on the deliverables of the later phases, such as design and coding, or on detailed process metrics. Moreover, these efforts have concentrated far more on the issue of 'building the product right' than 'building the right product', whereas both should be covered to ensure quality from the user's point of view [2]. Previously proposed quality goals for conceptual models [6, 14, 22, 25] have included many useful aspects, but unfortunately in the form of unsystematic bread and butter lists. Two recent frameworks [17, 20] have attempted to take a more structured approach to understanding the problem. Still, both these need more development before they can result in concrete guidelines for the requirements engineering process. A useful first iteration is to compare the two frameworks and see if they fit together, and possibly unite and extend them.

The rest of the paper is structured as follows: Section 2 reviews and compares the two frameworks. Then, section 3 establishes an extended framework based on the comparison. Section 4 concludes the paper. The terminology used in the papers follows the one usually used in the areas of conceptual modelling and requirements engineering. One should be aware of that the use of many terms in these areas differs significantly from their use in for instance logic programming.

2 Review and Comparison

We will briefly present the main parts of the two frameworks, before performing a comparison between them.

2.1 Lindland/Sindre/Sølvberg's Framework

The main structure of this framework is illustrated in Figure 1. The basic idea is to evaluate the quality of models along three dimensions — syntax, semantics, and pragmatics — by comparing sets of statements. These sets are:

- $\mathcal{M}$, the model, i.e., the set of all the statements explicitly or implicitly made in the model. The explicit model $\mathcal{M}_E$, consists of the statements explicitly made, whereas the implicit model, $\mathcal{M}_I$, consist of the statements not made, but implied by the explicit ones.

- $\mathcal{L}$, the language, i.e., the set of all statements which are possible to make according to the vocabulary and grammar of the modelling languages used.

- $\mathcal{D}$, the domain, i.e., the set of all statements which would be correct and relevant about the problem at hand. Hence, notice that the term domain is used somewhat differently from the usual. Here, it means the 'ideal' model/solution to the problem.

- $\mathcal{I}$, the audience interpretation, i.e., the set of all statements which the audience (i.e., various actors in the modeling process) think that the model consists of.

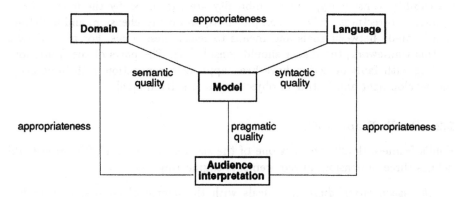

Fig. 1.: The framework by Lindland et al. (From [17])

The primary sources for model quality are defined using the relationships between the model and the three other sets:

- *syntactic quality* is the degree of correspondence between model and language, i.e., the set of syntactic errors is $\mathcal{M} \setminus \mathcal{L}$.

- *semantic quality* is the degree of correspondence between model and domain. If $\mathcal{M} \setminus \mathcal{D} \neq \emptyset$ the model contains invalid statements; if $\mathcal{D} \setminus \mathcal{M} \neq \emptyset$ the model is incomplete. Since total validity and completeness are generally impossible, the notions of *feasible validity* and *feasible completeness* were introduced. Feasible validity is reached when the benefits of removing invalid statement from $\mathcal{M}$ are less than the drawbacks, whereas feasible completeness is reached when the benefits of adding new statements to $\mathcal{M}$ is less than the drawbacks. The term drawback is used instead of the more familiar term cost in an effort to cover both purely economic issues and factors like user preferences and ethics.

- *pragmatic quality* is the degree of correspondence between model and audience interpretation (i.e., the degree to which the model has been understood). If $\mathcal{I} \neq \mathcal{M}$, the comprehension of the model is not completely correct. Usually, it is neither necessary nor possible that the whole audience understand the entire conceptual model — instead each group in the audience should understand the part of the model which is relevant to them. *Feasible comprehension* was defined along the same lines as feasibility for validity and completeness.

In addition to these primary quality concerns, it is pointed out that correspondence between domain and language, between domain and audience interpretation, and between language and audience interpretation may affect the model quality indirectly. These relationships are all denoted *appropriateness* as shown in Figure 1.

It is also argued that previously proposed quality goals such as minimality, traceability, consistency, and unambiguity are subsumed by the four goals of syntactic correctness, validity, completeness, and comprehension, and a distinction is made between goals and means to reach these goals. For more details on this framework, the reader should consult [17]. The parts of the framework dealing with fault detection have been applied in connection with integrating the development and testing of object-oriented software [18].

2.2 Pohl's Framework

Pohl's framework [20] which is one of the results of the NATURE-project [12] defines three dimensions of requirements engineering:

- *the specification dimension* deals with the degree of requirements understanding. At the beginning of the process, this understanding is opaque. The desired output of the RE process is a complete system specification, where completeness is measured against some standard, guideline, or model.

- *the representation dimension* deals with the degree of formality. Various languages can be used in the process; informal ones such as natural language,

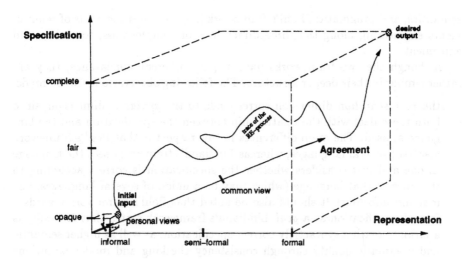

Fig. 2.: Pohl's framework (From [20])

semi-formal ones such as many graphical modelling languages, and formal ones (e.g., logic). At the beginning of the process, statements will usually be informal. Since formal representations allow reasoning and partial code-generation, these are more system-oriented. Hence, a transformation of informal requirements to a formal representation is desirable.

- *the agreement dimension* deals with the degree of agreement. The RE process has many stakeholders, and in the beginning each of these will have their personal views concerning the requirements to be made. The goal of the process is to reach agreement on the requirements. Detected conflicts must be solved through discussions among those affected.

The RE process can be characterized as an arbitrary curve within the cube spanned by these three dimensions, as illustrated in Figure 2. Pohl distinguishes between *original* RE problems, which are those caused by the three dimensions, and problems caused by approaches to solve the original problems, i.e., those related to methods, tools, social aspects, cognitive skills and economical constraints. Furthermore, the article discusses the computer support for RE in light of the three dimensions and discusses how the framework can be applied in analyzing RE methods, practise, problems, and process situations.

2.3 Overall comparison and critique

At first sight, the two frameworks may seem completely different. The terminology used is different. Lindland et al. [17] defines the quality of models (e.g., requirements specifications) according to the linguistic dimensions of syntax, semantics, and pragmatics, Pohl's framework [20] identifies the goals of requirements engineering along the three dimensions of completeness, formality, and agreement.

Although the two frameworks have a quite different appearance, they are rather similar in their deeper structure. The following observations can be made:

- the *representation* dimension corresponds to the *syntactic* dimension, since both these deal with the relationship between the specification and the language(s) used. The main differences in this respect is that Pohl's framework discusses several languages, whereas Lindland's framework sees the language as one and just considers whether the specification is correct according to the rules of that language (which may be a union of several languages, formal and informal). It should also be noted that Pohl's framework regards a formal specification as a *goal*. Lindland's framework states that formality is a *mean* to reach a syntacticly correct specification, as well as higher semantic and pragmatic quality through consistency checking and model executions of different kinds.

- the *specification* dimension corresponds to the *semantic* dimension, since both these deal with the goal of completeness. A notable difference here is that Pohl sees completeness as the sole goal (possibly including validity?), whereas Lindland's framework also identifies the notions of validity and feasibility. The reason for this discrepancy seems to be a somewhat different use of the term completeness, where Pohl uses the term relative to some standard, whereas Lindland et al. uses it relative to the the set of all statements which would be correct and relevant about the problem at hand.

- the *agreement* dimension is related to the *pragmatic* dimension, since both these deal with the specification's relationship to the audience involved. The difference is that Pohl states the goal that the specification should be agreed upon, whereas Lindland et al. aim at letting the model be understood. In a way these goals are partly overlapping. Agreement without understanding is not very useful in a democratic process. On the other hand, using the semiotic levels described in the FRISCO-report [16], it seems more appropriate to put agreement into the social realm, thus going beyond the framework of Lindland et al.

Although both frameworks contribute to improving the understanding of quality issues in requirements engineering, they still have several shortcomings. For instance, in Pohl's framework it appears that a formal, agreed, and complete specification is the goal of the requirements engineering phase. Although we support this as desirable, we — as argued in [17] feel that such goals are unrealistic and we need mechanisms for discussing when the specification/model is *good enough*. The notion of feasibility that is included in Lindland's framework addresses this aspect. In Pohl's framework such mechanisms are only implicitly included through the adherence to standards which potentially include them.

We also feel it is problematic that a completely formal representation is a goal of the RE process. It is not always desirable that all the products of a requirement specification process are formal. For instance, when developing a goal-hierarchy as used in, e.g., TEMPORA [23], it is not meaningful to formalise the high-level business goals, even if these are an important result of requirements engineering in order for the participants to understand and agree about the requirements to the information system. This kind of information is also of vital importance when the requirements to the information systems must be reevaluated during maintenance.

In Lindland's framework, on the other hand, the social aspect of agreement is currently not handled in a satisfactory way. Even if people understand the requirements, this does not mean that they will agree to them. When discussing agreement, the concept of domain as currently defined is also insufficient, since it represents some ideal knowledge about a particular problem, a knowledge not obtainable for the actors that are to agree.

3 Framework extensions

This section aims at extending Lindland et al.'s framework in order to include some of the good aspects of Pohl's framework and also hopefully eliminate the inherent shortcomings of the current version of Lindland's framework.

The key area for improvement is related to the relationships between the domain, model, and audience interpretations and the introduction of the social goal of agreement.

3.1 Background on social construction

Since 'agreement' was not thoroughly discussed in [17], we will first introduce our ontological position for discussing the concept. This will also influence some of the other relationships in the framework.

We base our treatment of agreement on the idea that 'reality' is socially constructed [1], an idea which is the foundation of most of the current theoretical discussion within social sciences [5], and which has received increased attention in the information systems community [8, 16, 24]. For a constructivist, the relationship between 'reality' and models of this reality are subject to negotiation among the audience, and may be adapted from time to time. This is in contrast to a more traditional objectivistic ontology, where the relationship between 'reality' and models thereof is obvious.

The mechanisms of social construction in an organization can briefly be described as follows [9]: An organization consists of individual social actors that perceive the world in a way specific to them. The *local reality* is the way the individual perceives the world that s/he acts in. Whereas some of this local reality may be made explicit and talked about, a lot of what we know about the world is tacit. The term 'individual knowledge' is below restricted to the *explicit* local reality of an individual actor.

When social actors act, they *externalise* their local reality. The most important ways the social actors of an organization externalise their reality, are to speak and to construct languages, artifacts, and institutions. What they do is to construct *organizational reality*: To make something that other actors have to relate to in their work. Finally, *internalisation* is the process of making sense of the institutions, artifacts, technology etc. in the organization, and making this organizational reality part of the individual local reality.

Whereas the development of a requirements specification based on a social actor's local reality is partly a process of externalisation of her/his reality, the process of developing conceptual models can also be looked upon as part of a sense-making process. The views of several actors are collected in a conceptual model and agreement about the validity of this is reached. It should also be noted that the ability and possibility for the different stakeholders to externalise their local reality will differ. Thus, in the words of Goguen one should think about requirements as " ...emergent, in the sense that they do not already exist, but rather emerge from interactions between the analyst and the client organization" [10].

In the framework of Lindland et al, 'reality' is represented by the domain, $\mathcal{D}$. The domain represents the perfect understanding of the problem. From the viewpoint of social construction, as well as the view of information systems engineering as a wicked problem [21], it can be questioned whether a perfect solution at all exists. This is not an important point, however, since the perfect solution is anyway stated to be unachievable. Hence, the domain $\mathcal{D}$ serves only as a useful conceptual fixpoint to make it easier to define quality terminology. To discuss the social aspects, the actors' understanding of the domain must be added to the framework, in the same sense as their understanding of the model was already introduced in the previous version of the framework.

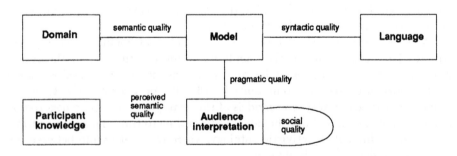

Fig. 3.: Extended framework

3.2 Extended framework

We are now ready to extend the framework of Lindland et al. The main concepts and their relationships are shown in Figure 3. The following sets are defined:

- $\mathcal{A}$, the audience, i.e., the union of the set of individual actors $A_1,...,A_k$ the set of organizational social actors $A_{k+1},...,A_n$ and the set of technical actors $A_{n+1},...,A_m$ who needs to relate to the model. The individual social actors being members of the audience is called the *participants* of the modelling process. An organizational social actor is made up of several individuals. The audience consists of all who need to understand the model during the RE process. The participants are a subset of the stakeholders of the process of developing the new or improved information system, a stakeholder being someone who potentially stands to gain or lose in the process. Stakeholders typically include project managers, system developers and analysts, financers, maintainers, and future users.

  A technical actor is typically a computer or computer program, which must "understand" part of the specification to automatically manipulate it. $\mathcal{A}$ is often evolving during the process of requirements engineering.

- $\mathcal{M}$, the model, i.e., the set of all statements explicitly or implicitly made in the model. At an early point of requirements engineering there may be one model for each participant, but usually fewer models which are the joint models of organizational actors exists. For each participant, the part of the model which is considered relevant for the actor can be seen as a projection of the total model, hence $\mathcal{M}$ can be divided into projections $\mathcal{M}^1,...,\mathcal{M}^k$ corresponding to the involved participants $A_1,...,A_k$. Generally, these projections will not be disjoint, but their union cover $\mathcal{M}$. The complete model will be evolving during the process of requirements engineering.

- $\mathcal{L}$, the language, i.e., the set of all statements that are possible to make according to the vocabulary and grammar of the modelling languages used. Several languages can be in use at the same time, corresponding to the sets $\mathcal{L}_1,...,\mathcal{L}_j$. A sub-language is related to the complete language by limitations on the vocabulary or on the set of allowed grammar rules or both.

  The set $\mathcal{L}$ can be divided into several subsets, e.g., $\mathcal{L}_I$, $\mathcal{L}_S$, and $\mathcal{L}_F$ for the informal, semi-formal and formal parts of the language, respectively. A language with formal syntax is termed semi-formal, whereas a language which also has formal semantics, is termed formal. Note that this does not imply that the language has a semantics based on formal logic.

- $\mathcal{D}$, the domain, i.e., the set of all statements which would be correct and relevant about the problem at hand. $\mathcal{D}$ denotes the ideal knowledge about the problem. The domain evolves during the requirements engineering process.

- $\mathcal{I}$, the audience interpretation, i.e., the set of all statements which the audience thinks that a model consists of. Various parts of the model will be of interest to various participants. Just like the model is projected into $calM^1,...,\mathcal{M}_k$ above, its interpretation can be projected into $\mathcal{I}_1,...,\mathcal{I}_k$ according to the interests of the participants.

– $\mathcal{K}$, the knowledge of the participants, i.e., the union of the sets of statements $\mathcal{K}_1,...,\mathcal{K}_k$, one for each individual social actor in the audience. The set $\mathcal{K}_i$ contains all possible statements that would be correct and relevant for addressing the problem at hand according to the knowledge of the actor A_i. $\mathcal{K}_i$ is a subset of the explicit internal reality of the social actor $\mathcal{K}^i$. $\mathcal{K}^i$ is also evolving during requirements engineering. $\mathcal{M}_i$ is an externalisation of $\mathcal{K}_i$ and is a model made on the basis of the knowledge of the individual actor. Even if the internal reality of each individual will always differ to a certain degree, the explicit internal reality concerning a constrained area might be equal, especially within groups of social actors [9, 19].

With this new framework in place, we have an increased potential for discussing specification quality. The primary goal for semantic quality is a correspondence between the model and the domain, but this correspondence can neither be established nor checked directly: to build the model, one has to go through the audience's knowledge of the domain, and to check the model one has to compare this with the audience's interpretation of the model. Hence, what we do observe at quality control is not the actual semantic quality of the model, but a perceived semantic quality based on comparison of the two imperfect interpretations.

Syntactic quality Syntactic quality is the correspondence between the specification and the language. The goal is syntactic correctness, $\mathcal{M} \setminus \mathcal{L} = \emptyset$, or for a given externalization, $\mathcal{M}_i \setminus \mathcal{L} = \emptyset$. Typical means to ensure syntactic quality is *formal syntax*, i.e., that the language is parsable by a technical actor in the audience, and the modeling activity to perform this is termed syntax checking.

Semantic quality For the semantic quality of the complete model $\mathcal{M}$, no major changes are necessary to the previous version of the framework. [17] defines two goals, feasible validity and feasible completeness.

Discussing perceived semantic quality, we get the following:

– *Perceived validity* of the model projection: $\mathcal{I}_i \setminus \mathcal{K}_i = \emptyset$.

– *Perceived completeness* of the model projection: $\mathcal{K}_i \setminus \mathcal{I}_i = \emptyset$.

The perceived semantic quality can change, for better or for worse, either as a result of changes in (the understanding of) the model, or as a result of changes in the knowledge about the domain. Notice that one way the knowledge of the actor can change, is through the internalization of another sub-model. Internalisation can be expressed crudely as a mapping between the sets of statements, being part of the explicit internal reality of an actor.

$$INT : \mathcal{K}_i \rightarrow (\mathcal{K}_i \cup \mathcal{N}) \subset \mathcal{M}_j \setminus (\mathcal{O} \subset \mathcal{K}_i) \cdot \qquad (1)$$

$i \neq j, \mathcal{O} \cap \mathcal{N} = \emptyset, \mathcal{K}_i \setminus \mathcal{N} = \mathcal{K}_i$

$\mathcal{N}$ and $\mathcal{O}$ above is sets of statements. $\mathcal{O}$ might be empty giving a monotonous growth of $\mathcal{K}_i$. If $\mathcal{O}$ is not empty there is a non-monotonous growth of $\mathcal{K}_i$.

Pragmatic quality Pragmatic quality can be defined largely the same way as before, the goal being comprehension, i.e. that the model is understood, not its understandability. [17] also defined this on behalf of various participant groups, since each such group will usually only be interested in a part of the model. Similarly, we can define individual comprehension: $\mathcal{I}_i = \mathcal{M}^i$, as the goal that the participant A_i understands the relevant part of the model.

For total comprehension, one must thus have $(\forall i, i \in [1...k]) \, \mathcal{I}_i = \mathcal{M}^i$, i.e., that every participant understands the relevant part of $\mathcal{M}$.

Total comprehension is also an unrealistic goal. Hence it is interesting to define feasible comprehension as the situation where comprehension can still be improved, but the drawbacks of doing this exceeds the benefits. This has been done in [17].

That a model is understood from the technical actor's point of view, means that $(\forall i, i \in [n + 1...m]) \mathcal{I}_i = \mathcal{M}^i$, thus all statements that are relevant to the technical actor to be able to perform code generation, simulation, etc. is comprehended by this actor. In this sense, formality can be looked upon as being a pragmatic goal, formal syntax and formal semantics are means for achieving pragmatic quality. This illustrates that pragmatic quality is dependant on the different actors. This also applies to social actors. Whereas some individuals from the outset are used to formal languages, and a formal specification in fact will be best for them also for comprehension (regardless of execution etc.), other individuals will find a mix of formal and informal statements to be more comprehensive, even if the set of statements in the model is in fact redundant.

Some of the means to achieve pragmatic quality have been identified earlier, namely formality, executability, expressive economy and aesthetics. The corresponding modelling activities are inspection, visualization, filtering, diagram layout, paraphrasing, explanation, execution, animation, and simulation. Another important activity is training the participants in the syntax and semantics of the modelling languages used.

Social quality Inspired by Pohl, we set up the goal for social quality as *agreement*. However, this is not straightforward to define. Four kinds of agreement can be identified, according distinctions along two orthogonal dimensions:

- agreement in knowledge vs. agreement in model interpretation.

- relative agreement vs. absolute agreement

Agreement in model interpretation will usually be a more limited demand than agreement in knowledge, since the former one means that the actors agree about what (they think) is stated in the model, whereas there may still be many issues they disagree about which have not been stated in the model so far, even if it might be regarded as relevant for one of the actors.

Relative agreement means that the various projections are consistent — hence, there may be many statements in the projection of one actor that are not present in that of another, as long as they do not contradict each other. Absolute agreement, on the other hand, means that all projections are the same.

Since different participants often have their expertise in different fields, relative agreement is a more useful concept than absolute agreement. On the other hand, the different actors must have the *possibility* to agree on something, i.e. the parts of the model which are relevant to them have to overlap to some extent.

However, it is not given that all participants will come to agreement. Few decisions are taken in society under complete agreement, and those that are are not necessarily good, due to e.g group-think. To answer this we introduce *feasible agreement*:

Feasible agreement: A situation of feasible comprehension where inconsistencies between statements in the different $\mathcal{I}_i$ are resolved by choosing one of the alternatives when the benefits of doing this is less than the drawbacks of working out agreement.

The pragmatic goal of comprehension is looked upon as a social mean. This because agreement without comprehension is not very useful, at least not when having democratic ideals. Obviously if someone is trying to manipulate a situation, agreement without comprehension is useful. The area of *model monopoly* [3] is related to this.

Some activities for achieving feasible agreement are:

- Viewpoint analysis [15]: This includes techniques for comparing two or more models and find the discrepancies.

- Conflict resolution: Specific techniques for this can be found in the area of computer supported cooperative work, see [4, 11] where argumentation systems are presented.

- Model merging: Merging two potentially inconsistent models into one consistent one.

The above activities can be done either manually, semi-automatically or automatically, for semi-automatic or automatic support, formal syntax and semantics are again useful. In addition is it useful to be able to represent inconcistency and disagreement directly in the model, and not only have to compare separate models.

4   Concluding Remarks

This paper has reviewed and compared two recent frameworks for disussing quality of requirement specifications: the framework of Lindland et al. in [17] and Pohl's framework in [20]. The comparision has shown that the frameworks have different appearances and uses different terminology, but the deeper structures of the frameworks are quite similar.

The main objective of the paper has been to push our understanding of quality aspects in requirements engineering one step further. The comparison of the two frameworks has been useful in that respect. In particular, the concept of agreement in Pohl's framework has inspired us to look deeper into the social process of building a specification.

In contrast to the previous version of the framework of Lindland et al. we are now able to discuss the quality of models where different social actors are developing their submodels based on individual domain knowledge. Furthermore, the process of merging different viewpoints is defined as contributing to social quality. Here, agreement among the actors is the major goal.

Table 1 shows an overview of the goals and means of the extended framework. The overview is based on a similar one in [17], but has been extended as discussed above.

Quality types	Goals	Means	
		Model properties	Activities
Syntactic q.	Synt. correctness	Formal syntax	Syntax checking
Semantic q.	Feasible validity Feasible compl.	Formal semantics Modifiability	Consistency checking Statement insertion Statement deletion
Perceived sem.q.	Perceived validity Perceived compl.		Statement insertion Statement deletion Audience training
Pragmatic q.	Feasible compr.	Expressive economy Aesthetics	Inspection Visualization Filtering Diagram layout Paraphrasing Explanation Audience training
		Executability	Execution Animation Simulation
Social q.	Feasible agreement	Conflict modelling	Viewpoint analysis Conflict resolution Model merging

Table 1.: Framework for model quality

Although the framework contributes to our understanding of quality issues with respect to requirement engineering, the contribution so far lies on a high level of abstraction. There are several interesting paths for further work by which the framework can be refined to become more directly useful for requirements engineering practitioners. Among others, the follow areas need further exploration:

- *development of further product metrics:* In the current framework quality goals are mainly defined as the degree of correspondence between various sets. Future work should concentrate on developing quantitative metrics so that the quality of the model, audience, and the domain knowledge can be more explicitly assessed. Some initial efforts in this direction are reported in [13].

- *development of process guidelines:* The framework gives an overview of decisions that will have to be made in the requirements engineering phase. Further work should result in guidelines that practitioners may use directly in concrete projects.

Since semantic, pragmatic and social quality are in practice immeasurable, process heuristics may be a more interesting issue to pursue than product metrics.

References

1. P. Berger and T. Luckmann. *The Social Construction of Reality: A Treatise in the Sociology of Knowledge.* Penguin, 1966.
2. B. W. Boehm. Verifying and validating software requirements and design specifications. *IEEE Software,* 1:75–88, 1984.
3. S. Bråten. *Dialogens vilkår i datasamfunnet (In Norwegian).* Universitetsforlaget, 1983.
4. J. Conklin and M. J. Begeman. gIBIS: A hypertext tool for exploratory policy discussion. *ACM Transactions on Office Information Systems,* 6(4):303–331, 1988.
5. B. Dahlbom. The idea that reality is socialy constructed. In Floyd et al. [8], pages 101–126.
6. A. M. Davis. *Software Requirements Analysis & Specification.* Prentice-Hall, 1990.
7. N. E. Fenton, editor. *Software Metrics — A Rigorous Approach.* Chapman & Hall, 1991.
8. C. Floyd, H. Züllighoven, R. Budde, and R. Keil-Slawik, editors. *Software Development and Reality Construction.* Springer Verlag, 1991.
9. R. Gjersvik. *The Construction of Information Systems in Organization: An Action Research Project on Technology, Organizational Closure, Reflection, and Change.* PhD thesis, ORAL, NTH, Trondheim, Norway, 1993.
10. J. Goguen. Requirements engineering: Reconciliation of technical and social issues. Technical report, Centre for Requirementss and Foundations, Oxford University, Cambridge, England, 1992.
11. U. Hahn, M. Jarke, and T. Rose. Group work in software projects: Integrated conceptual models and collaboration tools. In S. Gibbs and A. A. Verrijn-Stuart, editors, *Multi-User Interfaces and Applications: Proceedings of the IFIP WG 8.4 Conference on Multi-User Interfaces and Applications,* pages 83–102. North-Holland, 1990.

12. M. Jarke, J. Bubenko, C. Rolland, A. Sutcliffe, and Y. Vassiliou. Theories underlying requirements engineering: An overview of NATURE at genesis. In *Proceedings of the IEEE International Symposium on Requirements Engineering (RE'93)*, pages 19–31, 1993.

13. J. Krogstie, O. I. Lindland, and G. Sindre. Defining quality aspects for conceptual models. In E. D. Falkenberg et al., editor, *Information Systems Concepts, Proc. ISCO3, Marburg, Germany*. North-Holland, 1995.

14. C. H. Kung. An analysis of three conceptual models with time perspective. In Olle et al., editor, *Information Systems Design Methodologies: A Feature Analysis*, pages 141–168. North-Holland, 1983.

15. J. C. S. P. Leite and P. A. Freeman. Requirements validation through viewpoint resolution. *IEEE Transactions on Software Engineering*, 17(12):1253–1269, December 1991.

16. P. Lindgren ed. A framework of information systems concepts. Technical Report Interrim report, FRISCO, May 1990.

17. O. I. Lindland, G. Sindre, and A. Sølvberg. Understanding quality in conceptual modelling. *IEEE Software*, pages 42–49, April 1994.

18. J. D. McGregor and T. D.. Korson. Integrated object-oriented testing and development processes. *Communications of the ACM*, 37(9), 1994.

19. J. W. Orlikowski and D. C. Gash. Technological frames: Making sense of information technology in organizations. *ACM Transactions on Information Systems*, 12(2):174–207, 1994.

20. K. Pohl. The three dimensions of requirements engineering: A framework and its applications. *Information Systems*, 19(3):243–258, April 1994.

21. H. Rittel. On the planning crisis: Systems analysis of the first and second generations. *Bedriftsøkonomen*, (8), 1972.

22. G. C. Roman. A taxonomy of current issues in requirements engineering. *IEEE Computer*, pages 14–22, April 1985.

23. A. H. Seltveit. An abstraction-based rule approach to large-scale information systems development. In C. Rolland, F. Bodart, and C. Cauvet, editors, *Proceedings of the 5th International Conference on Advanced Information Systems Engineering (CAiSE'93)*, pages 328–351, Paris, France, June 8-11 1993. Springer Verlag.

24. J. Siddiqi. Challenging universal truths of requirements engineering. *IEEE Software*, pages 18–19, March 1994.

25. R. T. Yeh, P. Zave, A. P. Conn, and G. E. Cole Jr. Software requirements: New directions and perspectives. In C. Vick and C. Ramamoorthy, editors, *Handbook of Software Engineering*, pages 519–543. Van Nostrand Reinhold, 1984.

Modelling inheritance, composition and relationship links between objects, object versions and class versions

E. Andonoff*, G. Hubert**, A. Le Parc**, G. Zurfluh*

* Lab. CERISS, Univ. Toulouse I, 31042 Toulouse Cédex, France
Email : ando@cix.cict.fr

** Lab. IRIT pôle SIG, Univ. Toulouse III, 31062 Toulouse Cédex, France
Email : {ando,hubert,leparc,zurfluh}@irit.fr

Abstract. This paper presents a conceptual object-oriented model which allows to describe, in a unified framework, objects, object versions and class versions. Three kinds of classes are used for such a modeling: object classes, version classes and versionable classes. This paper approaches, in greater details, the outcomes of representing links between these different kinds of classes. The considered links are inheritance, composition and relationship links. Most of system managing object versions and/or class versions only partially approach this problem.

keywords. Object classes. Version classes. Versionnable classes. Inheritance. Composition. Relationship.

1 Introduction

The concept of version was introduced to describe the evolution of real world entities along time. The different states of entities are kept and correspond to their different versions. The concept of version is important in computer aided design, technical documentation or software engineering fields where managed data are time-dependent [2].

Many current database systems allow to manage versions. In these systems, versions are investigated at two abstraction levels: the object level and the class level. Some systems have studied versions at only one abstraction level. For example, Sherpa [14], O2 [20] or CloSQL [15] have studied this concept at the class level while Etic [9] has investigated it at the object level. Other systems, such as Orion [7] [12], Encore [19], Iris [3], Avance [4], OVM [10] or Presage [18] have studied versions at the two abstraction levels. But these studies are often (except Presage) carried out without analysing the outcomes of both managemement of class versions and object versions. Moreover, these studies partially deal with (or bypass) the study of links and cardinalities between versions: composition is partially approached while there is no work about inheritance and relationship.

On the other hand, current database design methods such as OMT [17], OOA [6], OOM [16], O* [5] do not propose solutions to model versions in their conceptual data models. Now, version modeling is an activity recovered from the conceptual level [11]. Indeed, to exactly describe the real world, a designer must be able to tell if an entity may evolve or if an entity class may evolve. So, he must have tools to model object and class versions in the conceptual data models he defines.

In this paper, we present a conceptual object model intended for object-oriented database modeling. This model enables us to describe, in a unified framework, objects, object versions and class versions. Three kinds of classes are used for such a modeling: object classes, version classes and versionable classes. Object class instances are objects of which one keeps only the last state. The instances of version classes are object versions where only the value evolves whereas the instances of versionable classes are object versions whose value and schema evolve (the different significant states are kept). This paper investigates, in greater details, the outcomes of modeling links between these different kinds of classes on objects and object versions. The considered links are inheritance, composition and relationship links. Moreover, operations on objects and classes are also discussed in this study.

This paper is organised as follows. Section 2 presents the main concepts of version and particularly the concepts of object and class versions. Section 3 describes the conceptual object model we have defined; it shows how we represent objects, object versions and class versions using three kinds of classes. Sections 4, 5 and 6 approach the outcomes of modeling inheritance, composition and relationship links between these various kinds of classes. Section 7 is the conclusion.

2 The Concepts

The version concept is studied in a unified way at two abstraction levels which are the object level and the class level.

2.1 Versions

In the real world, an entity has characteristics which may evolve during its life cycle: the entity has different successive states.

In object-oriented databases, a real world entity is described by a unique object. This object has a schema (i.e. a set of attributes and methods) and a value. The schema and the value describe the last entity state.

In a version context, an entity is not described by a unique object but by a set of objects (versions): it is possible to manage several entity states and not only the last one. A version corresponds to one of the entity states. The entity versions are linked by a derivation link; they constitute a version derivation hierarchy [11].

An entity class is described by a set of version hierarchies; each entity is described by only one hierarchy.

When created, an entity is described by only one version (called root version). The definition of every new entity version is done by derivation from a previous version. Such versions are called derived versions [11] (e.g. E1.v1 is a derived version from

E1.v0). Several versions may be derived from the same previous version. Such versions are called alternatives [11] (e.g. E1.v2 and E1.v3 are alternatives derived from E1.v1).

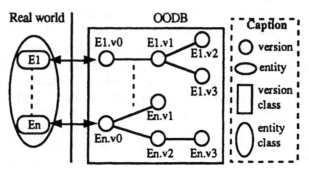

Fig. 1. Representing entities with versions

A version is either frozen or working. A frozen version describes a significant and final state of an entity. A frozen version may be deleted but not updated. To describe a new state of this entity, we have to derive a new version (from the frozen one). A working version is a version that temporarily describes one of the entity states. It may be deleted and updated to describe a next entity state. The previous state is lost for the benefit of the next state.

The default version of an entity [7] is a version pointed out by the database designer as the most representative version of the entity. It is unique for each entity and may be chosen among the set of frozen or working versions.

2.2 Object Versions and Class Versions

In object-oriented databases, versions may be considered at two abstraction levels: the object level and the class level. Evolution of objects may found expression in either value evolution or schema evolution. If an entity evolution is described by a set of versions having the same schema (there is only value evolution), one talks about object version. If an entity evolution is described by a set of versions which do not have the same schema (there is value and schema evolution), one talks about class version: these different versions belong to different classes. Value evolution consists in updating (in a partial or a total way) the attribute values of the considered object version. Schema evolution consists in adding new attributes or new methods, or in updating or deleting attributes or methods already defined, of the considered class version.

Class or object evolution is realized by deriving an object or a class version. Thus, derived or alternative object versions or class versions are created. These versions, like entity versions, are linked by a derivation relationship; they constitute a version derivation hierarchy (for objects and classes). The frozen, working and default version notions are available for object and class versions. The figure below illustrates object and class versions concepts.

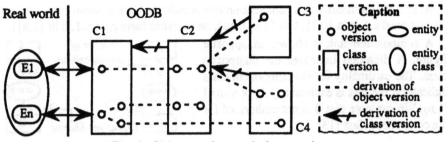

Fig. 2. Object versions and class versions

3 The Model

The data model we define is a conceptual model which takes its inspiration from the OMT object model [17]. It enables to describe objects, object versions and class versions.

3.1 Object Classes and Links

Class is the unique tool for modeling real world entities. A class gathers a set of objects having the same schema. The class schema describes the structure and behaviour of its objects. The structure is represented by a set of (monovalued or multivalued) attributes whose domain is a predefined class (integer, real...). Behaviour is described by a set of methods described by their signature. Classes may be linked by three kinds of links : inheritance links, composition links and relationship links.

3.2 Inheritance Links

Inheritance models *is-a* link between objects. It allows to gather the common properties (attributes and methods) of several classes, called subclasses, in a more general class, called superclass. Inheritance is the mechanism allowing to transfer properties from superclass to subclasses.

The model retains a specialization inheritance [1]: subclasses are described defining new properties or redefining inherited properties. The inheritance hierarchy of a class consists of the class itself and all the classes belonging to the inheritance hierarchy of its subclasses. Inheritance link is shown on opposite figure.

3.3 Composition Links

Composition models *is-part-of* link between objects. It is a basic modeling tool to describe complex objects [13]. A composition link is defined between two classes when life cycles of objects belonging to the two classes are dependent [5] (e.g. the creation of an object in a class causes the creation of an object in the other class). Composition links are either exclusive or shared. If a link is an exclusive one, a component object can only be a part of one composite object. If the link is a shared one, a component object can be a part of several composite objects.

At last, the cardinality of a composition link is indicated in a conventional way: on the one hand a,b (a in {0,1}, b in {1,n}), and, on the other hand c,d (c=1, d in {1,n}).

A composition link is shown on opposite figure. A diamond indicates the composite class. The cardinality for the component class indicates if the link is exclusive (1,1) or shared (1,n). We can note that 0 is not authorized for the component class [13].

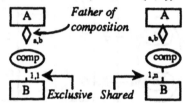

Composition links were studied in Orion. [13] introduces the dependent independent, exclusive and shared notions. The composition links we model correspond to the dependent exclusive and dependent shared composite references of Orion.

3.4 Relationship Links

Relationship models *is-linked-to* link between objects. A relationship link is defined between two classes when life cycles of objects belonging to the two classes are independent [5]. The cardinality of a relationship link is indicated as before.

Relationship links are shown as follows:

The relationship links we model correspond to the relationship links defined in OMT, OOA, OOM or O*, and to the independent exclusive and independent shared composite references defined in Orion.

3.5 Model Extensions

The model is extended to integrate the notions of object and class versions. In addition to object classes (whose instances are objects), it allows to model two other kinds of classes (whose instances are object versions): version classes and versionable classes.

Instances of version classes are object versions having only value evolution whereas instances of versionable classes are object versions having value and schema evolution. Version classes have a schema of which one keeps only the last state whereas versionable classes have a schema that may evolve (different significant and final states are kept). The different class versions describing schema evolution of a versionable class are linked by a derivation link. Object evolution is represented by a hierarchy of object versions belonging to one or more classes linked by a derivation link. We can observe that a versionable class is also a version class.

Version classes, versionable classes and derivation link between class versions of a versionable class are shown as follows:

Version class   *Versions of versionnable class*

A   A.v0 ← A.v1

A.v0

Versionnable class   *Derivation link*

Inheritance, composition and relationship links (previously shown between object classes) can be defined between the different kinds of classes. Different inheritance, composition and relationship cases are conceivable.

The constraints underlying these kinds of classes make some cases inconsistent or restrict the operations which can be performed on classes and their instances.

3.6 Operations

Operations which can be performed on classes (a) and their instances (b) are described in the following table :

operation class	derive (a)	update (a)	create (b)	delete (b)	derive (b)	update (b)
object class	no	yes	yes	yes	no	yes
version class	no	yes (*)	yes	yes	yes	yes (*)
versionable class	yes	yes (*)	yes	yes	yes	yes (*)

Class operations allow to create a new class deriving an existing one (derive) or to modify a class schema (update). Instance operations allow to create (from scratch) a new instance (create), to delete an existing instance (delete), to create a new instance deriving an existing one (derive) or to modify the instance values (update). We can observe that the update (*) operation can only be performed to unfrozen object versions (instances of version or versionable classes) or to unfrozen versionable classes. These operations are detailed in the following sections. The links defined between classes (inheritance, composition and relationships links) are also taken into account.

4 Inheritance

We first describe the different inheritance cases and then study the instance and class operations.

4.1 Inheritance Cases

A class belongs to one of the two following families : object or version. The object family consists of object classes. The version family consists of version and versionable classes. We can observe that a versionable class is less restrictive than a version class in term of evolution because it allows schema evolution in addition to value evolution.

We have defined two rules that indicate if an inheritance hierarchy is consistent. These rules allow to organize in inheritance hierarchies classes belonging to the same family (the instances of these classes evolve in a similar way: no evolution or value and/or schema evolution). These rules are the following :

- the subclasses and the superclass must belong to the same family, i.e. either object family or version family;
- the superclass category must not be less restrictive (in term of evolution) than its subclasses categories.

Inheritance cases checking these rules are described below. Any other case is forbidden.

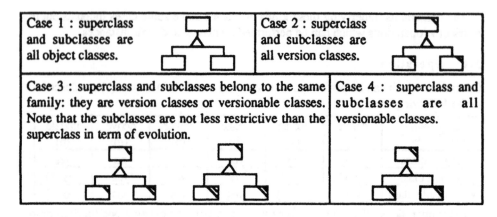

4.2 Operations

Instance operations are only performed on subclasses leaf of the inheritance hierarchy (the superclasses, i.e. the classes which are not leaf of a inheritance hierarchy, do not have their own instances). These instance operations (create, delete, derive and update) are available without restriction (as described in section 3.6).

With respect to inheritance cases, class operations (derive and update) may be forbidden or performed with or without restriction:

operations possible cases	derive superclass	derive subclass	update superclass	update subclass
case 1	no	no	yes (3)	yes (4)
case 2	no	no	yes (5)	yes (6)
case 3	no	yes (1)	yes (5)	yes (6)
case 4	yes	yes (2)	yes (5)	yes (6)

The following comments explain these different operations:

- (1) schema derivation is permitted in a versionable subclass. This derivation does not affect inherited attributes.
- (2) schema derivation is permitted in the versionable subclasses. If inherited attributes are updated in the subclass, then there is repercussion of this derivation on the superclass and on the other subclasses.
- (3) schema updating in a superclass causes schema updating in its subclasses. This updating is propagated on subclasses instances.
- (4) schema updating in a subclass is propagated on the superclass and the other subclasses if this modification affects inherited attributes. This updating is propagated on subclasses instances.
- (5) schema updating in a superclass is permitted if there are no frozen instances in its subclasses. In this case, the comment (3) is applicable.
- (6) schema updating in a subclass is permitted if the subclass has no frozen instances. In this case, the comment (4) is applicable.

5 Composition

We first describe the different composition cases and then study the instance and class operations. For space limitations, we only present the composition links whose cardinalities are (1,1/1,1), (1,1/1,n), (1,n/1,1) and (1,n/1,n). These cardinalities are the most restrictive ones, and, therefore, the most interesting ones.

5.1 Composition Cases

A composition link may be defined between the three kinds of classes: object, version and versionable classes. However, only the notion of object version must be considered in composition study. Indeed, instances of version and versionable classes are object versions. So, it is useless to distinguish version classes from versionable classes.

We have defined one rule which indicates if a composition link is consistent. This rule allows to organize in composition hierarchies the classes whose instances have similar life cycles (i.e. dependent). This rule imposes not to have a composite class which is version class, and a component class which is an object class.

The composition cases checking this rule are described below. Cases 1 and 3 are studied in the literature while case 2 is never approached.

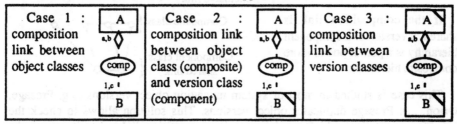

For each of the three previous cases, we study how the integrity constraints inherent in composition link cardinalities (they express the exclusive and sharing notions) are taken into account at both object level and object version level. Note that the chosen solutions limit the useless duplications of versions.

Case 1 : composition between object classes. This case is classic and is widely approached in the literature. The solution we retain is the one proposed in [13] (for more details, report to [13]).

Case 2 : composition between object class and version class. On the one hand, this case expresses a link between a composite class and one or more hierarchies of component object versions, and, on the other hand, this case expresses a link between one component object version and one (exclusive) or more (shared) composite objects.

If the composition link is exclusive, a component hierarchy is a part of only one composite object.

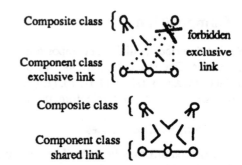

Composite class

Component class
exclusive link

forbidden
exclusive link

If the composition link is shared, a component hierarchy is a part of one or more composite objects.

Composite class

Component class
shared link

Case 3 : composition between version classes. On the one hand, this case expresses a link between a composite object version and one or more hierarchies of component object versions, and, on the other hand, this case expresses a link between a component object version and one (exclusive) or more (shared) composite object versions.

If the composition link is exclusive, a version of a component hierarchy is a part of only one composite hierarchy.

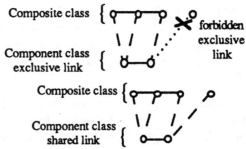

Composite class

Component class
exclusive link

forbidden
exclusive link

If the composition link is shared, a version of a component hierarchy is a part of one or more composite hierarchies.

Composite class

Component class
shared link

This case is studied in most of system managing object versions (e.g. Presage, Orion, ...). Presage duplicates object versions. This solution allows to check the integrity constraints which are inherent in composition links; but it causes the (useless) creation of several object versions describing the same object evolution states. The Orion solution consists in connecting the derived versions of an object to the component generic object. Such a technic limits object version duplication but it imposes to dynamically compute the derived versions.

5.2 Operations

Composition expresses that composite and component instance life cycles are dependent. So, some operations performed on instances (create, delete, derive) must be studied in details. The other ones are available as described in section 3.6.

Creation. The dependency of composite and component instance life cycles imposes to create one (or more) component instance(s) when creating a composite instance [13]. Exclusivity and sharing notions and the different composition cases must also be taken into account.

Case 1 : composition between an object class A and an object class B. This case is classic. We retain the solution proposed in [13].

Case 2 : composition between an object class A and a version class B. If the composition link is monovalued for A (1,1), when a new object "a" is created in the composite class A, it must be linked to a unique hierarchy of the component class B (i.e. to all the versions of this hierarchy). If the link is multivalued for A (1,n), when an object "a" is created in the composite class A, it must be linked to one or more hierarchies of the component class B.

If the link is exclusive (1,1), the hierarchy in B must be a new one. If the link is shared (1,n), the hierarchies in B are either existing or new hierarchies.

Case 3 : composition between a version class A and a version class B. If the composition link is monovalued for A, a root version "a" of a new hierarchy created in the composite class A must be linked to a unique version "b" of a hierarchy of the component class B. If the link is multivalued, the root version "a" can be connected to one or more version "b" of the component class B. These versions belong to distinct hierarchies.

If the link is exclusive, the version "b" of the component class B is either a root version of a new hierarchy, or a derived of a leaf version of a free hierarchy. A component hierarchy is described as free when it has no leaf versions linked to a leaf version of a composite hierarchy:

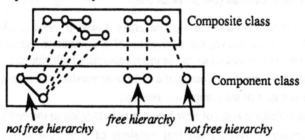

Fig. 3. Free hierarchies

If the link is shared, the versions "b" of the class B are either leaf versions of existing hierarchies, or root versions of new hierarchies.

Deletion. The dependency of composite and component instance life cycles imposes to delete one (or more) component instance(s) when deleting a composite instance [13]. Exclusivity and sharing notions and the different composition cases must also be taken into account.

Case 1 : composition between an object class A and an object class B. This case is classic. We retain the solution proposed in [13].

Case 2 : composition between an object class A and a version class B. If the composition link is exclusive, the deletion of an object "a" in the composite class A causes the deletion of all its component hierarchies in the component class B (i.e. the deletion of the versions belonging to these hierarchies). If the link is shared, the component hierarchies are only deleted if they do not compose other objects belonging to the composite class A.

Deleting a component hierarchy implies to connect the composite object to another component hierarchy (according to link cardinality).

Case 3 : composition between a version class A a version class B. If the composition link is exclusive, the deletion of a version "a" in the composite class A causes the deletion of its component versions "b" belonging to the component class B except if the component versions compose other versions ("aa") of the same composite hierarchy. On the other hand, if the link is shared, the component versions "b" are deleted only if they do not compose other versions.

The deletion of a component version causes the deletion of the corresponding composite versions which are frozen (several successive derived versions can have the same components). If the composite versions are working, they are not deleted but linked to other component versions.

Derivation. Derivation is an operation which can only be performed on instances of version classes. Only case 2 and case 3 are studied.

Case 2 : composition between an object class A and a version class B. A derived version in the component class is automatically linked to the same composite objects as the version it derives from (the previous one).

Case 3 : composition between a version class A and a version class B. If the composition link is exclusive, the derivation of a composite version causes the creation of a new version linked to one or more versions which can be :
- the same component versions as the composite version it derives from,
- derived versions of the component versions,
- versions which are roots of new hierarchies belonging to the component class,
- new versions derived from leaf versions of free component hierarchies (cf 5.2.1).

If a composition link is shared, the result of composite version derivation is a version which can also be linked to one or more leaf versions belonging to any component hierarchy.

Deriving a component version causes deriving all the linked composite versions. We can observe that this derivation does not cause the derivation of the other components of the composite object; the other (composition and relationship) links are not modified.

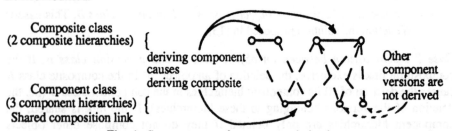

Composite class
(2 composite hierarchies) {

deriving component
causes
deriving composite

Component class
(3 component hierarchies) {
Shared composition link

Other
component
versions are
not derived

Fig. 4. Consequences of component derivation

6 Relationship

We first describe the different relationship cases and then study the instance and class operations. For space limitations, we only present the relationship links whose cardinalities are (1,1/1,1), (1,1/1,n) and (1,n/1,n). These cardinalities are the most restrictive ones, and, therefore, the most interesting ones.

6.1 Relationship Cases

A relationship link may be defined between the three kinds of classes: object, version and versionable classes. However, only the notion of object version must be considered in relationship study. Indeed, instances of version and versionable classes are object versions. So, it is useless to distinguish version classes from versionable classes. The relationship cases which must be studied are described below. Cases 1 and 3 are approached in the literature whereas case 2 is never investigated.

Case 1 : relationship link between object classes

Case 2 : relationship link between an object class and a version class

Case 3 : relationship link between version classes

For each of the three previous cases, we study how the integrity constraints inherent in relationship link cardinalities are taken into account at both object level and object version level. Note that the chosen solutions limit useless duplications of versions.

Case 1: relationship between object classes. This case is widely studied in the literature (OMT, OOA, OOM, O*, ...). It is not presented in this paper.

Case 2: relationship between an object class and a version class. On the one hand, this case expresses a link between an object and one or more hierarchies of object versions, and, on the other hand, this case expresses a link between an object version and one or more objects.

On the other hand, if the relationship link is monovalued for the object class A (1,1), an object of A must be linked to only one current hierarchy of B.

The current hierarchy for an object is the last hierarchy linked to it. If a relationship link is multivalued for the object class A (1,n), an object must be linked to one or more hierarchies of B.

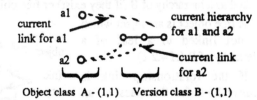

Fig. 5. Current hierarchies

If a relationship link is monovalued for the version class B, a version of B must be linked to a unique object of A. If the relationship link is multivalued for the version class B, a version of B must be linked to one or more objects of A.

Case 3 : relationship between version classes. This case expresses a link between an object version and one or more hierarchies of object versions.

If a relationship link is monovalued for the class A, a version of A is linked to only one hierarchy of B (and vice versa). If the relationship link is multivalued for the class A, a version of A must be linked to one or more hierarchies of B (and vice versa).

forbidden (card. 1,1). A version must be linked to only one hierarchy.

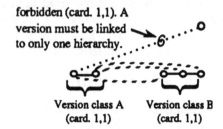

Version class A   Version class B
(card. 1,1)   (card. 1,1)

6.2   Operations

Operations performed on instances (create, delete, derive) must be studied in details. The other ones are available as described in section 3.6. The case 1 of relationship between object classes, widely studied in the literature (OMT, OOA, OOM, O*, ...), is not presented here.

Creation.

Case 2 : relationship between an object class and a version class. If the relationship link is monovalued for the object class A, a new object "a" created in A is linked to only one version "b" of the version class B. If the relationship link is multivalued for the class A, a new object "a" in the class A must be linked to one or more versions "b" of the class B. These versions belong to distinct hierarchies.

If the relationship is monovalued for the version class B, a new object created in the class A is linked to a version "b" of B which is either a leaf of a hierarchy of B not yet linked to an object belonging to A (if it exists), or versions derived from leaf versions of free hierarchies or a root of a new hierarchy of B. Multivaluation for the class B does not restrict the set of leaf versions which must be linked to an object "a".

If the relationship link is monovalued for the version class B, a new version "b" created in B (it is the root of a new hierarchy) is only linked to one object "a" of the object class A. If the relationship is multivalued for B, the new version "b" must be linked to one or more objects "a" of the class A.

Moreover, if the relationship link is monovalued for the object class A, the objects "a" which must be linked to the version "b" are either new objects of A which are not linked to a hierarchy of B (if they exist) or free objects.

A free object is an object which is not linked to a leaf of a hierarchy of B (cf 4.2.1).

If the relationship link is multivalued for the class A, an object of the class A can be linked to any version of the class B.

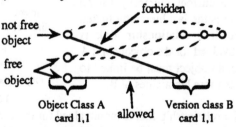

Object Class A   Version class B
card 1,1   allowed   card 1,1

Fig. 6. Free objects

Case 3: relationship between version classes. If the relationship link is monovalued for the version class A, a new version "a" created in A (it is a root of a new hierarchy) is linked to a unique version "b" of a hierarchy of the version class B.

If the relationship link is multivalued for the class A, a new version "a" created in A must be linked to one or more versions, each belonging to distinct hierarchies of the class B.

When the relationship is monovalued for the class B, the versions "b" linked to the version "a" are either leaves belonging to existing hierarchies of B not yet linked to a version of A (if they exists), or versions derived from leaf versions of free hierarchies, or roots of new hierarchies of B. Multivaluation for the class B does not restrict the set of leaf versions "b" which can be linked to the version "a".

Deletion. An instance (object or version) deletion is permitted when it is linked to objects or to working versions. On the other hand, if the instance is linked to frozen versions, deleting it causes the deletion of linked frozen versions. The relationship links are obviously deleted.

Derivation. Derivation is an operation which can only be performed on instances of version classes. Only case 2 and case 3 are studied.

Case 2 : relationship between an object class and a version class. If the relationship link is monovalued for the version class B, a new version "b" derived from a version belonging to a hierarchy of B is linked to a unique object "a" of the object class A. When the link is multivalued, the new derived version must be linked to one or more objects of the class B.

The objects "a" which must be linked to the version "b" are either objects linked to the version from which "b" is derived, or free objects (cf § 5.2.2).

Case 3 : relationship between version classes. When the relationship link is monovalued for the version class A, a new version derived from a version belonging to a hierarchy of A is linked to a unique version "b" of a hierarchy of B. Multivaluation for A allows to link the version "a" to one or more versions "b", each belonging to distinct hierarchies of B.

The versions "b" which can be linked to the version "a" are:
- versions linked to the version from which "a" is derived,
- derived versions from versions linked to the version from which "a" is derived,
- leaf versions belonging to hierarchies of B (if the link is multivalued for B) or derived versions from leaf versions of free hierarchies of B (if the link is multivalued for B),
- roots of new hierarchies.

When the relationship link is monovalued for B, the versions "b" which are linked to the version "a" must not be linked to versions belonging to other hierarchies of A. A multivalued relationship for B does not restrict the set of version "b" which can be linked to the version "a".

7 Conclusion

This paper has presented a conceptual model intended for object-oriented database modeling. This model allows to describe, in a unified framework, objects, object versions and class versions. Three kinds of classes are used for such a modeling: object classes, version classes and versionable classes. Object class instances are objects of which one keeps only the last state. The instances of version classes are object versions where only the value evolve whereas the instances of versionable classes are object versions whose value and schema evolve (the different significant states are kept).

This paper investigates, in greater details, the outcomes of modeling links between these different kinds of classes on objects and object versions. The considered links are inheritance, composition and relationship links. Their cardinalities are also taken into account. Moreover, operations on objects and classes are also discussed in this study. Such a study has never been done for conceptual models. But it is partially approached for logical models (database models):

- Inheritance and relationship are not investigated.
- Composition is tackled in most of system managing object classes. Composition between object classes (case 1) and composition between version classes (case3) are studied but composition between object class and version class (case2) is never met.

  On the one hand, we can observe that the solution we propose in case 1 is the same than the one proposed in Orion [13], and, on the other hand, we can observe that the solution we propose in case 3 avoids to duplicate versions describing the same states of an object evolution (Presage), and avoids dynamic computing of derived versions (Orion [8]): these are directly linked with their component objects.

Such a study allows to model object, version and versionnable classes from the conceptual level. This study can be re-used to extend the data models of the current object-oriented database design methods (OMT [17], OOA [6], OOM [16], O* [5], ...) so that they integrate version modeling capabilities.

References

1. M. Atkinson, F. Bancilhon, D. DeWitt, K. Dittrich, D. Maier, S. Zdonik. *The object-oriented database system manifesto*. 1st Int. Conf. on Deductive and Object-Oriented Databases, Kyoto (Japan), Dec. 1989.
2. D. S. Batori, W. Kim. *Modeling concepts for VLSI CAD objects*. ACM Transaction On Database Systems, Vol 10, n°3, 1985.
3. D. Beech, B. Mahbod. *Generalized version control in an object-oriented database*. 4th Int. Conf. on Data Engineering, Los Angeles (USA), 1988.
4. A. Bjornerstedt, C. Hulten. *Version control in an object-oriented architecture*. Object-oriented concepts, databases and applications, Edited by W. Kim, F. Lochovsky, Addisson-Wesley publishing company, 1989.

5. J. Brunet. *Modeling the world with semantic objects*. IFIP TC8 Int. Conf. on the Object-Oriented Approach in Information Systems, Québec, Oct. 1991.

6. P. Coad, Y. Yourdon. Object-oriented analysis. Yourdon Press publishing company, 1990.

7. H.T. Chou, W. Kim. *A unifying framework for version control in a CAD environment*. 12th Int. Conf. on Very Large Database, Kyoto (Japan), Aug. 1986.

8. H.T. Chou, W. Kim. *Versions and change notification in object-oriented database system*. 25th Int. Conf. on Design Automation, Anaheim, June 1988.

9. M.C. Fauvet. Définition et réalisation d'un modèle de versions d'objets. 5èmes Journées Bases de Données Avancées, Genève (Suisse), Sept. 1989.

10. W. Käfer, H. Schöning. *Mapping a version model to a complex object data model*. 8th Int. Conf. on Data Engineering, Tempe (USA), Feb. 1992.

11. R. Katz. *Toward a unified framework for version modeling in engineering databases*. ACM Computing Surveys, Vol 22, n°4, 1990.

12. W. Kim, H.T. Chou. *Versions of schema for object-oriented databases*. 14th Int. Conf. on Very Large Databases, Los Angeles (USA), Aug. 1988.

13. W. Kim. *Composite object revisited*. 14th ACM Int. Conf. on Managment of Data, Portland (USA), June 1989.

14. G.T. Nguyen, D. Rieu. *Schema evolution in object-oriented database systems*. Data and Knowledge Engineering, n°4, North-Holland publishing company, 1989.

15. S. Monk, I. Sommerville. *Schema evolution in object-oriented databases using class versionning*. ACM SIGMOD record, Vol 22, n°3, September 1993.

16. M. Rochfeld. *Les méthodes de conception orientées objet*. Conférence invitée, Congrès INFORSID, Clermont-Ferrand (France), May 1992.

17. M. Rumbaugh, M. Blaha, W. Premerlani, F. Eddy, W. Lorensen. *Object-oriented modeling and design*. Prentice-Hall publishing company, Englewood Cliffs, 1991.

18. G. Talens, C. Oussalah, M.F. Colinas. *Versions of simple and composite objects*. 19th Int. Conf. on Very Large Databases, Dublin (Ireland), Sept. 1993.

19. S. Zdonik. *Version management in an object-oriented database*. Lecture Notes in Computer Science n°244, June 1986.

20. R. Zicari. *A framework for schema updates in an object-oriented database system*. 7th Int. Conf. on Data Engineering, Kobe (Japan), April 1991.

Hypertext Version Management in an Actor-based Framework

Antonina Dattolo, Vincenzo Loia

Dipartimento di Informatica ed Applicazioni, Università di Salerno,
84081 Baronissi (SA), ITALY
{antos,loia}@udsab.dia.unisa.it

Abstract. In this work we discuss a number of issues for the design of
hypertext systems in an actor-based model of computation. We examine
how the "traditional" basic concepts which are at the basis of the design
of hypertexts can be re-visited under a new perspective of collaborative expert actors. The paper presents how some principles of high level
concurrent programming are applied as new methodologies for the design and realization of complex software, such as hypertext systems. By
adopting an actor-based framework, we gained powerful control on the
version management, which presents considerable difficulties in realization of hypertext systems. In this paper we present an initial prototype
implemented in a concurrent object-oriented language, realized on top
of Common Lisp Object System.

1 Introduction

In the last few decades we have witnessed a growing interest of the academic
and industrial communities towards hypertext and hypermedia systems [24]. The
wide range of applications of these "new" technologies has imposed their importance as indispensable features for computer-based systems. The work presented
in this paper is the result of experiences gathered in the last six years working
up to the design and implementation of complex programming environments.
In particular, we developed a software platform, named OPLA, suitable to conceive and implement large object-oriented logic programming. The architecture
consisted of a fast interpreter and compiler [19], enriched by a programming environment [20] designed to support the various activities which normally accom-
pany the code production (debug utilities, browsing, documentation facilities,
etc.). Owing to the increasing of number OPLA user groups, and to the strong
object-orientedness of the language, the need to strengthen the hypertext aspect
in documentation management became a key issue for the survival of the OPLA
platform itself. Before starting the implementation of this important requirement, we established the most important principles to follow in order to reduce
the possible costs and risks of the project. Some of these guide-lines were:

- design a general-purpose hypertext framework, in order to re-use it for other
  software applications (not strictly for programming environments),

- do not modify the underlying application, and, consequently, the basic implementation choices adopted to realize the interpreter, the compiler, and the other main components of OPLA,
- obtain something that could be specialized for program documentation, in particular for object-oriented logic programming.

To follow the previous trends we focused our attention in exploring a general design environment where we could test our ideas: we chose the concurrent object-oriented approach [25]. In fact, actor-based programming is starting to mature thanks to the boost derived from parallel computer technology and concurrent languages. Concurrent programming frees the programmer from specific hardware requirements. It enables to model multi-agent systems and to test how a distributed approach can solve problems in which the choice of a monolithic approach in handling computational efforts resulted in inadequate strategies. Programming software in actor-based frameworks has stimulated research in revisiting the foundations of Artificial Intelligence, by providing new schemes and methodologies to handle large-scale open systems [15]. Open Systems consist of a population of agents each of which are equipped with approximate knowledge and influence. These agents can share their knowledge and organize their activities to reach a common goal [7]. The concurrent, or distributed approach, is not new in the hypertext field, but its use has been limited in solving problems which generally occur in multi-user hypertext systems, where we have a concurrent, collaborative access to databases shared across a net of workstations and file systems [22, 27, 28]. Our approach is different: we have adopted the actor model as a general framework to design the basic components of a hypertext system, by sketching both the internal and the external activities by means of an extended communication of task requests sent through a web of intelligent actors. In order to stress the benefits that this approach provides, in this paper we do not discuss the advantages that our approach gives to support multiple users based activities for hypermedia systems, but we focus our attention on the advantages that an actor-based design and implementation can provide to a fast high-level, prototyping of open hypertext systems [8]. The paper is described as follows. In Section 2, after a brief introduction to the actor model, we present the main features of our framework, underlining the benefits that this approach provides with respect to more conventional tactics. Section 3 discusses the implementation details reported, by developing our system by means of an OOCP available on top of Common Lisp Object System, the ANSI specification of the object-oriented extension of Common Lisp [3]. As a key design issue, we discuss the approach studied to solve the version management problem. We conclude the paper showing further research directions of our project.

2   An Actor Model for Hypertext System

Generally a concurrent system has a kind of module (actor, object, guardian) which is invoked by (and only by) messaging. This module hides data from all other modules, i.e. there is no sharing data between modules. By messaging we activate light-weight processes within an addressed module. Sometimes these modules are known as "active objects" and programming with active object is nowadays named Object Oriented Concurrent Programming (OOCP at short). OOCP is represented by a large number of concurrent languages. The main entity at the basis of these languages remains the "actor". In this paper we assume a basic knowledge of the actor-based programming, directing the reader for a detailed description of the actor model to [2]. Before entering in to the method of implementation we would prefer to illustrate the actor-based model of our architecture. Essentially, a hypertext is a collection of heterogeneous objects (cognitive fragments viewed as texts, images, sounds,...) connected together by conceptual links. The user navigates this graph of concepts by browsing the nodes, and applying different actions. Owing to the richness of the resulting environment, hypertexts are characterized by numerous stimulant features, such as:

- strong fragmentation of information,
- high interactivity of information,
- instinctive recall to modifiability,
- natural approaches to retrieve information,
- openness towards other systems.

These important concepts generate several trade-offs for the implementation of hypertext systems. The most suffered constraint is known as "tyranny of the link" [12], which expresses the rigidity of the architecture which is not able to support in an appropriate way the cognitive activities offered by the hypertext. Recently, the need to improve the freedom of communication/handling of hypertext information, has stimulated the research community into providing new strategies suitable for dynamic evolution of the system [8, 9]. We argue that many difficulties remain unsolved in the realization phase because the underlying tools used as platforms for the design and implementation of hypertext do not reflect the concurrent, collaborative activities which exist at the basis of the system. In our proposal, the hypertext is conceived as an Open Information System [15], implemented by actors. The expertise, the knowledge, the actions of the system are spread among different classes of actors which work simultaneously and independently. This society of experts is animated by exchanges of messages, by means of which the actors can communicate. The communication is asynchronous because each actor keeps a mail-box to receive enquiries and it continues to function even when receiving messages.

3 Implementation

Our model of actor programming has been realized using an object-oriented concurrent language based on top of Common Lisp Object System, CLOS [3]. The concurrent extension of CLOS was named CLAS (standing for Common Lisp Actor System), and was initially tested and improved during the realization of a significant application [10]. Once the functionality of CLAS was proven, we decided to specialize the tried method as a tool for the design of hypertexts. The resulting system, named HYPERCLAS, is illustrated in the next paragraph.

3.1 A Tutorial Introduction to HYPERCLAS

HYPERCLAS allows the creation of populations of actors specialized in accomplishing tasks which generally occur in hypertext systems. Essentially, the complete architecture employed to design the hypertext system can be depicted with the following figure:

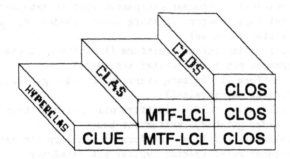

Fig. 1. The module composition of our platform.

As the reader can note, HYPERCLAS has been built thanks to three main modules: CLOS, Multi-Tasking Facility of Lucid Common Lisp (MTF-LCL), and CLUE [17]. This last module is exploited to manage the graphical window-based X11 interface. From the standpoint of actor handling, HYPERCLAS is composed of two levels:

- The first level consists of a module designed to solve all the problems which arise in concurrent programming, such as the management of concurrent access to resources, the scheduling of tasks, the binding of local or global data to a process, the locking or unlocking of a process, the creation of processes and their destruction. To accomplish these goals we defined a superclass, named `atomic-object`, specialized in handling mutual exclusion of processes. Thanks to this class the legal access to fields of actors is guaranteed.
- The second level realizes the actor model. The main difference between objects and actors consists in the fact that objects are seen as passive entities which communicate with other objects via active messages while actors are seen as active objects which exchange passive messages. Each actor is composed of a passive and active part, each of which is an object of CLOS.

The active part of an actor is an instance of a class task which encapsulates the interface with the host multitask system. This class contains a slot called *jeckill* whose function is to address the passive part of the actor, i.e. the class **actor**. Vice versa, in the class **actor** we refer to the active part by means of a slot hide. Let us provide the definition of the most general object of HYPERCLAS, the actor HypActor. The next code shows the definition of a "HypActor" actor. The meaning of this entity is similar to other well-known definitions, such as notecards, frames, nodes, etc..

```
(defclass HypActor(atomic-object)
  (hide      :initform () :reader get-hide :writer set-hide)
  (mbox      :initform () :reader get-mbox :writer set-mbox)
  (parcel    :initform () :reader get-parcel :writer set-parcel)
  (name      :initform "hactor" :initarg :name :reader get-name
             :writer set-name)
  (title     :allocation :class :initform () :initarg :title
             :reader get-title :writer set-title)
  (versionL  :initform () :initarg :versionL :reader get-versionL
             :writer set-versionL)
  (body      :allocation :class :initform nil :initarg :body
             :reader get-body :writer set-body)
  (fromActor :allocation :class :initform () :initarg :fromActor
             :reader get-fromActor :writer set-fromActor)
  (toActor   :allocation :class :initform () :initarg :toActor
             :reader get-toActor :writer set-toActor) ) )
```

Fig. 2. The data part description of the HypActor object.

This single object serves to collect some fundamental data. Following the code of Figure 2, we specify the role of these attributes:

- **hide** serves for addressing the active part of the actor.
- **mbox** is used to support communication with other actors.
- **parcel** maintains the current message.
- **name** identifies the actor.
- **title** stores the frame topic.
- **versionL** is used for versioning management.
- **body** contains the text related to the topic.
- **fromActor** enables to learn the address of the HypActors reachable from the current actor.
- **toActor** enable to learn the address of the HypActors from which it is possible to reach the current actor.

As the reader can note, the definition of the actor embodies (as in CLOS) only the data part. For each of these slots we have methods specialized in handling the corresponding slot. For example the methods :**initform**, :**reader**, and :**writer** are automatically generated by HYPERCLAS to accomplish operations of initialization, reading and writing, respectively. Naturally, we have other methods used by the HypActor outside its data part definition. In fact, the remaining behavioral part is detached from the actor data description, i.e. the implementation of the *scripts*, is done outside the class definition. This programming style, which derives from the initial CLOS proposal, leads to a more flexible model. In fact, the connection between data (actor/class definition) and operations (script/methods definition) is established by dynamic bindings and exploiting hierarchical structure. In this way the user can specify the structure of the actors via the **defclass** command, whereas the management of the contents is realized via the scripts definition, giving flexibility and efficiency in the separation structure/content. Before focusing our attention on the behavioral description of the actor, we will provide more information about the message passing strategies possible in HYPERCLAS.

3.2 Message Passing Protocol in HYPERCLAS

In HYPERCLAS message passing protocol is enriched with four schemes which fulfill the various needs to send a task to actors. These schemes are:

- **future**
  This option allows the handling of messages of a particular kind, the **future** message. The **future** is an answer to a message in form of a promise; the semantic of the **future** is equal to that of ACT-1 [18].
- **spray**
  We select this message passing when we want to apply multicasting messages.
- **express**
  An **express** is a message with the highest priority. If an actor receives this message while it is treating a normal one, then it stops the current task in order to handle the **express** request.
- **all**
  HYPERCLAS allows the creation of clones. A clone is a perfect duplication of the original actor. The difference between the two actors consists in the fact that a clone is always a passive entity, i.e. even though the clone survives in the system it is locked into for any message. If we want to escape from this rule, we can use the keyword **all**. In this case, the message is sent in multicast to all the active and passive actors.

Message passing is supported by means of the construct **send**. A general form of send appears as:
(send destinator kind-of-message task arguments)
where:

- **destinator** identifies the actor(s) to which the message is addressed;
- **kind-of-message** specifies the strategy by which the message must be sent on the web (**future, spray, express, all**);

- **task** determines (via the keyword :**selector**) the script which we want to trigger once the message is received by the destinator;
- **arguments** serves to specify (via the keyword :**args**) the arguments (if existing) to provide the script.

4 An Actor-oriented Versioning Management

The hypertext is an unstable resource. Users can create, destroy, modify nodes and links, changing small or large sections of the hypertext. In spite of these changes, some important laws must be observed:

- coherence of the information.
  For instance, when we cancel a node, we must reorganize the area of the hypertext in which this operation occurs. This task consists in eliminating the corresponding links, updating the contents, moving markers, testing the validity of such changes, etc..
- access to old versions of the hypertext.
  The return to previous cognitive instants must always be available, in order to reuse the information and to maintain the derivation history [14]. In particular, in systems which exploit concurrence, the version management is absolutely necessary to keep the consistence of data [22].

We use the term *version control* [16] to indicate the different control strategies suitable for handling the node-based version and the structure-based version. For a need of clarity, we use the term *configuration* with the same meaning as that adopted in software engineering [16], i.e. to indicate a specific state of the hypertext (generally, program) structure as a whole. The goal of this paragraph is to show as the versioning, one of the key issue among the functionality of a hypertext, is carried out by specialized scripts of actors. By providing chunks of HYPERCLAS code, we prove how the actor-based model is a powerful technique to handle this difficult trade-off. In detail, we illustrate our approach to manage the configuration problem. Such versioning faces the problems of updating all the hypertext in its current form [5]. We focus our attention on version control, omitting details about databases memory management. To better introduce the reader to our solution, we expose our main idea, sketching the behavior of the system with a simple example. We have organized this discussion in three subsections: the version creation, the version selection, and concluding remarks.

4.1 Version Creation

In Figure 3a, we can observe a general situation which occurs when the user decides to create a new state of the hypertext with a new version mark. The original nodes are identified by Ni, whereas the notation Nivj identifies a node Ni existing in a successive version *vj*.

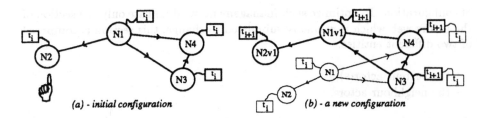

Fig. 3. The configuration of the hypertext fragment before the modification on the node N2 (a) and after (b).

Figure 3a depicts the state of the hypertext associated with a version labelled with t_i. Each node of the hypertext, i.e. each HypActor, contains, as local information, the list of all the versions to which it belongs (for simplicity we suppose that the only existing version is t_i). The cognitive activity of the user is located on the node N2. The user modifies the node and stores the new content. This command provokes a session-based versioning operation, with a new storing of the hypertext indicated by t_{i+1}. This situation triggers the script **replace-HypActor**. The action performed by this script is shown in the code of Figure 4.

```
(defmethod replace-HypActor((self HypActor) version newversion)
    (send (get-fromActor self) :spray
            :selector duplicate-actor                      1
            :selector set-version :args ())                1.1
    (send (get-toActor self) :spray
            :selector duplicate-actor                      2
            :selector set-version :args ())                2.2
    (duplicate-actor)                                      3
    (set-version ())                                       3.1
    (send (get-Controller self)                            4
            :future :selector new-context :args self)
    (send (get-fromActor self) :spray                      5
            :selector conc-version :args newversion)
    (send (get-toActor self) :spray                        6
            :selector conc-version :args newversion) )
```

Fig. 4. The behavior of HypActor defined by the script **replace-HypActor**.

The basic operation is to store the previous state of system, in order to recover it during a derivation history. The duplication is necessary to maintain old layers of configuration. To optimize such management, we duplicate only the section of the actors web which is probably submitted to change; this section is composed of two different entities:

- the current actor(s);
- the neighbour actors.

Regarding the neighbour actors, the possible alteration concerns the links, i. e., the incoming/outcoming links associated with the current actors. In our example (see Figure 3), this corresponds in duplicating the current node (N2), together with all its incoming/outcoming nodes (N1). This duplication consists in generating clones of the neighbouring HypActors, and of itself, as shown in lines 1-2-3. In our system, cloning is equivalent to freezing the actors. Cloned actors become passive entities. Though they exist, they are entities unknown to the rest of the system. In fact, when a HypActor H receives a message containing the request to trigger the script duplicate-actor, it creates the clone H', freezes the clone, and H remains the current, new active version of the HypActor.

Only a special message can resume the clones, as we will soon see. After all the HypActors have generated the corresponding clones, they reset the field version (see lines 1.1, 2.1, 3.1). In fact, these actors reflect a new configuration of the system, and thus they do not belong to the previous contexts. For example, in Figure 3b, the reader can observe that the node labelled with N2v1 identifies the node N2 in the version v1. Following the code of Figure 4, the current HypActor, addressed by the parameter self, (N2v1, in our example), informs a designed actor, named *Controller*, of the occurring of a new context (see line 4 of Figure 4). The importance of the Controller will be explained forthwith. For now, it is enough to know that this actor allows the identification of all the nodes belonging to a version. A new version is thus established. Now, it is necessary that all the active HypActors be admitted to this new configuration. This task is accomplished due to the messages sent on the net, corresponding to the lines 5-6. In Figure 3b, we sketch the configuration after the cloning of the nodes N1 and N2. The reader can observe that the new state is stressed by the fact that the nodes N3 and N4 now belong to both the configurations marked with t_i and t_{i+1}, whereas all the remaining nodes exist only in the latter version t_{i+1}. In order to distinguish the active from the passive entities, we use, in our graphical representation, the bold objects to depict the active actors. We underline the fact that an actor can be active only in one version. Thus, in the configuration t_{i+1} of Figure 3b, the incoming links for N4 come only from the nodes N1v1 and N3 (since the node N1 is invisible in such configuration). The mechanism discussed here is the reason adopted for the system creation versioning. The difference with a user-based creation versioning consists in the fact that in this last case is the user that decides when the storing of the hypertext occurs. For instance, let us suppose that the user alter the state of the nodes N3 and N4, and that, only after having modified N4, the user requires the creation of a new version. In this situation, following our mechanism, we obtain a new configuration, as shown in the Figure 5.

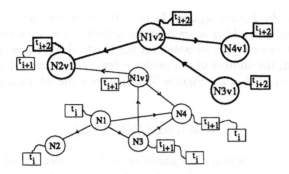

Fig. 5. The configuration identified by the mark t_{i+2}.

We stress the fact that only the active objects are cloned. The implementation of versioning exploits the parallel computation to the full. More in detail:

line 1 and 2.
The message is sent with the option "spray". In this way, both the incoming and outcoming actors, will create the cloned actors in a concurrent and asynchronous way. Thus, the fragment of the hypertext which must be stored is built in parallel. Thanks to the semantics of the script `duplicate-actor` we handle in a high level way, different configurations of the hypertext. The partition between active and passive societies of HypActors allows an efficient management of old contexts.

line 5 and 6.
In order to make the new configuration of the hypertext official each interested node is informed concurrently. The script `conc-version` broadcasts this message on the net until all the nodes acknowledge the reception of the message. In this way, although we do not copy the whole network, we extend the version mark over the whole network.

4.2 Version Selection

This activity enables the detection of a particular version of the hypertext. In our model the hypertext is represented by a population of active and passive HypActors. The active ones provide the last configuration. The remaining belong to suspended, past configurations, still living in our actor-based universe. In this section we explain how we can gather all the actors belonging to a designed configuration. Let us suppose that the user requires access to a configuration by providing a version identifier. The actor-based entity, named Controller, previously introduced, plays an important role in handling the version selection problem. Roughly speaking, this actor owns a panoramic view of the derivation history. In fact, everytime that a new version is established, the responsible actor informs the Controller about the new version. This message (see line 4 of Figure

4) is sent with the **future** option. In fact, the HypActor simply notifies this information, without asking more complex activity. If we observe the form of this message more carefully, we note that the Controller receives, in addition to the new version, the address of the sender actor. For instance, if we re-consider the situations depicted in the Figures 3b and 5, then the information sent to the Controller are:

$$(\ ... \ (\text{N2v1}, t_{i+1}) \ (\text{N3v1}, t_{i+2})$$

Thanks to this information, the Controller is able to identify all the other actors which share the same configuration. Let us provide an important script associated with the Controller.

```
(defmethod search-config((self Controller) (version mark))
  (send atomic-object :express :selector set-passive)
  (send (get-resp-actor self) [:spray :all] :selector wake-up :args mark))
```

Fig. 6. The script designed to select a configuration.

We can image the state of the system as a collection of active and passive HypActors. The first action consists in switching all the HypActors to passive entities[1]. This task is realized by the super-class **atomic-object**, which embodies all the basic elements of our actor-based universe. Among all these passive entities we have some *representative* HypActors, responsible of an occurrence of a new version. To this particular class, the Controller sends a message in multicast, containing a request to trigger the HypActor script **wake-up**. First of all, this script checks if the HypActor belongs to the specified version (given by the parameter **mark**). Only in this case, the HypActor becomes active, recognizing itself as element of the designed configuration. All the HypActors which have received this message, but which do not belong to the chosen configuration, remain automatically in a passive status. Vice-versa, any time that a HypActor matches with the configuration, it propagates this message to its neighbours. In this way we are able to identify all the actors belonging to the configuration.

To explain this mechanism in more detail, let us re-consider Figure 5. The reader is required to go back to the configuration identified by the mark t_{i+1}. In this case, the HypActors stimulated from the Controller are N2v1 and N3v1. Only N2v1 acknowledges its membership to the chosen configuration. The complete path of awakening of the HypActors is shown in the next figure (Figure 7).

We can note that our approach is not restricted to a time-based management. In fact, a very similar implementation of the **search-config** script is adopted

---

[1] The switch to active/passive status is carried out by special purpose routines of the host language. The general message passing protocol is employed in a transparent way in order to distinguish automatically active from passive entities (and viceversa).

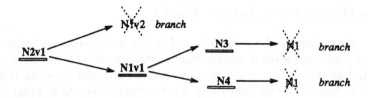

Fig. 7. Branching tree for selection of configuration marked t_{i+1}.

to handle situations in which the user requires access to versions of hypertext objects on the basis of their attribute values. Essentially, our model implicitly supports "composite object" management.

The separation structure/content, obtained by detaching scripts from the actor definition, allows the user to own, simultaneously, different logic views of the hypertext. For example, by defining an appropriate script which exploits the :spray option, we can address that portion belonging to a given configuration.

4.3 Concluding Remarks

Actor model represents a new strategy to conceive hypertexts. The novelty of our approach consists in a strong decentralization and distribution of control mechanisms operated on the nodes of hypertext. As result of this approach, the node is not more a passive container of knowledge [9], but it takes the role of active entity owning autonomous means to establish communication with corresponding neighbours. The usual separation between node and net versioning is broken: in our model we treat both aspects of versioning, gaining in simplicity and uniformity, avoiding the necessity to define separate resolution strategies [13]. Furthermore, our proposal offers a unique solution for node versioning, which, traditionally, is supported by distinguishing node, links and composites [14]. Our version group (that is, the set of all entities which are considered versions of the same entity [26]) is implicit, because any cloned HypActor knows its original node. An other interesting consequence of the clonation is that the system maintains the consistence of knowledge [12, 22], and allows, differently from Neptune [6] for instance, to track the derivation history, even though a new version is created with the outset in an old version. Our configuration definition, in some aspects similar to the concepts of context described in PIE [11] or in [26], is characterized by a different composition law of the layers. In fact, in our approach, the configuration (context) is not the sum [26] or the combination [11] of layers: the partition of the hypertext is carried out by appropriate awakening of populations of actors existing in the net. Moreover, in our approach we do not suffer of particular strategies to handle the links [13] , because they are seen as pure relations (acquaintances) between actors. As in [14], we recognize the importance to access versions of hypertext on the basis of their attribute values, and we support user-decided versioning and session based versioning, by differentiating their handling as stressed in [22].

5 Conclusions and Future Works

Owing to the richness of the design space of hypertext systems, the designers are faced with problems for the management of a large amount of heterogeneous data and control activities. This paper proposes a new methodology which is able to support the impact of this difficulty. Object-oriented concurrent programming offers high level tools to sketch software, characterized by strong dissemination of data and duties, as happens in hypertext systems. Moreover, OOCP enables to reach a fine grained control on multi-tasking facility, which nowadays represents a strategic property, due to the presence of multi-processor architectures. The work presented in this paper has been focused on the discussion of the version management. The approach illustrated presents several advantages:

- it exploits concurrent, asynchronous computation;
- it is described in a high level fashion by means of specialization of the HypActors behavior;
- it is general and thus it can be adopted in hypertexts as well as in engineering databases;
- it supports efficiently dynamical linking.

These benefits are due thanks to the underlying architecture, which is based on the actor-based programming paradigm. Our prototype has been tested with other versioning mechanisms [5], confirming the interest of our approach, but much research remains to do:

- improving HYPERCLAS with additional features in such a way to define a complete language framework suitable for distributed hypertext design;
- formulating a flexible model to handle multi-user collaborative activities. Actor-based paradigm constitutes a natural and attractive technique to solve difficult task rising from collaborative-based domains.

Acknowledgements
Authors wish to thank Anja Haake for helpfull suggestions provided on the topic of this paper and anonymous referees for their interesting remarks.

References

1. ABCL: ABCL: an Object Oriented Concurrent System. Edited by A. Yonezawa, MIT Press (1990)
2. G. Agha: Actors: A Model of Concurrent Computation in Distributed Systems. MIT Press, Cambridge, MA (1986)
3. D. G. Bobrow, L. DeMichiel, R. P. Gabriel, G. Kiczales, D. Moon, S. Keene: CLOS Specification; X3J13 Document 88-002R. ACM-SIGPLAN Not. **23** (1988)
4. DAI: Readings in Distributed Artificial Intelligence. Edited by A. Bond and L. Gasser, Morgan Kaufman (1988)
5. A. Dattolo, A. Gisolfi: Analytical Version Control Management in a Hypertext System. Proc. of Third CIKM, NIST, Gaithersburg, MD, ACM Press, November 29 - December 2 (1994) 132-139

6. N. M. Delisle, M. D. Schwartz: Contexts - A Partitioning Concept for Hypertext. ACM Transactions on Office Information Systems, **5**(2) (1987) 168-186

7. L. Evans, L. Anderson, G. Crysdale: Achieving Flexible Autonomy in Multiagent Systems. Applied Artificial Intelligence, **6**(11) (1992) 103-126

8. A. M. Fountain, W. Hall, E. Heath, H. C. Davis: MICROCOSM. Proc. of ECHT'90, INRIA, France, November (1990) 298-311

9. F. Garzotto, P. Paolini, B. Schawbe: HDM - A Model Based Approach to Hypertext Application Design. ACM Trans. on Inf. Systems, **11**(1) (1993) 1-26

10. A. Gisolfi, V. Loia: Designing Complex Systems within Distributed Architectures. Int. J. of Applied Art. Intelligence, **8**(3) (1994) 393-411

11. I. Goldstein, D. Bobrow: A Layered Approach to Software Design. Interactive Programming Environments, D. Barstow, H. Shrobe, E. Sandewall. Eds. McGraw-Hill (1984) 387-413

12. F. G. Halasz: Reflections on NoteCards: Seven issues for the next generation of hypermedia systems. CACM, **31**(7) (1988) 836-852

13. A. Haake: CoVer: A Contextual Version Server for Hypertext Applications. Proc. of ECHT'92, Milano, Italy, December (1992) 43-52

14. A. Haake, J. M. Haake: Take CoVer: Exploiting Version Support in Cooperative Systems. Proc. of INTERCHI'93, Amsterdam, April (1993) 406-416

15. C. Hewitt: Open Information Systems Semantic for Distributed Artificial Intelligence. Artificial Intelligence, **47** (1991) 79-106

16. R. H. Katz: Toward a Unified Framework for Version Modeling in Engineering Databases. ACM Computing Surveys, **22**(4) (1990) 375-408

17. K. Kimbrough, O. Lamott: Common Lisp User Interface Environment. Texas Instruments Inc., July (1990)

18. H. Lieberman: Concurrent Object-Oriented Programming in Act 1. OOCP'87 (1987) 9-36

19. V. Loia and M. Quaggetto: High level management of computation history for the design and implementation of a Prolog system. Software-Practice and Experiences, **23**(2) (1992) 119-150

20. V. Loia and M. Quaggetto: Integrating Object-Oriented Paradigms and Logic Program: The OPLA Language. Proc. of the Ninth KBSE, September 20-23, Monterey, CA, IEEE Press (1994) 158-164

21. Lucid: The Multitasking Facility: Lucid Common Lisp Advanced User's Guide. Lucid Inc. (1988)

22. C. Maioli, S. Sola, F. Vitali: Versioning issues in a Collaborative Distributed Hypertext Systems. Technical Report UBLCS-93-6, Bologna, April (1993)

23. V. Mashayekhi, J. M. Drake, W. Tsai, J. Rield: Distributed, collaborative software inspection. IEEE Software, September (1993) 66-75

24. J. Nielsen: Hypertext and Hypermedia. Academic Press (1990)

25. OOCP: Object Oriented Concurrent Programming, edited by A. Yonezawa and M. Tokoro, MIT Press (1987)

26. K. Osterbye: Structural and Cognitive Problems in Providing Version Control for Hypertext. Proc. of ECHT'92, Milano, Italy, December (1992) 33-42

27. D. E. Shackelford, J. B. Smith, F. D. Smith: The architecture and Implementation of a Distributed Hypermedia Storage System. ACM Hypertext '93 Proceedings, Seattle, Washington USA, November 14-18 (1993) 14-24

28. V. Tschammer, T. Magedanz, M. Tschichholz, A. Wolisz: Cooperative management in open distributed systems. Computer Communications, **17** (1994) 717-728

Modelling Ways-of-Working

Véronique Plihon, Colette Rolland

University of Paris I Panthéon-Sorbonne
C.R.I., 17 rue de Tolbiac
75013 Paris FRANCE
email : {vplihon , rolland}@masi.ibp.fr

Abstract. We propose in this paper, an approach for defining in a systematic manner, ways-of-working providing guidelines for the development of information systems. It is a modelling approach in which a given way-of-working is constructed by instantiation of a way-of-working model allowing to deal with a large variety of situations in a flexible, decision-oriented manner. The paper presents the way-of-working model and exemplifies the construction of a specific way-of-working based on the OMT methodology.

1   Introduction

Despite thirty years of constant improvements of Information Systems (IS) methodologies, the IS community is not satisfied with existing ways-of-working. They are too large-grained descriptions of the system life-cycle, unclearly defined, do not guide application engineers efficiently and consequently are not used as intended. They lack flexibility and cannot be easily adapted to the requirements of a specific project. One approach to solve the problem is to deal with methods as we deal with information systems, i.e. to engineer a method as a product subject to design, customisation, adaptation and evolution. This is the aim of *Method engineering*. Method engineering is defined in [8] as the engineering discipline to design, construct and adapt Information Systems Development Methods and CASE tools to specific projects.

Within the area of Method Engineering (ME) the formal description of a method takes an important place. Many definitions of a method have been proposed [2], [12], [17], [10] and most of them converge to the idea that a method is based on models (systems of concepts) and consists of a number of steps which must/should be executed in a given order. For example [15] proposes a framework for information systems development *methods* which comprises the *way of thinking* (the philosophy), the *way of modelling* (the models to be constructed), the *way of organising* (subdivided in the *way of working*, i.e. how to perform the development and the *way of control* i.e. how to manage the development) and the *way of supporting* (the description techniques and the corresponding tools).

In this paper we are concerned with the formal description of ways-of-working in the sense of the above framework. Our proposal consists of a *way-of-working model*, i.e. a set of generic concepts allowing to construct various ways-of-working for various methods in a structured and detailed manner. The way-of-working model plays the role of a theory and functions like a shell, a model from which specific ways-of-working can be generated by instantiation and then executed to guide the development of various projects.

Ways-of-working we want to generate are *guidance centred process models*. There is a need for such process models, in particular, in the early phase of Requirements Engineering (RE) and conceptual modelling. While performing highly intellectual and creative activities required to construct the system specification, application engineers need to be guided and advised, locally to handle the particular situations they are faced to, and globally, to monitor the flow of decisions they have to make. The required support is mainly based on heuristic knowledge. For this reason, our approach differs from the Software Engineering (SE) process modelling view which is focusing on process centred software environments (see a survey in [1]) for enforcing process performance that conforms to some preceptive software process definition [4].

The proposed way-of-working model corresponds to a certain way-of-thinking, a philosophy for process guidance which is decision and situation based. In other words, the underlying assumption of our way-of-working model is that the Information Systems Development (ISD) process is mainly a decision making process during which application engineers have to make decisions adapted to the situations they are faced to. Consequently the way-of-working intends to capture the types of situations the developer could encounter during ISD and to provide guidance, in each situation-type, on the decisions to make.

The way-of-working model focuses on the Requirements Engineering phase of systems development. It has been developed within the Process Theory of the NATURE[1] project and is being implemented as part of the CAPE (Computer Aided Process Engineering) environment to support process model definition, process guidance, trace and improvement.

For the sake of clarity, informal examples are used to illustrate the way-of-working structure; nevertheless a formal description of this process model, based on a decisions algebra can be found in [14].

The paper is organised as follows. The core of the paper deals with the presentation of the way-of-working model and its illustration to describe the OMT [13] method. This is made in section 2. Section 3 is a discussion of the approach. Conclusions are drawn in section 4.

2 The Way-of-Working Model

2.1 An Overview

The model we propose to support the construction of ways-of-working is centred around the concept of *context* which constitutes the basic building block of our approach. Contexts can be linked repeatedly in a hierarchical manner to define trees. A way-of-working is therefore a forest of trees as it is shown in the overview of the way-of-working model presented in the figure 1.

---

[1] This work is partly supported by the Basic Research Action NATURE (ESPRIT N°5363) which stands for Novel Approaches to Theories Underlying Requirements Engineering.

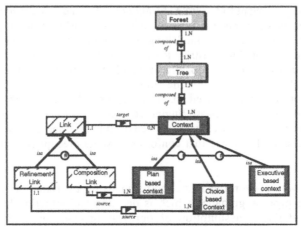

Figure 1 : Overview of the Way-of-Working Model

A *way-of-working* is represented as a collection of hierarchies of contexts that we refer to as a *forest*. A hierarchy of contexts, called a *tree*, represents a structured piece of knowledge for supporting decision making in the RE process; it is a process chunk which aims at supporting the application engineers in making the most appropriate decision according to the situation at hand. A tree is composed of *contexts* and *links*. Links allow to relate contexts in a recursive manner to construct hierarchies of contexts. As shown in figure 1, links are of two kinds : *refinement links* which allow to refine a large-grained context into a finer ones and *composition links* allowing to decompose a context into component contexts.

We detail in turn the notions of context, tree and forest and exemplify them with the OMT methodology.

2.2   The Notion of Context

A context is defined as a couple (situation, decision), where the *decision* represents a choice that an Application Engineer (AE) can make at a given point in time of the development process and where the *situation* is defined as the part of the product it make sense to make a decision on. A *decision* corresponds to an intention, a goal that the application engineer wants to fulfil while the situation is a part of the product under development the AE is working on. A context has also a type, namely executive, choice or plan. As we will see in the following, each type of context plays a specific role in a tree.

2.2.1 Executive-based Context
An executive-based context corresponds to a decision which is directly applicable through an action inducing a transformation of the product under development. For instance, in the OMT methodology, the creation of a candidate class is considered as an *action,* it materialises the implementation of the *executive-based context* <(Problem Statement Element), *Identify Candidate Class>*. Figure 2 is an instantiation of this *executive-based context* (<(A manager leads a department),

Identify Candidate Class>) showing the consequence of its execution on the product (the creation of the class Manager).

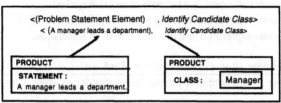

Figure 2 : An OMT Executive-based Context

Executive-based contexts are the atomic blocks of our ways-of-working. Non atomic blocks are built over contexts using refinement and composition links. Let us present first, choice-based contexts which are built with a refinement structure, explain their semantic and features.

2.2.2 Choice-based Context

When building a product, an application engineer may have several alternative ways to modify the product. Therefore, he/she has to select the most appropriate one among the set of possible choices. In order to model such a piece of knowledge, we introduce a second type of context, namely the *choice-based context.* The execution of such a context consists of choosing one of its alternatives, i.e. selecting a context representing a particular strategy for the resolution of the issue raised by the context.

For instance in the OMT methodology (figure 3), there are several ways to validate a class: by confirming, deleting or retyping the class into an attribute, an association or an operation.

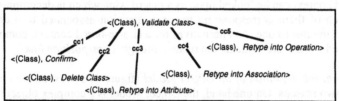

Figure 3: An OMT Choice-based Context

In our way-of-working model, arguments and choice criteria are defined to support or object to the various alternatives of a choice-based context. They are very helpful to support the application engineer while choosing the most appropriate strategy.
Table 1 gives a description of the arguments and choice criteria associated to the example of choice-based context introduced in figure 3.

---

arguments :
a1: The candidate class explicitly refers to a real world phenomenon relevant to the system.
a2: The candidate class expresses the same information than an existing object class and its name is less descriptive than the other.
a3: The candidate class is not in the scope of the problem.
a4: The candidate class is ill defined and not precise according to the scope of the problem.

a5: The candidate class expresses an implementation construct.

a6: The name of the candidate class describes an individual object, the class has no specific behaviour and represents an aspect or a property of an existing class.

a7: The candidate class represents something which is applied to the object.

a8: The candidate class expresses a role that is played in an association.

choice criteria :

$cc1 = a1$ $cc2 = a2 \vee a3 \vee a4 \vee a5$ $cc3 = a6$ $cc4 = a7$ $cc5 = a8$

Table 1: An example of Textual Description for a Choice -Criteria

As illustrated in the table above, *arguments* serve as a basis to define *choice criteria*. Each *choice criterion* is a condition for selecting one alternative, it is represented by a logical formula combining arguments. For instance, CC2 expresses that if a2 or a3 or a4 or a5 are true, then the context <(Class), *Delete Class*> should be chosen.

There are two major differences between the *choice-based context* and the *executive-based context* : the first one lies in the absence of any alternatives in the latter and the second is that a choice-based context has no direct consequence on the product under development.

Finally it is important to notice that the alternatives of a choice-based context are contexts too. In the case of figure 3 alternatives are executive-based contexts. But they could be choice-based contexts introducing what is referred to as a refinement link between contexts.

2.2.3 Plan-based Context

In order to represent situations requiring a set of decisions to be made to fulfil a certain intention (for instance to build the object model in the OMT methodology) the way-of-working model includes a third type of context called plan-based context. A plan-based context can be looked upon as a macro issue which is decomposed in sub-issues, each of them corresponding to a sub decision associated to a component decision of the macro one. As alternatives for a choice-based context, components of a plan-based context are contexts too related through a *composition link*.

For instance, *the definition of an Object Model* (figure 4) corresponds to a complex issue, for two reasons. On one hand, the Object Model is a complex object composed of a set of elements which are instances of concepts characterising the structure of the target system and, on the other hand, the "*Define an Object Model*" decision requires a set of decisions for identifying, validating and describing these elements.

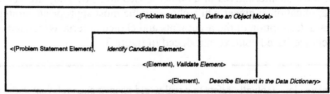

Figure 4: An OMT Plan-based Context

In the above example, the plan-based context <(Problem Statement), *Define an Object Model*> is decomposed into three choice-based contexts, namely: <(Problem Statement), *Identify Candidate Element*>, <(Element), *Validate Element*> and

<(Element), *Describe Element in the Data Dictionary>*. For achieving the intention of defining an Object Model, the application engineer should iterate several times on the three decisions "*Identify Candidate Element*", "*Validate Element*" and "*Describe Element in the Data Dictionary*".

The ordering of the component contexts within a plan is defined by a graph named *precedence graph*. There is one graph per plan-based context. The nodes of this graph are the component contexts while the links -called *precedence links (PL)*- define either the possible *ordered transitions* between contexts or their possible *parallel enactment*. Based on arguments, a choice criterion may be assigned to a link. The choice criterion defines when the transition can be performed. Figure 5 illustrates the notion of precedence graph for the OMT plan <(Problem Statement), *Define an Object Model>*.

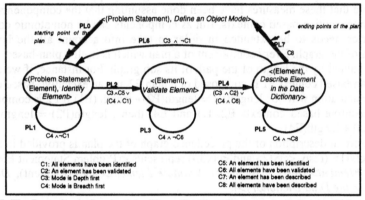

Figure 5: The Precedence Graph of the Plan <(Problem Statement), *Define an Object Model>*

One may observe in this graph that the validation of an element (i.e. the context <(Element), *Validate Element>*) is executed either if all the elements have been identified and if the mode chosen by the AE is *breadth first*, or if an element has been identified and if the AE wants to follow a *depth first* mode. This remark leads us to introduce the notion of *an execution path*, the AE can follow in a precedence graph, to execute a plan. A path comprises a set of precedence links and proposes a way to execute the plan which is most often, related to a particular mode (namely, breath first or depth first). Figure 5 defines two paths for the Object Model construction :

- If the AE chooses the *Depth first* mode, each time an element is identified, it is immediately validated and described in the Data Dictionary. Therefore, to build the complete Object Model, the AE should iterate on the execution of three decisions, namely "*Identify Element*", "*Validate Element*" and "*Describe Element in the Data Dictionary*". This path corresponds to a loop composed of the three component contexts of the plan and their relations PL2, PL4 and PL6.

- If the AE chooses the *Breadth first* mode, all the elements are first identified, by iterating on the context <(Problem Statement Element), *Identify Element>*. Following the precedence link labelled PL1, all the identified elements are then validated (PL3) and finally, all the validated elements are described in the Data Dictionary (PL5). In this path, Links PL2 and PL4 are used only once, whereas PL1, PL3, and PL5 are used as many times as there are elements to be created in the Object Model.

Thus, it is possible to evaluate the steps needed to create an Object Model. Apparently in the above description of paths, the depth first path requires less steps than the one defined for the breadth first mode. In fact it is possible to demonstrate that the size of both paths is the same. The component contexts are executed the same number of times, precedence links used in each case are different, but, as a link relates two component contexts, the same number of PL is used in both cases.

Let us illustrate this on a concrete example. Assuming the AE has to create an Object Model made of five elements, he will need to execute five times the three components of the plan. The total number of precedence links the paths are made of is the same : 16. The Depth First Path is equal to PL0+5PL2+5PL4+4PL6+PL7, and the Breadth First Path is equal to PL0+4PL1+PL2+4PL3+PL4+4PL5+PL7.

More generally, choice criteria impact the ordering of components, not the size of the path. Note that these measures have been done assuming that the components of the plan were executive-based contexts. But as components can be non atomic contexts, the metrics needs to be extended in order to take into account all the levels of deepness of the graph. Every component of a plan which is itself a plan-based context must be valued by the length of the path of its sub graph. For instance, if we assume that a plan-based context P1 is composed of a plan P2 and an executive-based context E1, the calculation will be : length(P1)= length(P2)+ length (E1) If P2 is composed of three executive-based contexts E2, E3 and E4, then : length(P2) = length(E2) + length(E3) + length(E4).

A more formal description of the precedence graph of the plan is provided in table 3, where <ctxt1> (resp. <ctxt2> and <ctx3>) represents <(Problem Statement Element), *Identify Element*> (resp. <(Element), *Validate Element*> and<(Element), *Describe Element in the Data Dictionary*>).

{PL0. { ([<ctxt1 > . PL2/(c3∧c5) . <ctxt2 > . PL4/(c3 ∧c2) . <ctxt3 > . PL6/(c3 ∧ (not c1))]*[<ctxt1 > . PL2/(c3 ∧c5) . <ctxt2 > . PL4/(c3 ∧c2) . <ctxt3 > . PL7/c8 ..])

∪ ([<ctxt1> . PL1/(c4∧ (not c5)) . <ctxt1 >]* . PL2/(c4∧c1) . [<ctxt2 > . PL3/(c4∧ (not c6)) . <ctxt2 >]* . PL4/(c4∧c6) . [<ctxt3 > . PL5/(c4∧ (not c8)) . <ctxt3 >]*. PL7/c8 ..) } }

*: 0 to n times ∪: union   . : Sequence ..: End of the Graph

Table 3 : An Example of Textual Description for a Precedence Graph

---

This description of a precedence graph shows the use of logical operators to represent all paths of the graph, and to combine precedence links and nodes of the graph. This particular example does not show the use of the "shuffle" operator required to describe parallel execution paths in a plan.

To sum up we can say that plan-based contexts allow to prescribe the way to solve complex issues by decomposing them in sub-issues. The precedence graph associated to each plan provides a detailed description of the different possible execution paths and make possible the measurement of the process performance. The metrics associated to precedence graphs help in the evaluation of process performance costs.

2.3 The Notion of Tree

As introduced in the two previous paragraphs, contexts are related through refinement and composition links. These links can be recursively used to define relations between contexts. This recursive building results in a hierarchy of contexts called a tree. Trees represent meaningful hierarchies of contexts which may be independent one from the others.

A *tree* has a root which is, either a choice-based context, or a plan-based context. It has 'n' levels (n ≥ 2). There is one level between a choice (resp. plan) based context and its alternatives (resp. components). The more global the root intention is, the more levels are required to support its decomposition and/or refinement. One may notice that the nodes of a tree are contexts of any of the three types : executive, choice or plan. This results from the fact that any component of a plan-based context or any alternative of a choice-based context may be a plan, an executive or a choice-based context. Moreover, whereas the intermediate nodes of trees can be either choice or plan-based contexts, executive-based contexts are always leaves of trees. The type of the leaves of the tree enable to verify whether the tree is complete or not: if all the leaves are executive, the tree is complete otherwise it is not. Figure 6 is an example of an OMT tree : the one which intends to guide the application engineer in constructing the Object Model.

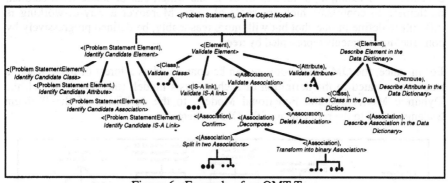

Figure 6 : Example of an OMT Tree

The issue of the above tree is to achieve the complete description of the static aspects of the Information System to be built. As shown in figure 6, several levels of refinement/decomposition of the root context, namely <(Problem Statement), *Define an Object Model*> are needed to achieve this complex issue. The complete definition of the Object Model is achieved by executing the components of the upper plan for each elements.

The first decomposition level of this tree have been discussed in the previous paragraph. It prescribes to organise the Object Model (OM) definition around three main decisions that the AE should make for all the OM elements. The way-of-working description suggests therefore to act in a plan composed of three contexts, namely, <(Problem Statement), *Identify Candidate Element*>, <(Element), *Validate Element*> and <(Element), *Describe Element in the Data Dictionary*>. The three component contexts are choice-based ones.

Each of their alternatives is associated to a specific kind of Object Model Element. For instance in the choice-based context <(Element), *Validate Element>*an element can be a class, an attribute, an association or an IS-A link, each of these concepts is related to an alternative of the above choice-based context. Thus, the alternatives are <(Class), *Validate Class>*, <(Attribute), *Validate Attribute>*, <(Association), *Validate Association>* and <(IS-A Link), *Validate IS-A Link>*.

Alternatives of the first component <(Problem Statement), *Identify Candidate Element>* are executive-based contexts and leaves of the tree. Similarly, alternatives of the third component, namely <(Element), *Describe Element in the Data Dictionary>* are executive-based contexts whereas the second component, namely <(Element), *Validate Element>* has alternatives which are choice-based contexts. The sub-trees of the tree have a variable depth. For instance, in the definition of an Object Model, the sub-tree dealing with Identification of Elements has two levels of depth, whereas the one dealing with Validation has five levels.

2.4   The Notion of Forest

A process model is usually composed of a collection of trees, that we call a *forest of trees*. The existence of multiple trees in a unique way-of-working comes from the independence of some contexts due to the independence of either situations or decisions. For example, a number of decisions which can be made from scratch, participate to contexts which are roots of trees. Moreover a way-of-working is difficult to define in one shot but will, more reasonably, be defined progressively by constructing fragments represented by trees.

For instance, the OMT methodology can be considered as a forest of trees, where a tree is associated to the definition of each analysis model, (the Object Model, the Dynamic Model and the Functional Model), to the definition of the Problem Statement, and to the refinement of the OMT schema.

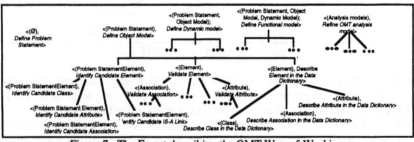

Figure 7 : The Forest describing the OMT Way-of-Working

To achieve the definition of an OMT schema, the application engineer needs to go through the forest depicted figure 7. The application engineer starts by describing the Problem Statement with users. Then, he/she creates the three analysis models and finally improves these models applying the refinement guidelines provided by the methodology. As the elaboration of the analysis models can be done in any order, the building of each analysis model is represented by an independent tree. In [13], the authors recommend however to start with the Object Model, because it is easier to elaborate and helps in the definition of the Dynamic and the Functional models.

The construction of the Object Model which aims to describe the structure of the future information system has already been presented in the paragraph 2.3. We focus now on the way-of-working to build the Dynamic Model. Figure 8 summarises the OMT guidelines to construct this model which aims at describing the system behaviour as a set of state diagrams.

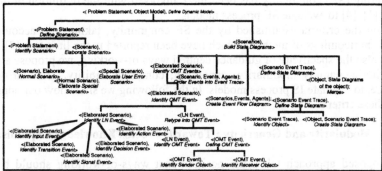

Figure 8 : The OMT Tree describing the Dynamic Model Elaboration

To achieve the building of *State diagrams*, the authors suggest to start with the elaboration of *scenarios* as descriptions of sequences of *events* expressed in natural language. *Scenarios* are built in an incremental way. Normal *scenarios* are defined first and then *special* cases are taken into account; finally the exceptions which could happen are also added to improve the *special scenarios*.

In our approach, the elaboration of a *scenario* is represented as a plan where each context deals with a specific aspect of the construction or the refinement of a scenario. The refinement can be done either immediately after the description of the *Normal scenario* or when the three analysis models have been created.
Scenarios are used as a basis to identify the *events* happening in the system life cycle and to build an *Event Trace Diagram* describing events, their ordering and impacts on actors. The knowledge presented in the *Event Trace Diagram* is summarised into the *Event Flow Diagram* where events and actors are related in a static manner (without representing the events ordering).
These diagrams are then used to build *State Diagrams*. A state diagram describes the *state transitions*, of an object, each transition comprising two states and an event with the action or activity it triggers. As the consequence of the event is a modification of the state of the object, the event is represented by an arrow linking the initial state of the object to the final state it will be transformed in. A *State Transition* is created for each event identified in the *Event Trace Diagram*, it can be nested in order to express complex behaviours. The nested State Diagrams are obtained through several refinements. When all the needed *State Diagrams* have been elaborated, they are merged to define a unique Dynamic Model.

3 Discussion

In the IS community, quality criteria have been defined for evaluating conceptual schema, [9], but very few efforts have been made for defining quality criteria of IS processes. Method comparisons [6], [7] focus, for the process aspects, on the number of activities a process model is made of, on how in depth the decomposition of activities is done, etc. This helps to compare the nature of activities, but does not contribute to defining quality criteria applicable to process models. The Software Engineering (SE) community has been more involved with the definition of quality criteria [1], [4] to evaluate SE process models.

Based on the criteria established by the SE community, taking into account the various shortcomings of methods which have been reported in the literature [3], [16], [5] and also the specificity of guidance centred ways-of-working, we propose a set of five criteria, namely modularity, genericity, comprehensibility, granularity and guidance, to evaluate IS process models. In the following we show how our approach meets these criteria.

3.1 Modularity and Genericity : Towards Process Knowledge Capitalisation

The proposed approach takes the position that ways-of-working should have a theoretical foundation which is provided in our case by the way-of-working model. This to ensure properties such as *modularity* and *genericity* .

Modularity has proved to be a key issue in many aspects of information and computer science. We believe that *modularity* of ways-of-working descriptions is useful to ensure an easy evolution and improvement of the method. It facilitates training of the methodology, makes easier the construction of a way-of-working by composing existing fragments and facilitates automation in a tool based environment.
Our approach structures a way-of-working into units such as contexts and trees which ensures modularity of process models descriptions. Modules of a way-of-working are obtained by applying the decomposition and refinement mechanisms to contexts. These notions are generic i.e. independent of a particular methodology and powerful enough to represent many various and complex situations in an homogeneous fashion.

The application of the approach for describing a number of existing ways-of-working [11] has demonstrated its genericity : similar process patterns appear several times in the same methodology and even in different methodologies. The properties of modularity and genericity introduce the idea of using *factorisation means* to allow both a more concise and meaningful description of a given way-of-working and to facilitate the reuse of generic process patterns.

In order to optimise the description of a way-of-working, contexts and trees sharing common features are factorised: If several contexts of the same type share common properties such as an intention or a product part of the same type we suggest to factorise them and to introduce a new higher abstraction level in the way-of-working description where guidelines are expressed at the factorised components level. This factorisation approach is illustrated in the following with the OMT methodology example. The stepwise approach recommended by the OMT methodology [13] corresponds to the plan sketched in the figure 10. The plan suggests to proceed in turn to the identification of each object model element.

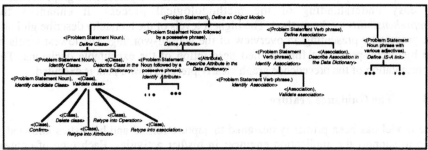

Figure 10 : The Way of defining an Object Model following a Step by Step Approach

The definition of each element, namely class, attribute, association and is-a link, is described in a two levels hierarchy of plans whose component decisions are of the same type, namely for the upper plan *"Identify ..."*, *"Describe ... in the Data Dictionary"*, and for the lower one *"Identify candidate..."* and *"Validate ..."*.

We suggest to apply a factorisation mechanism to reorganise this hierarchical description as shown in the figure 6. This transformation leads first, to create the "factorised" contexts <(Problem Statement), *Identify Candidate Element>*, <(Element) *Validate Element>* and <(Element) *Describe in a Data Dictionary>*, second to relate them at a new level in the hierarchy to express things at the factorised level and third, to introduce choice-based contexts allowing to select the alternative appropriate to the element to be defined as a refinement of the factorised contexts. These alternatives are then refined as in the initial description using the two level plan based description.

This factorisation attitude leads to a more synthetic description of a way-of-working but also helps in identifying generic process chunks that can be reused in other methodologies. For instance, the generic context <(Problem Statement Element), *Identify Element>* has been instanciated for the definition of other ways-of-working (e.g. O*, E/R., OOA).

3.2 The Granularity Feature

The ability to describe ways-of-working *at different levels of granularity*, in a uniform manner is provided by the recursive application of refinement and decomposition mechanisms on contexts. High level intentions such as *"the definition of an OMT schema "* or lower level ones such as *"the identification of an event of the OMT dynamic model "* are modelled using the same concept (*context*) and can be hierarchically connected using the refinement and decomposition mechanisms. We believe that this is a powerful feature for modelling complex process situations which are not supported by most existing process models. As alternatives of choice-based contexts and components of plan-based contexts are contexts too, the way-of-working model provides an elegant solution to solve the granularity problem by describing hierarchies of contexts.

3.3   The Comprehensibility Capability

The *graphical representation* used to represent trees and precedence graphs leads to an easy understanding of the methodological process. It enhances the *comprehensibility* of the method. The highest levels of the hierarchy describe globally the process by presenting an overview of the way-of-working. The lowest levels of the hierarchy provide a fine-grained description of the executable decisions. The representation of the precedence graph clearly presents how a plan is executed.

3.4   The Guidance Feature

The model has been primarily designed to capture formal and heuristics knowledge able to support the application engineer in his/her activities. Each type of context provides a specific guidance. Executive-based contexts automate the execution of actions. Arguments and choice criteria advise the AE when he/she has to make a choice. Modes and approaches make guidance within a plan more flexible. Finally the various levels of granularity enable to guide the AE from the beginning to the end of his/her work.

4   Conclusion and Future Work

In this paper, an approach for defining ways-of-working in a structured and systematic manner has been presented, exemplified with the OMT methodology and evaluated against five quality criteria. The approach leads to construct ways-of-working able to represent a large variety of situations in a decision oriented manner, with a reasonable level of genericity, at various levels of detail, in a modular and hierarchical manner. The graphical representation of the way-of-working makes its understanding by the application engineer easier and enhances the guidance capabilities. Finally the factorisation mechanism helps optimising the way-of-working description and the discovery of reusable process chunks. In addition, metrics can be defined to measure the cost of using a given way-of-working. As illustrated in section 2.2.3, metrics can be used to compare different paths in a precedence graph. It can be defined for the whole hierarchy in order to calculate the time needed to build an application and to compare two paths in a given hierarchy or to compare several methodologies.

We are looking for the introduction of new features such as dynamic change which has been identified as a key issue of SE process models. We are currently implementing the approach in *a CAPE Environment* able to monitor method engineers in the definition of ways-of-working, and to guide application engineers in the use of ways-of-working for elaborating high quality products. Another topic of research work is to define *a complete set of metrics* for evaluating and comparing methodological processes. Finally, we are populating a *library of reusable process chunks* which will be the basis of a *meta-methodology* for defining a new way-of-working within a specific methodology.

References

1. P. Armenise, S. Bandinelli, C. Ghezzi, A. Morzenti, *A survey and assessment of software process representation formalisms*, Int. Journal of Software Engineering and Knowledge Engineering,Vol. 3, No. 3, 1993.
2. Brinkkemper S, "Formalisation of Information systems modelling", Ph.D. Thesis, University of Nijmegen, Thesis Publishers, Amsterdam, 1990.
3. Bubenko J.R., Bubenko J.A., "Information System Methodologies - A Research View", in Olle T.W., Sol H.G., Verrijn-Stuart A.A. (Eds.) : "Information Systems Design Methodologies : Improving the practice, North-Holland, Amsterdam, The Netherlands, 1986, pp 289-318.
4. M. Dowson, *Software Process Themes and Issues*, IEEE int. conf. , 1993.
5. L.J.B. Essink, *A Conceptual Framework for Information System Development Methodologies*, Memorandum INF-86-34, Univ. Twente, Enschede, The Netherlands, 1986.
6. Goor G. van den, Brinkkemper S., Hong S.; "Formalization and comparison of six Object Oriented Analysis and Design Methods", Report Method Engineering Institute, University of Twente, 1992.
7. Iivari J., "Object-oriented information sytems analysis: A comparison of six object-oriented analysis methods", IFIP Int. Conf. on "Methods and associated Tools for the Information Systems Life Cycle" (A-55), North Holland, 1994.
8. Kumar K., Welke R. J., "Methodology Engineering : A prposal for situation-specific Methodology Engineering", Challenges and strategies for research in Systems Development , J. Wiley & sons Ltd., 1992, pp. 257-269.
9. Lindland O.I., Sindre G., Solvberg A., "Understanding Quality in Conceptual Modeling", IEEE software, March 1994.
10. Lyytinen K., Smolander K., Tahvanainen V.-P., "Modelling CASE Environ-ments in sytems Work", CASE89 conference papers, Kista, Sweden, 1989.
11. Plihon V., "The OMT,The OOA ,The SA/SD,The E/R ,The O* , The OOD Methodology" NATURE Deliverable DP2, 1994.
12. Prakash N., "A Process View of Methodologies", Proc 6th Int. Conf. on "Advanced Information Systems Engineering" (CAISE), Sprg. Vg,1994.
13. J. Rumbaugh, M. Blaha, W. Premerlani, F. Eddy, W. Loresen : "Object-oriented modeling and design", Prentice Hall international, 1991.
14. Schwer S. R. , Rolland C. ,"Formalization of the Information System Design Process", Internal Report C.R.I., 1994.
15. Seligmann P.S., Wijers G. M., Sol H.G., "Analyzing the structure of I.S. methodologies, an alternative approach", in Proc. of the 1st Dutch Conference on Information Systems, Amersfoort, The Netherlands, 1989.
16. Sol H.G.: "Kennis en ervaring rond het ontwerpen van informatiesystemen", Informatie, Vol. 27, N°3, 1985.
17. Wynekoop J.d., Russo N.L., "System Development methodologies: unanswered questions and the research-practice gap", Proc. of 14th ICIS Orlando, USA, 1993, pp. 181-190.

Modelling Communication between Cooperative Systems

Frank Dignum[1] and Hans Weigand[2]

[1] Eindhoven University of Technology, Dept. of Mathematics and Computer Science,
P.O.box 513, 5600 MB Eindhoven, The Netherlands,
tel.+31-40-473705, email: dignum@win.tue.nl
[2] Tilburg University, Infolab, P.O.box 90153, 5000 LE Tilburg, The Netherlands,
tel.+31-13-662806, email: h.weigand@kub.nl

Abstract. In cooperative systems many of the obligations, prohibitions and permissions that govern the behaviour of the system exist as a result of communication with users and/or other systems. In this paper we will discuss the role of illocutionary logic and deontic logic in modelling these communication processes and the resulting norms. The combination of illocutionary and deontic logic can be used to reason about communication structures. It is also possible to model the authorization relations, on the basis of which orders and requests can be made, and the delegation of these authoritizations in this logic.

1 Introduction

In recent years there has been a growing interest in cooperative systems or co-operating *agents*(see e.g. [Po93]). However, little has been said about how these cooperating agents influence each other's behaviour. Each agent has certain capabilities, actions that it can perform. These actions can be material, such as opening a window, or communicative, such as providing some piece of information. Each agent also has an agenda containing the actions to be performed by the agent, instantly or at some designated time. In a normative system this agenda consists of the obligations of the agent. We assume that the agenda is not fixed but can be manipulated by the agent. The agent can add new obligations to the agenda (typically done on the request of another agent). He can also remove actions by performing them or by violating the obligation. In the latter case he usually is obliged to perform some new action that compensates for the violation. The description of the obligations and the manipulation of the obligations has been the subject of research in normative systems and deontic logic (see e.g. [MW93]).

The interaction between agents can most easily be seen in the cases where a particular service is rendered from one agent to the other. A (simple) example of such a service is illustrated in the following picture.

In general we can distinguish three phases of communication. The first phase is the negotiation about the terms of the contract. In this phase authorizations can be established on the basis of which some actions can be performed in the

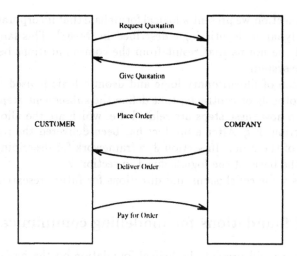

Fig. 1. ordering procedure

following phases. In the above figure this corresponds to the requesting and sending of a quotation. Here, sending a quotation implies authorizing the customer to order some products on some specified conditions. The second phase consists of the acceptance of the contract. I.e. the authorizations and obligations that follow from the contract. In the above example this is included in the order which implies an acceptance of the quotation. The last phase is the fulfilment of the contract. I.e. following a protocol according to the terms agreed upon in the contract. In the example this corresponds to the actual order, delivery and payment sequence.

In this paper we will show that the communication processes described above (including the resulting norms) can be modelled using illocutionary logic and deontic logic.

Illocutionary logic [SV85] is a logical formalisation of the theory of speech acts [Se69] and is used to formally describe the communication structure itself. A first attempt to model communication using speech acts is made in the method SAMPO [LL86], but this does not include the deontic aspects. In [Lee88], Lee presents a language and modelling technique for deontic rules, but these model procedures rather than communication structures.

The fundamental reason for the use of deontic concepts is that coordination of behaviour always requires some form of mutual commitment. If an agent does not execute an action, he has committed himself to, this causes a violation of the contract. Because the action should be executed in the future, it cannot be guaranteed, so the interpretation "it will happen in all future courses of events" is too strong, but the interpretation "it will happen in some course of events" is too weak. Interpreting the formula "α is obligatory" as: 'not doing α violates a commitment", we get a more precise meaning of what it is that something is on an agent's agenda.

In the next section we present a logical formalism that incorporates the speech acts into the dynamic deontic logic described in [Me88]. This language can be used to model the norms that result from the communications between agents in a normative system.

The combination of illocutionary logic and deontic logic is used to build communication protocols or contracts, that define the subsequent steps in the communication and how these steps are related. I.e. which are the allowed reactions to a certain action. E.g. After a product has been delivered the reaction should be a payment of the order. In section 3, a framework for describing contracts is presented on the basis of the logic defined in section 2.

Section 4 gives some conclusions and directions for future research.

2 Logical foundations for modelling communication

In this section we will present the logical foundation on the basis of which the communication processes between agents can be modelled. The logical language is based on the dynamic deontic logic described in [Me88], which is extended to include speech acts as formalized in illocutionary logic.

2.1 The language

We start with a language based on the Dynamic Deontic Logic Language given in [Me88]. We will only give a short overview.

We start by defining a language of parameterized actions L_{act}

Definition 2.1 The language L_{act} of actions is given by the following BNF:

$$\alpha :: - \underline{a}|\alpha_1 \cup \alpha_2|\alpha_1 \& \alpha_2|\overline{\alpha}|\mathbf{any}|\mathbf{fail}$$

The $\underline{a}$ stands for the atomic actions in the system, like "order(i,j,p)", which states that agent i orders p from agent j. The first parameter indicates the subject of the action. The meaning of $\alpha_1 \cup \alpha_2$ is a choice between α_1 and α_2. $\alpha_1 \& \alpha_2$ stands for the parallel execution of α_1 and α_2. The expression $\overline{\alpha}$ stands for the non-performance of the action α. The **any** action is a universal or "don't care which" action. Finally the **fail** action is the action that always fails (deadlock). This action does not lead to a next state.

The language L_{act} can be used to describe actions within dynamic deontic logic. The language of dynamic deontic logic (L_{dd}) is given in the following definition.

Definition 2.2 The language L_{dd} of dynamic deontic logic is given by the following BNF:

$$\Phi :: - \phi|\Phi \vee \Psi|\Phi \wedge \Psi|\neg\Phi|[\alpha]\Phi|B(i,\phi)|I(i,\alpha)|I(i,\phi)$$

Where ϕ is a first order logic formula and α an element of L_{act}.

The intuitive meaning of $[\alpha]\Phi$ is that after the execution of α, Φ necessarily holds. The meaning of $B(i, \phi)$ is that agent i believes ϕ. $I(i, \alpha)$ means that agent I intends to perform α and $I(i, \phi)$ means that agent i intends to bring ϕ about. Due to a lack of space we did not include temporal aspects in the logical language. One way to do this in a simple way is described in [WMW89].

The deontic operators are defined by the following abbreviations (cf. [Me88, WMW89]):

Definition 2.3

$$O_{ij}(\alpha(i)) = \overline{[\alpha(i)]Violation_{ij}}$$
$$F_{ij}(\alpha(i)) = [\alpha(i)]Violation_{ij}$$
$$= O_{ij}(\overline{\alpha(i)})$$
$$P_{ij}(\alpha(i)) = \neg[\alpha(i)]Violation_{ij}$$
$$= \neg F_{ij}(\alpha(i))$$

Where $Violation_{ij}$ are special predicates indicating the violation of an agreement between i and j. So, the agent i is obliged to agent j to perform the action $\alpha(i)$ if not doing $\alpha(i)$ by i leads to a violation of i with respect to j, i is forbidden to do $\alpha(i)$ by j if doing $\alpha(i)$ leads to a violation of i with respect to j. i is permitted to do $\alpha(i)$ by j if i is not forbidden to do $\alpha(i)$ by j.

In order to model the communication between agents in a normative system the language L_{dd} has to be extended to incorporate speech acts as described in illocutionary logic. Before we introduce the speech acts, first we introduce two special relations involving agents. One relation implements a power relation between two agents and the other one implements an authorization of an agent to perform some action.

The power relation is the most primitive relation of the two. There exists a power relation between the agent i and the agent j with respect to action α, if i has the power to order j to perform the action α. For instance, the boss can order his secretary to type a letter for him. Note that he might not have the power to order his secretary to make coffee for him! We assume that the power relation is persistent and is only changed in special occasions, like when a manager is appointed.

The power relation can also be defined with respect to a proposition. This means so much as that i has the power to convince j of the truth of ϕ. For instance, a student will (usually) consider the statements of a teacher to be true.

The power relation defines a partial ordering on the class of agents for every action α. This ordering is reflexive (self-power) and transitive but not necessarily total.

Notation: if i has power over j with respect to α we write: $j <_\alpha i$. If i has power over j with respect to the truth of ϕ we write $j <_\phi i$.

The second relation is the authorization relation. This relation can be established for a certain time with mutual agreement (under certain restrictions). For instance, I can agree that a company can order me to pay a certain amount of money after they delivered a product. This relation ends after I pay the money. The authorization relation is modelled using a special predicate.

Notation: if i is authorized to do α we write: auth(i,α).

We will now continue by extending the language of actions to include the speech acts. A speech act is formalised as an illocutionary point (indicating the goal of the speech act) with three parameters: the Speaker, the Addressee, and the content. We distinguish the following basic speech acts (based upon [SV85, Aus62]):

Definition 2.4
DIR(i,j,α) – i does a request to j for α
COM(i,j,α) – i commits himself to j to do α
ASS(i,j,ϕ) – i asserts to j proposition ϕ
DECL(i,j,ϕ) – i declares and informs j that ϕ holds from now on

From these basic speech acts we can construct other basic speech acts by e.g. using the logical negation of actions.

Definition 2.5
FOR(i,j,α) = DIR(i,j,$\overline{\alpha}$) – i forbids j to do α
PER(i,j,α) = DECL(i,j,$P_{j,i}(\alpha(j))$) – i permits j to do α

There might be some dispute over the question whether the declarative DECL has an Addressee parameter, since if it succeeds, the effect will be a change of the world and not of the knowledge of the Addressee only. Depending on the preparatory conditions, it is not necessary that there is an Addressee at all. However, in general it makes little sense to do a declarative speech act and not inform anybody. Hence the Addressee should be understood here as the agent (or set of agents) that is informed.

Declaratives can only be used for specific institutionalized speech acts, so the propositional content is usually rather restricted. In practice, a limited number of specific declaratives will be distinguished, such as the "authorization" action that we will introduce in section 2.2.

Speech acts can be grounded in three different ways: charity, power and authorization. (See also [DW92] for a similar distinction as an improvement to the completely power based CSCW tool Coordinator ([FGHW88])). For instance, a directive (DIR) can be made on the basis of charity, which means it is a request, or on the basis of a power relation or authorization (in which cases it is an order). Hence for each basic speech act we distinguish three variants, indicated by a subscript c,p or a. So, DIR_a stands for an authorized request, whereas DIR_p stands for an order based on power. Similarly for assertives and declaratives. For commissives, the distinction seems to be not very relevant and we ignore it here. Likewise, when the distinction of the powerbase of a speech act is not important, we will ignore the subscript.

The language of all acts is now defined in two steps. First we define the set of all speech acts L_{Sact}.

Definition 2.6
1. All basic speech acts are elements of L_{Sact}.
2. If $\alpha \in L_{Sact}$ then also $IP(i,j,\alpha) \in L_{Sact}$ and $IP(i,j,\overline{\alpha}) \in L_{Sact}$ where $IP \in \{DIR, COM\}$

Note that this is a recursive definition. So, we can have speech acts about speech acts, etc.
The language of actions L_{ACT} can now be defined as:

Definition 2.7

$$L_{ACT} = L_{act} \cup L_{Sact}$$

The speech acts of L_{Sact} as defined above do not contain all elements of speech acts that are identified in illocutionary logic.
The propositional content conditions are not modelled at this moment. They can be modelled through a refinement of the language L_{Sact} which renders only those speech acts syntactically correct that comply to the propositional content conditions. In an Information System environment, the propositional content conditions are contained in the data model.

The preparatory conditions (ϕ) and the intended effects (ψ) of a speech act (α) can be modelled through the following schema:

$$\phi \rightarrow [\alpha]\psi$$

Which means that if ϕ is true then ψ will hold after α has been performed. The intended effects of the speech acts are described by means of deontic and epistemic operators, while the preparatory conditions refer to either the authorization relation or the power relation. We have the following general preparatory conditions and intended effects for the basic speech acts. Of course, for speech acts mentioning specific actions there might be more conditions and effects.

Axiom 2.8
1. $([DIR_p\ (i,j,\ \alpha)]\ O_{ji}(\alpha)) \leftarrow j <_\alpha i$
2. $([DIR_a\ (i,j,\ \alpha)]\ O_{ji}(\alpha)) \leftarrow \text{auth}(i, DIR(i,j,\alpha))$
3. $[COM(i,j,\alpha)]\ O_{ij}(\alpha)$
4. $[DECL_a\ (i,j,\phi)]\ \phi \leftarrow \text{auth}(i, DECL(i,j,\phi))$
5. $[DECL_p\ (i,j,\phi)]\ \phi \leftarrow j <_\phi i$
6. $([ASS_a\ (i,j,\phi)]\ B(j,\phi)) \leftarrow \text{auth}(i, ASS(i,j,\phi))$
7. $([ASS_p\ (i,j,\phi)]\ B(j,\phi)) \leftarrow j <_\phi i$

The last of the above properties expresses the fact that a person can be authorized to assert some facts. If this person asserts such a fact the effect is that the Addressee(s) will believe that fact (which is not the same as making the fact true, which happens with a declaration!).

The axioms describe the effects of power and authorization speech acts, but not of those based on charity. This is correct, although we might add some politeness rules that say that a message is always replied. For example, a request based on charity would be replied by either a commissive or an assertion of the effect that the agent does not commit himself:

$$[DIR_c \; (i,j, \; \alpha)] \; O_{ji}(COM(j,i,\alpha) \cup ASS(j,i,\neg O_{ji}(\alpha))))$$

In a formal context we assume that an agent is always sincere and thus we have:

Axiom 2.9
[DIR(i,j,α)] I(i,α) – any DIR speech acts expresses that i intends α to happen
[DECL(i,j,ϕ)] I(i,ϕ) – any DECL speech acts expresses that i intends to bring about ϕ (by the speech act)
[ASS(i,j,ϕ)] B(i,ϕ) – any ASS speech act expresses that i believes ϕ

So the effect of a DIR_c is at least that the agent knows about the subjects intention, and this can trigger him to commit himself.

2.2 The dynamics of authorization

If the subject is not authorized, it can not issue a DIR_a speech act sucessfully. In that case, it can try to attain an authorization first. This can be done by means of a DIR_c (i,j,DECL(j,i,auth(i,DIR(..)))) , that is, a request for authorization of the other party. If the other party complies to the request, that is, grants the authorization, the subject gets authorized from that time on. This example shows that the system should not only formalize authorized behavior itself, but also the creation of authorizations, and, for that matter, the deletion. The crux of the formalization is that authorizations can only be made and retracted by an act of the other party. Because the establishment of authorizations is an important and frequently occurring speech act we introduce the following notation:

$$AUT(i,j,\alpha) == DECL_a(i,j,auth(j,\alpha))$$

So, AUT(i,j,α) means that i gives authorization to j to do α. Of course, this speech act is only successful if i is authorized to give this authorization. For that reason, we have to presuppose the following axiom:

Axiom 2.10
1. $auth(i,AUT(i,j,DIR_a(j,i,\alpha(i))))$
2. $auth(i,AUT(i,j,ASS_a(j,i,p)))$

that says that each agent is authorized to authorize other parties as far as actions and beliefs of the agent himself are concerned. This is irrespective of whether the granting of authorizations is forbidden by for example a higher power. If that would be the case, the authorization would still be successful, although the agent might be punished for it.

The ability to retract an authorization should be left to the subject of the authorization. If i has granted j an authorization, it is only j who can retract the authorization. For this purpose, we introduce a new declarative RTR:

$$RTR(i,j,\alpha) == DECL_a(i,j,\neg auth(i,\alpha))$$

The preparatory condition of RTR is that the authorization does exist. By axiom, every agent is authorized to retract authorizations given to him. If an agent has first granted an authorization, and then wants to retract it, he must ask the other party to do so. Of course, the agents may have made appointments. For example, the agent who grants the authorization may ensure himself of the authorization to request the retracting. The effect is that he can have the authorization retracted whenever he wants.

2.3 "Ordering" in logic

In this section we will show how the example given in section 1, about ordering products, can be formally described in the logic developed sofar. Each of the arrows from figure 1 (i.e. each of the messages between the customer and the company) is modelled with a logical formula. The whole contract including the request for quotation can be modelled by the following formulas:

1. $[DIR_c(i,j,\text{give-quotation}(j,i,g,p))]O_{ji}(\text{give-quotation}(j,i,g,p) \cup \text{refuse}(j))$
   After a request for a quotation (i.e. a directive based on charity) the company is obliged to give the quotation or send a refusal. Here we assume some business rule that such a request is always answered.

2. $[\text{give-quotation}(j,i,g,p)] auth(i,DIR_a(i,j,\text{deliver}(j,i,g,p)))$
   If a company gives a quotation for a certain price (p) the client is authorized to order the product (g) for that price.

3. $auth(i,DIR_a(i,j,\text{deliver}(j,i,g,p))) \rightarrow$
   $[DIR_a(i,j,\text{deliver}(j,i,g,p))](O_{ji}(\text{deliver}(j,i,g,p)) \wedge$
   $[\text{deliver}(j,i,g,p)]auth(j,DIR_a(j,i,\text{pay}(i,j,p))))$
   If a customer is authorized to order a product for a certain price (i.e. a quotation has been given for that price) then the company is obliged to deliver the product after the customer has ordered it. (This follows directly from the axioms 2.8.) But after delivery of the product, the company is authorized to order the customer to pay for it.

4. $O_{ji}(\text{deliver}(j,i,g,p)) \rightarrow [\text{deliver}(j,i,g,p)]\neg auth(i,DIR_a(i,j,\text{deliver}(j,i,g,p)))$
   If a company has to deliver a product and actually does it, the customer is no longer authorized to request delivery of the product. (One might omit this formula or replace it with a formula that limits the validity of the quotation to a period of time).

5. $auth(j,DIR_a(j,i,\text{pay}(i,j,p))) \rightarrow [DIR_a(j,i,\text{pay}(i,j,p))]O_{ij}(\text{pay}(i,j,p))$
   If an order has been delivered (and authority acquired to request payment) a request for payment induces an obligation for the customer to pay. (This follows directly from the axioms 2.8.)

6. $O_{ij}(\text{pay(i,j,p)}) \rightarrow [\text{pay(i,j,p)}]\neg\text{auth}(j, DIR_a(j,i,\text{pay(i,j,p)}))$
   Finally, after the customer has paid, the company cannot request another payment again.

Although the above formulas describe the exchange between the customer and the company exact and complete, they are not very readable. In the next section we will show a language that is based on the logic introduced in this section, but has a more readable syntax and structures the (speech) acts to form transactions and services.

3 Contracts and communication protocols

In this section we will give an overview of the formal specification language CoLa (Communication Language), which is based on the logic described in section 2 and on the language presented in [We93]. Due to space limitations, this overview will not be extensive neither complete, but will be given by illustrating how the example from section 1 can be modelled in this language.

The protocols that are specified in CoLa are independent from the applications, but in contrast to traditional communication protocols, they capture the complete communication logic, not just a set or ordered set of messages. The contracts specified in CoLa are managed by a Contract Manager, which is a process responsible for the proper dealing with the communication, including (a) the transaction management, including compensation; (b) the set-up of new contracts, and adaptation of active ones. It follows that these aspects therefore do not have to be specified in the contracts themselves. For instance, we do not have to specify in the contract what happens if a message does not arrive through some hardware failure. Handling this kind of communication problems is typically a task for the Contract Manager and can be specified (generically) in that place. We will not consider the Contract Manager in this paper, but assume it to be present.

The contracts as specified in CoLa are units of cooperation between two or more agents, and have a three-level organization: messages, transactions and services.

Messages are defined using primitives such as request, assert, and authorize. These message types have pre-defined semantics as described in section 2, in terms of obligations and authorizations.

The agents that are involved in the contract and the messages that each of them uses as explicit speech act during the execution of the contract are specified at the start of the contract. The messages that are not defined here are implemented as implicit speech acts executed through some other action. For instance, the commitment of the company to deliver a product in this contract is not modelled as an explicit speech act. It is only implicit through the actual delivery of the product. Note that this is a choice made for this contract indicating that in this case there is no need to send a message indicating that the company commits itself to deliver the product.

For our example the explicit speech acts are as follows:

149

```
agents X: customer; Y: company

MESSAGES(X to Y)

  request_quotation == quotation.request_c;
  place_order/3     == request_a(partno,quantity,price);
  place_order/2     == order.request_c(partno,quantity);

MESSAGES(Y to X)

  refuse_quotation == quotation.refuse;
  give_quotation   == quotation.authorize;
  refuse_deliver   == order.refuse;
  request_payment  == pay.request_a;
```

The messages that are specified here correspond to the speech acts that are used
in the contract (either explicitly or implicitly). For instance, "request_quotation"
is defined as a request_c (corresponding to DIR_c in the logic), which is defined
local within the transaction "quotation". We do not specify all actions that are
used in the contract, but only the speech acts. So, the actions deliver and pay
are not specified at this place!

Messages that are aimed at the establishing (or adapting) a certain deontic
statement (that is, a conjunction of obligations and authorizations) are grouped
together in transactions. A typical example of a transaction is a request of the
client followed by a commit, or refuse, of the server. For each transaction, there
is a successful termination, indicated by the goal of the transaction, and non-
successful terminations. In the example we have the following transactions:

```
TRANSACTIONS
transaction quotation
  isa get_authorization(order(Partno, Quantity, Price));

transaction get_authorization(Alfa:action)
messages
    request_c(auth(Alfa));
    authorize(Alfa), refuse(authorize(Alfa));
goal
    authorize(Alfa)
end-transaction;
```

The above states that the transaction "quotation" is a specialization of the
transaction "get_authorization". This generic transaction is defined as a request
(based on charity) to get authorization, followed by an authorization or a refusal.

```
transaction order
messages
    request_c(deliver(Partno,Quantity));
```

```
    commit(deliver(Partno,Quantity,Price)),
    refuse(deliver(Partno,Quantity));
    accept(commit(deliver(Partno,Quantity,Price)))
goal
    {commit(deliver(Partno,Quantity,Price)),
        accept(commmit(deliver())) }
end_transaction;
```

The "order" transaction is defined for the cases where no quotation was given before. The request to deliver a product is therefore based on charity. The company then commits itself to deliver the product against a certain price (or refuses to deliver) after which the price has to be accepted by the customer.

```
transaction delivery (O: order)
messages
    declare(delivered(O));
    accept(delivered(O));
goal
    accept(delivered(O))
end-transaction;

transaction invoice(O: order)
messages
    request_a(transfer_money(O));
    commit(transfer_money(O));
goal
    commit(transfer_money(O))
end_transaction;
```

Finally, transactions that deal with the same deontic statements are grouped together in one service. The service, centered around an object, specifies how the object - the deontic statement - can be created, how it can be removed and, possibly, how it can be modified. In general, there are several ways in which the object can come into being or is removed. In the service, it is possible to specify also the consequences of a certain action, such as sanctions for not satisfying the obligation.

```
SERVICES
service quote
provided by Y
object
    auth(X,place_order/3)
attributes
    Partno: num(9);
    Quantity: integer;
    Price: money;
    Expiration_date: date
```

```
created by
    quotation
removed by
    expire(Expiration_date)
    withdraw            => {auth(X,request(sanction)) };
end-service;
```

The service "quote" is given by the company to the customer. It is centered around the authorization of the customer to order a product for a certain price. The authorization pertains to a certain product, quantity and price that are given in the attributes. The expiration date indicates when the offered quotation expires. The authorization is created by the quotation transaction and removed by the passing of the expiration date. It can also be removed by a withdrawal of the company, but this gives the customer the authorization to request some compensation.

```
service supply
provided by Y
object
    obl(Y,deliver)
attributes
    Partno: num(9);
    Quantity: integer;
    Price: money
created by
    place_order(Partno, Quantity, Price)
    order(Partno,Quantity)
removed by
    delivery        => {auth(Y,request_payment)};
    cancel_order    => {obl(X,pay(fine)) };
end-service;
```

The obligation for the company to deliver a product arises either directly from an authorized order message (after a quotation has been made) or from the order transaction (an order without previous quotation, followed by a commitment of the company).

```
service payment
provided by X
object
    obl(X,pay)
created by
    invoice
removed by
    transfer_money
    expire(date)    => {obl(X,pay(fine)) }
end-service
```

The last "service" of the contract concerns the payment of the order. After the delivery of the products, the company is authorized to request payment. This is done through the transaction "pay". This transaction always ends with an obligation of the customer to pay if the company is authorized to request payment. Note that if the message "request_payment" is used to create the obligation directly, this would result in an obligation to pay for the customer whenever the company asks for it, which is obviously not what we want.

The obligation to pay is not directly created by the delivery of the product, but arises from a request for payment which is authorized through the delivery of the product. This construction makes the contract more flexible than usually is the case where delivery of a product means a direct obligation to pay for it.

We now have described all the components of the contract in CoLa. The contract itself is the set of messages, transactions and services together.

It can be seen from the above that CoLa provides a means to describe the communications between agents and the resulting obligations and authorizations in a structured way, which makes it very suitable to describe contracts as given in the example above.

4 Conclusions

Although deontic logic has been applied in the field of Information Systems before, the dynamics of normative systems has received almost no attention. In this paper we have explored the way how deontic statements are created and adapted in communication processes, and the role they play in the regulation of communication itself. We have distinguished three different perspectives, corresponding with three validity claims that communicative agents can make: charity, authorization, power. As in human social systems, these perspectives can complement each other in the organization of interoperable computer systems.

We have shown how authorizations for specific acts can be requested, granted and also retracted, thereby creating a dynamic environment for establishing and derogating authorized norms.

Contracts were presented as a way of modularizing the normative specifications. The contracts can be described in CoLa, which provides a structured high level way to specify the contracts.

Both the negotiation phase to establish the contract as well as the contract itself can be modelled using our formalism.

Several open issues are left for further research. One is the use of conditions. In the deontic/illocutionary logic given in section 2, all deontic statements were unconditional. In practice, a certain obligation or authorization only obtains under certain conditions: a specific event, a specific time or time slot etc. In the directive that creates a certain deontic statement, an extra parameter "condition" should be added. We have not worked this out yet.

A second topic is the delegation and inheritance of authority. Under which conditions is it possible to delegate the authority to perform a certain action? Under which conditions is authority inherited through a power relationship?

A third topic of future research is the elaboration of contracts. In this paper, a contract is a set of norms. A contract gives rise to a certain communication process or protocol. Such a protocol can be implemented in a computer-computer or human-computer interface. Protocols are based on the essential speech acts given in the contract, but usually contain other speech acts as well, such as acknowledgement and reminding. A given protocol can be tested for completeness with respect to the basic contract, and also for internal completeness: whether every communicative obligation that is created, or can be created, is materialized in a possible communicative action.

A last topic for further research that we want to mention here is the relation between different contracts. One contract can be a specialisation of another contract or an extension of that contract. Also an agent can have contracts with different parties at the same time. We should be able to prove that these contracts are mutually consistent.

References

[Aus62]   J.L. Austin *How to do things with words* Oxford: Clarendon Press, 1962.

[DW92]   J.L.G. Dietz and G.A.M. Wiederhoven A comparison of the linguistic theories of Searle and Habermas as a basis for communication supporting systems *Linguistic Instruments in Knowledge Engineering (Riet, R.P van de, and R.A. Meersman (eds)* North-Holland, 1992.

[FGHW88] F. Flores, M. Graves,B. Hartfield,T. Winograd Computer Systems and the Design of Organizational Interaction *ACM Trans. on Information Systems* Vol.6, No.2, 1988.

[Lee88]   R. Lee Bureaucracies as Deontic Systems, *Trans. on Office Information Systems* Vol.6, No2, 1988, pp87-108.

[LL86]   E. Lehtinen, K. Lyytinen Action Based Model of Information Systems *Information Systems*, Vol.12, No3, 1986, pp299-317.

[Me88]   J.-J.Ch. Meyer A different approach to deontic logic: deontic logic viewed as a variant of dynamic logic, *Notre Dame Journal of Formal Logic* 29(1), 1988, pp.109-136.

[MW93]   J.-J.Ch. Meyer and R. Wieringa (eds.) *Deontic Logic in Computer Science* Wiley Professional Computing, 1993.

[Po93]   R. Power *Cooperation among organizations : the potential of computer supported cooperative work* Springer, Berlin. 1993.

[SV85]   J.R. Searle and D. Vanderveken *Foundations of illocutionary logic* Cambridge University Press. 1985.

[Se69]   J.R. Searle *Speech Acts* Cambridge University Press. 1969.

[We93]   H. Weigand Deontic aspects of communication *Deontic Logic in Computer Science (Meyer, Wieringa eds)* Wiley Professional Computing, 1993.

[WMW89] R.J. Wieringa, J.-J.Ch. Meyer and H. Weigand *Specifying dynamic and deontic integrity constraints* Data & Knowledge Engineering 4, 1989, pp.157-189.

Challenges in Applying Objects to Large Systems

Juha-Markus Aalto

Nokia Telecommunications, Cellular Systems
Mobile Switching, Network Management Systems
Hatanpäänvaltatie 36 A, 33100 Tampere, Finland
Juha-Markus.Aalto@ntc.nokia.com

Abstract. Object-orientation seems to be the winning approach in the war of software development paradigms. Compilers for the C programming language have been largely updated to support the object-oriented C++, modern CASE tools and software development methods are designed for object-oriented approaches, and more and more software development organizations believe that objects help them to cut costs and improve software quality.

A natural consequence of the popularity of object-oriented methods and tools is that today they are also used for developing large systems. This paper discusses how object technology affects the success factors of an organization developing large systems. This paper is based on experiences in institutionalizing object-oriented technology in the development organization of a large network management system called the Nokia OMC.

1   Introduction

Typically, examples in software engineering books show how a software engineering methodology can be applied to a relatively *small* application. This is usually done in order to keep the examples readable. Examples serve to clarify the author's ideas of how a specific approach can and should be applied under certain circumstances. The suggested text book approaches usually provide more or less half-baked ideas rather than real solutions to software process challenges. Unfortunately, many organizations develop also large systems on the basis of these books although a number of issues need to be solved before any of the proposed methods can successfully be applied to large projects.

The development of large systems differs considerably from that of small ones. The main differences are:

- Large systems are complex and require so much effort that they cannot be created by one individual; organized teams are needed. Good communication is essential both between and within these teams.
- Large systems are typically developed incrementally: New features are developed by reusing existing software. Enhancements to existing features are common;

changes in customers' business needs often bring about new software requirements.

- Large systems are often mission critical systems, such as air traffic control systems and telecommunications infrastructures. They are extremely important for the customer's business, and the quality of the delivered systems needs to be particularly high to ensure maximum reliability.
- The customers of companies developing large systems are typically other companies, not consumers. Therefore, the large systems need to fit into the business activity of the user organization.

The Nokia OMC is one of the leading network management systems for managing digital GSM networks. It is an example of a large system developed using object technology. It consists of more than one hundred concurrently running processes with over 1.000.000 LOC written in C++. The development of the system takes place in parallel main projects that each have several sub-projects. Each main project produces a release which consists of features that implement an increment to the functionality of the existing system. The size of an increment is typically 200.000 - 300.000 LOC. The Nokia OMC is a mission critical system for network operators who use it in building and monitoring their networks. Therefore, the requirements for software quality are high, and the functionality of the system needs to closely match the business activity of the operators.

A talented individual or two can implement outstanding applications using any methods (or none) if the problem domain is well understood and the application size is in the range of 10.000 - 100.000 LOC. Large systems, such as the Nokia OMC require a wide range of knowledge about the problem domain, and the technical complexity increases so much that the heroic efforts of one or a few gurus are not enough. The success of an organization developing large systems seems to mostly depend on the following factors:

- a competitive *product* matching the customers' needs,
- an effective and efficient *process*,
- feasible *technology* used in product and in its development,
- capable and motivated *personnel*, and
- carefully maintained *software assets*.

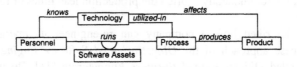

Fig. 1. Important success factors of a system supplier.

The relationships of the success factors are depicted in Figure 1. Perhaps the most important factor is that the *product,* in other words, the system to be developed, matches the customer's needs. A prerequisite for this is that the *process* that implements the system is effective in ensuring that all requirements are caught and implemented efficiently. Furthermore, the efficient implementation of the process is highly dependent on the skills and motivation of the *personnel*. Another basic competitive requirement is that the right *technology* is used in the product and in its development. The *software assets* of the system, such as code and documentation, are the results of the process that will be reused several times in the future. That property needs to be kept in good shape so that it can be further processed and sold to customers over several years.

This paper views the applicability of object-oriented approaches to software engineering from the viewpoint of the above-mentioned success factors that are important in developing large systems. Some problems recognized in popular methodologies, such as Object Modeling Technique (OMT) [13], Fusion [4] and Object-oriented Software Engineering [10], are highlighted. Solutions for these problems have been developed by Nokia Telecommunications and Nokia Research Center. The resulting methodology is called OMT++ [2], and it is based on the above mentioned methodologies.

2   Product Viewpoint

Nobody wants to buy a product that does not fulfill the needs of its users. A company developing such a product is soon out of the market place. The most critical phase in software development is therefore the requirements definition phase, during which the requirements for the system to be developed are identified, analyzed and documented. If the system is purchased by another company, which is typical for large systems, the system should make a part of the customer's business activity automatic or more manageable in order to improve the performance of the company. To be able to analyze and evaluate customer requirements, we need to understand the business activity of the customer.

Business process re-engineering (BPR) is an approach to business development in which all business related activities of a company are re-thought. Typically, the operations of the company are modeled as chains of activities that add value to the customer's business. These chains are called *core business processes*, and the idea is to streamline these processes and automate them using information technology. Typical goals are to dramatically shorten the production lead times or to reduce costs.

Jacobson has described how a company can re-engineer its operations using a modified use case approach of the *Object-oriented Software Engineering* (OOSE) method [10] called *Object-oriented Business Engineering* [11]. Business modeling techniques used in business engineering can also be utilized in software development, not only in business process re-engineering. A software supplier can 'reverse engineer' the relevant business processes of the customers in order to understand their business environment. The results can be utilized in software requirements analysis so that the software features can be well integrated in customers' business needs. Our on-going work has already verified the feasibility of a similar approach: It is possible to establish a continuous, traceable path from the customers' business processes to user interface actions, as depicted in Figure 2.

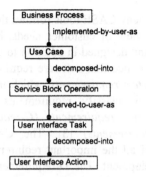

Fig. 2. From business processes to user interface actions with OMT++. The service blocks are sub-systems that are responsible for a set of closely related services.

It is likely that new object-oriented approaches to business area analysis will be published in the near future in addition to Object-oriented Business Engineering, since the object-oriented methods offer suitable modeling facilities for this purpose. It is also likely that business area analysis will constitute a front end for the requirements definition of other methods, too, in addition to OOSE and OMT++.

Business process modeling helps mostly in finding process related *functional requirements*. However, they are not the only requirements for software: there are also *non-functional* ones which correspond the requirements for the technical characteristics of the system, such as capacity, response times, reliability, and maintainability. The non-functional requirements are mostly related to the technical constraints of the target environment. However, quite a few of them can be derived from attributes of business processes such as business volumes, frequencies of operations, and the number of persons related to each activity.

Most of the object-oriented methods do not address non-functional requirements in particular, although they constitute an essential part of the specification work of applications. The hierarchy of customer needs (analogous to Maslow's one for human beings) for a new software system seems to be as follows:

1. First, the most essential functionality must exist and provide some useful results.
2. When the system is able to provide some results, the requirements concentrate on the stability of the system for long periods of time.
3. The capacity of the reliable and stable system must then be adequate and scaled up as the use and number of users increase.

4. In order to make full use of the capacity, the performance of the system must meet the users' daily needs.
5. When the system is reliable and fast enough to deal with its capacity, the user interface must be sufficiently flexible to ensure effective and pleasant use.

For instance, the life-cycle of many CASE tools follows the pattern above. Of course, the above list is a simplified view of customer needs, but it shows that there are several things to be analyzed and designed in addition to the objects and functions of the system. It is important to notice that software requirements are only part of all requirements known as the *system requirements*, which may be related to hardware, for instance. Another way to classify requirements is to divide them into *customer/user-oriented software requirements (C-requirements)* and *developer-oriented requirements (D-requirements)* [3]. The C-requirements provide the customer with a description of all the important requirements that are adequate for commitment to software development. The D-requirements are typically elaborated from C-requirements, and they provide the developer with a description of all the significant requirements adequate for the design and implementation of the software.

Most object-oriented analysis methods described in the text books, such as [13], concentrate on modeling facilities, especially conceptual modeling (e.g. object modeling). In addition to that, the methods have some notations for representing dynamic behavior and data transformations in the system. However, the requirements representation is only one part of the requirements definition. In particular, most of the suggested object-oriented analysis methods provide limited facilities for:

- identifying the requirements based on business area analysis,
- eliciting information related to requirements from people (including fact-finding and validation of results),
- deriving software requirements from system requirements,
- analyzing end-user tasks for user interface specification,
- identifying software development constraints,
- classifying requirements as mandatory or desirable requirements, and
- evaluating the feasibility of requirements.

Standards such as IEEE Standard 830, IEEE Guide to Software Requirements Specification [8] give valuable guide-lines on how to document the requirements. The popular object-oriented methods described in textbooks do not seem to address the documentation of requirements in general and non-functional requirements in particular. These kinds of elements from the traditional software engineering discipline need to be added to object-oriented methods in order to make them applicable to industrial strength system development, which fulfills the requirements necessary for the development of products that match customer needs.

3 Process Viewpoint

Successful implementation of large software systems requires a well-defined and managed software process. The process descriptions of the textbooks for object-oriented approaches are usually too loosely defined. Some examples of daily problems not addressed by object-oriented methods - in addition to the previously mentioned deficiencies in the requirements definition process - are:

- Detailed document templates with check-lists for the artifacts are not provided.
- Specification practices of the user interface are often neglected, although usability is one of the most important elements of the system from the user's point of view.
- Software architecture guidelines are vague, and rules for decomposing a large system into processes and libraries are not presented.
- Project management issues are not discussed in detail. However, OOSE and Fusion provide some tips for project planning.
- Although most of the effort is put in modifying the existing software, all existing methods provide proper support for the development from new only. Jacobson et al. [10] discuss this problem extensively, but provide no 'silver bullet' for solving it.

A process model suitable for developing large systems must scale up so that the complexity of the system and the implementation projects can be managed. The process must be defined well enough to be repeatable and produce reusable artifacts that can be processed in future projects. Flexibility in division of labor is also important, especially in large projects, where specialization is required to successfully carry out various activities such as analysis, architectural design, and user interface specification. As an example, Jacobson et al. explain the difference between the OOSE book and their Objectory process description: The book provides only fundamental ideas of the process and a simplified version of it; a detailed process description with examples takes up about 1200 pages [10]. Our experiences of adapting OMT to OMT++ support this view; a lot of effort is needed to establish a solid software process documentation that is detailed enough.

A detailed process description does not guarantee success, though. The greatest challenge also in object-oriented software development is the *institutionalization* of the new process model, which means major changes in work methods. Successful institutionalization requires strong and large management commitment, adequate funding, readiness for change, and resources for training and support. However, these outward circumstances are not available for all software engineering organizations.

Many organizations claim that they use some methodology such as Structured Analysis/Design, but very few of them really follow the process model. The 'use' of the methodologies usually means that some part of the modeling facilities (such as object diagrams) are used. Bill Curtis has estimated that about 75% of organizations were at initial level 1 of the Capability Maturity Model for Software, CMM, in 1994 [7]. This leads to the conclusion that about 75% or organizations starting to use object-oriented approaches will face severe problems when taking them into use. Software process models based on object-orientation (or any models) cannot be institutionalized if there are no feasible ways of introducing changes into the organization and verifying their implementation.

In order to facilitate institutionalization, the object-oriented methods need to be adapted to fit into the organization's existing processes. Obviously, they also need to be extended to support the individual needs of the company's software development, such as the large system issues. In the development of OMT++, we have recognized that software engineers need detailed guidelines for implementing features effectively in a large existing system. There are close connections between the four important elements in software development: software process, software architecture, software components, and the tools used, as depicted in Figure 3. A process model explains the chain of activities leading to achievement of the expected artifacts. A model of the system architecture is needed to illustrate the implementation structure of the system: What should be modified, and how new functionality should be added. The architecture of the system should be supported by a suitable set of components forming a platform for applications, and tools should be available for making everything as automated as possible.

The existing object-oriented approaches are on a general level and they do not usually rely on any particular software architecture model. We have successfully integrated the process model in an architecture framework based on the Model-View-Controller approach in OMT++ [9]. In addition, we have integrated tools such as a GUI builder together with the process model [12]. Our experiences suggest that process models, architecture models, components, and tools should not be considered as separated issues; they should be integrated in an integral whole. An approach called *design patterns* [6] seems a promising way of documenting the experience related to integrating these elements of software development.

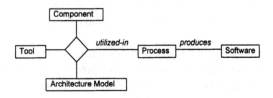

Fig. 3. Elements of software development.

4   Technology Viewpoint

The right technology solutions are essential for the success of the product in the long run. This is particularly true for large systems which may live for decades. Because of the rapid development of software technology, any part of the current systems may need to be totally rewritten within the next ten years. We may not be able to avoid that, but we may be able to avoid another risk: choosing immature technology that the customers do not want to buy now or even in a couple of years. If we loose a customer once due to unsuitable technology, our window of opportunity may close, pushing us out of the market place.

From the software supplier's point of view, the main benefits of object technology are derived from the expected improvements in the productivity of work. The elements of object-technology used in carrying out that work consist of:

- Computer-Aided Software Engineering (CASE) tools, and
- components (both Commercial-off-the-shelf (COTS) and internal reusable components).

Although tools are getting better all the time, they cannot be considered mature in general. CASE tool vendors have problems in implementing support for methods due to the absence of rigorous semantics. For instance, code generation and reverse engineering facilities of object-oriented design CASE tools are moderate. Another problem is capacity: Large-scale object models are not truly supported, because the methods do not support them either.

Good programming environments for C++ with all necessary facilities, such as compilers, symbolic debuggers, and browsers, are available. Yet the standardization situation of the C++ programming language is a problem. Features such as templates and exceptions are not properly standardized, and the implementations of the compilers have deficiencies. These deficiencies decrease the portability of systems implemented in C++. In order to minimize the problems related to the immature definition of C++, the use of these C++ features should still be avoided.

Today, implementation tools can probably be selected so that the selected tools are still supported after, say, five years. The main stream object-oriented programming languages, C++ and Smalltalk, seem to be safe selections due to extensive support of tool vendors. Selecting any other object-oriented programming language to develop systems - which are maintained for years - is a risk.

The number of available COTS components is strongly dependent on the programming language used. C++ is often the best choice, since many of the component interfaces are defined using C programming language or C++. An important factor in large scale development is that the internal components can be used now and in the future. To make this possible, only tools and programming languages having high credibility should be used.

Most customers are not interested in the implementation tools used in the development of their system. However, the customers want to know that the credibility of the used technology is adequate. From the customer's point of view, the most important third-party software is the database management system. Object databases are considered to replace relational databases like object-orientation is replacing functional decomposition. Although object databases have several advantages, they are not considered better than relational databases in all types of applications [1]. An important commercial aspect is that many customers of large systems already have some legacy system in place. It is likely that they are not even willing to administer object databases in the near future. It will take some time before the credibility of object database products is so high that customer organizations are willing to include them in their information management policies. This is an example of a solution that is attractive for the development organization but may not be so attractive for practical reasons.

5   Personnel Viewpoint

Competent and motivated personnel is, no doubt, one of the most important success factors of any expert organization. There are great differences in the individual productivity of work depending on the experience and skills of software engineers. Attitudes and the culture created by personnel contribute strongly to the future of the organization: Readiness for change and for learning new things is important in software engineering, where new technology brings changes continuously. On the other hand, positive changes in processes often increase motivation, if the pace of the changes is not too fast.

Object-orientation also represents a change for many companies and individuals. Currently, it seems to be quite difficult to recruit personnel with a suitable skill-base for object-oriented software development. It may be relatively easy to find a C++ programmer, but although the programmer knows the syntax, he or she may not have internalized the idea of object-oriented programming in the first place. Maybe the 'worst case' is an experienced C++ programmer who has not internalized the concepts of object-oriented development, but who has a lot of experience of the 'wrong' way of designing C++ programs. In any case, an employer cannot be really sure about the object-oriented capabilities of job seekers. We have found it necessary to give all newcomers extensive training in object-oriented thinking, analysis, design, and programming.

It is unfortunate that there is no one or even a few winning 'industrial methods' among object-oriented approaches. OMT seems to be popular when considering the notations used in software engineering articles, for instance. However, none of the methods is as dominating as Structured Analysis/Structured Design (SA/SD) among approaches based on functional decomposition. Furthermore, when we consider the fact that the methods are not detailed enough to establish a repeatable process, it is obvious that any employer faces problems when trying to recruit a software analyst or designer who could immediately start using objects in a productive way. This jeopardizes the first schedule-critical projects implemented by newcomers.

An organization developing large systems needs to assure that the capabilities of the personnel are adequate. Since object technology is still a new thing for many companies and university training programs, it is harder to find suitable people for projects implemented using object technology than for projects using traditional methods.

6   Software Assets Viewpoint

In OMT++, a *feature* is a product characteristic offered to customers which fulfills a set of customer requirements. A feature may consist of other features, i.e. the concept is hierarchical. Features often correspond to a set of use cases, but features are not only functional. A feature may be, for instance, a different solution to the same functional need, such as an open communications interface instead of an existing proprietary interface.

Large systems, such as the Nokia OMC, are developed in increments so that new features are designed on top of the existing system. Features are the units that are analyzed, designed, implemented, and tested. The mass of code and related documentation such as specifications, design documents, test cases, and customer documents, comprise the *software assets* of the company that are needed to develop new features. The software development of large systems relies extensively on the large-scale reuse of software assets. If they deteriorate, their reuse will become less productive, and the quality of the software will decline. The future of the organization will thus be endangered if the software assets are not properly managed.

Large systems need to be decomposed into *sub-systems* in order to manage their complexity. The need for a proper product breakdown structure is two-fold. First, we need to manage the set of features provided by a complex system through a structure mapped to the customers' needs. Only if the features of the product are understood as a whole, the evolution of the product parts can be managed consistently. If a holistic view to the product is missing, it is quite impossible to establish any clear strategy that would ensure that the system is competitive also in years to come. Secondly, we need to decompose the technical complexity into manageable pieces in order to make the construction of the system possible.

The object-oriented methods today give little support for managing the characteristics of a large system. Decomposition into sub-systems is typically seen only in the design phase, although the classification and management of requirements call for a product breakdown structure already in the analysis phase. Some methods, such as Coad-

Yourdon OOA [5] and OOSE [10], provide facilities for decomposing the object model into parts (called *subjects* by Coad and Yourdon and *sub-systems* by Jacobson et al.) but even they do not seem to give any practical guidelines on how to allocate functional requirements to sub-systems. As a consequence, the traceability of functional requirements is lost because they cannot be traced to sub-systems.

It is not feasible to decompose large systems into sub-systems in the design phase so that one object class contains all behavior (i.e. attributes and operations) related to it. One 'real world' object may be viewed from dozens of perspectives and it may have hundreds of operations and attributes in a large system. The same operation names may even have different meanings depending on viewpoints. On the other hand, independence of decomposed parts is one of the golden rules of any architecture design. In large system development, dozens of software development groups might need to access the same entity object class if all behavior relating to it were centralized into one single class allocated to one sub-system. That would make the maintenance of these software assets quite impossible. The same goes for the division of labor in software development.

In OMT++, the system is decomposed into sub-systems, which are called *service blocks*, first in the analysis phase. The sub-system division is mainly based on the views that the users of the system have of objects of the problem domain. This product breakdown structure makes it possible to develop service blocks independently and coordinate their dependent product characteristics. In the design phase, service blocks providing implementation services are created in order to establish a layered architecture. They provide services for application designers. Each service block in the design phase consists of *program blocks*, which are either *libraries* or *processes*. The program blocks are the key-elements in software configuration management, and they consist of *files* to be managed by revision control mechanisms. This product breakdown structure is depicted in Figure 4.

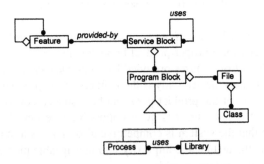

Fig. 4. Concepts of product breakdown structure in OMT++.

Large system development with OMT++ is thus based on features which are allocated to service blocks, which in turn are implemented by communicating processes developed using a set of libraries. Unfortunately, such key-concepts are almost totally missing from existing methods, or they are supported only by 'work-arounds'. For instance, there is no notational support for all these concepts. It goes without saying that traceability issues or pragmatic guidelines are not addressed by methods such as OMT, OOSE and Fusion. As emphasized earlier in this paper, the methods described in the respective text books concentrate on developing software from new; maintenance of software assets is not properly described in them.

However, object-oriented approaches to software development offer a good foundation for creating software based on stable concepts expressed in terms of objects. The main challenge faced in large-scale use of these methods is scaling them up. In addition to that, analysis and design models need to be separated in order to allow easy and secure updating of both of them as enhancements and new features are implemented. All document templates need to be considered from the maintenance point of view: How easy it is to add new functionality, which other models need to be updated, etc. These are the challenges of methodologists who deal with large object projects aiming at enhancing the reuse of software assets.

7 Conclusions

Nokia Telecommunications and Nokia Research Center have developed a methodology called OMT++ [2], which supports the development of the large systems in particular. OMT++ is based on OMT, OOSE and Fusion. The observations of this paper are based on experiences of developing OMT++, and on the information provided by text books about these popular methods [13], [10], [4]. The findings concentrate on situations where the methods are applied to large projects. However, many of the findings apply to small organizations as well.

Object technology has several advantages, but many unresolved issues need to be addressed before it can be fully utilized in the development of large-scale systems. In this paper, these issues were discussed from perspective of the success factors that are important for an organization developing large applications. The main findings were:

- From the *product perspective,* object-oriented analysis methods need to be supplemented with practices for identifying and documenting non-functional requirements as well. Business process modeling seems to be a suitable front end for the requirements definition process; it helps in finding the functional requirements in particular. The modeling facilities of object-oriented methods seem to be well suited for this kind of business modeling.

- From the *process perspective,* the object-oriented methods are too loosely defined if a repeatable, managed process is what is expected. The object-oriented methods support development from new, but give little support for incremental development of large systems. Object-orientation calls for a new way of thinking, and this, in turn, requires that the organization can manage the change. The immaturity of most software engineering organizations causes trouble in the institutionalization of object-oriented technology. Its buy-in can be facilitated by pragmatic guide-lines which not only define the process steps, but also integrate the use of tools, software components, and the architecture model in the process.

- There are two *technology perspectives*: that of the customers and that of the development organization. The tools used in development are maturing, but several problems still exist, mostly related to the loose definition of methods. Those technology solutions that are attractive to development organizations, such as object databases, may not be so attractive for user organizations. Correct timing and the selection of a product with high credibility are of vital importance to long term success of systems which may be used and developed for decades.

- The new way of thinking is a challenge from the *personnel perspective* - both for employees and employers. Individuals need to develop their skill-base in order to be productive in utilizing the possibilities provided by objects. Employers will face problems in recruiting for some years, in other words, as long as the majority of job-seekers has inadequate knowledge of object-orientation. Large projects requiring a lot of resources need to establish wide training programs in order to create a suitable skill-base for the organization.

- Object-oriented methods are problematic from the *software assets perspective* as far as the development of large systems is concerned. Basic concepts of large systems such as feature, process, and library do not constitute a part of the concepts of the methods. In practice, support for requirements traceability ends when a system is divided into sub-systems. Since concepts, such as process, are missing, no pragmatic support is provided for mapping objects to processes by methods such as OOSE, OMT or Fusion. They are mostly meant for developing one application from scratch. A solid product breakdown structure needs to be established in order to manage the functionality provided by the product as a whole also in the long run. This kind of manageable structure enables productivity gains through the large-scale reuse, and provides a basis for the product structure which can be enhanced by new features for years to come. When the functionality becomes manageable, another great challenge is posed by the system architecture. The existing methods do not give clear guide-lines for developing a robust software architecture for systems having hundreds of communicating processes and thousands of classes.

It seems quite obvious that object-orientation will be the mainstream software development approach of this decade. Many challenges still call for pragmatic solutions in order to make objects into productive building blocks for large systems.

8   Acknowledgments

This paper has been reviewed by my colleagues Ari Aalto, Ari Jaaksi, Hannu Pahkala and Sari Hänninen from Nokia Telecommunications, by Ilkka Haikala from Tampere

University of Technology, and by Kalle Lyytinen from the University of Jyväskylä. I would like to thank them all for their valuable comments on the earlier versions of this paper. I would also like to thank the reviewers, Pasi Rajala and Pertti Tapola from Nokia Telecommunications for the valuable debates which have helped me in preparing this paper.

References

1. A. Aalto: Data Management Solutions in an Object-oriented Application. Licentiate thesis, Tampere University of Technology, 1994 (in Finnish).
2. J-M. Aalto: A. Jaaksi: Object-oriented Development of Interactive Systems with OMT++. In: R. Ege, M. Singh, B. Meyer (Eds.): Proceedings of the Fourteenth International Conference TOOLS Santa Barbara 1994. Prentice-Hall, 1994.
3. J. Brackett: Software Requirements. SEI Curriculum Module SEI-CM-19-1.2, Carnegie-Mellon University, 1990.
4. D. Coleman, P. Arnold, S. Bodoff, C. Dollin, H. Gilchrist, F. Hayes, P.Jeremaes: The Fusion Object-Oriented Analysis and Design Method. Prentice Hall, 1994.
5. P. Coad, E. Yourdon: Object-oriented Analysis. Prentice-Hall, 1991.
6. E. Gamma, R. Helm, R. Johnson, J. Vlissides: Design Patterns: Elements of Reusable Object-oriented Software. Addison-Wesley, 1994.
7. W. Gibbs: Software's Chronic Crisis. Scientific American. September, 1994.
8. IEEE: IEEE Guide to Software Requirements Specification. ANSI/IEEE Std 830-1984. IEEE, 1984.
9. A. Jaaksi: Implementing Interactive Applications in C++. Software Practice and Experience. John Wiley & Sons, 1995 (in print).
10. I. Jacobson, M. Christerson, P. Jonsson, G. Övergaard: Object-oriented Software Engineering - a Use Case Driven Approach. Addison-Wesley, 1992
11. I. Jacobson, M. Ericsson, A. Jacobson. The Object Advantage. Business Process Re-engineering with Object Technology. Addison-Wesley, 1994
12. V. Punkka: Intelligent Reusable User Interface Components. The X Resource, Issue 13. O'Reilly & Assoc. Inc., 1995.
13. J. Rumbaugh, M. Blaha, W. Premerlani, F. Eddy, W. Lorensen: Object-oriented Modeling and Design. Prentice-Hall, 1991.

Feasibility of Flexible Information Modelling Support

T.F. Verhoef[1] and A.H.M. ter Hofstede[2]

[1]ID Research
Kastanjelaan 4
NL-3833 AN Leusden
The Netherlands
e-mail: DVerhoef@idr.iaf.nl

[2]Department of Information Systems
University of Nijmegen
Toernooiveld 1
NL-6525 ED Nijmegen
The Netherlands
e-mail: arthur@zeus.cs.kun.nl

Abstract

The necessity of CASE tools for system development is beyond dispute. The current generation of CASE tools, however, is too inflexible to provide adequate modelling support. One of the proposed solutions to this problem is the development of so-called *CASE-shells*. A CASE shell is a method independent CASE tool, which may be instantiated with a specific method to become a CASE tool supporting that method. As such, a CASE shell provides complete flexibility. This paper does not address the benefits of CASE shells, as they are completely clear, but focuses on the *feasibility* of this concept from a theoretical as well as a practical point of view.

1 Introduction

CASE tools are currently considered to be an indispensable part of the systems engineer's toolkit. Justification of CASE tools is no longer subject of debate. and [Flo86]). Naturally, the range of the required facilities should be thoroughly understood before using automated tools, see also [BS87]. In this reference an environment (automated or not) is proposed supporting the *practising information engineer* in the use of suitable techniques, depending on the current situation. CASE tools, however, have the problem that the view of the information systems development life cycle to be supported has been *hard-coded* in these tools, and therefore cannot be changed or customised to include also knowledge that is based upon information engineers' practical experience. By consequence, information engineers are left with the problem of finding a way of applying these rigid tools in their information engineering practice.

From the mid-1980s onwards, research has focused on this problem. It is claimed that automated tools are preferably built according to a *CASE shell* architecture.

Such an architecture allows for the modification and extension of the tool's behaviour as the tool includes explicit and adaptable method knowledge. As a consequence, information engineers are able to adapt support tools to their working styles instead of the other way around. Crucial for the development of a CASE shell is the availability of a suitable and formally defined technique for the representation of method knowledge. Such a technique is referred to as a *meta-modelling technique*. Method knowledge represented in a CASE shell according to such a technique is called a *meta-model*.

The concept of a CASE shell is not new. Commercial products such as Toolbuilder of IPSYS Software, Virtual Software Factory of Systematica and MetaDesign of Meta Software Corporation or academic products such as RAMATIC [BBD+89], Metaview [STM88] and MetaPlex [CN89], claim to generate CASE tools tailored to specific methods and organisations. Even a tool exists (MetaEdit [SLTM91]), that supports the modification of meta-models. However, all these shells focus on the support of modelling techniques and hardly pay attention to the modelling process (the importance of which is stressed in [KDH86], [Pot89], [WH90], and [LM86], among others). Furthermore, the degree of support of modelling techniques which they offer is limited, due to the low expressive power of the meta-modelling techniques used.

The focus of this paper is on the *feasibility* of flexible support of information modelling in the early phases and as such on the feasibility of CASE shells. Flexible support is of course considered to be feasible if its benefits outweigh its realisation effort. As the benefits are clear, this feasibility study focuses on the effort needed to realise adequate flexible support. This effort is determined by the complexity of the modelling knowledge to be captured in general, and the diversity needed to support *individual* information engineers. As a result, it is important to know (1) the complexity of information modelling in the early phases and (2) the extent to which flexibility is needed in these phases.

With respect to the first research question, it can be remarked that the early phases of systems development are still poorly understood (cf. [GC88]). Activities in these stages are characterised by incompleteness and vagueness [Bel85]. Terminology is often fuzzy and not standardised. Therefore, a prerequisite for dealing with the first research question is a language in which information modelling concepts can be adequately expressed, i.e. an adequate meta-modelling technique. State-of-the-art meta-modelling techniques, as described in [AC92], [HÖ92], [Bri90], and [SLTM91], are not fully suited for this purpose. They do not have sufficient expressive power to capture information modelling concepts and relations between these concepts, and tend to neglect the modelling process. In addition to that they rarely have a formal semantics and therefore only tend to add to the current confusion with respect to information modelling (see also [HW92]). In section 2, focus is on the various aspects of information modelling and their relations, essential for flexible support. In section 3, techniques are described that are capable of formally describing the aspects described in section 2. Focus in this section is not on the techniques as such, but rather on the *inherent* complexity of an adequate meta-modelling technique.

With respect to the second research question, it can be remarked that relatively little is known about the diversity of information modelling processes in practice and the corresponding degree of flexibility needed for adequate support. Empirical studies reported in the literature (e.g. [Gui90a], [Gui90b], [Bal87], [Wij91] and [BB93]) show that information modelling knowledge as applied by *experienced* information engineers turns out to deviate from modelling knowledge described in textbooks, regarding both modelling concepts and the way models using these concepts are constructed. These studies served as a starting point for the experiments described in section 4, which focused more closely on the precise behaviour of information modelling experts and the degree of flexibility needed for adequate support.

In section 5 the findings of the previous sections are summarised and the feasibility of adequate flexible support of information modelling processes in the early phases is addressed. The question arises whether the concept of a CASE shell is a realistic goal, given the inherent complexity of an adequate meta-modelling technique and the desired degree of flexibility.

2   A View on Information Modelling

Information modelling processes can be looked upon from many different perspectives, depending on the underlying goal. From a management point of view, resources, deadlines, and quality requirements are important. From a collaboration perspective, the focus will be on communication between individuals in groups. Given our goal, the investigation of the feasibility of flexible support, *knowledge* about the information modelling processes to be supported is important. This knowledge has to be reflected in flexible information modelling support environments. Therefore, this section addresses our view on information modelling by exploring the structure of the repository of a CASE shell.

Essentially, three orthogonal dimensions are recognised within the repository. In its most elementary form, the structure of the repository of a CASE shell can thus be represented as a 2×2×2 cube, see figure 1. These dimensions are discussed subsequently.

It is important to realise that the *combination* of these, as such relatively well-known, dimensions poses significant demands on the, by consequence inherent, complexity of meta-modelling techniques necessary for adequate information modelling support. Section 3 may be interpreted as a justification for this statement.

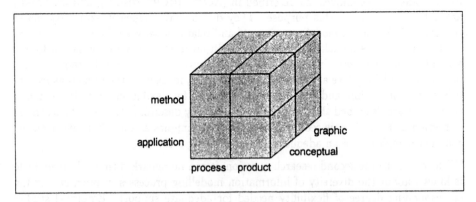

Figure 1: Information modelling dimensions

The first dichotomy is that of *method* level versus *application* level, also referred to as *types* versus *instances*. The method level is concerned with knowledge which may be *used* by information engineers. The method level controls the ways how information modelling processes may be performed, and defines which products may result from those information modelling processes. The application level is concerned with information which *results from* projects for specific organisations and applications by a specific group of information engineers. The application level is an *instantiation* of the method level.

The second dimension is that of *process* versus *product*: in order to provide information modelling support, it is necessary to have knowledge about the (intermediary) products and their relationships on the one hand, and about the underlying modelling process on the other hand. In other words, both questions "*what* should be produced?" and "*how* should it be produced?" should be answered. In [Wij91], the process side is referred to as the *way of working*, while the product side is referred to as the *way of modelling*.

Knowledge about information modelling processes is structured by several key concepts. It is necessary to know which *tasks* may be performed as part of an information modelling process. Tasks can be large tasks: "Perform the Business Area Analysis" within the Information Engineering method, and can be minor tasks: "Add a total role constraint to an Information Structure Diagram" within the NIAM method ([NH89]). These examples show that *decomposition* is a key concept too: tasks may be decomposed into subtasks. Knowledge about information modelling processes also concerns the flow of control: which tasks may be performed next?

Knowledge about information modelling products shows the structure of and the relationships between information modelling products. Examples of information modelling products are a "list of requirements", a "CRUD matrix", a "cardinality constraint", and an "organisation hierarchy". Examples of structure and relationships: "attribute types belong to entity types" and "organisation hierarchies consist of organisation units".

This completes the discussion of the second dimension. It should be clear that the two dimensions are orthogonal: both knowledge about information modelling processes and knowledge about information modelling products exist at method level and at application level. To clarify this, it may be specified, at method level, that the following tasks are to be performed: (i) "Select manager for interview session", (ii) "Interview manager", and as a result (iii) "Refine organisation model". These three tasks may be succeeded by the decision (iv) "Is the organisation model at the desired level of detail?", which triggers task (i) if the outcome is negative, and which leads to continuation if the outcome is positive. Correspondingly, execution of these tasks in a specific project, at application level, may lead to dozens of specific interviews and specific model refinements. Analogously, a notion such as "entity type" on the method level, may lead to many instances on the application level, e.g. "Customer" and "Article".

The third dichotomy concerns the difference between *conceptual* and *graphical* knowledge. Evidently, models must be represented in one way or another: diagrams, matrices, tables, lists, and program specifications are examples. A clear distinction should be made between the *modelling concepts* and their *external notation*. In [SBL89] it is argued that some methods allow alternative equivalent notations for one and the same modelling concept, but that on the other hand similar graphical and textual topologies can represent different types of modelling concepts.

A similar argumentation is valid for the process oriented view on information modelling. If one looks at some of the commercially available CASE tools, one observes different ways of model manipulation, for example, how entities can be created in entity relationship diagrams. In IEW one action within the ERD window suffices to create an entity. In Excelerator a menu selection has to be performed first, after which one can point at the location preferred.

This third distinction is particularly important for CASE shells. In some way or another, it has to be specified how models appear on the screen and how actions can be performed on these represented models. Furthermore, the specification of graphical knowledge allows information engineers to change the user interface of tools to their own preferences.

Again, it should be clear that this third axis is orthogonal in relation to the two previous ones. Both knowledge about information modelling processes and information modelling products have graphical counterparts. Modelling concepts such as data flows and organisation units are related to graphical notions such as arrows and boxes. Conceptual tasks such as additions of model components lead to graphical interaction patterns such as menu selections, object clicking and dragging, and so on.

3   Complexity of Meta-Modelling

A *meta-modelling technique* is a technique in which modelling knowledge can be expressed. As such, a meta-modelling technique should at least be capable of capturing the various perspectives on information modelling as described in the previous section. This implies that a meta-modelling technique should have sufficient *expressive power*. There are, however, other requirements that meta-modelling techniques have to fulfil.

As a meta-model should not be ambiguous, a meta-modelling technique should be *formally defined* (both syntax and semantics, see also [HW92]). It has to *abstract from implementation details*. Meta-models often need to be validated with modelling experts, therefore a meta-modelling technique should support the construction of *comprehensible* meta-models (e.g. offer graphical representations, decomposition mechanisms etc.). Finally, for the development of CASE-shells meta-models should be *executable*.

In this section, (partial) meta-modelling techniques for the various perspectives on information modelling are outlined. As stated before, the goal of this section is to stress the inherent complexity of meta-modelling rather than to provide an in-depth treatment of the various techniques. This section reflects the view on information modelling presented in the previous section. Section 3.1 concerns the representation of product oriented knowledge, section 3.2 concerns the representation of process oriented knowledge. Both these sections exclude the representation of graphical knowledge, so they are restricted to conceptual knowledge.

3.1 Representing a Way of Modelling

Modelling techniques in general contain concepts with complex structures and their models usually have to satisfy quite complex rules. To capture these structures and rules, a powerful data modelling technique is required, together with a powerful constraint modelling technique. In this section the data modelling technique PSM and the constraint modelling language LISA-D are highlighted. The Predicator Set Modelling technique (PSM) has been specifically defined with the representation of complex structures, often needed for meta-modelling, in mind. PSM is defined in [HW93], and LISA-D in [HPW93].

The elementary notions of object type, relationship, and role are assumed to be well-known. For their graphical representation, the NIAM style has been adopted. First, the necessity of *complex* objects and object inheritance is illustrated by several meta-modelling problems. Subsequently, attention is paid to constraints to represent *complex* rules in product knowledge.

3.1.1 Object Composition

Knowledge about information modelling products can be characterised as structured in a complex way. For example, the information modelling product "entity-relationship diagram" consists of a large variety of information model components. To describe these composition relationships between modelling concepts, PSM offers three representation mechanisms for object composition: set types, sequence types, and schema types.

An instance of a *set type* is a set of instances of its *element type*. As a simple example of the use of set types in the context of meta-modelling, consider the total role constraint in NIAM. An example of such a constraint is depicted in figure 2.

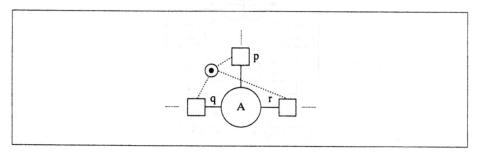

Figure 2: A sample total role constraint in NIAM

In this figure the total role constraint requires every instance of entity type A to participate in at least one of the roles p, q and r. Syntactically, a total role constraint is nothing more (or less) than a *set* of roles. Total role constraints have no other identification than their constituing roles. In a meta-model of NIAM, the total role constraint should therefore be modelled as a set type having an object type "Role" as its element type (see figure 3).

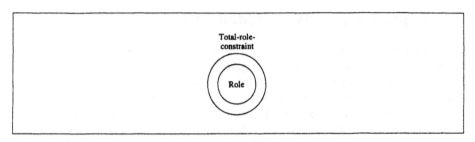

Figure 3: An example of a set type in the context of a meta-model of NIAM

Sequence types can be compared to set types. The differences are that, in the case of sequence types, the ordering of elements is important and elements may occur more than once. An instance of a sequence type is a sequence (tuple) of instances of its element type. A clarifing example of the use of sequence types is given in [Hof93] where a meta-model of JSD entity structure diagrams is explored. This meta-model captures the fact that an action can be decomposed into a *sequence* of other actions.

The third and most complex representation mechanism within PSM is schema objectification. Schema objectification allows to define part of a schema as an object type (referred to as *schema type*). Schema objectification can thus be seen as a decomposition mechanism. An instance of a schema type is an instantiation of the associated schema part. Schema types are particularly important for meta-modelling as they allow for a natural representation of decomposition constructs in modelling techniques. As an example of a schema type, consider the meta-model of Activity graphs as shown in figure 4.

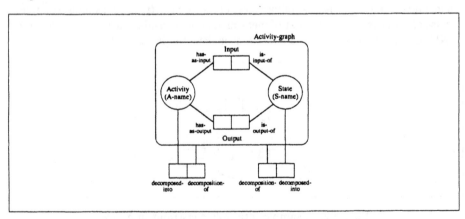

Figure 4: An example of a schema type in the context of a meta-model of activity graphs

Activity graphs are bipartite directed graphs consisting of activities and states. States can be input and output for activities and can be compared to flows in DFDs. Both states and activities can be decomposed into other activity graphs. Figure 4 shows the use of the concept of Schema type to represent the meta-model of Activity graphs. "Activity graph" is a schema type, the decomposition relation is reflected by the binary relationships to "Activity" and "State".

3.1.2   Object Inheritance

PSM offers two representation mechanisms for the representation of inheritance of properties between modelling concepts: specialisation and generalisation.

Specialisation, also referred to as subtyping, is a mechanism for representing one or more (possibly overlapping) subtypes of an object type. Intuitively a specialisation relation between a subtype and a supertype implies that the instances of the subtype are also instances of the supertype. Specialisation relations are organised in so-called specialisation "hierarchies". The top of a specialisation hierarchy is referred to as the *pater familias*. Identification of subtypes is derived from their supertypes, as object types inherit all properties from their ancestors in the specialisation hierarchy. Graphically, each specialisation relation is represented as an arrow. Specialisation is useful in the context of meta-modelling as it allows the definition of specific subsets of instances of certain object types for which only specific relations are important.

Generalisation is a mechanism that allows for the creation of new object types by uniting existing object types. For generalisation it is typically required that the generalised object type is covered by its constituent object types (or *specifiers*). Furthermore, properties are inherited "upward" in a generalisation hierarchy instead of "downward", which is the case for specialisation. This also implies that the identification of a generalised object type depends on the identification of its specifiers. Generalisation allows for the specification of recursive structures. In the context of meta-modelling this is important as e.g. document structures often are of a recursive nature. Graphically, generalisation is represented by means of dashed arrows.

3.1.3   Constraints

PSM offers a number of graphical constraint types for the representation of rules which hold for modelling products. Examples can be found in the meta-model of Yourdon DFDs presented in figure 5. This meta-model also demonstrates the need for the many type construction mechanisms in PSM. First the DFD concepts which appear in this meta-model are clarified.

According to [You89], a DFD pictures a system as a network of functional processes. The main components of a DFD are processes, flows, data stores, and terminators. A process transforms input into output. Processes have a process specification or are decomposed into a DFD. Each process has a number. Control processes are a special kind of process. A control process does not process data, but coordinates other processes. The operation of a control process is modelled by means of a state transition diagram. Terminators represent external processes communicating with the system under consideration. Data stores model collections of data "at rest". Data stores may be external, which means that they are used for communication with the outside world.

Flows represent data "in motion". Several types of flows exist. A simple flow has a source and a destination. Processes, data stores and terminators can be source or

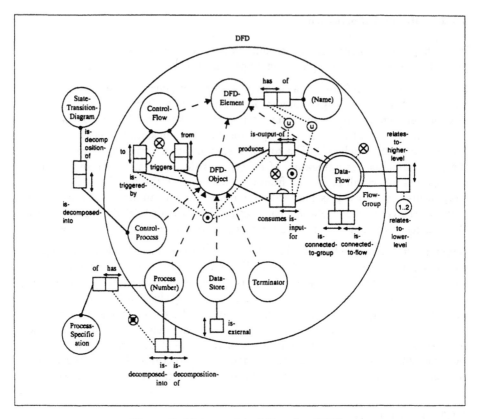

Figure 5: Meta-model of Yourdon DFDs

destination of simple flows. A complex flow consists of a set of flows converging to one other flow or a flow diverging into a set of other flows. Control flows represent triggers, i.e. signals or interrupts.

Some of the graphical constraints in this meta-model deserve some further explanation. We only explain some of the graphical constraints in figure 5. The *total role* constraint on the role named "has" attached to the object type "DFD-Element" expresses that each instance of this object type has to have a "Name". The two *exclusion* constraints attached to binary relationship types express that the source and the destination of a "Data-Flow" are different and that the source and the destination of a "Control-Flow" are different. The two *uniqueness* constraints each over two relationship types, express that no two "Data-Flows" with the same "Name" have the same "DFD-Object" as destination and that no two "Data-Flows" with the same "Name" have the same "DFD-Object" as source. The *occurrence frequency* constraint on the role with role name "relates-to-lower-level" expresses that a "Data-Flow" is related to at most two other "Data-Flows" on a lower decomposition level. The exclusion constraint attached to the set type "Flow-Group" states that a "Data-Flow" does not occur in more than one "Flow-Group".

Of course, there are many other constraints that have to be fulfilled. These constraints, however, are too complex to be expressed using the graphical constraint types offered by PSM. It should even be noticed that the strive for expressing the most complex constraints graphically might decrease the comprehensibility of the meta-model under consideration. Figure 5 provides a good example of a meta-model which cannot be grasped at once, even in spite of the fact that only a minority of the constraints applicable are represented graphically.

The language LISA-D has been introduced for the representation of constraints that cannot be graphically expressed in PSM. LISA-D expressions exploit the natural language basis of PSM to improve comprehensibility. In meta-models, complex constraints often occur. We do not treat the language LISA-D within the scope of this paper, but refer to [Hof93].

3.2 Representing a Way of Working

This section addresses several constructs for the representation of a way of working. As stated in section 2, a way of modelling and a way of working are closely related. Therefore, attention is also paid to the representation of relationships between a way of modelling and a way of working.

To represent knowledge about information modelling processes adequately, constructs are needed that allow for the description of moments of choice, sequence, parallelism, synchronisation, and iteration. *Task structures* (formally defined in [HN93]) contain constructs for expressing these task dependencies. In figure 6, the main concepts of task structures are graphically represented. They are discussed subsequently.

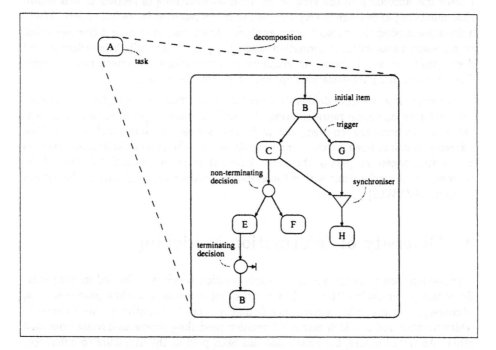

Figure 6: Graphical representation of task structure concepts

The central notion in task structures is the notion of a *task*. A task is defined as something that has to be performed in order to achieve a certain goal: the realisation of (part of) some information modelling product. A task can be defined in terms of other tasks, referred to as its *subtasks*. This *decomposition* may be performed repeatedly until a desired level of detail has been reached. Tasks with the same name have the same decomposition, e.g. the tasks named B in figure 6. Performing a task may involve choices between subtasks, *decisions* represent these moments of choice. Decisions coordinate the execution of tasks. Two kinds of decisions are distinguished, *terminating* and *non-terminating* decisions. A decision that is terminating, may lead to termination of the execution path of that decision. If this execution path is the only active execution path of the supertask, the supertask terminates as well.

Triggers, graphically represented as arrows, model sequential order. In figure 6 the task with name G can start after termination of the top task named B. *Initial items* are those tasks or decisions, that have to be performed first as part of the execution of a task that has a decomposition. Due to iterative structures, it may not always be clear which task objects are initial. Therefore, this has to be indicated explicitly. Finally, *synchronisers* deal with explicit synchronisation. In figure 6 the task named H can only start when the tasks with names C and G have terminated.

3.3 Conclusions

This section has given a flavour of the complexity of the representation of modelling knowledge, according to the view on information modelling of section 2. It is shown that modelling knowledge is very complex to be represented in its full variety. Mechanisms are needed to represent complex object structures, to represent complex rules, to represent tasks within information modelling processes in all their orderings and decompositions, and to represent graphical representations and interaction patterns. Furthermore, many interrelationships exist between these items.

At the same time, we have deliberately used the term "flavour". To offer one coherent toolkit for an adequate representation of modelling knowledge, even more representation mechanisms are required, such as those described in [Hof93] and [HV94]. This reference restricts itself to the formal definitions for the representation mechanisms *within* the conceptual part of the cube. A first attempt to a formal definition of the representation mechanisms within the graphical product oriented part of the cube is given in [HVNW92].

4 Diversity of Information Modelling

This section focuses on the second research question which is addressed in this paper. Since this paper deals with flexible support of information modelling processes, it is, of course, necessary to know how much flexibility is needed, in other words, to know in which manner and to which extent information modelling processes deviate from each other. As stated before, little attention has been paid in the literature to differences and similarities between information modelling processes. This section discusses the insight gained while comparing information modelling processes, both in theory and in practice. For a detailed discussion of both the approach and the results, see [Ver93].

4.1 Results

This section discusses the insights gained by representing the modelling knowledge as it is *prescribed* in the Yourdon method handbook of [You89], and by representing the modelling knowledge of the Yourdon method as it has been actually *applied* by three expert information engineers in two project situations. The representation of prescribed modelling knowledge and applied modelling knowledge has resulted in seven meta-models. These meta-models have enabled us to compare the individual experts' actual behaviour. Comparison has taken place, not only to grasp the diversity of information modelling processes, but also to compare the practice of information modelling processes to the so-called stick of reference. Methodological considerations about the experimental setting chosen and its justification are given in [Ver91] and in [Ver93].

Given our focus on the early stages, emphasis has been on *data-flow diagrams* (DFDs) and *entity-relationship diagrams* (ERDs) while using a product oriented view on modelling knowledge in Yourdon, and on *constructing the essential model* while viewing Yourdon's modelling knowledge from a process oriented perspective.

4.1.1 A Product Oriented Perspective

Focusing on a *way of modelling* in Yourdon, the main modelling concepts are similar over the model type variants. For example, every ERD consists at least of entity types and relationships. DFDs always consist of processes and data stores, with flows between them. Although the main modelling concepts are similar, we observed that at the same time each model type variant has its own modelling concepts. Comparing the prescribed model type variants to the applied ones, we observed that some prescribed modelling concepts, such as complex data flow and associative object type, are not applied at all. At the same time, the experienced information engineers used *more refined modelling concepts*. Examples are customer and supplier rather than external party, and planning, control, preparation, transformation, and termination processes, rather than just processes. Finally, the applied model type variants contain more concepts which serve communication purposes (e.g. sample value) or which provide quantitative information (e.g. frequency and volume). In addition to ERDs and DFDs, several *other modelling concepts* were used by the experts as well, in particular to create a (sometimes only mental) model of organisational aspects during the problem analysis stage. These non-diagramming concepts are found only in the applied ways of modelling. Some typical examples are: problem cause, organisation unit, information need, and requirement. We observed that several *different graphical notations* are used to denote one modelling concept. Three external notations for the modelling concept relationship within ERDs were seen. One of the information engineers even used two different graphical notations during one knowledge acquisition session. Clearly, the choice of a fixed set of graphical notations is not considered to be a matter of relevance during the problem analysis stage.

4.1.2 A Process Oriented Perspective

Consecutive modelling tasks gradually lead to more structured models, both in the prescribed *way of working* and in the applied ways of working. In the course of modelling processes, more, and more refined modelling concepts are used, and the intermediate models have to satisfy a growing number of verification rules. The nature of modelling tasks changes from free to structured.

The applied ways of working differ from the reference book to a large extent with regard to the *order* in which modelling tasks are performed. The prescribed way of working is characterised by an almost strictly linear order of modelling tasks. The actual application shows an opportunistic order, which is determined by characteristics of the problem domain and of the problem at hand, as well as by the expert's preferences. The information engineers reformulated their approach several times during the course of the knowledge acquisition sessions. In some cases, they even scheduled a number of tasks to be performed in advance. In most cases, however, they only stated that they preferred to pay attention to a specific part of the problem domain, usually to fill clear lacunae in their insights in the problem domain. Their momentary needs strongly influenced the order in which the several modelling techniques were used. Modelling techniques were used as a means to increase insight or to communicate insights, be it in the problem domain or in a specific solution scenario.

The experts showed *individual* ways of working. This is clearly demonstrated by the relative dominance of data modelling and process modelling. One of the applied ways of working can be characterised as data driven, one as process driven, whereas the third shows an equilibrium between the two.

Various *process modelling strategies* have been applied: input driven process modelling, output driven process modelling, and data driven process modelling. From an input driven point of view, processes handle events, and lead to other processes. From an output driven point of view, processes result in fulfilling information needs, and other processes are necessary to deliver the input for these processes. From a data driven point of view, processes manipulate data, i.e., create, read, update, and delete instances of entity types, relationships, and attributes.

Various *data modelling strategies* have been applied too: noun driven data modelling, object driven data modelling, and process driven data modelling. In the noun driven strategy, each noun in the description is considered to be a candidate entity. In the object driven strategy, objects in the real world are related to each other. Each object is questioned for the necessity of storing information on it. The process driven strategy investigates each operating process for entity types, and integrates the resulting partial data models.

As a final observation, the experts incorporated *user participation* as an essential ingredient in their ways of working. They often validated their results with respect to correctness and completeness. They focussed on comprehensibility of intermediate information models, by adding sample values or quantitative data.

4.2 Conclusions

This section summarises the findings and insights with regard to the diversity of information modelling processes in practice. It can be concluded from the individual meta-models that the information engineers differ from each other to a considerable extent, both in their way of modelling and in their way of working. This is a remarkable conclusion since the information engineers were expected to work according to the same underlying information systems development method.

Furthermore, it can be concluded that detailed insights in similarities and differences between information engineers have been gained, but at the expense of a time-intensive approach. The six elicitation sessions led to voluminous text protocols, each including about 150 pages of text and about 30 diagrams, some of which went through several stages. Due to the bulky text protocols, the interpretation task and the conceptualisation task have been time-intensive for the knowledge engineer. This observation is even reinforced by the fact that the representations of the information engineers' way of working do not have a high level of granularity: within the context of creating a diagram, the representations indicate that the diagrams went through several stages, but they do not reach the level of manipulating individual objects.

5 Epilogue

As stressed in the introduction of this paper feasibility of flexible information modelling support is dependent on (1) the complexity of information modelling in the early phases and (2) the extent to which flexibility is needed in these phases. The more complex information modelling is, and the more diverse information modelling processes are in practice, the more effort is needed to realise flexible information modelling support and the less feasible this goal is.

Section 3 dealt with the first research question and demonstrated the inherent *complexity* of a meta-modelling technique capable of describing all the relevant aspects (as defined in section 2) of information modelling methods. Information modelling products are in general quite complex due to decomposition mechanisms, complex structures and complex rules. In addition to the rules that information modelling products (syntax) have to satisfy, their formal meaning (semantics) must be also described. In case of a data model this means that the meta-model should capture which instantiations satisfy the constraints specified and in case of a process model, this means that all possible process executions have to be defined on the meta-level. Information modelling processes may be quite complex if modelling tasks may be performed in parallel. Furthermore, a formal and complete description of the precise effect information modelling processes may have on the various products (and vice versa) turns out to be difficult. Finally, both information modelling processes and products not only have to be approached from a conceptual point of view, but also from a representational point of view. Information modelling products may have complex associated representations and information modelling processes may have complex associated graphical interactions. This relation between the conceptual part of a meta-model and its representational part is essential for flexible support, but has hardly been investigated.

Section 4 dealt with the second research question and demonstrated the inherent *diversity* of information modelling in the early phases. The ways of modelling *and* the ways of working applied by the observed experienced information engineers differ to a large extent. Each information engineer uses its own rules, heuristics, graphical representations and so on. This means that for adequate flexible support, meta-models have to be constructed for each *individual* information engineer. Clearly, this is not feasible, especially since capturing the method followed by an experienced information engineer turns out to be a very time-consuming and difficult task.

These problems may be partially solved if one is less ambitious. To achieve flexible support, it is necessary to find an adequate way to decrease the level of ambition whilst approaching this area. To be more precise, it is necessary to diminish the specification effort effectively. The easiest (and least satisfactory) approach is to neglect aspects of information modelling knowledge. For example, by *not* paying attention to the modelling process or by *not* paying attention to representational aspects. This approach has been used in the development of all "state-of-the-art" meta-modelling techniques mentioned in section 1. None of these techniques address the modelling process. In [VHW91], the modelling process *has* been addressed. This reference, however, neglects the representational aspects of information modelling. A more promising approach would be to exchange complete freedom for "controlled flexibility". Those specifying the knowledge base are then provided with a (pre-specified) generic meta-model, which may be adapted to one's needs by the application of a number of pre-defined meta-model transformations. Another promising approach to reduce the large specification effort is triggered by our observation that a detailed way of working of information engineers is difficult to acquire and requires a lot of effort to describe. Perhaps, it is best not to try to support this level in all details. Alternative support could then be achieved by offering a number of predefined operations. We consider such a *building block* approach to be an interesting issue for future research.

Summarising, it is clear that unrestricted, adequate, flexible support of information modelling is, practically speaking, impossible to achieve. Sometimes, however, restrictions (e.g. when complete graphical support is not needed) may be perfectly acceptable. To balance benefits and efforts of flexible information modelling support, a research agenda has been presented, centered around the level of ambition to be realised.

References

[AC92]   T. Araujo and R. Carapuça. Issues for a Future CASE. In B. Theodoulidis and A. Sutcliffe, editors, *Proceedings of the Third Workshop on the Next Generation of CASE tools*, pages 225–243, Manchester, United Kingdom, 1992.

[Bal87]   J.M. Ballay. An experimental view of the design process. In W.B. Rouse and K.R. Boff, editors, *System Design: Behavioral Perspectives on Designers, Tools and Organizations*, pages 65–82, Amsterdam, The Netherlands, 1987. North-Holland.

[BB93]   J.P. Bansler and K. Bødker. A Reappraisal of Structured Analysis: Design in an Organizational Context. *ACM Transactions on Information Systems*, 11(2):165–193, 1993.

[BBD⁺89]   P. Bergsten, J.A. Bubenko, R. Dahl, M. Gustafsson, and L-Å. Johansson. RAMATIC - a CASE shell for implementation of specific CASE tools. Technical report, SISU, Stockholm, Sweden, 1989. First draft of a contribution to section 4.4 of the TEMPORA T6.1 report.

[Bel85]   L. Belady. MCC: Planning the Revolution in Software. *IEEE Software*, 2(6), 1985.

[Bri90]   S. Brinkkemper. *Formalisation of Information Systems Modelling*. PhD thesis, University of Nijmegen, Nijmegen, The Netherlands, 1990.

[BS87]   D. Benyon and S. Skidmore. Towards a Tool Kit for the Systems Analyst. *The Computer Journal*, 30(1):2–7, 1987.

[CN89]   M. Chen and J.F. Nunamaker Jr. MetaPlex: An integrated environment for organization and information systems development. In J.I. DeGross, J.C. Henderson, and B.R. Konsynski, editors, *Proceedings of the Tenth International Conference on Information Systems*, pages 141–151, Boston, Massachusetts, December 1989.

[Flo86]   C. Floyd. A Comparative Evaluation of System Development Methods. In T.W. Olle, H.G. Sol, and A.A. Verrijn-Stuart, editors, *Information Systems Design Methodologies: Improving the Practice*, pages 19–54. North-Holland, Amsterdam, The Netherlands, 1986.

[GC88]   R. Guindon and B. Curtis. Control of Cognitive Processes during Software Design: What Tools are Needed? In *Proceedings of the Conference on Human Factors in Computing Systems CHI'88*, pages 263–268, 1988.

[Gui90a]   R. Guindon. Designing the Design Process: Exploiting Opportunistic Thoughts. *Human-Computer Interaction*, 5:305–344, 1990.

[Gui90b]   R. Guindon. Knowledge exploited by experts during software system design. *International Journal of Man-Machine Studies*, 33:279–304, 1990.

[HN93]   A.H.M. ter Hofstede and E.R. Nieuwland. Task structure semantics through process algebra. *Software Engineering Journal*, 8(1):14–20, January 1993.

[HÖ92]   M. Heym and H. Österle. A Reference Model for Information Systems Development. In K.E. Kendell, K. Lyytinen, and J.I. DeGross, editors, *Proceedings of the IFIP WG 8.2 Working Conference on the Impact of Computer Supported Technologies on Information Systems Development*, pages 215–239, Minneapolis, 1992.

[Hof93]   A.H.M. ter Hofstede. *Information Modelling in Data Intensive Domains*. PhD thesis, University of Nijmegen, Nijmegen, The Netherlands, 1993.

[HPW93]   A.H.M. ter Hofstede, H.A. Proper, and Th.P. van der Weide. Formal definition of a conceptual language for the description and manipulation of information models. *Information Systems*, 18(7):489–523, 1993.

[HV94]   A.H.M. ter Hofstede and T.F. Verhoef. Flexible Support of Information Modelling: Is the Game worth the Candle? Technical Report CSI-R9406, Computing Science Institute, University of Nijmegen, Nijmegen, The Netherlands, May 1994.

[HVNW92] A.H.M. ter Hofstede, T.F. Verhoef, E.R. Nieuwland, and G.M. Wijers. Integrated Specification of Method and Graphic Knowledge. In *Proceedings of the Fourth International Conference on Software Engineering and Knowledge Engineering*, pages 307–316, Capri, Italy, June 1992. IEEE Computer Society Press.

[HW92]   A.H.M. ter Hofstede and Th.P. van der Weide. Formalisation of techniques: chopping down the methodology jungle. *Information and Software Technology*, 34(1):57–65, January 1992.

[HW93]   A.H.M. ter Hofstede and Th.P. van der Weide. Expressiveness in conceptual data modelling. *Data & Knowledge Engineering*, 10(1):65–100, February 1993.

[KDH86]   E. Knuth, J. Demetrovics, and A. Hernadi. Information System Design: On Conceptual Foundations. In H.J. Kugler, editor, *Information Processing 86*, pages 635–640, Amsterdam, The Netherlands, 1986. North-Holland.

[LM86]   P.C. Lockemann and H.C. Mayr. Information System Design: Techniques and Software Support. In H.J. Kugler, editor, *Information Processing 86*, Amsterdam, The Netherlands, 1986. North-Holland.

[NH89]   G.M. Nijssen and T.A. Halpin. *Conceptual Schema and Relational Database Design: a fact oriented approach*. Prentice-Hall, Sydney, Australia, 1989.

[Pot89]   C. Potts. A Generic Model for Representing Design Methods. In *Proceedings of the 11th International Conference on Software Engineering*, pages 199–210, Pittsburgh, Pennsylvania, 1989.

[SBL89]   A.G. Sutcliffe, W.J. Black, and P. Loucopoulos. System Specification Semantics: Defining the knowledge captured by structured system development methods in conceptual models. In E.D. Falkenberg and P. Lindgreen, editors, *Information Systems Concepts: an In-depth Analysis*, pages 53–77, Amsterdam, The Netherlands, 1989. North-Holland.

[SLTM91]   K. Smolander, K. Lyytinen, V-P. Tahvanainen, and P. Marttiin. MetaEdit: A Flexible Graphical Environment for Methodology Modelling. In R. Andersen, J.A. Bubenko, and A. Sølvberg, editors, *Proceedings of the Third International Conference CAiSE'91 on Advanced Information Systems Engineering*, volume 498 of *Lecture Notes in Computer Science*, pages 168–193, Trondheim, Norway, May 1991. Springer-Verlag.

[STM88]   P.G. Sorenson, J.-P. Tremblay, and A.J. McAllister. The Metaview System for Many Specification Environments. *IEEE Software*, pages 30–38, March 1988.

[Ver91]   T.F. Verhoef. Structuring Yourdon's Modern Structured Analysis. In V.-P. Tahvanainen and K. Lyytinen, editors, *Proceedings of the Second Workshop on the Next Generation of CASE Tools*, pages 219–313, Trondheim, Norway, May 1991.

[Ver93]   T.F. Verhoef. *Effective Information Modelling Support*. PhD thesis, Delft University of Technology, Delft, The Netherlands, 1993.

[VHW91]   T.F. Verhoef, A.H.M. ter Hofstede, and G.M. Wijers. Structuring modelling knowledge for CASE shells. In R. Andersen, J.A. Bubenko, and A. Sølvberg, editors, *Proceedings of the Third International Conference CAiSE'91 on Advanced Information Systems Engineering*, volume 498 of *Lecture Notes in Computer Science*, pages 502–524, Trondheim, Norway, May 1991. Springer-Verlag.

[WH90]   G.M. Wijers and H. Heijes. Automated Support of the Modelling Process: A view based on experiments with expert information engineers. In B. Steinholz, A. Sølvberg, and L. Bergman, editors, *Proceedings of the Second Nordic Conference CAiSE'90 on Advanced Information Systems Engineering*, volume 436 of *Lecture Notes in Computer Science*, pages 88–108, Stockholm, Sweden, 1990. Springer-Verlag.

[Wij91]   G.M. Wijers. *Modelling Support in Information Systems Development*. PhD thesis, Delft University of Technology, Delft, The Netherlands, 1991.

[You89]   E. Yourdon. *Modern Structured Analysis*. Prentice-Hall, Englewood Cliffs, New Jersey, 1989.

A Meta-Model for Business Rules in Systems Analysis

H. Herbst

herbst@ie.iwi.unibe.ch
Institute of Information Systems, Research Unit 'Information Engineering', University of Berne
Engehaldenstrasse 8, CH-3012 Berne, Switzerland*

Abstract. Commonly used methodologies for systems analysis are data- or function-oriented and are sufficient for information systems which will be implemented on passive database management systems (DBMS). In the last years, several research prototypes of active DBMS and active mechanisms in commercially available DBMS have been developed. To fully use the potential of these rule-based mechanisms, a rule-based systems analysis methodology seems necessary. This paper defines and structures business rules as a main component of such a methodology and presents a meta-model for business rules; furthermore, an outlook on the implementation of the meta-model in a repository system is given.

1 Introduction

Many current database research projects are focusing on the specification and implementation of databases which provide active components (cf. [StHH87]; [DaBM88]; [WiCL91]; [Gatz94]; [ChMi93]). First results of this research are already available in commercial DBMS such as CA-Ingres, Oracle or Sybase (cf. [KnHS94]). In connection with this progress on the implementation level, the importance of treating business rules on the conceptual level has been emphasized (cf. [Appl84]; [VLLS88]; [BBSG90]; [Mori93]; [KnHe93]). Though the term *business rule* is often referred to, it is defined and used rather differently and often restricted to semantic integrity constraints (cf. e.g. [Appl88]; [SaVo91]). However, business rules do not only cover data integrity but may also impose restrictions on organizational dynamics; therefore, we define business rules with reference to [BBSG90] as statements about how the business is done, i.e., about guidelines and restrictions with respect to states and processes in an organization [HeKn94].

In [HKMS94] a comparison of selected function-oriented, data-oriented, and object-oriented methods revealed the lack of an approach for a convenient graphical specification of business rules at the conceptual level. To complete the ongoing research dealing with the graphical representation of business rules (cf. e.g. [Tana92], [MaOd92]) we focus on the administration of business rules in a repository and try to derive graphical views from it.

---
* The work presented in this paper has been partially supported by the Swiss National Science Foundation, Priority Program Informatics, Project 5003-034330.

2   Business Rules

2.1   Systems Analysis Focusing on Business Rules

A main purpose of systems analysis is to collect all relevant information about the universe of discourse [Pohl93]; these facts are primarily about processes and about the structure and manipulation of data objects. Business rules as defined above encompass both aspects; therefore, we want to treat business rules as a central element of systems analysis and adapt the process of systems analysis accordingly (cf. Figure 1). In this process facts are collected in the real world (e.g. by interviews or document analysis) and specified as business rules and data structures. After verifying the specifications, they can be used in systems design and implementation. The first part of the process may be supported by a repository system which encompasses funcionalities to store, retrieve, validate represent, and manipulate the relevant meta-data including business rules.

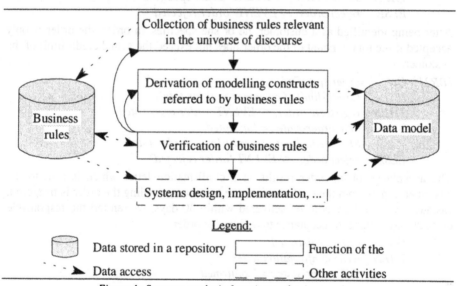

Figure 1: Systems analysis focusing on business rules

2.2   The Structure of Business Rules

Business rules can be represented according to the structure of rules in active databases (cf. [DaBM88]) using the three basic components event, condition and action (ECA) [TsKL90]. Several case studies to extract business rules from practically applied information systems (cf. [KnHS94]) revealed the need for an extension of this structure to ECAA:

• *Event*: When has a business rule to be processed?
• *Condition*: What has to be checked?
• *Then-Action*: What has to be done if the condition is true?
• *Else-Action*: What has to be done if the condition is false?

These basic component types of business rules can be further classified into several subtypes [HeKn94] which is especially relevant for the definition of a syntax for describing business rules in a repository.

The ECAA structure allows to specify single business rules (e.g. encompassing static integrity constraints) and the definition of entire processes consisting of business rules. The importance of events with respect to processes is emphasized in [Stre94] and [Sche94]. For specifying processes, the action component of a rule has to be linked to raised events which trigger other business rules; this link is specified within the action component.

To illustrate the scope and different types of business rules, we introduce some examples which may be relevant in an order processing system. In this system we want to specify the process of order entry and some constraints for the treatment of orders. In the first stage of the order processing we want to assure that a person who calls to put an order is a customer:

[BR1] *ON* *phone call of a person*
   IF   *(person is a registrated customer)*
   THEN *specify order, ⇨ EVENT 'order specified'*
   ELSE *reject order, ⇨ EVENT 'order rejected'*

After being identified as a customer, he or she specifies an order; the order is only accepted if the total amount of the order does not exceed the actual credit limit of the customer:

[BR2] *ON* *order specified*
   IF   *(credit-limit of customer > order-total)*
   THEN *registrate order, ⇨ EVENT 'order registrated'*
       SET order-state := 'accepted'
       SET credit-limit := credit-limit - order-total
   ELSE *reject order, ⇨ EVENT 'order rejected'*

The acceptance of an order results in a confirmation letter which is sent to the customer. Apart from the confirmation, the task of assembling the order is triggered. Because every order has to be delivered within 30 days, we remind the responsible clerk 20 days after the acceptance to deliver the order.

[BR3] *ON* *order registrated*
   THEN *write confirmation letter*
       SET order-state := 'confirmed'

[BR4] *ON* *order registrated*
   THEN *assemble order, ⇨ EVENT 'order assembled'*

[BR5] *ON* *20 days AFTER [order registrated]*
   IF   *order not assembled*
   THEN *remind responsible clerk*

Finally, the order is delivered to the customer who is expected to pay the order total within 30 days.

[BR6] *ON* *order assembled*
   THEN *deliver order, ⇨ EVENT 'order delivered'*

[BR7] *ON* *30 days AFTER [order delivered]*
   IF   *(order not paid)*
   THEN *remind customer, ⇨ EVENT 'customer reminded'*

[BR8]　*ON*　　*order paid*
　　　　THEN　*SET order state = 'closed', ⇨ EVENT 'order closed'*
　　　　　　　SET credit-limit := credit-limit + order-total
　　　　　　　SET closure date := today()

After payment the order is closed and kept in the system for ten years.

[BR9]　*ON*　　*10 years AFTER [order closed]*
　　　　THEN　*attempt to delete order, ⇨ EVENT 'order deletion attempted'*

To prevent an erase of an order prior to this delay event, the following rule is specified:

[BR10]　*ON*　　*order deletion attempted*
　　　　IF　　*order closure date > (today() - 10 years)*
　　　　THEN　*reject deletion of order*
　　　　　　　issue message „Orders must be kept for 10 years"
　　　　ELSE　*delete order, ⇨ EVENT 'order deletion'*

To ensure that no customer is deleted while having an order, the following business rule may be specified:

[BR11]　*ON*　　*customer deletion attempted*
　　　　IF　　*∃ order related to customer*
　　　　THEN　*reject deletion of customer*
　　　　　　　issue message „Deletion not possible because of existing orders"
　　　　ELSE　*delete customer, ⇨ EVENT 'customer deleted'*

These examples show the close relation of business rules to the concepts of 'workflow management' (cf. e.g. [Heil94]) and 'business process re-engineering' [HaCh93]; therefore, the meta-model presented in this paper includes a submodel 'process' (cf. section 3.2.4).

2.3　Abstraction and Specialization of Business Rules

An IS may encompass plenty of business rules; therefore, mechanisms for reducing the complexity have to be provided. One possibility to achieve this is a leveled approach for the specification of business rules, i.e., their generalization and specialization of business rules. In [DeMa78] a balancing rule for leveled dataflow diagrams (DFD) is specified: The parent and the child diagram have to be *balanced*, i.e., „data flows into and out of the parent bubble are equivalent to data flows into and out of the child diagram". An adaptation of this rule on the specialization of business rules is that on both levels the triggering event and the raised events have to be identical.

In our concept, different levels for specifying business rules are allocated to (sub)processes encompassing a specific subset of all business rules (cf. Figure 2). This allocation allows a reuse of business rules on different levels (e.g. the business rule 'BR-4' in Figure 2). The reused business rules always raise the same events but they may trigger different business rules, depending on the subset of business rules which define the current subprocess.

Because the concept of business rules incorporates these different abstraction levels, allows the description of concurrent activities and explicitly incorporates the time dimension (event types 'time event', 'interval events', 'periodical events' and 'delay events'), the model can be classified as dynamic (cf. [MeBS94]).

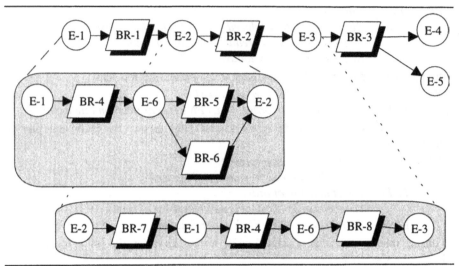

Figure 2: Specialization of business rules

3 A Meta-Model for Business Rules

The meta-model presented in this chapter is assigned to the second layer of the IRDS standard [ANSI89] and describes therefore information about the meta-structure of facts to be stored in the data dictionary. The meta-model is discussed in two parts: the first is about the core of the meta-model including the two submodels *'Business Rule'* and *'Modeling constructs'* and the second deals with the embedding of business rules into further submodels.

3.1 The Core of the Meta-Model

3.1.1 Submodel 'Business Rule'

The submodel 'Business rule' consists of the four meta-entity-types *Business rule, Event, Condition* and *Action* (cf. Figure 3). Every business rule has exactly one event, at most one condition and one or two actions (then/else). Furthermore, business rules can be specialized and generalized which leads to a recursive m:n relationship on *Business rule*. Events and conditions can be complex and have therefore also recursive m:n relationships. As shown in the examples actions of business rules may raise events which is depicted in the meta model as a relationship between the meta-entity-types *Action* and *Event*.

3.1.2 Submodel 'Modeling Construct'

The submodel 'Modeling construct' encompasses the meta-entity-types for the specification of a conceptual data model. The most popular data model for conceptual modeling is the Entity Relationship Model; therefore, we incorporate into the submodel 'Modeling construct' the meta-entity-types *entity type, relationship type* and *attribute* (cf. Figure 3). The semantic of the relationship between components of business rules and modeling constructs is e.g. the retrieval, modification, derivation or deletion of the data of a modeling construct. The following relationships between components of business rules and modeling constructs are possible:

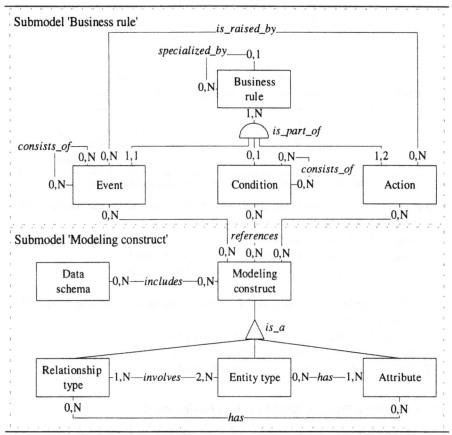

Figure 3: Submodels 'Business rule' and 'Modeling construct'

- Relationship between *Event* and *Modeling construct*: Data related events (which may also be part of a complex event) make reference to modeling constructs within the universe of discourse.
- Relationship between *Condition* and *Modeling construct*: The specification of conditions always refers to modeling constructs whose content has to be retrieved for the evaluation of the condition.
- Relationship between *Action* and *Modeling construct*: An action may explicitly refer to modeling constructs.

These relationships between modeling constructs and business rules may be depicted e.g. in an Entity-Relationship-Event-Rule (ER^2) diagram [Tana92].

As discussed in the description of a business rule based systems analysis (cf. Figure 1), modeling constructs can be derived from a collection of business rules and afterwards structured in a conceptual data model (cf. Figure 4).

The submodels *'business rule'* and *'modeling construct'* allow a data view on the meta model focusing on the relationship between modeling constructs and business rules; it can be regarded from the following points of view:

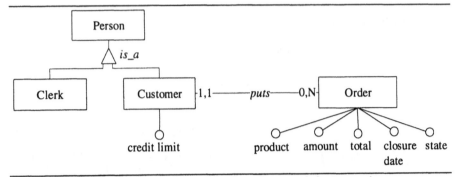

Figure 4: Data model resulting from the example business rules

1. Business rule ⇨ modeling construct: Which impact has a specific business rule on modeling constructs?

    Example: The business rule [BR2]

includes	*registration of order*	*(≡ insertion)*
	order state	*(modification)*

    ...

2. Modeling construct ⇨ business rule: Which business rules use a specific modeling construct?

    Example: The entity type 'Order' is referenced by

[BR2]	*Event, action*	*(modification)*
[BR3]	*Event, action*	*(modification)*

    ...

3.2 Embedding Business Rules into their Environment

3.2.1 Overview

Business rules as defined and exemplified above describe how the business is done; however, to obtain an integrated view on the universe of discourse they have to be embedded into their own environment. Therefore, the meta-model consists of several submodels linked to the central submodel 'business rule'. Figure 5 shows the relationships between the submodel 'business rule' and the other submodels:

- 'Modeling construct': As discussed above, business rule components may refer to modeling constructs.
- 'Origin': A business rule has at least one origin.
- 'Organizational unit': Each component of a business rule is processed within an organizational unit.
- 'Process': Business rules may be an element of a process, which consists of at least one business rule. Processes are furthermore linked to organizational units.
- 'Software component': Components of business rules may be implemented in a software component as e.g. a module or a stored procedure.

These relationships allow a classification of business rules [HeKn94] which is briefly discussed within the sections describing the submodels.

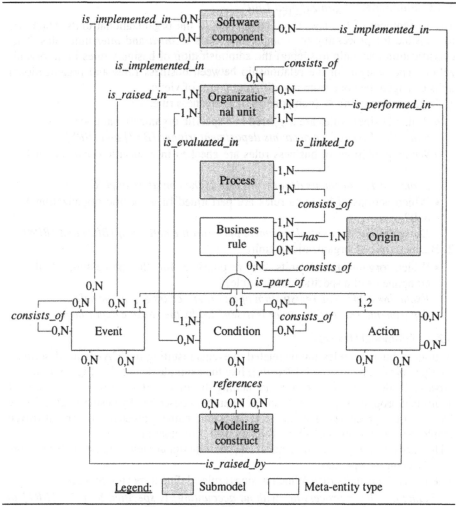

Figure 5: Embedding business rules

3.2.2 Submodel 'Origin'

Business rules may originate outside or inside an organization. Externally originating rules can be further divided into *natural facts* which are eternally fixed and (e.g. legal) *norms* which are specified by the society and may change. Internal origins can be either *primary* or *secondary*; an origin is primary if its content is originally described in a source document, whereas a secondary origin has previously been derived from another source. The knowledge about the origin of a business rule allows among others an analysis from the following two viewpoints:

1. Origin ⇨ business rule: Which business rules originate from a specific origin (e.g. in case of modifications of real world rules from a specific origin)?

2. Business rule ⇨ origin: Where does a specific business rule originate from (e.g. for checking the consistency between the implementation and the real world)?

3.2.3 Submodel *'Organizational Unit'*

The assignment of business rule components to the organizational units which are responsible for processing the components leads to *intra* and *inter* unit rules. This classification may help to support the administration of business rules in an organization. The analysis of the relationship between business rules and organizational units can again be done from two different points of view:

1. Organizational unit ⇨ (components of a) business rule:

   • Which business rules are triggered in a specific organizational unit?
   Example: Tasks of the accounts department trigger [BR7] and [BR8]

   • Which conditions of business rules are checked in a specific organizational unit?
   Example: The accounts department checks the condition of [BR7]

   • Which actions of business rules are performed in a specific organizational unit?
   Example: The accounts department performs the actions of [BR7] and [BR8]

2. Business rule ⇨ organizational unit:

   • Which organizational units are responsible for the processing of the components of a specific business rule?
   Example [BR4]: The registration of an order occurs e.g. in the sales department, whereas the order is assembled by the storage department.

3.2.4 Submodel *'Process'*

Actions of business rules can be related to events resulting in ECA-chains describing the dynamic of processes (cf. [Sche94]) like the example depicted in Figure 6. Such a process is defined by starting and ending business rules; however, because of additional properties, processes can not be entirely described by business rules. These facts about processes include e.g. process name, process owner, involved employees/organizational units and relationships to other processes.

The focus on the process dynamics, i.e., the functional view, can be analyzed from two different viewpoints:

1. Process ⇨ business rule: Which business rules define a specific process?
   Example: Order processing (without accounting) is specified by rules [BR1] to [BR7]

2. Business rule ⇨ process: Which processes are referred to by components of a business rule?
   Example: Within the order specification a reservation for the ordered products is done. This reservation could reduce the available stock below a threshold and cause the reordering of the concerned product. [BR1] would therefore be a part of the order processing and would simultaneously trigger the process of reordering the product from our supplier.

The integrated consideration of the data and functional view leads to information about the modeling constructs to which a process refers.

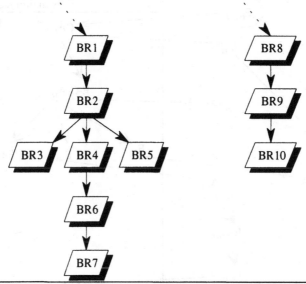

Figure 6: Order processing described by business rules

The representation of the process in Figure 6 shows that most activities are linked through actions raising events and triggering the next business rules. Only between the rules [BR7] and [BR8] no link exists because [BR8] is triggered by the user event 'order paid' which cannot be raised by an action of another business rule of the enterprise. Therefore, the completion of the process depends on raising this event. The diagram shows the importance of this view on business rules because among others it indicates such critical points where the continuation of a process depends on an event from the environment.

3.2.5 Submodel *'Software Component'*

The process depicted in Figure 6 delivers no information about the distribution of business rules between the computer system and its environment, i.e., the real world. To obtain this information, the ECA components of the business rules have to be assigned to software components (e.g. functions or database triggers) and/or the system environment (cf. Figure 7), resulting in $2^3=8$ types of rules. This assignment can be determined from the following viewpoints:

• Description of the *current* system (systems survey)
• Description of *possible* assignments (alternatives analysis)
• Description of the *planned* assignments (analysis of target systems).

As stated in [Poo92], high-level business policies are normally transformed into low-level computational representations and are „buried deep within the system program code". To support the maintenance of an IS, the examination of the *current assignments* helps to find the (possibly redundant) implementations of a specific business rule: the modification of e.g. an organizational guideline leads to the determination of business rules originating from this document; afterwards, the actual implementation can be derived by regarding the relationship to software components.

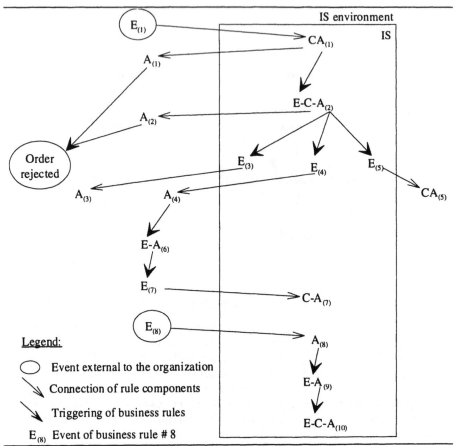

Figure 7: Order processing with assignment of the ECA components to software components and/or the system environment.

The analysis of *alternatives* is only necessary for defining a planned assignment if the current system is not satisfying. The possible assignment especially depends on the question if it is feasible to implement a rule component within an IS. For determining the *planned assignment* of the components, several aspects have to be taken into account [HeKn94]:

- *Flexibility*: Rule components implemented in a computer system are processed very strictly; this may prevent adequate actions in exceptional situations.
- *Consistency of the rule enforcing*: The disadvantage mentioned above may also be regarded as an advantage, because those components implemented in computer systems are always processed in the same consistent way.
- *Data*: How difficult is it to store all data needed for computer based processing of a rule component?
- *Complexity*: Is it possible to implement the logic of a component with acceptable expenses (e.g. non-feasible algorithms)?
- *Number of interactions*: The amount of interfaces necessary for processing a business should be minimized. One should strive for a homogenous rule proces-

sing and assign the whole business rule either to the IS or to its environment.
- *Desirability*: Beneath technical aspects one has to determine whether the control on processing a specific rule component should be left to a computer system (e.g. with respect to ethical reasons).

4 The Implementation of the Meta-Model within a Repository System for Business Rules

The repository system based on the meta-model described is currently being implemented using the repository system Rochade, whose functionalities allow the specification of the meta-model and the implementation of a graphical user-interface for its manipulation.

Repository systems have to provide some basic application independent functionality (cf. [Myra94]); some additional functionality resulting from the specific use for business rule based systems analysis can be derived from Figure 1. For the basic administration of the main submodels 'Business rule' and 'Modeling construct', the repository system has to support the tasks

- business rule registration,
- verification of the business rules (e.g. checking for loops),
- derivation of modeling constructs,
- specification of the data structure and
- verification of the consistency between business rules and modeling constructs.

To cope with the large number of verbally described business rules, the repository system has to provide functionalities for detailed analysis as the ones discussed above. These analysis may result in written output or can be partially visualized using graphical notations as e.g.

- the overview on the relationship between business rules and modeling objects with ER^2 diagrams [Tana92] or the dynamic of a specific entity type with Entity Life History diagrams [DoCC92]
- the dynamics of business rules with original or adapted Petri-Nets (cf. e.g. [Tana92];[TsGH94]), event-driven process chains [HoKS93], State-Transition Diagrams [Lipe89] or Event Schemes [MaOd92].

Further functions of the repository system will probably include the manipulation of the other submodels.

5 Conclusions and Outlook

Business rules are an important element of IS but rather neglected in commonly used methodologies of systems analysis. According to research in the area of active databases and to proposals for graphical representations of rules implemented in those databases, a meta-model for the treatment of business rules on the conceptual level is proposed. In this meta-model business rules are embedded into their environment which leads to various possibilities for analysis and administration of business rules. This embedded business rules as a technique for systems analysis fulfill requirements of systems users and analysts as e.g. the ones described in [McGi92]. The meta-model is currently being implemented using the commercial repository system Rochade [HeMy95]. The functionality of the business rules repository system allows an easy administration of a large amount of business rules;

furthermore, several graphical representation of views on the meta-data is implemented within Rochade. The business rule repository will subsequently be applied on a large case study encompassing approximately 750 business rules from an insurance application.

References

[ANSI89]   ANSI, American National Standard X3.138-1988: Information Resource Dictionary System (IRDS), New York: American National Standard Institute 1989.

[Appl84]   Appleton, D.S., Business Rules: The Missing Link, in: Datamation 30 (1984) 16, pp. 145 - 150.

[Appl88]   Appleton, D.S., Second Generation Applications, in: Database Programming & Design 1 (1988) 2, pp. 48 - 54.

[BBSG90]   Bell, J., Brooks, D., Goldbloom, E., Sarro, R., Wood, J.: Re-Engineering Case Study Analysis of Business Rules and Recommendations for Treatment of Rules in a Relational Database Environment, Bellevue Golden: US West Information Technologies Group 1990.

[ChMi93]   Chakravarthy, S., Mishra, D., Snoop: An Expressive Event Specification Language for Active Databases, Technical Report UF-CIS-TR-93-007, University of Florida, 1993.

[DaBM88]   Dayal, U., Buchmann, A.P., McCarthy, D.R., Rules Are Objects Too: A Knowledge Model for an Active, Object-Oriented Database Management System, in: K.R. Dittrich (Eds.), Advances in Object-Oriented Database Systems, Berlin et al.: Springer 1988, pp. 129 - 143.

[DeMa78]   De Marco, T., Structured Analysis and System Specification, New York: Yourdon 1978.

[DoCC92]   Downs, E., Clare, P., Coe, I., Structured Systems Analysis and Design Method - Application and Context, 2nd ed., Englewood Cliffs: Prentice-Hall 1992.

[Gatz94]   Gatziu, S., Events in an Active Object-Oriented Database System, Hamburg: Dr. Kovac 1994.

[HaCh93]   Hammer, M., Champy, J., Reengineering the corporation, New York: Harper Business 1993.

[Heil94]   Heilmann, H., Workflow Management: Integration von Organisation und Informationsverarbeitung, in: HMD (1994) 176, pp. 8 - 21.

[HeKn94]   Herbst, H., Knolmayer, G., Ansätze zur Klassifikation von Geschäftsregeln, Working Paper 46, Institute of Information Systems, University of Berne 1994, to appear in: Wirtschaftsinformatik 37 (1995).

[HKMS94]   Herbst, H., Knolmayer, G., Myrach, T., Schlesinger, M., The Specification of Business Rules: A Comparision of Selected Methodologies, in: A.A. Verrijn-Stuart, T. W. Olle (Eds.), Methods and Associated Tools for the Information System Life Cycle, Amsterdam et al.: Elsevier 1994, pp. 29 - 46.

[HeMy95]   Herbst, H., Myrach, T., A Repository System for Business Rules, Working Paper 57, Institute of Information Systems, University of Berne 1995.

[HoKS93]   Hoffmann, W., Kirsch, J., Scheer, A.-W., Modellierung mit Ereignisgesteuerten Prozessketten, Working Paper 101, Institute of Information Systems, University of Saarbrücken 1993.

[KnHe93]   Knolmayer, G., Herbst, H., Business Rules, in: Wirtschaftsinformatik 35 (1993) 4, pp. 386 - 390.

[KnHS94]   Knolmayer, G., Herbst, H., Schlesinger, M., Enforcing Business Rules by the Application of Trigger Concepts, in: Proceedings Priority Programme Informatics Research, Information Conference Module 1, Berne 1994.

[Lipe89]   Lipeck, U.W., Dynamische Integrität von Datenbanken, Grundlagen der Spezifikation und Überwachung, Berlin et al.: Springer 1989.

[MaOd92]   Martin, J., Odell, J., Object-Oriented Analysis & Design, Englewood Cliffs: Prentice-Hall 1992.

[McGi92]   McGinnes, S., How Objective is Object-Oriented Analysis?, in: P. Loucopoulos (Ed.), Proceedings of the Forth International Conference on Advanced Information Systems Engineering, Berlin et al.: Springer 1992, pp. 1 - 16.

[MeBS94]   Van Meel, J.W., Bots, P.W.G., Sol, H.G., 'A Hard Core for Soft Problems' - A Business Engineering Case Study within the Amsterdam Municipal Police Force, in: A. Verbraeck, H.G. Sol, P.W.G. Bots (Eds.), Proceedings of the Fourth International Conference on Dynamic Modelling and Information Systems, Delft: Delft University Press 1994, pp. 239 - 270.

[Mori93]   Moriarty, T., The Next Paradigm, in: Database Programming & Design 6 (1993) 2, pp. 66 - 69.

[Myra94]   Myrach, T., Konzeption und Stand des Einsatzes von Data Dictionaries, Heidelberg: Physica 1995.

[Pohl93]   Pohl, K., The Three Dimensions of Requirements Engineering, in: C. Rolland, F. Bodart, C. Cauvet (Eds.), Proceedings of the Fifth International Conference on Advanced Information Systems Engineering, Berlin et al.: Springer 1993, pp. 275 - 292.

[Poo92]   Poo, C.-C. D., A Framework for Software Maintenance, in: P. Loucopoulos (Ed.), Proceedings of the Forth International Conference on Advanced Information Systems Engineering, Berlin et al.: Springer 1992, pp. 88 - 104.

[SaVo91]   Sandifer, A., Von Halle, B., Linking Rules to Models, in: Database Programming & Design 4 (1991) 7, pp. 13 - 16.

[Sche94]   Scheer, A.-W., Wirtschaftsinformatik - Referenzmodelle für industrielle Geschäftsprozesse 5th. edition, Berlin et al.: Springer 1994.

[StHH87]   Stonebraker, M., Hanson, E., Hong, C.-H., The Design of the POSTGRES Rules System, in: Proceedings of the IEEE International Conference on Data Engineering 1987, pp. 365 - 374.

[Stre94]   Streng, R.J., BPR needs BIR and BTR: The PIT-framework for Business Reengineering, in: Proceedings of the Second SISnet Conference, Barcelona 1994.

[Tana92]   Tanaka, A.K., On Conceptual Design of Active Databases, PhD Thesis, Georgia Institute of Technology 1992.

[TNCK91]   Tanaka, A.K., Navathe, S.B., Chakravarthy, S., Karlapalem, K., ER-R: An Enhanced ER Model with Situation-Action Rules to Capture Application Semantics, in: T.J. Teorey (Ed.), Proceedings of the 10th International Conference on the Entity Relationship Approach, San Mateo: E/R Institute 1991, pp. 59 - 75.

[TsGH94]   Tsalgatidou, A., Gouscos, D., Halatsis, C., Dynamic Process Modelling Through Multi-Level RBNs, in: A. Verbraeck, H.G. Sol, P.W.G. Bots (Eds.), Proceedings of the Fourth International Conference on Dynamic Modelling and Information Systems, Delft: Delft University Press 1994, pp. 327 - 341.

[TsKL90]   Tsalgatidou, A., Karakostas, V., Loucopoulos, P., Rule-Based Requirements Specification and Validation, in: B. Steinholtz, A. Sølvberg, L. Bergman (Eds.), Proceedings of the Second Nordic Conference on Advanced Information Systems Engineering, Berlin et al.: Springer 1990, pp. 251 - 263.

[VLLS88]   Van Assche, F., Layzell, P., Loucopoulos, P., Speltincx, G., Information systems development: a rule-base approach, in: Journal of Knowledge Based Systems 1 (1988) 4, pp. 227 - 234.

[WiCL91]   Widom, J., Cochrane, R.J., Lindsay, B.G., Implementing Set-Oriented Production Rules as an Extension to Starburst, in: Proceedings of the 17th International Conference on Very Large Databases, pp. 275 - 285.

Metrics in Method Engineering

Matti Rossi[1] and Sjaak Brinkkemper[2]

[1] University of Jyväskylä
Department of Computer Science and Information Systems
P.O. Box 35
SF-40351 Jyväskylä
Finland
Internet: mor@jyu.fi

[2] University of Twente
Centre for Telematics and Information Technology
P.O. Box 217
NL-7500 AE Enschede
Netherlands
Internet: sjbr@cs.utwente.nl

Abstract. So many software development methods have been introduced in the last decade, that one can talk about a "methodology jungle". To aid the method developers and evaluators in fighting their way through this jungle we propose a systematic approach for measuring properties of methods. We describe two sets of metrics, which measure the complexity of diagrammatic specification techniques on the one hand, and of complete systems development methods on the other hand. Proposed metrics provide a relatively fast and simple way to analyse the technique (or method) properties, and when accompanied with other selection criteria, can be used for estimating the cost of learning the technique and the relative complexity of a technique compared to others. To demonstrate the applicability of the metrics, we have applied them to 34 techniques and 15 methods.

1. Introduction

Recent years have witnessed the appearance of new software development paradigms and methods. Examples of these are object-oriented analysis and design methods, and business process reengineering methods. However, we feel that there is room for improvement in the analysis of these methods and in understanding their use and functionality. Though, some attempts have been made to compare existing methods (e.g. see [Cha91]), the studies lack rigor and sound conceptual foundation, and they are mostly based on ad hoc feature analysis techniques. Some recent attempts [Son92, Hon93] have proposed more systematic approaches, based on a common formal metamodel of method, that hold the promise of a more systematic and analytic way to compare methods. Yet, they are still mainly used for making tabular comparisons of method's parts and properties.

Simultaneously there is a lack of CASE tools to support these methods. Brinkkemper and Tolvanen [Bri89, Tol93] have tackled the problem of adaptation of methods by metamodelling. The rapid growth of the number of both methods and their support environments has led to the proposition of a new area called Computer Aided Method Engineering, or CAME for short [Slo93, Kum92]. *Method engineering* is defined here, according to Heym & Österle, as the disciplined process of building, improving or modifying a method by means of specifying the method's components and their relations [Hey93].

We claim that by using a metamodel and a CAME environment for method engineering, we can achieve two goals simultaneously: first we can compare the methods analytically, and second, we can try out these methods in a situation, where methods have a platform that supports the storage and representation of descriptions made with these tools. Earlier work in this area has mainly concentrated on constructing method modelling (or metamodelling) languages [Bri90, Tol93] or building support environments for them [Che91, Sor88, Smo91b]. Earlier attempts to use metamodels for method comparison [Oei94] have mainly concentrated upon mapping metamodels into some "supermethod" or comparing metamodels by identifying their common parts [Hon93]. Instead we try to find quantitative measures, that can be computed without human judgement.

In this paper, we try to establish an approach which is systematic, automatic and easy to use for method measurement. We propose a metric approach and present a suite of metrics for methods. These metrics measure the complexity of the method or technique. Complexity is here classified into two categories: the complexity of learning and understanding the method, which is caused by the number of different constructs used in a technique or method [Tei80], and the complexity of the products, which is caused by the number of describing properties of objects and relationships.

The metrics can be used at least in two purposes, first, by method engineers to check the method properties and second, by method users to aid in the selection of methods, based on their measurable properties. The first aspect should be emphasized at the current status of method development, as we see a rapid appearance of new method categories, such as object-oriented [Boo94, Coa91] or business engineering methods [Dav90]. There is a clear push to develop new methods and consequently the method developers are in a hurry to come up with their own developments and variants of methods in the "fashionable" categories. The second aspect is more problematic, because the metrics by themselves cannot be used to judge the "goodness" or the appropriateness for the task of the method, instead they should be used together with approaches such as metamodel hierarchies [Oei94] and classification frameworks [Iiv83].

To test our claims we apply proposed metrics over a variety of well known methods. As a by-product, a set of tools for analysing methods within the MetaEdit CAME tool are introduced. The adaptation of the metrics into other CAME (and CASE) environments should be straightforward.

This paper is organized as follows. In the next section, we present the metamodelling technique used to describe techniques. In section 3, we present the proposed metrics and in section 4 these metrics are applied to a number of techniques and methods in the MetaEdit environment. The last section discusses the results and proposes some future directions for research.

2. Methods and the method engineering environment

Techniques of interest here consist of traditional graphical formalisms, such as Data Flow Diagrams, Entity Relationship Diagrams or Object Diagrams. Thus these techniques describe the object systems by objects and their relationships. In most cases the relationships and objects can have attributes or properties. The techniques usually describe only one aspect of an object system (such as data flows or state changes etc.). There is also a need to apply multiple views to describe the object system. In those cases we use organised sets of techniques, called *methods*. Methods contain several techniques, their interconnections and the use process of these techniques, but we currently limit our investigation to meta data models of the techniques and methods. An example of a method is Object Modelling Technique [Rum91] which consists of several techniques such as Class Diagrams, Data Flow Diagrams and Object State Diagrams. We chose those because their popularity and generality in the class of OO methods.

To be able to compare and analyse techniques, we need a way to describe them. This systematic way is called here a metamodelling technique. We use here the OPRR metamodelling technique, proposed by Welke [Wel92] and enhanced by Smolander [Smo91] to model the techniques and methods. The use of one metamodelling language gives us a neutral and non-biased basis to compare the properties of techniques, and it provides a common background for the formulation of metrics. Because we have also a CAME and a CASE shell environment, MetaEdit, which incorporates the OPRR model [Smo91b], we can develop automatically OPRR models and generate prototype support environments for a specified technique. In the following sections we describe the CAME environment, the static structure and the concepts of the OPRR technique and develop a model of OMT Class Diagrams [Rum91] using the OPRR technique.

2.1. The metrics environment

We have earlier developed tools for method engineering in Metaedit, one of which is a tool for developing methods with OPRR graphically (see [Ros94b]). It has been used to develop new methods for MetaEdit itself. We have currently implemented a collection of nearly forty development techniques [Ros94].

To test the metrics proposed in this paper, and to demonstrate the applicability of automating metrics computation procedures, we have implemented a metrics calculation package by using MetaEdit's report definition capabilities. List of techniques and methods, with the obtained metrics values is in Appendixes 1 and 3. The metrics computations and graphical outputs were produced using SPSS for Windows statistical package [SPS94].

2.2. The definition of the OPRR technique

The acronym OPRR comes from the words Object, Property, Role, and Relationship which are the *meta-types* in OPRR [Smo91]. Welke [Wel88] defines the meta-types in the following way:

- *Object* is a "thing" which exists on its own. Examples of objects are process, flow, store, source, module, etc.

flow, store, source, module, etc.

- *Properties* are the describing[qualifying characteristics associated with the other meta-types. Typical properties include name,description, etc.

- *Relationship* is an association between two or more objects. For example, there may be a relationship between a source and a process meaning that the process *uses* the source.

- *Role* is the name given to the link between an object and its connection with a relationship. From the example above, the process would be the *user* and the source would be the *origin* of the data.

Formally, a meta-model of a technique can be defined in OPRR as a six-tuple $M = \langle O,P,R,X,r,p \rangle$, where

O   is a finite set of object types
P   is a finite set of property types
R   is a finite set of relationship types
X   is a finite set of role types

r   is a mapping $r:R \to \bigcup_{l=2}^{\infty} \left\{ \bigcup_{j=1}^{i} \{X \times \wp(O)\} \right\}$

In other words, r is a total mapping from the relationship types to sets of cartesian products. This mapping shows the bindings of the relationships to their roles and of the roles to object types, that can act in those roles.

p   is a mapping $p:NP \to \wp(P)$, where $NP = \{O \cup R \cup X\}$ is the set of *non-property types*. In other words, NP is a partial mapping from the non-property types to all subsets of property types. The mapping defines the property types associated with the non-property types.

In the sequel we will use indexes, e.g. O_T and M_T to indicate the meta model of a particular technique T. As said earlier we consider a method M to be a set of techniques. The meta model of the method is thus $M_{\mathcal{M}} = \bigcup_{T \in \mathcal{M}} M_T$, because we omit here the interconnections between methods. The metamodel of a method has been added to the original OPRR definition in [Smo91] to allow a simple handling of methods, which contain sets of techniques.

2.3. OPRR Definition of an example technique

We use here the definition of OMT method's Class Diagram technique [Rum91] as a source of metric values. OMT is an object-oriented method, which uses extensively graphical diagrams to describe information systems. The Class Diagrams are used for analysing and modelling class hierachies and the associations between classes. Their representations are depicted in Figure 3. Classes are connected to each other by Inheritance, Aggregation or Association relationships. Classes are connected to Objects by Instantiation relationships.

The Class Diagrams have been formally specified using the OPRR model. The result is the graphical OPRR model depicted in figure 2. (See [Smo91, Ros94b] for the definition of the graphical OPRR technique).

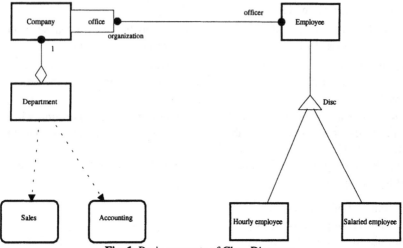

Fig. 1. Basic concepts of Class Diagrams.

The model contains some "dummy" objects in addition to those mentioned above to handle ternary relationships of the method with the binary OPRR relationships. The same method definition can be expressed in a sixtuple $M_{CD} = \langle O, P, R, X, r, p \rangle$ shown in table 1.

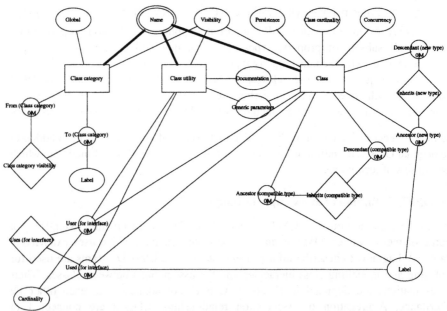

Fig. 2. Part of the OPRR Model of the Class Diagram technique of OMT]Ros94/

O= {Class, Disjoint divider, Divider, Object, Subclass group}

P= {Class name, Group name, ID, Object name, Aggregation name, Association name, Attributes, Discriminator, Link Attributes, Operations, Ordered, Qualifier, Role name, Cardinality}

R= {Aggregation 1 to 1, Aggregation 1 to M, Association (optional to 1), Association (optional to many), Association (optional to optional), Association 1 to 1, Association 1 to many, Association many to many, Generalisation, Generalisation/Specialisation, Instantiation, Qualified association 1 to 1, Qualified association 1 to many, Qualified association many to many, Specialisation}

X= {Ass 1 part, Ass M part, Ass opt part, Assembled to, Gen_from, Gen_to, Generalisation part, Instantiates, Part of, Qualified 1 part, Qualified M part, Specialisation_part, Superclass_part, is instance of}

r= {<Aggregation 1 to 1, {<Assembled to, {Class }>, < Part of, {Class}>}>
<Aggregation 1 to M, {<Ass M part, {Class, Class }>, < Assembled to, {Class}>}>,
<Association (optional to 1), {<Ass 1 part, {Class }>, < Ass opt part, {Class}>}>,
<Association (optional to many), {<Ass opt part, {Class }>, < Ass M part, {Class, Class}>}>,
<Association (optional to optional), {<Ass opt part, {Class }>, < Ass opt part, {Class}>}>,
<Association 1 to 1, {<Ass 1 part, {Class }>, < Ass 1 part, {Class}>}>, <Association 1 to many, {<Ass M part, {Class, Class }>, < Ass 1 part, {Class}>}>, <Association many to many, {<Ass M part, {Class, Class }>, < Ass M part, {Class, Class}>}>,
<Generalisation/Specialisation, {<Specialisation_part, {Class }>, < Generalisation part, {Class}>}>, <Instantiation, {<is instance of, {Class }>, < Instantiates, {Object}>}>,
<Qualified association 1 to 1, {<Ass 1 part, {Class }>, < Qualified 1 part, {Class}>}>,
<Qualified association 1 to many, {<Qualified 1 part, {Class }>, < Ass M part, {Class, Class}>}>; <Qualified association many to many, {<Ass M part, {Class, Class }>, < Qualified M part, {Class}>}>}

p= {<Class, {Class name, Operations, Attributes}>, <Disjoint divider, {ID, Discriminator}>, <Divider, {ID, Discriminator}>, <Object, {Object name, Attributes}>, <Subclass group, {Group name}>, <Ass 1 part, {Role name}>, <Ass M part, {Qualifier, Cardinality, Role name, Ordered}>, <Ass opt part, {Role name}>, <Assembled to, {Role name}>, <Qualified 1 part, {Qualifier, Role name}>, <Qualified M part, {Qualifier, Role name, Cardinality}>}

Table 1. OPRR definition of Class Diagrams

This example will be used in the following chapters as a source to define metric values.

3. Metrics for techniques and methods

This chapter outlines a number of metrics and their purpose. The metrics are derived and enhanced from metrics proposed in the earlier literature on the complexity of specification techniques [Tei80]. We describe the metrics on two levels: the technique level, which describes the characteristics of one technique and on the method level, which describes the complexity of a set of techniques.

Complexity is here classified into two categories: the complexity of learning and understanding the method, which is caused by the number of different constructs used in the technique or method [Tei80], and the complexity of the products, which is caused by the number of describing properties of objects and relationships. We are not trying to derive normative values such as "quality" or "learnability" from the measures, because these are not direct numerical attributes of the models [Fen94].

To avoid reported problems of design and specification metrics [Alb83, Hen81] i.e. poor theoretical foundations, being hard to analyse, and being flawed derivatives of code measures [Kit91, Roc94], we try to present the thing to be measured, a formal mathematical basis of the metric for the measure and guidelines for the interpretation of the obtained values. Also the metrics are defined so that they are directly computable from the properties of the methods [Fen94].

For each metric the following is described: The formula for computing the metric, a brief explanation of the metric and the expected values of the metric and their interpretation. The expected values are given as box-plots, that have been obtained from the collection of techniques. The collection is represented in appendix 1. A box-plot is a five number summary of (minimum, lower quartile, median, higher quartile, maximum) [Tuk77]. The box-plot gives an interval, where the values should locate. If tighter intervals are needed, one could use for example box-plots or medians and variances from a category of techniques. For example in case of Class Diagrams we could use a group of object description methods. The box-plots can be found in Appendix 2.

The quartiles and median give the range of expected values for a given metric and most of the methods will fall into the range between a lower and upper quartile. If we find a significantly lower or higher value, there will be a need to analyse the reasons for that, and either change the method model or accept the the model as it is.

The metrics suggested here are not expected to produce nice regressions, and to infinitely come closer to a certain numerical value, as in traditional software science [Hal77]. The obtained metric values have the usual properties of metric data, i.e. the distributions are discrete, heavily skewed and there are a lot of outliers [Kit91], which make the usual statistical techniques unsuitable. Thus we apply data analysis and outlier analysis to unterstand the reasons for abnormal values. As Kitchenham points out, [Kit91] the interpretation of the results makes metric values meaningful, not their comparison with some arbitrarily given values. Yet, to make the judgements easier, we have derived some guiding values from the available material. The comparison of metric values between methods of similar species should be particularly fruitful.

3.1. Technique level

We assume a technique $M_T = \langle O_T, P_T, R_T, X_T, r_T, p_T \rangle$. We use the function $n(A)$ to denote the number of elements in the set of A. As all sets are considered to be finite (see section 2), this function always yields finite numbers.

Independent measures. The first measure is the number of object types used per technique. This measure, and the following two, are used while analysing the complexity of the technique on the basis of the number of concepts to be learned. They were suggested already by Teichroew et al. [Tei80]. The greater the number, the more complicated the technique. On the other hand, the technique with more concepts should also be able to capture more precise or detailed information about the object system, as claimed by Oei and Falkenberg [Oei94].

    1. $n(O_T)$

The *count of object types per technique*. This metric shows the number of individual object types used to specify object systems. In the case of Class Diagrams, we find out that $n(O_{Class\ Diagram}) = 5$. This can be compared to the box-plot in appendix 2, and this shows, that the value is somewhat big, in the maximum line.

2. $n(R_T)$

The *count of relationship types per technique*. This is the number of concepts, which are used for describing connections between objects. The value $n(R_{\text{Class Diagram}}) = 15$ is marked as extreme value in the box-plot. The reason for the big number is partially the way of modelling the particular method in OPRR, because all the subtypes of relationships with different cardinalities have been modelled with separate relationship types. The reason for this choice is that the technique has been modelled for use with a CASE tool and the relationships with different graphical appearance have been modelled as different types.

The reader should notice, that the lower quartile and the minimum have the same value (1), and thus the number of relationship types tends to be quite low, between 1 and 5 for most techniques.

3. $n(P_T)$

The *number of property types per technique*. The value $n(P_{\text{Class Diagram}}) = 14$, is in the upper quartile line, but most CASE tools allow the specification of various properties per object or relationship type, so $n(P_T)$ can be rather high in comparison to $n(O_T)$ and $n(R_T)$. The reader should notice, that this is not the construct used directly in the following metrics, because the next metrics count properties per object, or a relationship type.

The following three metrics (formulae 5, 7 and 9) suggest metrics, that measure the complexity of the description of the object or relationship types.

4. $P_0(M_T, o) = n(p_T(O))$, where $o \in O_T$

5. $P_0(M_T, o) = \dfrac{1}{n(O_T)} \sum_{o \in O_T} P_0(M_T, o)$

The fourth formula is the *number of properties for a given object type*. It is defined separate by, in order to be able to define the method level summaries later. The fifth formula is the *average number of properties per object type*. This metric shows the average internal complexity of the object types in technique. The value $P_0(M_{\text{Class Diagram}}) = 2$ is quite typical, and it seems that most of the techniques fall into the range between one to three properties per object type.

6. $P_R(M_T, e) = n(p_T(e)) + \sum_{x \in r_T(e)} n(p(x \cdot i))$, where $i = (1,0)$ and $e \in R_T$

7. $\overline{P}_R(M_T) = \dfrac{1}{n(R_T)} \sum_{e \in R_T} P_0(M_T, o)$

The sixth formula is the *number of properties of a relationship type and its accompanying role types*. The inner sum of the equation counts the number of properties for all the role types associated with the current relationship type. Formula seven counts the *average number of properties per relationship type*. This metric shows the complexity of the interface between object types. The value $\overline{P}_R(M_{\text{ClassDiagram}}) = 4.0$ is quite normal.

8. $R_0(M_T, o) = n\left(\left\{e \in R_T : o \in \bigcup_{x \in fr(e)} (x \cdot j)\right\}\right)$, where $j = (0,1)$ and $o \in O_T$

9. $\overline{R}_o(M_T) = \dfrac{1}{n(O_T)} \sum_{o \in O_T} n(R_0(M_T, o))$

Formula 8 gives the *number of relationship types that can be connected to a certain object type*. Formula 9 gives the *average number of relationship types that can be connected to a given object type*. This metric measures, how complicated it is to select the right connection between object types. For example a requirements analysis technique can just use one connection type, whereas a detailed design technique can present a large number of slightly different relationship types.

This metric was chosen instead of, for example the average number of object types, that can be connected by a given relationship type, because in the usual use the developers are faced with the selection of a relationship type between objects instead of making first a relationship and then selecting object types for the relationship. The value for $R_0(M_{Class\ Diagrams}) = 4.4$, which is in the upper quartile line and shows, that the method has quite simple descriptions of the interfaces between objects (formula 7 above), but a high number of relationship types in the interface. The result can be interpreted that the complexity of using the relationships in this method is in the selection of the right relationship type and not in describing further the connection the relationship represents.

Aggregate metrics. The independent metrics above described the individual characteristics of techniques. In this section we propose some aggregate metrics, that can be used to measure the overall complexity of the technique.

10. $C(M_T, o) = \dfrac{P_0(M_T, o)}{\displaystyle\sum_{\{R_1 \in R: \exists b \in r: (R_1 = b \cdot i) \wedge (\exists \sigma \in (b \cdot j): (o \in \sigma \cdot j))\}} P_R(M_T, e)}$, where $i = (1,0)$ and

$j = (0,1)$

11. $\overline{C}(M_T) = \dfrac{1}{n(O_T)} \sum_{o \in O_T} C(M_T, o)$

The quotient (formula 10) shows the division of work in this technique, i.e. are things described by their internal properties, or external connections. The quotient will get higher values if there are many properties and a few relationship types with a few properties. The value for $\overline{C}(M_{Class\ Diagram}) = 0{,}91$ is quite close to the median line, and it shows that the method gives considerable importance to external connections.

12. $C'(M_T) = \sqrt{n(O_T)^2 + n(R_T)^2 + n(P_T)^2}$

The total conceptual complexity of a technique is not a straightforward measure, but we use the sum vector of the individual complexity factors of formula 1, 2 and 3. We propose to use it as the complexity vector in a xyz-coordinate system, that can be compared with other techniques.

In figure 3 we show the xy-plot of objects and relationships. It shows that Class Diagrams are more complex than average in number of relationships, but average in number of objects.

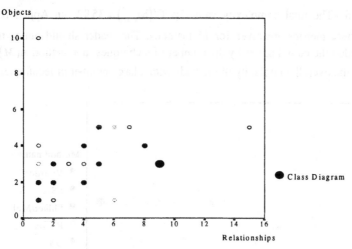

Fig. 3. Object / Relationship for Techniques

3.2. Method level metrics

Methods are here treated as collections of individual techniques, and thus we are omitting the problems related to the complexity of interconnected methods, due to the used meta modelling techniques inability to tackle with multiple techniques and their connections. This area clearly needs to be addressed in the future, but currently there is a lack of formal models of method interconnections as well as clear and unambigious decription of these interconnections in the methods [Kel94]. Thus method level complexities are simply summaries of individual technique complexities.

The cumulative complexities for method are counted first for each of the object, relationship and property types.

$$13. \quad n(O_m) = \sum_{T \in \mathcal{M}} n(O_T)$$

$$14. \quad n(R_m) = \sum_{T \in \mathcal{M}} n(R_T)$$

$$15. \quad n(P_m) = \sum_{T \in \mathcal{M}} n(P_T)$$

The following are the aggregate complexity metrics for the method level.

$$16. \quad \overline{C}(\mathcal{M}) = \sum_{T \in \mathcal{M}} \overline{C}(M_T)$$

$$17. \quad C'(\mathcal{M}) = \sqrt{n(O_M)^2 + n(R_M)^2 + n(P_M)^2}$$

The cumulative complexity can either be defined as the cumulative value of each individual technique's complexity, or we can take the sum vector of the totals of formulae 13, 14 and 15. The cumulative complexity returns a value, that explains the total complexity of the method. The sum vector identifies the "style" of the method, i.e. whether it describes the object systems by the properties, or relationships or objects, and whether these are used in a coherent and consistent style.

The values for OMT are the following: $n(O_{OMT}) = 13$, $n(R_{OMT}) = 19$ and $n(P_{OMT}) = 26$. The total complexity value is: $C'(M_{OMT}) = 35.92$. In Appendix 3 the values of these metrics are given for 15 methods. The reader should notice that we haven't divided the complexities by the number of techniques in a method $n(\mathcal{M})$. This would hide the overall complexity of methods with a large number of techniques.

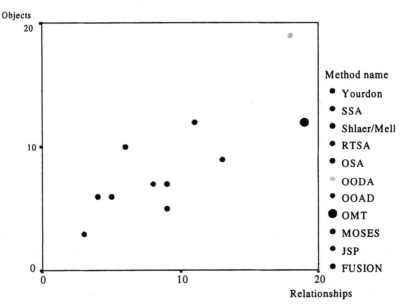

Fig. 4. Object / Relationship for Methods

On the method level it can be useful to check out the balance of individual techniques in the methods: i.e. if one of the techniques is very heavily loaded (i.e. has much more concepts than others), or the parts of the method are very different in style, this should be made explixit. In the case of OMT the Class Diagrams use 14 of the total of 19 relationship types and the other measures also have highest numbers in CD's. This means that the CD's are hard to learn and they are probably quite important for the method, because the main attention in development has been devoted to them. The checking ot the balancing can be done by counting the methods internal variances of each of the metrics and pointing out strange or extraordinary values.

4. Discussion and future research

In this paper we have proposed a set of metrics to evaluate the complexity of software development techniques and methods. By doing so we wish to guide and instruct the method developers to understand and analyse more systematically methods they suggest. Our goal is to establish one set of instrumental tests, that can be easily, and in a cost effective manner, used in evaluating methods. The proposed metrics are relatively simple due to the fact, that they are easier to understand and there is not much point in developing more complex metrics before we know more about the nature and measuring of methods.

One interesting comparison could be made between the implementations of the same techniques or methods in different CASE tools. This could show some differences in the complexity of the use of one technique in different tool environments. Similarly the various implementations of rule checking in Entity Relationship diagramming and Data Flow diagramming in CASE tools has been compared by Vessey [Ves92]. The metrics have been applied here only with OPRR-models, but their adaptation for ER-based metamodels in other CASE tools should be straightforward.

The metrics proposed here analyse only the conceptual part of the techniques, and they should be accompanied with a set of metrics for the complexity of the resulting models. The analysis of resulting models could be used to verify the method complexity. There should be a negative correlation between the complexity of the method and the size of the produced models, if the methods conceptual complexity leads into greater expressiveness [Oei94]. We believe, that there is a balance between learnability and expressive power of the method, and the organisations selecting methods should be aware of the fact, that more powerful methods are harder to learn, but can be more effective for experienced users.

Furthermore the metrics should be tested by method developers and in that way we could reach a set of metrics that can predict the properties of techniques such as learnability and model size.

The limitations of the approach proposed here are: first, there is no way of representing constraints of the technique in OPRR and OPRR can only model the static aspects of the techniques. Secondly, OPRR is not capable of dealing appropriately with interconnected methods. Third, our values should be complemented with empirical experience from practical applications of methods in use.

In the future we'll have to consider integrated methods and derive metrics for them. In that work we'll need better understanding of integration of techniques and how that complicates, or simplifies, the methods. Also we should gather empirical material about the learnability of different techniques and their implementations and about the use of different constructs in different techniques.

Acknowledgements

We would wish to thank Steven Kelly for assistance in formalising the metrics, other members of MetaPHOR team, Design Methodology Research Group of University of Twente and anonymous reviewers.

References

[Alb83]   Albrecht, A. J., J. E. Gaffney, "*Software Function, Source Lines of Code, and Development Prediction: A Software Science Validation,*" IEEE Transactions on Software Engineering 9(6) (1983) pp.639--647.

[Boo94]   Booch, G., "Object-Oriented Analysis and Design," Benjamin]Cummings, Redwood City, California (1994).

[Bri89]   Brinkkemper, S., M. de Lange, R. Looman and F. H. G. C. van der Steen, *"On the Derivation of Method Companionship by Meta-Modelling,"* Imperial College, London, UK (1989).

[Bri90]   Brinkkemper, S., *"Formalisation of Information Systems Modelling,"* Thesis Publishers, Amsterdam (1990).

[Cha91]   Champeaux, D. de, *"A comparative study of Object Oriented Analysis Methods,"* Technical report Research Report, HP Laboratories (1991).

[Che91]   Chen, M., J. F. Nunamaker Jr. and G. Mason, *"The Architecture And Design Of A Collaborative Environment For Systems Definition,"* DATA BASE (1991) pp.22--28.

[Coa91]   Coad, P., E. Yourdon, *"Object-Oriented Analysis,"* Yourdon Press, Englewood Cliffs, New Jersey (1991).

[Dav90]   Davenport, T. H., J. E. Short, *"The New Industrial Engineering: Information Technology and Business Process Redesign,"* Sloan Management Review (1990) pp.11--26.

[Fen94]   Fenton, N., *"Software Measurement: A Necessary Scientific Basis,"* IEEE Transactions on Software Engineering 20(3) (1994) pp.199--206.

[Hal77]   Halstead, M., *"Elements of Software Science,"* Elsevier North-Holland (1977).

[Hen81]   Henry, S., D. Kafura, *"Software Structure Metrics Based on Information Flow,"* IEEE Transactions on Software Engineering 7(5) (1981) pp.510--518.

[Hey93]   Heym, M., H. Österle, *"Computer-aided methodology engineering,"* INFORMATION AND SOFTWARE TECHNOLOGY 35(6/7) (1993) pp.345--354.

[Hon93]   Hong, S., G. van den Goor and S. Brinkkemper, "A Comparison of Six Object-Oriented Analysis and Design Methods," in *Proceedings of the 26th Hawaiian Conference on Systems Sciences*, IEEE Computer Science Press (1993).

[Iiv83]   Iivari, J., P. Kerola, "A sociocybernetic framework for the feature analysis of information systems development methodologies," in *Information Systems Methodologies: A Feature Analysis*, North--Hollland, Amsterdam (1983).

[Kel94]   Kelly, S., K. Smolander, *"Evolution and Issues in MetaCASE,"* Information and Software Technology (1994).

[Kit91]   Kitchenham, B., "Metrics and measurement," in *Software Engineer's reference book*, Butterworth-Heinemann, Oxford (1991).

[Kum92]   Kumar, Kuldeep, Richard J. Welke, "Methodology Engineering: A Proposal for Situation Specific Methodology Construction," in *Challenges and Strategies for Research in Systems Development*, John Wiley & Sons, Washington (1992).

[Oei94]   Oei, J. L. H., E. D. Falkenberg, "Harmonisation of information systems modelling and specification techniques," in *Methods and Associated Tools for the Information Systems Life Cycle*, Elsevier Science publishers (1994).

[Roc94]   Roche, John M., *"Software Metrics and Measurement Principles,"* Software Engineering Notes 19(1) (1994) pp.77--85.

[Ros94]   Rossi,   M.,   J.-P.   Tolvanen,   *"Metamodeling   approach   to   method comparison: A survey of a set of ISD methods,"* University of Jyväskylä, Jyväskylä (1994).

[Ros94b] Rossi, M., *"The MetaEdit CAME environment,"* University of Sunderland press, Sunderland (1994).

[Rum91]   Rumbaugh, J., M. Blaha, W. Premerlani, F. Eddy and W. Lorensen, *"Object-Oriented Modeling and Design,"* Prentice--Hall, Englewood Cliffs, NJ, USA (1991).

[Slo93]   Slooten, Kees van, Sjaak Brinkkemper, "A Method Engineering Approach to Information Systems Development," in *Procs. of the IFIP WG 8.1 Working Conference on the Information Systems Development Process,* North-Holland, Amsterdam (1993).

[Smo91]   Smolander, Kari, "OPRR: A Model for Modelling Systems Development Methods," in *Next Generation CASE Tools,* IOS Press, Amsterdam, the Netherlands (1991).

[Smo91b] Smolander, Kari, Kalle Lyytinen, Veli-Pekka Tahvanainen and Pentti Marttiin, "MetaEdit --- A Flexible Graphical Environment for Methodology Modelling," in *Advanced Information Systems Engineering, Proceedings of the Third International Conference CAiSE'91, Trondheim, Norway, May 1991,* Springer-Verlag, Berlin (1991).

[Son92]   Song, X., L. Osterweil, *"Towards Objective and Systematic Comparisons of Software Design Methodologies,"* IEEE Software (1992).

[Sor88]   Sorenson, Paul G., Jean-Paul Tremblay and Andrew J. McAllister, *"The Metaview System for Many Specification Environments,"* IEEE SOFTWARE (1988) pp.30--38.

[SPS94]   SPSS, , *"SPSS for Windows 1.0 Reference Guide,"* SPSS Inc., Chicago, USA (1994).

[Tei80]   Teichroew, Daniel, Petar Macasovic, Ernest A. Hershey III and Yuzo Yamamoto, "Application of the entity-relationship approach to information processing systems modeling," in *Entity-Relationship Approach to Systems Analysis and Design,* North-Holland (1980).

[Tol93]   Tolvanen, J.-P., K. Lyytinen, *"Flexible method adaptation in CASE environments - The metamodeling approach,"* Scandinavian Journal of Information Systems 5(1) (1993) pp.51-77.

[Tuk77]   Tukey, J. W., *"Exploratory Data Analysis,"* Addison Wesley, Reading, MA (1977).

[Ves92]   Vessey, I., S. L. Järvenpää and N. Tractinsky, *"Evaluation of Vendor Products: CASE Tools as Methdology Companions,"* Communications of the ACM 35(4) (1992) pp.90-105.

[Wel92]   Welke, R. J., "The CASE Repository: More than another database application," in *Challenges and Strategies for Research in Systems Development,* Wiley, Chichester UK (1992).

Appendix 1. Values obtained from 34 techniques

This table lists the values of 34 techniques modelled by OPRR in the MetaEdit environment. The table shows the name of the method, the name of the technique and the values obtained for the formulae, which are referred by their number in the main text.

Method	Technique	1	2	3	5	7	9	11	12
Yourdon	Entity Relationship Attribute Diagram	3	2	6	2,33	1,67	,50	1,44	7
Yourdon	Data Flow Diagram	3	2	6	1,67	2	1	,42	7
Yourdon	Structure Chart	1	1	4	2	1	2	,67	4,24
Yourdon	State Transition Diagram	3	1	5	2	1	4	,40	5,92
OODA	Class Diagram	3	9	10	4,67	5	1,44	,70	13,78
OODA	Module Diagram	10	1	4	3	1	1	1,50	10,82
OODA	Object Diagram	1	6	8	5	6	4	,17	10,05
OODA	Process Diagram	2	1	6	4	1	3	1	6,40
OODA	State Transition Diagram	3	1	4	1	1	3	,25	5,10
JSP	Data Structure Diagram	1	1	3	3	1		3	3,32
JSP	Program Structure Diagram	2	2	5	2,50	1,50		1,75	5,74
OOAD	Object Oriented Analysis and Design	3	5	6	2,33 ·	4	1	,37	8,37
OOAD	Service Chart	3	2	7	2,67	2	,50	,89	7,87
OOAD	Object State Diagram	1	1	3	2	1	1	1	3,32
OMT	Class Diagram	5	15	14	2	4,40	4	,91	21,12
OMT	Data Flow Diagram	3	3	8	1,67	3	2	,19	9,06
OMT	State Diagram	4	1	4	1,50	1	2	,50	5,74
FUSION	Object Model	4	4	8	2	2,25	,75	,54	9,80
FUSION	Object Interaction Graph	2	1	7	3	1	3	,75	7,35
MOSES	O/C Model	4	8	10	4,50	6	1,88	,67	13,42
MOSES	Event Model	1	1	6	3	1	4	,60	6,16
Shlaer/ Mellor	Information Structure Diagram	2	4	8	2,50	2	5	1,06	9,17
Shlaer/ Mellor	Action Data Flow Diagram	2	4	7	2,50	3	1,75	,30	8,31
Shlaer/ Mellor	State Transition Diagram	3	1	5	2	1	4	,40	5,92
OSA	Object Behavior Model	3	4	6	3	4	1	,38	7,81
OSA	Object Interaction Model	1	2	4	1	2	2,50	,14	4,58
OSA	Object Relationship Model	5	7	11	1,80	2,20	1,57	,75	13,96
Goldkuhl	Activity model	5	5	8	1,60	2,80	,20	,55	10,68
Demeter	Demeter	3	2	5	4	2	,50	1,33	6,16
Express	EXPRESS-G	5	6	13	2,20	4	2,67	,14	15,17
SSA	Structured Systems Analysis	3	2	10	3	2	2	,50	10,63
SSA	Entity Relationship Attribute Diagram	3	2	6	2,33	1,67	,50	1,44	7

RTSA	Real-Time Structured Analysis	5	7	4	2,20	4,20	1	,30	9,49
RTSA	Entity Relationship Attribute Diagram	3	2	6	2,33	1,67	,50	1,44	7
RTSA	Structure Chart	1	1	4	2	1	2	,67	4,24
RTSA	State Transition Diagram	3	1	5	2	1	4	,40	5,92

Appendix 2. Boxplots for Techniques

The 5-point box-plots can be read as (from left to right): bar representing minimun, box starting from lower quartile, in the box there is the median bar and end of the box is the upper quartile, fifth bar is the maximum. The outliers are indicated by a marker with the name of the technique (objects number with the * indicating Booch module diagrams is an example). **Notice**, that the scales differ from figure to figure to ease the reading of the boxes.

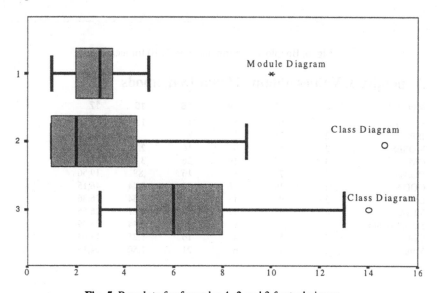

Fig. 5. Boxplots for formulae 1, 2 and 3 for techniques

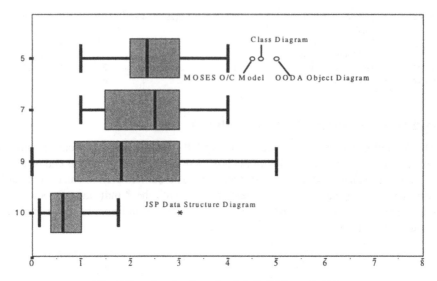

Fig. 6. Boxplots for formulae 5, 9, 7, 10 for techniques

Appendix 3. Values obtained from 15 methods

Method	n*	13	14	15	16	17
FUSION	2	6	5	15	1,20	17,15
JSP	2	3	3	8		9,06
MOSES	2	5	9	16	2,11	19,58
OMT	3	12	19	26	3,58	35,92
OOAD	3	7	8	16	,88	19,56
OODA	5	19	18	32	2,44	46,15
OSA	3	9	13	21	1,54	26,36
RTSA	4	12	11	19	1,27	26,65
Shlaer/Mellor	3	7	9	20	3,44	23,39
SSA	2	6	4	16	1,25	17,63
Yourdon	4	10	6	21	1,50	24,16

---

* n is the number of techniques in the method

InfoHarness: Use of Automatically Generated Metadata for Search and Retrieval of Heterogeneous Information

Leon Shklar*‡, Amit Sheth†, Vipul Kashyap†‡, and Kshitij Shah*‡

shklar@cs.rutgers.edu

Abstract. The *InfoHarness*™ system is aimed at providing integrated and rapid access to huge amounts of heterogeneous information independent of its type, representation, and location. This is achieved by extracting metadata and associating it with the original information. The metadata extraction methods ensure rapid and largely automatic creation of information repositories. A stable hierarchy of abstract classes is proposed to organize the processing and representation needs of different kinds of information. An extensible hierarchy of terminal classes simplifies support for new information types and utilization of new indexing technologies. InfoHarness repositories may be accessed through Mosaic or any other HyperText Transfer Protocol (HTTP) compliant browser.

1.0 Introduction

The accelerating explosion in the amounts and variety of information has made the knowledge about its existence, location, and the means of retrieval very confusing. The information ranges from software artifacts to engineering and financial databases, and comes in different types (e.g., source code, e-mail messages, bitmaps) and representations (e.g., plain text, binary). This information has to be accessed through a variety of vendor tools and locally developed applications.

There have been attempts to address this problem by building information repositories that depend on relocating and reformatting the original information [20]. Such approaches require the design and maintenance of ever-changing format translators. The initial conversion of information requires substantial human and computing resources. Maintaining the repositories presents the additional dilemma of either creating new and updating existing information in the uniform format, or continuously managing changing data in different formats. The latter may be partially remedied through recent efforts in the uniform representation of heterogeneous documents [29], but this does not help with arbitrarily formatted data.

Our main objective in constructing the InfoHarness system is to provide rapid access to huge amounts of heterogeneous information in a distributed environment without any relocation, restructuring, or reformatting of data. Many researchers have investigated the use of metadata to support run-time access to the original information [1,3,8,9,11, 12,13,19,26]. Others [5,11,21,27] have investigated the use of data mining for the automatic extraction of metadata. We refine and synthesize some of the ideas contained in these efforts to provide advanced search and browsing capabilities without

---

*   Bell Communications Research, 444 Hoes Lane, Piscataway, NJ 08854
†   LSDIS, Department of Computer Science, University of Georgia, Athens, GA 30602-7404
‡   Computer Science Department, Rutgers University, New Brunswick, NJ 08902
™ InfoHarness is a trademark of Bell Communications Research, Inc.

imposing constraints on information suppliers or creators. Further, we propose and develop a *stable* abstract class hierarchy, which need not be modified to define terminal classes that accommodate new types of information and new indexing technologies.

InfoHarness has been designed with an open, extensible, and modular architecture. The InfoHarness prototype is now operational and on trial at Bellcore for building repositories of heterogeneous software artifacts [25], accessing geo-spatial data, and a variety of other applications. It supports the largely automatic generation of InfoHarness repositories, and provides access to the physical information from Mosaic and other World-Wide Web (WWW [2]) browsers through an HTTP gateway. We expect to make the system available on the Internet in the first half of 1995.

The key features of InfoHarness include:
- Providing advanced search and browsing capabilities without restructuring, reformatting, or relocating information.
- An extensible terminal class hierarchy to model arbitrary formatted information.
- The ability to utilize third-party indexing technologies.
- Extensive use of metadata for mapping logical views of information to physical files.
- A high-level declarative language [26] to provide power and flexibility in controlling the metadata generation process (now under development).

In this paper, we have analyzed *content-based* and *content-descriptive* metadata and their utility in the search, retrieval and browsing of information. Content-based metadata is based on the content of documents (e.g., the document vectors in the LSI index and the complete inverted WAIS index). Content-descriptive metadata serves to describe documents and includes *domain-independent* metadata (e.g., the location and size of a document) and *domain-dependent* metadata which abstracts or attempts to capture the semantic meaning of information. We also take a look at the classification of metadata based on their utility (a modified version of the one in [3]) and see how various attempts at using metadata (including the one in InfoHarness) conform to the classification.

The organization of the paper is as follows. In section 2, we discuss the role of metadata in providing transparent access to information. In section 2.1, we discuss the organization of metadata. In section 2.2, we define the notions of stability and extensibility of a class hierarchy. These notions are based on the ability of subclasses to inherit general methods from their superclasses and customize them for their own use. The customization is performed by writing ad-hoc stand-alone programs as discussed in section 2.3. In section 2.4, we discuss attribute-based access and retrieval of information. In section 3, we discuss the InfoHarness architecture. We begin with an overview (section 3.1), and then concentrate on indexing and searching of InfoHarness repositories (section 3.2) and on browsing information (section 3.3). In section 4 we discuss related efforts. Conclusions and plans for future work are presented in section 5.

2.0 Transparent Data Access through Metadata

An important advantage of InfoHarness is that it provides access to a variety of heterogeneous information without making any assumptions about the location and representation of data. This is achieved by creating metadata and associating it with the original information. Metadata for different media types is often defined as derived properties of the media, which are useful in information access or retrieval [5]. It establishes relationships between *information units* (defined below) and portions of physical information that present logical units of interest for end-users.

An *information unit* (IU) is a metadata entity that encapsulates a logical unit of information. It represents the lowest level of granularity of information available to Info-Harness. The IU may be associated with a file (e.g., a man page), a portion of a file (e.g., a C function or a database table), a set of files (e.g., a collection of related bitmaps), or any request for the retrieval of data from an external source (e.g., a database query).

An *InfoHarness object* (IHO) is defined recursively as one of the following:
- A *simple* IHO, composed of a single IU.
- A *collection* IHO that contains a set of references to other InfoHarness objects.
- A *composite* IHO that combines a simple IHO and a set of references to other IHOs.

Each IHO has a unique object identifier that is recognized and maintained by the system. An IHO that contains an IU has to store the locations of both the data and the retrieval method, as well as any parameters needed by the method to retrieve the encapsulated data. In addition, each IHO may contain an arbitrary number of attribute-value pairs (e.g., owner, last update, security information, decryption method).

Each IHO that references a collection of other IHOs stores unique object identifiers of the members of the collection (its *children*). An IHO that both contains an IU and references a collection is called a *composite object*. An example of the composite object is this paper's abstract combined with the collection containing references to postscript and latex versions of the full paper.

IHOs that encapsulate indexed collections store information about locations of both the index and the query method. Any indexed collection may make use of its own data retrieval method that is not a part of InfoHarness. As a result, an InfoHarness Repository may be created from existing heterogeneous index structures.

An InfoHarness Repository (IHR) is a set of IHOs that are known to a single Info-Harness server. These IHOs are not necessarily members of the same collection. An IHO may be a member of any number of collections (its *parents*). Each IHO that has one or more parents always contains unique object identifiers of its parent objects. An IHO that does not have any parent is unreachable from any other IHO and may only be accessed if it is used as an initial starting point (or *entry point*) in the IHR traversal.

2.1 InfoHarness Class Hierarchy

This section describes the InfoHarness class hierarchy (Figure 1). The *Abstract Classes* provide method sharing between groups of terminal classes. The *Terminal Classes* are classes that cannot be subclassed and are instantiated as InfoHarness objects. Examples of Terminal Classes include encapsulators of external viewers, as well as the Wide-Area Information Service (WAIS) [16] and Latent Semantic Indexing (LSI) [6] indexing tools. The InfoHarness class hierarchy is utilized to instantiate terminal classes to IHOs. We can say that it represents an implicit organization of the metadata.

The abstract class hierarchy (Figure 1) has been constructed to serve two purposes:
1. Support for heterogeneous data and independent indexing technologies.
2. Support for both server-side and client-side run-time processing of information.

The distinction between the *Server Processing* class and the *Client Processing* class is based on the differences in processing information while the rationale for their subclasses is in data representation.

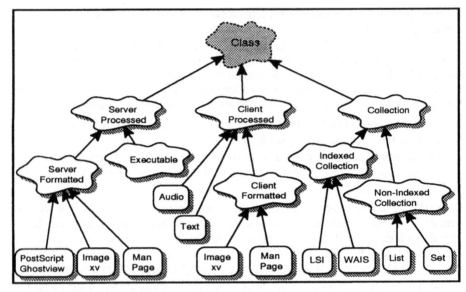

Fig. 1. InfoHarness Class Hierarchy with Sample Terminal Classes.

Server Processing

The *Server Processing* abstract class helps to group IHOs with IUs, which are accessed at run-time by running a process on the server. The subclasses of this class are the abstract classes *Server Formatted Data* and *Executable*. The subclasses of *Server Formatted Data* serve to access physical data by running external viewers. The abstract class *Executable* represents IUs that encapsulate application programs.

Client Processing

For instances of terminal subclasses of *Client Processing*, data is first transferred to the client and then processed. Most of the data types may be defined by instantiating either a subclass of *Server Processing* or a subclass of *Client Processing*. The exceptions are *Audio* and *Text* that are always defined by instantiating the *Client Processing* class.

- *Audio:* The special treatment of audio files is determined by the need to play the recording on the client machine for it to be heard.
- *Text:* The special treatment of text is for convenience in presenting plain text, as well as documents that use a mark-up language known to the client program.

Collections

Each instance of the *Collection* class stores a set of parent-child relationships between the IHOs. In addition, instances of the *Indexed Collection* class are associated with a physical index that is used at run-time to select members of the collection. Instances of the *Indexed Collection* class are presented to the end-user through a query interface, while instances of *Non-Indexed Collection* are presented as a full list of members.

2.2 Issues of Stability and Extensibility

In this section we discuss the properties of the InfoHarness class hierarchy that are important for supporting new data types and new indexing technologies.

Stability of the Abstract Class Hierarchy

The abstract class hierarchy in InfoHarness is stable in nature; i.e., we do not foresee the need for additional abstract classes to model different kinds of processing. Whenever an appropriate terminal class is defined, it inherits data access and representation methods from an existing abstract class. The abstract classes may thus be made part of the server implementation. The terminal class hierarchy is open and extensible, as discussed in the next section.

Extensibility of Data Types

The InfoHarness class hierarchy is open in that new terminal classes may be defined to accommodate the vast variety of information. The new classes utilize methods inherited from the abstract classes. These methods are customized by writing ad-hoc stand-alone programs that are invoked at run-time. In the future, the customization will be performed through interpreting statements of a declarative type definition language.

Terminal classes are not part of the InfoHarness implementation and reflect design choices made by InfoHarness administrators. These choices may be determined either by the availability of data or by the availability of tools used to view the data. It is possible to define two different terminal classes, *Man Page* (descendant of *Server Processing*) and *Man Page* (descendant of *Client Processing*), as subclasses of *Server Formatted Data* and *Client Formatted Data* respectively. These classes may either be used for accessing different sets of man pages or for providing end-users with alternative ways of accessing the same data.

Extensibility of Indexing Strategies

Just as new terminal classes may be defined to support new data types, new terminal classes may also be defined to support independent indexing technologies. The only additional complication is in maintaining the mapping between two different member identifications: the one known to the indexing algorithm and the one known to InfoHarness. It is fairly easy to support WAIS [16], LSI [6,7], and similar indexing technologies by defining appropriate terminal classes. In the present version of InfoHarness, we default to LSI indexing, which is discussed further in section 3.2. In the same section, we discuss the selection of an appropriate indexing strategy depending on the size of a collection, frequency of modification, etc.

2.3 Metadata Extraction

In this section, we discuss the extraction of content-based and content-descriptive metadata. The content-descriptive metadata is composed of IHOs and their relationships. Each IHO in an IHR may have multiple children, as well as multiple parents. The physical data that is associated with information units is not part of the IHR. The generation of an IHR amounts to the generation of both content-descriptive and content-based metadata, the latter by indexing physical information declared to belong to indexed collections.

The IHR generation is supported by the *generator* program, which accepts as inputs both the location and the desired representation of data, and outputs the set of IHOs and their relationships. The generator commands may be either written down by InfoHarness administrators, or created automatically by interpreting IRDL statements. Detailed discussion of IRDL is beyond the scope of this paper and may be found in [26].

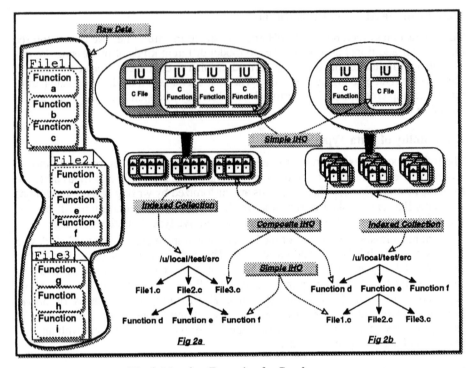

Fig. 2. Metadata Extraction for C code.

Consider the simple example of creating an indexed collection of man pages. Given the location of man pages, their desired run-time representation, and the desired indexing technology, the generator program performs the following actions:

1. Creates IUs associated with individual man pages.
2. Creates an IHO for every IU created in step 1.
3. Invokes an independent indexing tool to index the man pages.
4. Creates an IHO associated with the index, and adds parent-child relationships from this IHO to each object created in step 2.

By definition, IUs represent the smallest pieces of information retrievable through Info-Harness. Consider the example of an e-mail system that stores messages in individual files. Making this information available through InfoHarness involves defining information units that have one-to-one correspondence with physical files. On the other hand, in the case of *RMAIL* files, a single file contains multiple messages and each message is associated with an information unit.

To better understand the process of metadata extraction, we discuss the metadata generation for *C* code (Figure 2). To encapsulate individual functions and perform indexing based on comments and function names, the extractor has to perform some basic parsing to recognize comments, function blocks, etc. Function signatures, which uniquely identify individual functions, are stored as values of the *name* attribute of encapsulating objects. Function names are used to qualify file names in the *location* attribute. Similar work has been done in [4] where information about functions and variables is extracted after code analysis. There have also been earlier efforts to index *C* code based on comments [22].

The next step is to encapsulate and index C files, and create parent-child relationships between the collection IHO and the child objects (Figure 2a). The latter are composite objects that reference collections of simple objects, which encapsulate individual functions. Alternatively (Figure 2b), it may be desirable to index the individual functions and establish parent-child relationships between the indexed collection and function IHOs, as well as between function IHOs and file IHOs.

A recent addition to the InfoHarness type library is the $C++$ extractor. Since $C++$ code has much more information of interest than C code, it is correspondingly more complex to write a $C++$ extractor. Parse trees are generated and traversed to separate out information units, which encapsulate functions, class definitions, class-subclass relationships, and individual methods.

Additional extractors for unstructured image data and structured data in the form of relational and object oriented databases are being designed. Some of these offer significant research challenges.

2.4 Attribute-based Access and Retrieval

We have considered the following kinds of metadata:
1. content-based metadata,
2. content-descriptive metadata,
   2.1. domain-independent metadata,
   2.2. domain-dependent metadata.

Examples of content-based metadata include full-text indices of InfoHarness collections. In the case of LSI, these indices have the form of document vectors (section 3.2). The extraction of content-descriptive metadata was discussed in section 2.3. Examples of content-descriptive metadata may include *location, ownership, creation-date*, etc. The content-descriptive metadata is inferred without performing the semantic analysis.

In the future, we are planning to support more intelligent querying to accommodate naive users. This may require capturing the semantic content of information by describing the meaning and possible usages of individual documents. For this, we need to characterize the *domain* of information represented by a set of IHOs, for example, the domain of software artifacts. While content-based metadata is stored as a set of vectors, the content-descriptive metadata is represented as a set of attribute-value pairs. The attributes may capture domain aspects, as well as characteristics of physical data.

One approach to capturing domain-dependent descriptive metadata for structured databases is described in [18]. The attributes, which are referred to as contextual coordinates, are selected judiciously from domain-specific ontologies. These are then used to construct contexts that capture the assumptions implicit in the design of the object classes in a database. The contexts are used to perform inferences on the information content of the databases without actually retrieving the data.

We are investigating extending the above approach to semi-structured and unstructured data. Additional generalization effort may be well worth it due to the limitations of content-based access, as in the following example:

Consider a paper titled *"Use of Automatically Generated Metadata for Search and Retrieval of Heterogeneous Information"* that is to be presented at the conference in Jyvaskyla, and let it be identical to the one that you are reading with the only exception that it does not contain section 2.4. Then, it would not contain the words *conference* and *Jyvaskyla*.

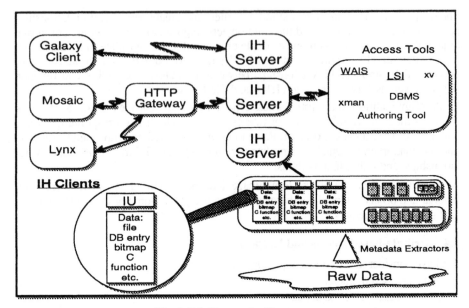

Fig. 3. InfoHarness Architecture.

Consider the following keyword-based query:

Query = *conference Jyvaskyla*

The above mentioned paper will not be retrieved! The problem may, of course, be remedied by creating additional descriptive attributes and associating them with the paper. Work is also underway to mutually scale results obtained from attribute-based and content-based queries.

3.0 InfoHarness Architecture

The InfoHarness system architecture provides a platform for integrating information in a distributed environment by encapsulating existing and new information, without converting, restructuring or reformatting the physical data. Through this object-oriented encapsulation, the system provides an integrated view and access to diverse and heterogeneous information. The system allows the use of independent tools for accessing, retrieving, browsing, and administering the information encapsulated by IHOs that are stored in InfoHarness repositories.

3.1 Architecture Overview

As shown in Figure 3, the main components of the current implementation of the Info-Harness architecture are:

1. The InfoHarness Server (IH Server) that uses metadata to traverse, search, and retrieve the original information.
2. The HTTP Gateway that is used to pass requests from HTTP clients to the IH Server and the responses back to the clients.
3. The Repository Generator that is used for the off-line generation of metadata that represents the desirable view on the structure and organization of the original information. This metadata is used by the Server for the run-time search and retrieval.

Independent tools for accessing and displaying information (e.g., xv, xman, etc.), and for indexing information (e.g., Wide-Area Information Server (WAIS), Bellcore's Latent Semantic Indexing (LSI)), are not part of InfoHarness.

At run-time, users of HTTP-compliant clients may issue query, traversal, or retrieval requests that are passed on to the Gateway, which performs the following operations:

1. Parses the request, and reads input information when the request is associated with an HTML form.
2. Establishes a socket connection with the IH Server, generates and sends out a request, and waits for a response.
3. Parses the response, converts it to a combination of HTML forms and hyperlinks, adds the HTTP header, and passes the transformed response to the Mosaic browser.

The IH Server processes requests based on the meta-information. The same physical data may be treated differently depending on its type. For example, consider two alternative types, both designed to represent man pages: *man_to_html* and *xman*. In the first case, the IH Server will pass the man page location to a *man_to_html* converter and send the generated HTML back to the HTTP gateway. In the second case, the server will pass the man page location directly to the *xman* browser and notify the gateway program.

The Gateway does not perform any format conversions of the original information. It only converts to HTML those parts of the response that either contain the portion of metadata that is currently being searched or traversed by the end-user, or error messages and notifications.

The InfoHarness architecture is open, modular, extensible and scalable. InfoHarness implements the abstract type hierarchy that does not have to be modified to support a new data type, or a new indexing technology. The methods associated with abstract classes are general enough because they are data-driven and may invoke independent programs. The definitions of terminal classes are also data-driven and are not part of the implementation, which makes the system capable of supporting arbitrary information access and management tools (e.g., browsers, indexing technologies, access methods).

The system addresses the goals of scalability and interoperability in a large and geographically distributed environment by supporting multiple servers and multiple clients, and by decentralizing the administration of information repositories.

3.2 Indexing and Searching InfoHarness Repositories

InfoHarness supports both indexed and non-indexed collections. Indices are generated on the bags of words that are contained within portions of physical data that are encapsulated by member IHOs. InfoHarness can support different indexing strategies (Latent Semantic Indexing (LSI), WAIS, etc.). LSI is discussed in the next section, followed by a brief review of alternative indexing technologies and guidelines for their selection.

Latent Semantic Indexing

A fundamental deficiency of many information retrieval methods is that the words used for searching are rarely the same as the words used for indexing. The fact that there are many ways of describing the same object (synonymy) means that many relevant objects will be missed, thus affecting the *recall*. The fact that the same word can be used to refer to different things (polysemy) means that irrelevant objects will be retrieved, thus affecting the *precision*.

LSI's [6,7,28] approach is to take advantage of implicit higher order structure in the association of terms with documents. It uses the singular-value decomposition that arranges the term space to reflect the major associative patterns in the data and ignore the smaller and less important influences.

Each term and document is represented as a vector in the k-dimensional factor space. A query, just as a document, initially appears as a set of words. It is represented as the weighted sum of its component term vectors and placed at the centroid of its term vectors. The scaled query representation is compared against the representations of all indexed documents, the nearest of which (those with the highest cosines) are selected.

Alternative Indexing Techniques

As mentioned earlier in the paper, InfoHarness can support multiple indexing technologies. We are developing formal criteria and guidelines for selecting the ones that are the most appropriate for particular applications.

LSI is a statistical technique which correlates words on the basis of their occurrence patterns in the documents. It also does the clustering of words based on the statistical analysis, which form the dimensions of the multi-dimensional vector space. The WAIS index [16] is a complete inverted index on the document contents and does not involve any statistical analysis. We are currently investigating the following criteria for choosing between these technologies:

- *Size of a Collection:* The WAIS indexing technique is preferred if there are just a few documents in the collection. Statistical techniques like LSI require a large sample space to prevent meaningless answers at the time of query processing.
- *Frequency of Modification:* WAIS is also preferred if the collection is modified frequently (addition, deletion and update of documents). This is because extensive statistical computations are required by LSI to recompute the word clusters.
- *Types of Queries:* The WAIS index is suitable for keyword-based queries but not for finding documents that do not contain the exact keywords (e.g. searching for *car* it may not be possible to retrieve documents containing the word *automobile*). The LSI index supports such "semantic" searches.
- *Domain Structure of Information:* It would be advantageous to use LSI if all documents are from the same domain or display a typical usage correlation pattern or structure. If the documents are chosen at random from different domains, WAIS is likely to work better.

3.3 Browsing Information

This section addresses browsing physical data, which may range from plain text to multimedia information. We distinguish between browsing metadata and browsing the encapsulated physical data. Browsing methods are determined by types, which are assigned by the metadata extractors at the pre-processing stage.

Each IHO contains relevant information about the encapsulated physical data, as well as the relationships with other IHOs. This structure is presented to the user, who can choose to retrieve the physical data or to traverse parent-child relationships. Browsing methods act upon the data retrieval request after determining the physical location of information. A browsing method may or may not invoke a presentation tool. Independent browsers are used to browse through postscript documents, image files, etc.

The relationships between information units and physical files are different for types, as described in section 2.3. The extractor methods understand these relationships and generate the metadata accordingly. The search and browsing methods obtain this very same knowledge from IHOs and their relationships. The browsing methods are specific to the representation of the physical information. For example, an image viewer may be invoked for image files and an audio player for sound files. The user need not have any knowledge about ways of launching the appropriate tool. Hypertext browsing can also be supported if the original document is a hypertext.

3.4 Query Processing in InfoHarness

In the previous sections we have identified two ways of accessing IHOs in InfoHarness repositories. They are as follows:

- *Attribute- based Access:* This has been discussed in section 2.4 of this paper and involves querying documents based on their attributes, which may contain information not captured in their contents (e.g., ownership, publisher, etc.).
- *Content-based Access:* This involves querying for documents based on their contents (e.g., presence of keywords, presence of patterns, etc.). Querying indices built from the contents of documents is an example of content-based access. We are planning to further simplify adding support for third party indexing technologies.

We are currently investigating different ways of meaningfully combining results obtained from attribute-based and content-based queries.

4.0 Related Work

Hypermedia systems like Intermedia [30] focus more on browsing than on retrieval. As for database systems, the original data has to be converted into internal representations that are usually proprietary. On the other hand, traditional file systems lack the ability to represent inter-file relationships. Huge and growing amounts of heterogeneous information call for a more versatile system.

InfoHarness shares some of its objectives with RUFUS [26]. The RUFUS system has an extensible object-oriented data model, storage system, and associated search and display methods for a variety of predefined file types. RUFUS users can also search, browse, filter and display the imported data objects. The system automatically classifies data files and extracts type-specific attributes. In InfoHarness, its information units may be associated with files, sets of files, or portions of these files. This approach is more flexible in providing finer control at interpreting data.

Metadata is being increasingly used by researchers in multimedia, text and structured databases as an aid in the quest for seamless interoperability. Chen et al [5] define metadata as derived properties of the media which are useful for information access or retrieval. In the meta-database project at RPI [12], a metadata management approach is adopted to achieve a global synergy between various component databases. Bohm and Rakow [3] have classified metadata according to their nature and related it with their different intended purposes. The comparison of this classification with the approach used in InfoHarness is discussed further in the section. Kiyoki et al [19] implement a semantic associative search for images based on the keyword metadata representing the user's impression and the image's content. Anderson and Stonebraker [1] have developed a metadata schema for satellite images. Jain and Hampapur [13] have proposed an intermediate representation for audio-visual information.

In InfoHarness, we have emphasized the extensive use of automatically generated metadata. Bohm and Rakow [3] have proposed a novel classification of metadata and have drawn a distinction between the metadata and its organization. They have also established the relation between the intended use of metadata and its classification. The same perspective is reflected in the hierarchical organization of InfoHarness objects and classes as illustrated in Figure 1. The overlap between the classification in [3] and our approach is as follows:

- *Representation of Information Types:* This is achieved in InfoHarness through various encapsulators for different kinds of information. It is also one of the rationales for the proposed organization of metadata. In [1], metadata is used to support two perspectives of satellite image data: a computer scientist's and an earth scientist's.
- *Content-based Metadata:* This type of metadata refers to the metadata extracted from the physical information based on its content. Vectors associated with textual documents in an LSI-indexed collection are examples of content-based metadata. Vectors proposed for text and audio documents in [10], time-indices of keywords and location of keywords in a text image based on word spotting [5], and the data features in [13] also follow the content-based approach.
- *Content-Descriptive Metadata:* This is being planned as an extension to InfoHarness (section 2.4). Content-descriptive metadata has been used in [18] for information resource discovery and query processing in Multidatabases. The domain-dependent Q-features and the content-independent meta-features in [13] are examples of content-descriptive metadata for audio-visual information.
- *Document Composition:* This type of metadata is created at the time of extraction when the parent child relationships between different IHOs are being established. This perspective is reflected in the structure of composite IHOs.
- *Document Location:* This information is represented as an attribute for all kinds of IHOs supported by the InfoHarness system.
- *Document Collection Metadata:* The information associated with a full-text index is a type of metadata associated with the collection of documents as a whole.
- *Presentation Requirements:* Different technical settings on the client and the server sites demand more flexible document-processing mechanisms. In the InfoHarness system, the idiosyncrasies are captured as metadata. This perspective is reflected in the abstract classes Client Processing and Server Processing in Figure 1.
- *Browsing:* In the InfoHarness system, browsing takes place through the association relationships between information units and physical data. These associations are captured by the metadata (section 3.3). In [11], the metadata is represented through objects with their associated relationships and attributes. These relationships are used for browsing through the associated media objects (images and video).

5.0 Conclusions and Future Work

The important advantage of InfoHarness is in providing flexible access to arbitrary heterogeneous information without any relocation or reformatting. The InfoHarness Abstract Type Hierarchy is stable in the sense that it does not have to be modified to support new user-specific terminal classes. This hierarchy has been constructed to achieve the dual flexibility in the representation, as well as the presentation of data.

Our current work is directed toward further automation of the generation of Info-Harness repositories. However, it is not our intention to direct the generation of the repositories by the analysis of physical data alone. We intend to develop a declarative Repository Definition Language [26]. Statements of this language, combined with the physical data, together would determine the structure of InfoHarness repositories.

We are also performing investigations aimed at improving the scalability of search by meaningfully combining the results of querying independent (possibly heterogeneous) indices that reference different collections of objects.

6.0 Acknowledgements

The authors want to thank Chumki Basu, Satish Thatte, Gomer Thomas, and Andrew Werth for their comments to the draft of the paper.

References

1 J. Anderson and M. Stonebraker, "SEQUOIA 2000 Metadata schema for Satellite Images", (to appear) SIGMOD Rec., special issue on Metadata for Digital Media, December 1994.

2 T. Berners-Lee et al, "World Wide Web: The Information Universe", Electronic Networking: Research, Applications and Policy", 1(2), 1992.

3 K. Bohm and T. Rakow, "Metadata for Multimedia Documents", (to appear) SIGMOD Record, special issue on Metadata for Digital Media, December 1994.

4 Y-F. Chen, M. Nishimoto and C. Ramamoorthy, "The C information abstraction system", IEEE Transactions on Software Engineering, March 1990.

5 F. Chen, M. Hearst, J. Kupiec, J. Pederson and L. Wilcox, "Metadata for Mixed-Media Access", (to appear) SIGMOD Record, special issue on Metadata for Digital Media, December 1994.

6 S. Deerwester, S.T. Dumais, G.W. Furnas, T.K. Landauer and R. Hashman, "Indexing by Latent Semantic Indexing", Journal of the American Society for Information Science, 41(6), 1990.

7 S. T. Dumais, G. W. Furnas, T. K. Landauer, S. Deerwester, and K. Harshman, "Using latent semantic analysis to improve access to textual information", Proceedings of the 1988 CHI Conference, 1988.

8 G. Fischer and C. Stevens, "Information access in complex, poorly structured information spaces", Proceedings of the 1991 CHI Conference, 1991.

9 F. Garzotto. P. Paolini, and D. Schwabe. "HDM - A Model-Based Approach to Hypertext Application Design", ACM Trans. on Inform. Systems, 11(1), 1993.

10 U. Glavitsch, P. Schauble and M. Wechsler, "Metadata for Integrating Speech Documents in a Text Retrieval System", (to appear) SIGMOD Record, special issue on Metadata for Digital Media, December 1994.

11 W. Grosky, F. Fotouhi and I. Sethi, "Content-Based Hypermedia - Intelligent Browsing of Structured Media Objects", (to appear) SIGMOD Record, special issue on Metadata for Digital Media, December 1994.

12 C. Hsu, "The Meta-database Project at Renesselaer", SIGMOD Record, special issue on Semantic Issues in Multidatabases, 20(4), December 1991.

13 R. Jain and A. Hampapur, "Representations for Video Databases", (to appear) SIGMOD Record, special issue on Metadata for Digital Media, December 1994.

14 Y. Kane-Esrig, L. A. Streeter, W. Keese, and G. Casella, "The relevance density method in information retrieval", Proceedings of the 4th International Conference on Computing and Information, 1992.

15 Y. Kane-Esrig, L. Shklar, and C. St. Charles, Using Multiple Sources of Information to Search a Repository of Software Lifecycle Artifacts, Proceedings of the Bellcore Conference on Electronic Document Delivery, NJ, May 1994.

16 B. Kahle and A. Medlar, "An Information System for Corporate Users: Wide Area Information Servers", Connexions - The Interoperability Report, 5(11), Nov. 1991.

17 V. Kashyap and A. Sheth, "Semantics-based Information Brokering: A step towards realizing the Infocosm", Technical Report DCS-TR-307, Department of Computer Science, Rutgers University, March 1994.

18 V. Kashyap and A. Sheth, "Semantics-based Information Brokering", Proceedings of the 3rd International Conference on Information and Knowledge Management (CIKM), Gaithersburg, MD, November 1994.

19 Y. Kiyoki, T. Kitagawa and T. Hayama, "A meta-database System for Semantic Image Search by a Mathematical Model of Meaning", (to appear) SIGMOD Record, special issue on Metadata for Digital Media, December 1994.

20 T. Landauer, D. Egan, M. Lesk, C. Lochbaum and D. Ketchum, "Enhancing the usability of text through computer delivery and formative evaluation: the Super-Book Project", In C. McKnight, A. Dillon and J. Richardson, (eds) "Hypertext: A Psychological Perspective", Chicester: Ellis Horwood, 1993.

21 C.J. Matheus. P.K. Chan, and G. Piatetsky-Shapiro, "Systems for Knowledge Discovery in Databases", IEEE Trans. on Knowledge and Data Eng., Dec. 1993.

22 V. Sembugamoorthy, L. Streeter, and Mary Leland, "Igrep: A real World Prospective on Locating Software Artifacts for Reuse", Proceedings of the 5th Annual Workshop on Software Reuse (WISR'92), Palo Alto, CA, 1992.

23 A. Sheth and J. Larson, "Federated Database Systems for Managing Distributed, Heterogeneous, and Autonomous Databases", ACM Comp. Surveys, 22(3), 1990.

24 L. Shklar, "XReuse: Representation and Retrieval of Heterogeneous Multimedia Objects", Proc. of Bellcore Object-Oriented Symposium, Arlington, VA, June 1993.

25 L. Shklar, S. Thatte, H. Marcus, and A. Sheth, "The InfoHarness Information Integration Platform", Advance Proceedings of the Second International WWW Conference '94, Chicago, October 17-20, pp. 809-819, *http://www.ncsa.uiuc.edu/SDG/ IT94/Proceedings/Searching/shklar/shklar.html*.

26 L. Shklar, K. Shah, and C. Basu, "Putting Legacy Data on the Web: A Repository Definition Language", To appear in the Proceedings of the Third International WWW Conference'95, April 1995, Darmstadt, Germany, *http://www.igd.fhg.de/ www/www95/www95.html*.

27 K. Shoens, A Luniewski, P. Shwartz, J. Stamos, and J. Thomas, "The Rufus System: Information Organization for Semi-Structured Data", Proceedings of the 19th VLDB Conference, Dublin, Ireland, 1993.

28 L. A. Streeter and K. E. Lochbaum, "Who knows: a system based on automatic representation of semantic structure", Proceedings of RIAO 88: User-oriented context-based text and image handling, M.I.T., Cambridge, MA, 1988, pp.379-388.

29 John R. Rymer, "Distributed Object Computing", Distributed Computing Monitor, Vol. 8, No. 8, Boston, 1993.

30 N. Yankelovich, B. Haan, N. Meyrowitz and S. Drucker, "Intermedia: The concept and construction of a seamless information environment", IEEE Computer, 21(1), January 1988.

Designing the User Interface on Top of a Conceptual Model

Matti Pettersson

Department of Computer Science, University of Tampere
P.O.Box 607, FIN-33101 Tampere
mpe@cs.uta.fi

Abstract: The paper shows how a conceptual model represented as a combination of an Entity-Relationship diagram and a Petri net can be used in user interface design. We first discuss how the conceptual model can contribute to the design of usable systems in general. We then describe the specification of the interface as a refinement process from the events of the conceptual model to the operations of the interface.

1 Introduction

One of the critical issues in software engineering is how to get user interface design as an integral part of software development. Traditionally software engineering methods seem to take quite diverse standpoints. Some methods suggest that user interface design is part of the requirements engineering, some consider it as being part of the implementation.

Within HCI literature it is often stated that an interactive system should be built on a conceptual model [24, 8, 17]. However, there seems not to be any consensus of the role of such models. Possible interpretations vary from an overall description of the application domain to an implementation concept (as an example see the discussion reported by Cockton, [5]). The point of view taken in this paper is that the designer of a direct manipulation interface needs a model of the application domain as the interface should show the user the concepts and behaviour of the application domain on the screen [23, 24, 17, 12]).

There is not much discussion in HCI literature how a conceptual model in general or a model of the application domain can be built and represented and how exactly it relates to the user interface design (c.f. [14] as an exception see [1]). The techniques used to describe user interfaces seem to suppose that the user interface is an independent part of the software and start the design from scratch (as an example see [10]).

Conceptual modeling is often discussed within information system research and particularly within the data base community, where several analysis methods have been suggested to modeling of the concepts and behaviour of the application domain (as an example see [18]). Heuser, Peres and Richter [11] use a combination of Entity–Relationship modeling [3] and Petri nets [19, 22] to describe static and dynamic features of the application domain, respectively. In this paper we show how user interface design can benefit from representations created in the form of a conceptual model in general. Moreover, we show how the user interface can be specified on top of a conceptual model. The benefit of the approach described is that it shows how the user interface design can be viewed as a continuation of the modeling of the application domain, both conceptually and methodologically. The method described is in a trial use in a project, where a weather monitoring system is being developed to support road maintenance activities depending on changing weather conditions. The system consists of several graphical workstations connected to a large data base.

The organization of the paper is as follows. We first introduce the conceptual model modified from [11]. We then discuss the usefulness of the model from the point of view of user interface design. We then proceed by a general discussion of interactive systems as the details of using the model as a basis for user interface design depends on the type of interaction we are aiming at. Finally we show a specification of the user interface as a Petri net.

2 Conceptual model

Figure 1 shows the conceptual model from [11]. The part of Figure 1 drawn in heavy lines displays an E–R diagram for the IFIP working conference case study [18]. Entities and relationships are represented as usually. Light lines, circles and boxes are added to model the dynamics of the system as a Petri net. They describe the events that manipulate the data within the system.

A simplest form of a Petri net appears towards the lower left corner of Figure 1. It consists of two circles, or places, and of a box, or a transition. Places are labeled "Receipt open" and "Receipt closed". Transition is labeled "Close". There is a token, or marking, in "Receipt open" indicating the state of the receipt. Transition "Close" corresponds to the event of closing the receipt. When the transition "Close" fires, the token is moved from its input place "Receipt open" to its output place "Receipt closed" to indicate the new state of the receipt. In the model, the letter 'e' labels the edges describing the path the token is moved. In a Petri net, the firing of a transition is possible if, and only if, there is a token in each of its input places and there is no token in any of its output places. This is the mechanism controlling the firing of transitions.

The type of net in Figure 1 is actually a condition/event net. The tokens within the net are tuples of the form <x1,...,xn>, where x1,...xn are variables. Each place can contain several tuples of the same type as long as the values of the variables differ. And instead of a token, the transitions (or events) move sets of tuples while firing. Each tuple corresponds to a data item. For example, event "Submit paper" inserts a set of tuples of the form <pap, top> to place "Submitted paper with topic". Tuple <pap, top> represents an item consisting of a paper and its topic. Event "Submit paper" has no input places, so from the system's point of view submitting is always possible. Whether the papers submitted are sent to referees or ignored depends on the state of the receipt. Event "Receive paper" is enabled only when the receipt is open, otherwise event "Ignore late paper" is enabled.

Note the double–head arrows. They are used to represent restoring actions. In a Petri net, the token is no more available in its original place after the transition has fired, unless the transition explicitly restores the token. For example, event "Receive paper" would take the token from "Receipt open" thus effectively closing the receipt, with the exception that the token would not end to "Receipt closed". But as restoring actions are quite common in practice, a special symbol is used for it.

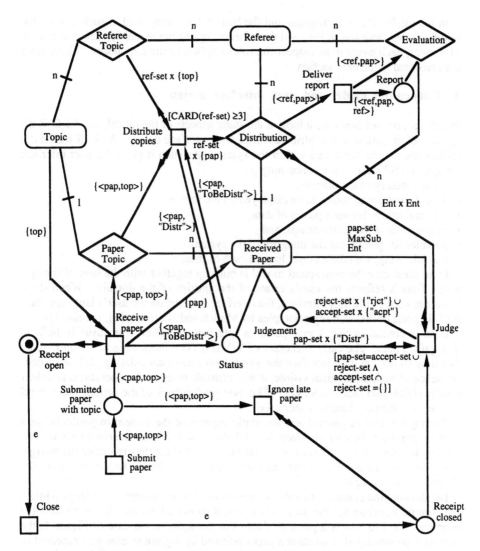

Figure 1. Conceptual model for the IFIP working conference case study.

In a condition/event net, there are two additional mechanisms to control the firing of the events. The first one is variable instantiation. All instantiations of a variable related to a certain tuple must be the same around an event. For example, there are several instantiations of variable "top" around event "Receive paper". Firing of the event takes each tuple available in "Submitted paper with topic" and compares it against the topics of the conference in "Topic". If a match can be found, the tuple is moved forwards as indicated by the arrows leaving the event.

The second mechanism to control the transitions is conditions associated with events. In Figure 1, conditions appear in brackets, '[]'. For example, the condition associated with event "Distribute copies" states that each paper should be distributed to at least three referees.

In the model, the E–R diagram and the Petri net are integrated in such a way, that beside circles, both the entities and the relationships of the model can serve as places. Moreover, each event must respect the rules implicit in the ER–model. These rules are discussed in the next section.

3 Conceptual model and user interface design

In this section, we first take a look at the static aspects of the model, i.e. the E–R diagram and discuss how it contributes to the user interface design. An E–R model describes the data manipulated within the system. As such it gives the user interface designer useful information concerning
- the vocabulary of the domain,
- the data and the attributes to be displayed on the screen,
- the connections between pieces of data,
- cardinalities of the relationships, and
- the rules for preserving the integrity of the system.

In the following, we take a closer look at each of these.

In an ideal case the conceptual model is built up together with the user of the system. Thus it reflects the user's terms of the entities of the domain. When these terms are used in the user interface, the interface is based on the user's language, thus fulfilling one of the usability principles by Molich and Nielsen ([15], see also [16]).

Data is central in direct manipulation interfaces. Systems are usually built to manipulate data. The early successes of WYSIWYG editors were based on the fact that they showed at their interface the data the user was manipulating [23]. As a consequence of making the data visible, it was possible to make the operations and their results visible and more direct [12]. The user got feedback of the actions in a natural way and her memory load was decreased.

Taking the data in general and the static aspects of the system in particular as a starting point for the user interface design helps in keeping the interface easy to control by the user. The sequences of operations remain short thus reducing the navigation effort and the number of steps needed while moving from a task to the next. Dialogue remains simple.

By showing the connections between pieces of data, a conceptual model provides a meaningful structure for the data. Moreover, it shows all the possible ways how the user may want to access a piece of data. For example, in the case of Figure 1, the user may be interested in whether a paper refereed by a given referee was accepted or not. In practice, it may be impossible to incorporate all possibilities under one graphical interface, without visualizing the whole SQL. The first task of the user interface designer is to try to catch the essence of the system under development. In this particular case, the essence might be managing papers in the referee process, which suggests that it is plausible to focus on paper objects in user interface design.

Cardinalities of the relationships are important for the design of the user interface. Cardinalities differing from 1:1 suggest that the interface must be capable of showing several data items instead of only one. As an example consider showing the referees of a given paper. Moreover, systems based on the model must not override the cardinalities in the model. For example, the model in Figure 1 states that no more than one paper should be distributed to any referee. Thus the system based on the model should not allow distributing more than one paper per referee. The user interface may be designed in such a way that it makes this constraint visible. This prevents errors thus increasing the usability of the system [15].

An E–R model includes some integrity rules implicitly. An example is the referential integrity rule stating that an entity participating in a relationship, must exist [7]. For example, it is not allowed to have an entry in "Paper Topic" relationship, if there are no corresponding paper and topic entries in the system. From the point of view of the user interface design this means that the existence of the entries must be checked at some point of interaction. Part of the design is to decide upon the policy to be followed to maintain the rule.

The dynamic part of the conceptual model shows the actions the system should take to manipulate the data described by the static model. Part of the actions may be automatic, whereas some of them require interaction with the user. The user interface designer's task is to turn the actions requiring user's activity into a user interface. Moreover, the model shows the prerequisites and consequences of actions, as the user expects them to be.

The dynamic part of the model also makes explicit the conditions that must be met in order to fire the event. This helps designing error messages that are both precise and constructive. Precise error messages provide the user with exact information about the cause of the problem. Constructive error messages provide meaningful suggestions to the user about what to do next [15].

There are several proposals of how the components of the interface relate to the components of the application. The problem is that there is usually no one–to–one correspondence between the components of the two types. Data from an application object is displayed by several interface objects and an interface object shows data from several application objects. Properties of the objects of the two domains can not easily be put together in one object.

One possible solution is to go to the attribute level, where a correspondence can be found more easily. This is suggested in [8]. However, from the point of view of designing the interface, it is not desirable to consider the interface as consisting of separate attributes, each of which can be controlled by the user, but to try to keep attributes and operations relating to one application object close to each other.

A correspondence can be found between user's operations at the interface level and the events of the system. For each event of the system requiring user's activity there must be at least one operation or a sequence of operations in the interface to fire the event. One of the challenges of user interface design is, how to make these operations visible to the user. This suggests a model of an interactive system, where the events requiring user's activity connect the user interface and the system and serve as a starting point to user interface design. A direct manipulation interface assumes close interaction between the user interface and the rest of the system. How exactly this interaction can be implemented is discussed in the next section.

4 Interaction between the interface and the system

One of the important discussions around user interfaces in the 80's was the discussion of the architecture of interactive systems. The Seeheim model of interactive systems [9] got a status of some kind of a standard. The basic idea was to separate the user interface part of the system from the rest of the application and then further divide the interface in three parts, each having a role of its own in the processing of the exchange between the user and the system. The architecture was an analogy from compilers. The tasks of the components were to do lexical, syntactic and semantic analyses to user's input and provide as a feedback information of the success and failure of each step, and finally show the results of the computation.

The evolution towards graphical, direct manipulation interfaces questioned the applicability of the Seeheim model. It turned out that the separation was not as simple as in the case of command or menu based interfaces [26]. A direct manipulation interface should give the user continuous feedback of the state of the system as a whole. In a sense it blurs boundaries between the feedback types. However, we maintain that the separation to the interface and to the rest of the system is both possible and feasible, but not in the mechanistic way suggested in the Seeheim model (see also the discussion in [6]).

The separation does not make sense from the users' point of view [14]. In many cases we cannot point to a set of concepts and say that these are the interface concepts and to another set of concepts and say that these are the system concepts. A direct manipulation interface shows the semantic (or system) concepts in its interface [24]. But the separation is possible, in principle, from the technical point of view as different features of objects (or concepts) are central in the interface and in the rest of the system. From the point of view of the interface, the visual appearance and visual behaviour of the objects and the spatial relations between objects are central. From the point of view of the rest of the system, the state of the objects appearing as values in the data structures of the system is central.

For example, Bødker [2] discusses whether the size of a font is a system concept or an interface concept. Quite correctly she argues that it is both. But from the point of view of the interface it is central how a character of a certain font type and size is displayed and at what point of the screen. From the point of view of the system, the font type and size are only values at a certain point in the data structure of the system.

The maintainability of the system seems to be the most important benefit from the separation. In itself, it increases the modularity of the system in a meaningful manner as not all modifications cross the boundary. A portion of changes consists of changes either in the interface only or in the system only. Unfortunately there are no figures available to describe what the actual portions might be. A successful separation also increases the portability of the software between windowing environments.

Moreover, if the development project relies on some method of system analysis, the implementation should maintain the results of the analysis. In case of a change in requirements, it is easier to modify the system, if there is a clear connection between the results of the analysis and the code that implements the system. For example, if object analysis is used to find the most suitable objects to describe the application domain, the objects should be easily found at the code level too. The common method of deriving system objects from interface object classes usually requires decomposing the application domain objects into several interface objects as there is no one–to–one relationship between the interface objects and the application domain objects. For the same reason, decomposing the interface inside application domain objects spreads the interface all around the code, which again decreases maintainability and portability of the system.

The separation of the application objects from the interface objects may of course in object oriented code increase the number of objects and the communication overhead, but for example, C++ programming language has tools to make this communication as efficient as references within an object.

Separating the interface leads to another problem requiring a solution: which part, the system or the interface (or both) has the control [4]. A common solution in graphical environments is that the interface has the control. This is a feasible solution as in this way it is easier to implement the system so that the user is given the sense of controlling the system and not the other way around.

Letting the user have the control over the system does not mean that the user should be able to do anything she likes independently of the state of the system, even if many of us would like an automatic teller machine which gives us money regardless of the balance of our account. As the conceptual model in Figure 1 describes, each action, the user wants to take with the aid of the system has a set of conditions, to be checked before the operation may be executed. Whatever the type of the interface, the task of the interface is to give the user feedback on whether the function she wants to execute can be executed or not. Typical to a direct manipulation interface is an attempt to check the conditions associated with the operations as early as possible, in order to keep the user informed of the state of the system. This check may in some cases be done even beforehand. As an example consider the dimmed choices in your favourite menu based word processor.

This requirement for direct manipulation interfaces means that there must be a continuous interaction between the interface and the system. There are two consequences. First, the model for an interactive system should not only show that there are two components, the interface and the system, but show also how the components interact with each other. Second, the system and the interface cannot be layered on top of each other in a mechanistic way, but rather the design of the interface should be seen as a refinement from the actions in the system to the operations of the interface [20].

5 User interface specification

In this section, we show how the user interface can be specified as a refinement from the events of the conceptual model in Figure 1. The structure of the Petri net allows the refinement of each event separately. In practice, the interface designer may want to consider the events in parallel as they may be parts of the same interface, having its own dynamics too, like sequencing of dialog boxes or selecting suitable tools for an operation. In this paper we deal with only one event to keep the size of the example small.

In the following section we specify an interface for assigning referees to papers. In some designs it may be considered an automated function, but in this paper we assume that the user wants to have a tight control over the assignment process and thus it should be interactive. The starting point for the user interface design is "Distribute copies" event in Figure 1. The following preconditions for the event can be derived from the conceptual model:
- Paper is drawn from "Paper Topic".
- Paper status is "ToBeDistr".
- Referee is drawn from "Referee Topic".
- Referee's topic and paper's topic must match.

The event has also a set of post conditions:
- Each paper–referee pair formed is inserted to "Distribution". No pair may appear more than once.
- A paper must be distributed to at least 3 referees.
- Paper's status is changed to "Distr".
- Each referee must not refer more than one paper.

Let us assume that we want to specify a user interface, where referees are assigned to papers by dragging them (or labels with their names) with the mouse on top of the papers. The interface shows a list of papers and a list of referees available. The topics are visible in both lists. The user presses the mouse button on top of a referee's name and drags the name on top of the paper she wants to be distributed to the referee.

No usability tests have been done to test whether the solution works or not in practice and a detailed evaluation falls beyond the scope of this paper. The good point is that all the referees and and papers are visible at the same time. Moreover the interface is quite symmetric in the sense that it does not force the user to select either the paper first or the referee first. Problems may arise if the number of papers and referees increases, but then perhaps the visibility of papers and referees may be limited to one topic at a time. If even this is insufficient, then the process might be automated.

The specification refines the actions in the conceptual model to the level of interface operations. These operations are mouse presses on various graphical elements like buttons, boxes etc. The graphical elements are usually included in user interface toolkits, so the specification may rely on these components. In practice, this means that the specification does not tell us how the user moves the cursor on top of a button and how she presses the button. But the specification should show what happens when the user presses the button.

In the case of a drag operation, we must specify how the suboperations, pressing the mouse button, moving the mouse and releasing the mouse button relate to each other and how the system responds to the suboperations. A drag operation should be standard within an environment and thus needs no specification, but cloning (Pettersson, 1991, 25]. Let us assume that the drag operation starts by the press of the mouse button on an object and ends when the mouse button is released on top of another object. Between these events mouse may be moved at the screen. The drag may be interrupted by releasing the mouse button outside any object. So, there are operations of three types: mouse down, move and mouse up. Each operation generates a point describing the location of the mouse at the moment the event takes place. An overall schema of the drag operation is given in Figure 2.

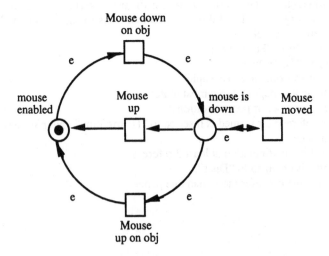

Figure 2. An overall schema for the drag operation.

The next step is to embed the general schema in the context of "Distribute copies" event. Each pre and post condition of the "Distribute copies" should be bound to the suboperations of the drag. There is no general rule how the connecting should be done, rather it depends on the semantics of the operations and the places.

The result of the embedding is shown in Figure 3. In reality, some of the conditions may seem to be unnecessary in the sense, that some combinations may be excluded by the user interface design. For example, the rule that each referee must not have more than one paper to be refereed, may be easily implemented in that way in our exemplary user interface. When the referee is moved on top of the paper, it disappears from the list of referees. However, in Figure 3, we have faithfully included all conditions appearing in the conceptual model. We have also included some details from the conceptual model that are actually not used, to keep the figure more readable.

The explanation of the specification is as follows. The user presses the mouse button. The first condition (Actually, there is no order defined in a Petri in which the conditions should be checked, but here we describe the process in the order that seems natural. In reality ordering should be considered while implementing the interface.) is that the mouse is enabled for this particular operation. The condition bounds the operation to the rest of the interface. Next, if the coordinates of the point the mouse is in at the moment of pressing is within the area of a referee, "Mouse down on ref" event starts to fire.

First it is checked that no other papers are assigned to the referee. In the specification this is described as inserting a tuple consisting of the referee and of any paper to place "Distribution". If this can be done without violating the cardinality constraint, the referee is accepted as selected referee and the tuple is taken back. Selecting the referee enables "Mouse moved", "Mouse up" and "Mouse up on pap" events. If the mouse is moved "Mouse moved" event fires. If the mouse is moved on top of an undistributed paper the paper is highlighted (Feedback is not shown in Figure 2). When the mouse is released on top of a paper, the paper becomes selected. The tuple corresponding to the referee and to the paper selected is added to "Distribution". If the cardinality of the referees assigned to the paper equals three, the status of the paper becomes "Dist" (distributed).

Notice that we have changed the original model at this point. The original model says that "at least three". The specification in Figure 2 limits the number to three referees exactly. This limitation can be relaxed, by not considering the status of the paper while assigning referees, i.e. extra referees can always be assigned to a paper, but the status is changed when there are enough referees (The status is needed elsewhere to check that all papers have been distributed). The need for the modification is a result of assigning the referees interactively, one by one and not all in parallel as is assumed in the conceptual model. (As a matter of fact it is problematic, how assignment could be done without considering an upper limit for the number of referees per paper.)

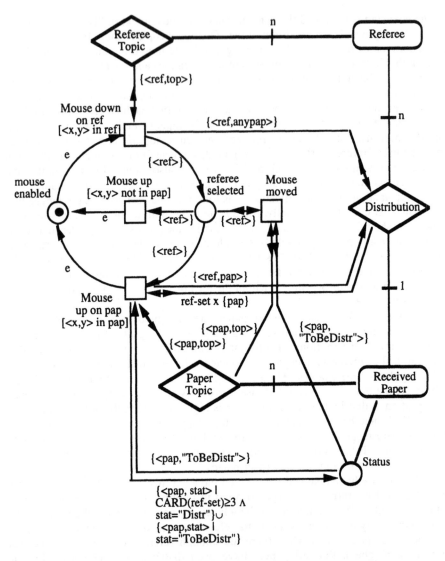

Figure 3. A specification of the interface for the "Distribute copies" event.

The next step in the specification process would be the specification of the feedback associated with each operation of the user. This was partially done in the description above. However, the exact specification of the feedback is out of the scope of this paper.

6 Related work

Petri nets have been used to model user's interactions with the system [27], but not on a model of the application domain. Pettersson [20] uses a layered model to describe the user interface as a Petri net. The lowest layer, the application model represents the application domain, but there is no representation of the static aspects. Janssen, Weisbecker and Ziegler [13] combine the ER model with a variant of a Petri

Janssen, Weisbecker and Ziegler [13] combine the ER model with a variant of a Petri net, but they model the dialogues directly, without considering the dynamics aspects of the application domain.

Quite similar to the use of Petri nets is the approach presented by Sukaviriya, Foley and Griffith [25]. They use pre and post conditions associated with each action on lexical, syntactic and semantic levels. Our approach is different as we consider the specification of the dialogues as a refinement process from the dynamics of the application domain to the domain of the user interface.

7   Conclusions

In this paper we show how the conceptual model of the application domain can be used as a starting point for specifying the user interface. The conceptual model used in this paper was based on a combination of the Entity–Relationship model and of a Petri net [11]. The model seems to be a suitable starting point for specifying the user interface as it shows both the static and dynamic aspects of the application domain. Moreover, as Petri nets are capable of describing parallel processes, strict ordering of events can be avoided in the conceptual model. Thus it supports user interface design, where the user has the control over the system and not vice versa.

The specification process described in the paper is a kind of refinement process from the events of the conceptual model to the operations of the interface. However, it is not a pure refinement in the usual sense. The user interface designer has to consider also the dynamics of the user interface as a whole.

References

1.   Braudes R.E. (1991), Conceptual modelling: a look at system–level user interface issues, in Karat J. (ed.), Taking Software Design Seriously, Academic Press.
2.   Bødker S. (1987), Through the interface—a human activity approach to user interface design, *DAIMI PB–224, Aarhus University*.
3.   Chen P.P. (1976), The entity relationship model: towards a unified view of data, *ACM Transactions on Data Base Systems, Vol. 1, No. 1*.
4.   Cockton G. (1987), Interaction ergonomics, control and separation: open problems in user interface management systems, *Report No. AMU8711/02H, Scottish HCI Centre*.
5.   Cockton G. (1992), Critical issues: Conceptual design, Larson J. and Unger C. (Eds.) Engineering for Human-Computer Interaction.
6.   Coutaz J. (1993), Software architecture modeling for user interfaces, Amodeus Project Document: SM/WP33.
7.   Date C.J. (1982), An introduction to database systems, Addison–Wesley.
8.   Foley J.D. and van Dam A. (1982), Fundamentals of Interactive Computer Graphics, Addison-Wesley.
9.   Green M. (1985), Report on dialogue specification tools, in *Pfaff (1985)*.
10. Green M. (1986), A survey of three dialogue models, *ACM Transactions on Graphics, Vol.5, No.3*.
11. Heuser C.A., Peres E.M. and Richter G. (1993), Towards a complete conceptual model: Petri nets and Entity–Relationship diagrams, *Information Systems, vol.18, No.5, pp 275-298*.

12. Hutchins E.L., Hollan J.D. and Norman D.A. (1986), Direct manipulation interfaces, in *Norman D.A. and Draper S.W. (Eds.), User Centered System Design*, Lawrence Erlbaum Associates.
13. Janssen C., Weisbecker A. and Ziegler J. (1993), Generating user interfaces from data models and dialogue net specifications, in *Proceedings of the Interact'93 Conference*.
14. Kuutti K. and Bannon L. (1993), Searching for unity among diversity: exploring the "interface" concept, in *Proceedings of the Interact'93 Conference*.
15. Molich R. and Nielsen J. (1990), Improving a human–computer dialogue, *Comm.ACM, Vol.33, No.3, pp. 338-348*.
16. Nielsen J. (1993), Usability Engineering, Academic Press.
17. Norman D. (1984), Stages and levels in human–machine interaction, *International Journal of Man–Machine Studies, Vol.21, pp. 365-375*.
18. Olle T.W., Sol H.G. and Verrijn-Stuart A.A. (Eds) (1982), Information systems design methodologies: A comparative review, North-Holland.
19. Peterson J.L. (1981), Petri net theory and the modelling of systems, Prentice–Hall.
20. Pettersson M. (1991), Specifying the user interface, *Lic.thesis, University of Tampere, Department of Computer Science*.
21. Pfaff G.E. (ed.)(1985), User Interface Management Systems, Springer-Verlag, Berlin.
22. Reizig W. (1984), Petri nets, An introduction, Springer–Verlag.
23. Shneiderman B. (1983), Direct manipulation: a step beyond programming languages, *IEEE Computer, (August 1983)*.
24. Shneiderman B. (1987), Designing the user interface, strategies for effective human-computer interaction, Addison–Wesley.
25. Sukaviriya P.N., Foley J.D. and Griffith T. (1993), A second generation user interface design environment: the model and the runtime architecture, in *Proceedings of the Interact'93 Conference*.
26. Tanner P. and Buxton W. (1985), Some issues in future user interface management systems (UIMS) development, in *Pfaff (1985)*.
27. van Biljon W.R. (1988), Extending Petri nets for specifying man-machine dialogues, *International Journal of Man–Machine Studies, Vol.28, No.4, pp 437-455*.

Graphical Representation and Manipulation of Complex Structures Based on a Formal Model

G. Viehstaedt   M. Minas

Lehrstuhl für Programmiersprachen
Universität Erlangen-Nürnberg
Martensstr. 3, 91058 Erlangen, Germany

Abstract

Complex information structures can often be represented by diagrams. Diagrams (e.g., trees for hierarchical structures, or graphs for finite state machines) are useful as part of user interfaces of information systems and CASE tools. Beyond representation, manipulation by interactively editing diagrams should be possible. The implementation of editors for diagrams should be supported by a tool and based on a formal model. This paper gives an overview of our generator for diagram editors. An editor for a certain kind of diagrams is generated from a specification, which includes a grammar to describe the structure of diagrams. The user of a diagram editor, however, doesn't have to be concerned with the grammar, but can manipulate diagrams in a very convenient way.

1 Introduction

An easily comprehensible representation of complex structures is getting more and more important for the users of information systems as well as for software engineers using a CASE tool. A significant and increasing share of the effort for implementing these systems goes into the user interface. The available interface builders for so-called Graphical User Interfaces (GUIs), however, mainly focus on widgets like buttons, menus, etc., and aren't very graphical. This assessment was also made in a recent *CACM* issue on GUIs [7]:

What the market considers a GUI is little more than a glorified menu system, having no graphics. This leaves the graphical representation of the application domain as an exercise for the developer, ...

Diagrams usually have a semantical meaning for the application. Thus, changes to a diagram have to be transformations from one consistent state into another. The set of valid diagrams, called a *diagram class*, should be described by a formal model. A diagram class can, e.g., be the set of graphs for entity-relationship diagrams or finite state machines, or the set of all Nassi-Shneiderman diagrams (NSDs). Editing is done in a syntax-directed way, which ensures that the result of a change is again a valid diagram. Such an editor for diagrams is refered to as *diagram editor*.

Many user interface tools provide no help for diagrams. Some tools, e.g., Garnet [8], support simple kinds of diagrams. The structure of valid diagrams, however, isn't specified formally, but more or less hidden in the code. There are only very few systems for generating a diagram editor that are based on a formal model. In the *PAGG* system [4] layout of diagrams is troublesome and editing inconvenient. The *Constraint* system [9] uses a grammar model based on context-free grammars and constraints for automatic layout of diagrams. A disadvantage is that context-free grammars don't permit direct representation of multidimensional relationships, as needed for the layout of diagrams. Furthermore, the editing capabilities are very restricted.

DiaGen, a generator for diagram editors, will be outlined in this paper. The very natural and convenient way of editing will be illustrated in the next section. Section 3 gives an overview of the system. The grammar model for specifying the structure of diagrams and layout are the topic of Section 3.1. User interaction with diagrams will be briefly addressed in Section 3.2.

2   Editing diagrams

A diagram editor for Nassi-Sheiderman diagrams (NSDs), which was generated with *DiaGen*, serves for demonstrating the way of editing.[1] An NSD mainly consists of lines and text blocks for statements and conditions. These diagram elements can be selected in different ways, which are stated in the specification and thus adapted to the particular editor. For our sample editor it has been specified that subsequent selected statements (which may be complex) are automatically combined into a single entity called a *group*. In Fig. 1 a group of two subsequent statements is selected, as indicated by the handles.

As an example, we now want to remove this group from its position and insert it into the upper NSD as the first statements of the *while*. Fig. 2 shows the result. One way to achieve this is to press the *Cut*-button, and then select the line immediately below the *while*'s condition to indicate the position for insertion. Finally, the *Insert*-button has to be pressed.

---

[1] A graphical language for database queries would be a similar example, but NSDs are more familiar and don't require further explanations.

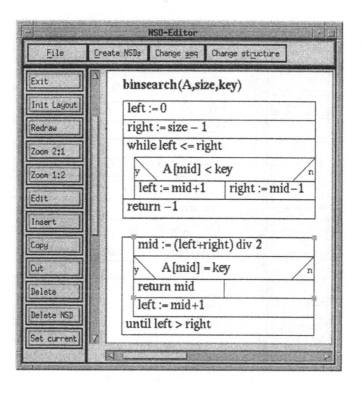

Fig. 1. *Editing state with two NSDs. A group of two subsequent statements (consisting of a simple statement and an if) is selected in the lower NSD.*

This editing style is solely based on selection and pressing buttons or choosing menu items. It is the only way of editing possible in diagram editors which can be generated with other tools like PAGG [4] or Constraints [9].

With *DiaGen* diagram editors with much more convenient editing operations can be specified. E.g., the modification from Fig. 1 to Fig. 2 can also be made by simply pressing the mouse button while the mouse pointer is located over the selected group, dragging this group to its destination, and releasing the mouse button over the line below the *while*'s condition. We will refer to this editing style as *direct manipulation* of diagrams.

In the same way any part of a diagram can be removed and inserted at any other spot. A diagram part can be made a new NSD of its own in a similar fashion by moving it around and releasing the mouse button outside any other NSD. Of course, an entire NSD can also be inserted into another diagram.

A number of other editing operations by direct manipulation have been specified for the NSD editor. E.g., the *then-* and *else*-branch of an *if* can be switched

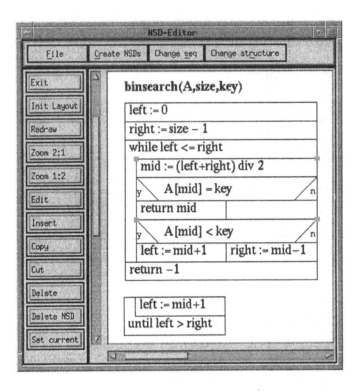

Fig. 2. *Situation after moving the group selected in Fig. 1 to the beginning of the while.*

by pressing the mouse button over the *if*'s triangle with '*y*' inside, dragging it to the right, and releasing it over the corresponding '*n*' (or the other way around). Another example of direct manipulation is to change a *while* into an *until* by moving the *while*'s condition down to the end of the *while* and releasing the mouse button there. Similarly, an *until* can be modified into a *while*.

3 The generator *DiaGen*

DiaGen generates a diagram editor for some diagram class (e.g., NSDs) from a specification, which consists of the parts shown in Fig. 3. A major part is the grammar for the diagram class. Section 3.1 will describe a sample grammar. Some particular diagram shown on the screen is internally represented in the diagram editor by a derivation graph, which is the main data structure (see Fig. 3). Layout conditions are attached to grammar productions in the specification. They constrain the values of layout attributes and thus determine a diagram's layout. The terminal symbols in a derivation graph are mapped on the

Diagram Editor

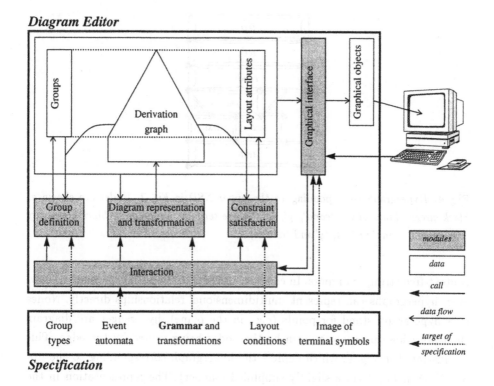

Fig. 3. *Overview of a diagram editor generated with DiaGen and its specification.*

screen. Their image is composed of primitive elements (lines, text, etc.) and also part of the specification. The remaining parts of a diagram editor's specification in Fig. 3 are needed for user interaction.

3.1 Diagram structure and layout

A diagram class, i.e., the syntactic structure of diagrams which will be edited, is specified by a hypergraph grammar. A *hypergraph* is a generalization of a graph, in which edges are *hyperedges*, i.e., they can be connected to any (fixed) number of nodes [1]. Each (hyper)edge has a type and a number of connection points that determine how many nodes the hyperedge is connected to. We say the edge *visits* these nodes. The familiar directed graph can be seen as a hypergraph in which all (hyper)edges visit exactly two nodes.

Context-free hypergraph grammars are analogously defined as context-free (string) grammars and have similar properties [3]. Terminal and nonterminal hyperedges are used in hypergraph grammars instead of alphabet symbols in

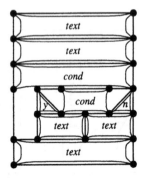

Fig. 4. *Hypergraph corresponding to the upper NSD in Fig. 1. Nodes are shown as black circles. Lines, 'text', 'cond', 'y', and 'n' are terminal hyperedges. Lines have arity 2, 'text' and 'cond' arity 4, 'y' and 'n' arity 3.*

context-free string grammars. In contrast to context-free string grammars, however, hypergraphs can represent multidimensional relationships directly. Nodes in a hypergraph stand for points (e.g., in the plane), hyperedges are diagram elements whose position is given by the nodes being visited by the edge. This is illustrated in Fig. 4, which depicts the hypergraph corresponding to the upper NSD in Fig. 1 (in a slightly simplified manner). The representation in the PAGG and Constraint systems [4, 9], which don't use hypergraphs, would be significantly more complicated.

Each production in a context-free hypergraph grammar consists on its left hand side (lhs) of a hypergraph with a single nonterminal edge and the nodes visited, see Fig. 5. The lhs of production P_1 is the *starting graph* of the grammar. The right hand side (rhs) of every production is an arbitrary hypergraph of terminal and nonterminal hyperedges. Application of a production to a hypergraph is similar to context-free string grammars, too: if the lhs is a subgraph of the hypergraph, this subgraph is removed and replaced by the rhs. The resulting hypergraph is said to be *derived* from the first hypergraph. In order to specify which rhs node replaces which lhs node, corresponding nodes of the lhs and the rhs are labeled with the same letters. A sample derivation sequence is shown in Fig. 6. Context-free hypergraph productions are sufficient for the NSD example. There are also context-sensitive productions for specifying diagram structure, but they aren't addressed here.

The diagram class given by a (context-free) hypergraph grammar is the set of derivation graphs that are derivable from the starting graph and consist of terminal hyperedges only. Just these derivation graphs are mapped on the screen such that the user of a diagram editor only sees valid diagrams. Furthermore,

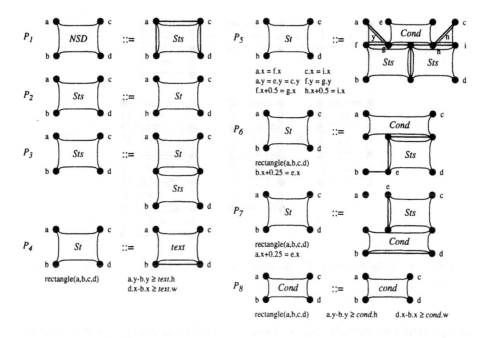

Fig. 5. *Context-free hypergraph grammar for NSDs. Terminal hyperedges are the same as in Fig. 4. Nonterminals 'Sts' and 'St' stand for statement sequence resp. statement, 'Cond' for condition. 'rectangle(a,b,c,d)' is used as shortcut for 'a.x = b.x, c.x = d.x, a.y = c.y, b.y = d.y'.*

the user isn't aware of the grammar productions and deals with diagrams in an application-oriented way, as shown in Section 2.

Hypergraph grammars can describe the syntactic structure of diagrams, but layout requirements aren't included. For context-free (string) grammars this problem can be solved by *attribute grammars* [5], i.e., by assigning attributes to grammar symbols and functional dependencies to productions that determine the attribute values. *Constraints* were made popular by Borning [2] for layout in interactive environments. Constraints are conditions automatically maintained by the system. They permit a very high level specification of layout. The advantage of constraints is that they have a multidirectional nature, whereas in attribute grammars changes are propagated only into one direction. Vander Zanden [9] combined constraints with context-free (string) grammars by assigning attributes to grammar symbols, and by adding constraints, which have to be equations, to each production in order to determine the attributes' values.

Hypergraph grammars are attributed in a similar way. However, not only edges, which correspond to alphabet symbols in context-free (string) grammars,

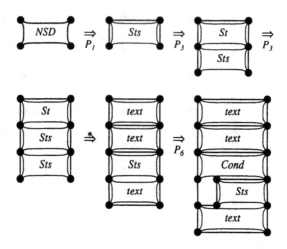

Fig. 6. *Part of the derivation for the hypergraph in Fig. 4 using the productions from Fig. 5.*

carry attributes, but also nodes. Since any number of hyperedges can be connected to a node, node attributes are common attributes for all hyperedges visiting this node. The advantage is that with using hypergraphs only few constraints are needed compared to [9]. Furthermore, constraints can be linear inequalities in *DiaGen*. Equations determine relations between attribute values in a definite way, whereas inequality constraints permit a whole range of values as solutions. This is a convenient way to combine automatic layout of diagrams provided by the system with user-defined modifications. More details on layout and the incremental algorithm for constraint satisfaction built into our generator can be found in [6].

The constraints for layout of NSDs are shown in Fig. 5. Every node has attributes x and y for the node's position. They are refered to by $n.x$ and $n.y$ for a node labeled n. The only edge attributes needed are *text.h*, *text.w*, *cond.h*, and *cond.w* for the mimimal height and width of text blocks and conditions. The values of the edge attributes are determined by the size of the text actually contained in the terminal symbol. There are no constraints needed for productions P_1, P_2, and P_3. Just those in Fig. 5 are sufficient for layout due to node attributes, which are shared among all visiting hyperedges.

3.2 User interaction and transformations

The main feature concerning user interaction is that a diagram can be modified very conveniently in a direct manipulation style by just moving diagram ele-

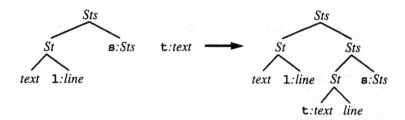

Fig. 7. *Sample transformation rule in the NSD editor for inserting text t at line 1. For applying this rule the lhs has to match the diagram's current structure. The rhs describes the modification.*

ments around on the screen. This isn't the case for other systems like PAGG or Constraints [4, 9], in which editing operations have to be chosen from a menu. In a diagram editor generated with *DiaGen* the interaction module (see Fig. 3) is responsible for the reaction on a user's actions with mouse and keyboard. They can, e.g., cause selection of diagram elements, layout changes, or transformations of the diagram's structure.

A transformation is a transition from a set of diagrams to another set of diagrams. The structure of one or more diagrams can be changed, but the user of a diagram editor only sees valid diagrams, i.e., diagrams belonging to the specified diagram class. In contrast to [9], transformations in DiaGen can be complex and consist of several primitive steps. This enables more powerful transformations and reuse of primitives. E.g., many tranformations in the NSD editor are based on primitives for deleting or inserting a sequence of (compound) statements.

An example of a simple transformation rule in the NSD editor is given in Fig. 7. Transformation rules describe the modification of the derivation which stands behind each diagram being displayed on the screen. In these rules a derivation (like that in Fig. 6) is written as a tree. A transformation consists of a sequence of rules. The user of a diagram editor indicates by mouse and keyboard actions which transformation shall be applied and the location where this shall be done. In the above example the user would indicate the *text* t and the *line* 1 where t has to be inserted.[2] The system tries to apply the transformation by matching the left hand sides of the transformation's rules in the sequence given. The first matching lhs determines the modification to be made. Different rules in a transformation take care of different contexts of the positions indicated by the user (here *text* t and *line* 1). In the current implementation

---

[2] This can be achieved by dragging *text* t to *line* 1 and releasing the mouse button there.

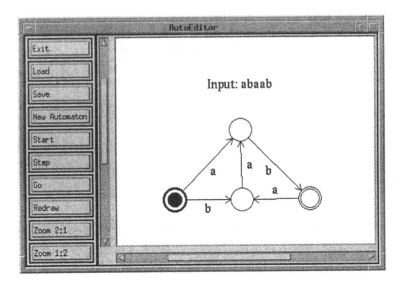

Fig. 8. *Simple automaton after pressing button* Start. *The initial state is marked by a thick border line, the final state by a double border line.*

the programmer of a diagram editor, i.e., the user of our generator, has to make sure that transformations, which are part of an editor specification, contain all relevant rules. If the programmer fails to provide a complete set of rules, this only means that for certain contexts a transformation doesn't cause any change. An analysis during parsing the specification would be helpful to prevent such pitfalls.

Transformation rules as illustrated in Fig. 7 are sufficient for tree structured diagrams like NSDs. For other diagram classes, e.g., finite state machines, a context-free hypergraph grammar (see Fig. 5) is too weak. In such cases context-sensitive productions resp. transformations are needed. This is possible in *DiaGen*, but not detailed here since the principle is about the same as for the transformations described above.

In diagram editors generated with *DiaGen* transformations can also be used to specify execution of a diagram, as in our sample editor for finite state machines. A user first constructs an automaton with its states and transitions. Some states can be marked as final states, one as the initial state. Fig. 8 shows the situation after constructing an automaton and pressing button Start. The user was asked to provide an input string for the automaton, and the current state was set to the initial state. If there is a suitable transition for the currently first character in the input string, each press on button Step causes a transition

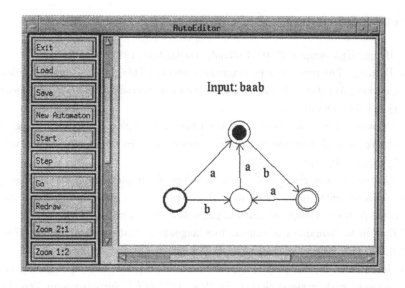

Fig. 9. *Situation arising from Fig. 8 after pressing button* Step *once.*

and removes the first character from the input. Pressing Step once yields Fig. 9. Button Go continues execution until either the input is finished, or a transition for the current input character is impossible.

4 Conclusions

Sophisticated user interfaces should permit the representation and easy manipulation of complex structures by a diagram editor. *DiaGen* has been presented as a tool for generating diagram editors from a specification. A diagram class is specified by a formal model based on hypergraph grammars. This kind of grammar is useful for describing multidimensional relationships between diagram elements. Furthermore, layout of diagrams is defined on a high level by constraints. Editing can be done in a very convenient way by direct manipulation. Complex editing operations and execution of a diagram can be specified in *DiaGen*. Nevertheless, a diagram edited by the user always is in a consistent state, which is a hypergraph in the formal model. This hypergraph can be used by other parts of the application.

A prototype of *DiaGen* has been implemented. Future work will be to generate more sample editors and link them to applications.

References

1. C. Berge. *Hypergraphs*. North-Holland, Amsterdam, 1989.
2. A. Borning. The programming language aspects of ThingLab, a constraint-oriented simulation laboratory. *ACM Transactions on Programming Languages and Systems*, 3(4):353–387, October 1981.
3. F. Drewes and H.-J. Kreowski. A note on hyperedge replacement. In H. Ehrig, H.-J. Kreowski, and G. Rozenberg, editors, *Lecture Notes in Computer Science*, volume 532, pages 1–11. Springer, 1991.
4. H. Göttler. Graph grammars, a new paradigm for implementing visual languages. In N. Dershowitz, editor, *Rewriting Techniques and Applications*, volume 355 of *Lecture Notes in Computer Science*, pages 152–166. Springer, 1989.
5. D.E. Knuth. Semantics of context-free languages. *Mathematical Systems Theory*, 2(2):127–145, 1968.
6. M. Minas and G. Viehstaedt. Specification of diagram editors providing layout adjustment with minimal change. In *Proc. 1993 IEEE Symposium on Visual Languages*, pages 324–329. IEEE Computer Society Press, 1993.
7. A. Morse and G. Reynolds. Overcoming current growth limits in UI development. *Communications of the ACM*, 36(4):73–81, April 1993.
8. B.A. Myers, D.A. Giuse, R.B. Dannenberg, et al. Garnet - Comprehensive support for graphical, highly interactive user interfaces. *Computer*, 23(11):71–84, November 1990.
9. B.T. Vander Zanden. Constraint grammars - a new model for specifying graphical applications. In K. Bice and C. Lewis, editors, *Proc. CHI'89*, volume 20 of *SIGCHI Bulletin*, pages 325–330, March 1989.

Providing Integrated Support for Multiple Development Notations

John C. Grundy and John R. Venable

Department of Computer Science, University of Waikato
Private Bag 3105, Hamilton, New Zealand
email: jgrundy@cs.waikato.ac.nz or jvenable@cs.waikato.ac.nz

Abstract. A new method for providing integrated support for multiple development notations (including analysis, design, and implementation) within Information Systems Engineering Environments (ISEEs) is described. Our method supports both static integration of multiple notations and the implementation of dynamic support for them within an integrated ISEE. First, conceptual data models of different analysis and design notations are identified and modelled, and then merged into an integrated conceptual data model. Second, mappings are derived from the integrated conceptual data model, which translates data changes in one notation to appropriate data changes in the other notations. Third, individual ISEEs for each notation are developed. Finally, the individual ISEEs are integrated via an integrated repository based on the integrated conceptual data model and mappings. An environment supporting integrated tools for Object-Oriented Analysis and Extended Entity-Relationship diagrams is described, which has been built using this technique.

1 Introduction

1.1 Integrated ISEEs

A software system can be modelled using a variety of notations, such as Object-Oriented Analysis and Design (OOA/D) diagrams, Extended Entity-Relationship (EER) diagrams and Data Flow Diagrams (DFDs). The choice of modelling notation is often dependent on the kind of problem and organisational and designer preferences. Some problems suit being modelled using object-oriented techniques while others are more easily conceptualised using entity-relationship and data flow diagrams. The use of different notations for different (or the same) parts of a problem offers several advantages: the most appropriate notation can be used for each part; the same design can be expressed using different notations; different designers can communicate about the same design using different notations; and organisations using different notations can collaborate on projects. Integrated ISEE support for using different notations on the same project is necessary, however, to provide consistency management between each notation, and thus produce a consistent design for the problem as a whole. In fact, integrated ISEEs enable the use of multiple notations. Without them, effective use of multiple notations would not be feasible.

1.2 Our Approach

Providing integrated support for multiple development notations (whether to support single or multiple phases of development), requires both static and dynamic integration. We define static integration as the conceptual integration of the description languages (or notations) that are used by the system developers. This defines the requirements for how concepts in one notation map onto another notation. Dynamic integration is concerned with how changes to one system description are propogated to all other system descriptions, using the same or different notations.

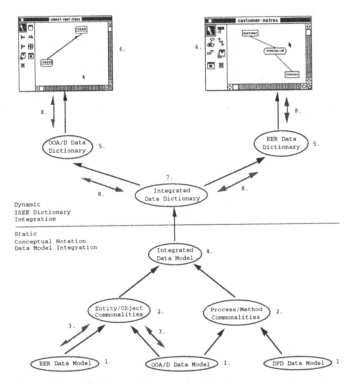

Fig. 1. Integrating design notations via a hierarchical data model.

We present a new approach which supports both static and dynamic integration of multiple notations, illustrated in Fig. 1. The first 4 steps achieve static integration: 1) The conceptual data models of different design notations are identified and documented. 2) Commonalities between aspects of these notations' conceptual data models are identified, resulting in partial intgerated data models. 3) Dynamic mappings between different notation components are identified i.e. how changes to data in one model are translated into changes to the other. 4) Several levels of partial data models are built up and collected to describe an integrated data model for all of the design notations.

The second 4 steps achieve dynamic integration of design and implementation tools for the different notations, with the conceptual data models and mappings used to implement an ISEE encorporating all of the notations. 5) Individual tools for each notation are developed with the tool repository based on the notation's conceptual data model. 6) Editors for this repository are developed, including multiple textual and graphical notation views. 7) The integrated data model (and possibly the intermediate partial data models) are used to define an integrated repository. 8) Data changes in one notation's repository are propagated to other notation repositories via the integrated repository, with change translation as specified by the mappings defined in step 3.

In the following sections, related research in integrating design notations is discussed, and then an environment which incorporates integrated OOA/D and EER tools, called OOEER, is illustrated. The development of conceptual data models for individual OOA/D and EER notations, and an integrated conceptual data model, is briefly described with mappings between the notations. Two previously developed OOA/D and EER environments are introduced and the implementation of OOEER by integrating these environments is decribed. The paper concludes with a brief discussion of experience with this integrated tool and future research directions.

2 Related Research

Integrated ISEEs (or Integrated CASE tools and programming environments) allow designers to analyse, design, and implement Information Systems from within one environment, providing a consistent user interace and consistent repository (data dictionary). They help to minimise inconsistencies that can arise when using several separate tools for information systems development [17, 13].

Some work has been done on the static integration of notations. Wieringa [18] has compared JSD, ER modelling and DFD modelling, and examined the possibilities of integrating different aspects these methods. Data modelling has been used to compare different notations [11] and support methodology engineering [10]. Process-modelling has also been applied to compare and integrate notations [14]. There has been little work at developing detailed integration of individual notations, and little has been done to translate conceptually integrated notations into tool-based implementations.

Limited dynamic notation integration is supported by many CASE tools, such as Softare thru Pictures™ [17] and TurboCASE™ [15]. These ICASE environments allow developers to analyse and design software using a variety of different notations, with limited inter-notation consistency. For example, entities from an EER model can be used as objects in an OOA model, with name and attribute changes kept consistent. Such tools do not generally support complex mappings between the design notations, such as propagating an EER relationship addition to corresponding OOA diagram. This greatly limits their usefulness for supporting integrated development using different notations. The implementation of these environments is generally not sufficient to allow different design notations to be effectively integrated, and consistency between design and implementation code is often not maintained.

FIELD environments [13] utilise selective broadcasting, involving propagating messages between separate Unix tools, to keep muliple tool views conistent. FIELD can not effectively integrate different design notation tools, as it provides no integrated repository. As more tools are added the translation process becomes complex and difficult to implement. Dora [12] provides abstractions for keeping multiple textual and graphical views consistent under change. These views share the same repository and hence can more easily be kept consistent. Dora does not provide any mechanism for propagating changes between views which can not be directly applied by the environment. Thus some changes made to a design which can not be automatically implemented in another notation by the environment can not be supported.

Two key methods are thus required for dynamic integration: (1) utilising an integrated repository and (2) providing additional support for ensuring consistency between aspects which cannot be automatically kept consistent by the environment. Aspects that require human intervention to maintain consistency should be indicated by the environment to the notation/tool user. This relies on being able to identify aspects that can be automatically kept consistent and those which require human intervention. Doing so requires effective static integration by identifying commonalities and change mappings between the notation's conceptual data models.

3   A User's Perspective of OOEER

We have built an ISEE, called OOEER, which integrates the OOA/D and EER design notations, in addition to supporting object-oriented program implementation and relational schema definition. Unlike most CASE tools, OOEER propagates all changes made to OOA/D diagrams to related EER diagrams, and vice-versa. This not only includes simple mappings, such as entity, object and attribute addition, renaming and deletion, but also all relationship manipulation in both models. While the environment can only partially infer required changes to some diagrams when other notation diagrams are modified, it always informs designers of such changes made, to assist them in maintaining inter-notation consistency.

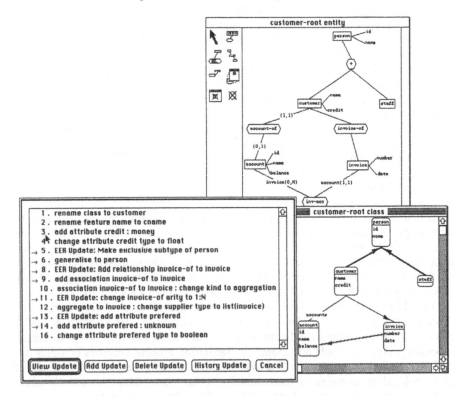

Fig. 2. The integrated OOEER environment.

A screen dump from OOEER is shown in Fig. 2. This shows an OOA view ('customer-root class') and an EER view ('customer-root entity') for an invoicing Information System. The dialog shows the modification history for the customer class. Items highlighted with a '→' were actually made to the EER customer entity, and were automatically translated to the OOA customer class by OOEER.

The OOA/D notation is based on [9]. Bold, arrowed lines represent generalisation relationships, thin lines represent aggregation and shaded lines represent association. Client/supplier relationships are represented by shaded lines with caller/called method names and (optional) method arguments. The EER notation is based on Chen's ER model [1]. Square icons represent entities with optional named attributes connected to the icon. Diamond-shaped icons represent relationships with optional role names and arities on the connecting lines. Subtyping is exclusive ('-') or inclusive ('+').

All of these views are kept consistent by OOEER. If a designer changes information in an OOA view, this change is propagated to all other views which share the changed information (OOA/D, EER and implementation views). Where the environment can automatically make an appropriate change to keep these views consistent, the change is performed. For example, if the customer class were renamed in the OOA view, the customer entity, method class name, and relational table would also be renamed. The reverse is also true if any of the other views with this information are updated.

For some view edits, OOEER can not directly update other affected views. For example, when a relationship is added between two entities in an EER view, the OOA view requires a relationship to be added. The EER update does not, however, specify whether this relationship should be an association or aggregation relationship. OOEER by default adds an association relationhip between the two classes in the OOA view, but colours this relationship, indicating the designer needs to add further information. In Fig. 2, change #8 was made to the EER view, while OOEER autoamtically made change #9 to the OOA view. The designer can view the description(s) of the EER view change(s) made which affect the OOA view, and which could not be fully implemented by the environment. The designer then manually changes the new OOA relationship to an aggregation relationship (change #10).

Fig. 2 shows some other EER changes on the customer entity and its relationships, which have been (semi-)automatically translated into OOA view updates. Some changes made in the EER view require the designer to further modify the OOA view, to ensure it is correct. For example, making a customer entity an exclusive subtype of the person entity (change #5) is directly translated into generalising the customer class to the person class (change #6). Changing the arity of a relationship (change #11), can not be automatically implemented by OOEER. Instead, the designer is informed of the EER change by the presence of this change description. The designer then must manually change the type of the aggregation relationship between the customer and invoice classes to list(invoice) (change #12), to implement this OOA/D relationship. Similarly, if an untyped attribute is added to the customer entity (change #13), OOEER translates this into an attribute addition to the customer class (change #14). The designer then must manually define an appropriate attribute type (change #15).

OOEER also supports editable, textual object-oriented program views and relational schema views. These are kept consistent with the graphical views by expanding the change descriptions at the start of the textual view, as shown in Fig. 3. These inform programmers of changes that need to be made to keep the implementation view consistent. Designers can select change descriptions and request the environment try to automatically update the view, or can manually implement an appropriate change and then delete the change description. Thus unlike most CASE tools, OOEER supports integrated design and implementation views. In total OOEER supports fully integrated OOA, OOD, EER and debugging graphical views, and class definition, class contract, method implementation, relational schema and general documentation textual views.

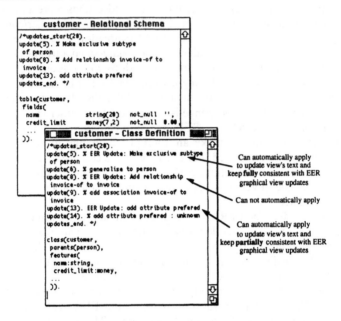

Fig. 3. OOEER textual view consistency.

4 Conceptual Data Model Integration

The first 4 steps in the tool integration process for OOEER involve developing conceptual data models for the OOA/D and EER notations, and mappings between them. We have developed these conceptual models, and a hiearchical, integrated conceptual model, using a conceptual data modelling language called CoCoA [16]. Fig. 4 shows the conceptual data models for OOEER's EER and OOA/D notations.

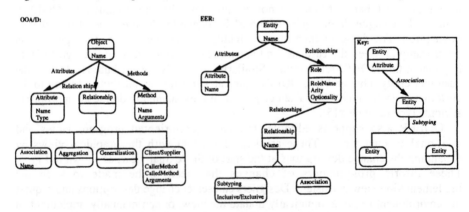

Fig. 4. Separate conceptual data models for OOA/D and EER notations.

The OOA/D notation has named objects, with a collection of named/typed attributes and methods with arguments. Generalisation relationships indicate an object is generalised to another object, aggregation relationships indicate an object is composed of other object(s), and association relationships indicate an object is related to other object(s) in some way. Client-supplier relationhips define method calling protocols.

The EER notation defines named entities which have a collection of named attributes. Entities are linked by named relationships, each entity fulfilling a particular role in the relationship. The role links between an entity and a relationship may be named, may hold a cardinality (1:1, 1:N or M:N), and may have an optional or manditory flag. Subtyping relationships between entities have inclusive and exclusive flags.

The integrated OOEER conceptual data model integrates the notation of entity/attribute and object/attribute into a single entity/object notion. EER relationships and OOA/D relationships are integrated by being described as sub-types of a relationship notion, liked to entity/objects by a role, as shown in Fig. 5.

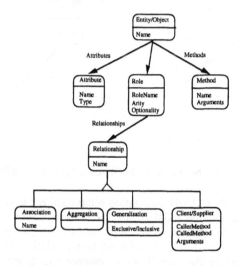

Fig. 5. An integrated data model for OOA/D and EER modelling.

5 Mappings Between Notation Data Models

There are some simple mappings between OOA/D information and EER information, which we term *direct* mappings. These are illustrated in Fig. 6. An entity corresponds directly to an object and an entity name to an object name. Entity attributes also correspond directly to object attributes. in OOEER, EER entities are thus described by an OOA/D object with the same name as the entity name. Similarly, object attribute names directly equate to entity attributes. To maintain consistency, when an entity/attribute is added or deleted, a same-named object/attribute is added or deleted.

Many CASE tools support these direct mappings. Many other mappings also exist between these notations, which we term *indirect* mappings, i.e. an EER change can be translated to the integrated repository, but the resulting change on the integrated model cannot be directly translated to the OOA/D model, and similar for some OOA/D to EER changes. For example, the OOA/D notation specifies the type of an attribute but the EER notation does not. Changes to an attribute's type are thus either ignored by the EER notation or a description of the OOA/D change is presented to users. A similar approach is used for object methods, which have no EER concept.

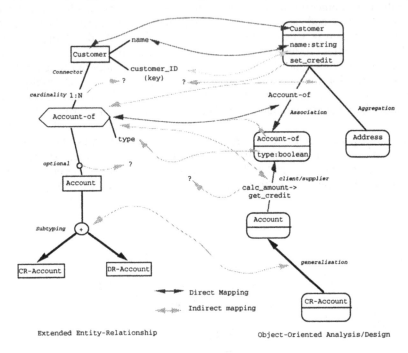

Fig. 6. Mappings between OOA/D concepts and EER concepts.

Creation and deletion of OOA/D association relationships can be directly translated into EER relationship addition and deletion. The reverse is not always true: if an EER relationship is created, this may be implemented by an OOA association or aggregation relationship. Such an inferred OOA relationship needs a change description documenting the inferal, so a designer can appropriately make it an aggregation or association relationship. EER relationships of greater than binary cardinality, or with attributes, must be implemented by OOA/D objects, as must an EER M:N relationship, via an objet and two 1:N connections.

EER subtyping relationships loosely correspond to OOA/D generalisation/inheritance relationships. Mutually inclusive and exclusive EER subtypes are not, however, supported in the OOA/D notation. A change to this inclusive/exclusive state of an EER subtype thus can't be directly reflected in OOA/D relationships, and a change description is needed to document this indirect mapping.

The OOA/D notation has no concept of EER primary or foreign keys. Changing an OOA/D attribute which corresponds to part of a EER primary or foreign key must be documented, as it impacts on the EER model semantic correctness. If a relationship implemented by foreign key(s) is deleted, an indication should be given to the designer that EER attributes should be removed or ammended. A notation's formal semantics must thus be considered when determining automatic and semi-automatic translations.

Further indirect mappings exist when translating changes between the EER and OOD notations. The OOD client/supplier relationship may implement an EER relationship or may document a method call between two objects. Adding, removing or changing a client/supplier relationship can thus only be indicated by a change description in the EER model. The designer decides on whether an EER relationship change is needed. EER 1:1 and 1:N relationships may be implemented as OOD reference-typed attributes or as generic collection classes. Various other mappings between the EER notation and OOD notation, are not discussed further here but are supported by OOEER.

6 Tool Implementation and Integration

6.1 MViews

We have developed MViews, which provides abstractions for implementing integrated ISEEs [3, 5]. New environments are constructed by specialising object-oriented framework classes to describe the repository and program representation for ISEEs. Software system data is described by a graph-based structure, with graph *components* (nodes) specifying e.g. classes, entities, attributes and methods, and *relationships* (edges) linking these components to form the system structure. Multiple views of this repository are defined using the same graph-based structure. These views are rendered and manipulated in concrete textual and graphical forms.

Fig. 7 illustrates the structure of SPE, an integrated ISEE for object-oriented software development, developed using MViews [6]. The repository describes classes, attributes and methods (features), inter-class relationships, and implementation code. SPE multiple views include graphical OOA/D and textual implementation and documentation views.

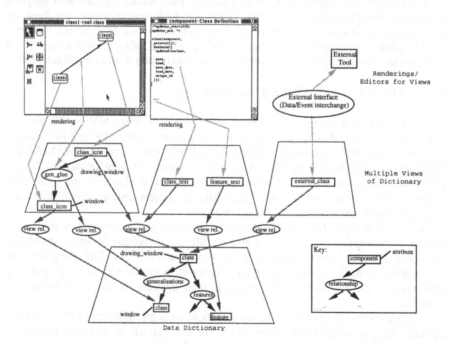

Fig. 7. Example of implementing an integrated ISEE using MViews.

MViews components support very flexible inter-component consistency managenent by generating, propagating and responding to *change descriptions* whenever a component is modified. A change description documents the exact change in the state of a component and is propagated to all relationships the component participates in. These relationships respond to change descriptions by applying operations to themselves or other components, forwarding the description to related components, or ignoring the component update. Most ISEE consistency management facilities are supported by this technique, including flexible multiple view consistency, constraints, attribute recalculation, undo/redo, and version control and cooperative work [7].

MViews is implemented in Snart, an object-oriented extension to Prolog. Environment implementers specialise Snart classes to define new environment data dictionaries, multiple views, and view renderings and editors. Snart is a persistent language, with objects dynamically saved and loaded to a persistent object store, making repository and view persistency management transparent for ISEE implementers. External tools not built using MViews can be interfaced to the integrated environment by using extenal views.

SPE was implemented as an ISEE for developing Snart programs [6]. It supports analysis, design, implementation, debugging and documentation of object-oriented programs using graphical and textual views. Views are kept consistent via the shared repository, so information in one view is always consistent with other representations in other views. This includes keeping analysis and design views bi-directionally consistent with implementation views, not supported by most ISEEs. SPE has been used to model large object-oriented software applications, including architectural building model frameworks and the MViews and SPE frameworks.

MViewsER was implemented as an ISEE for EER modelling, and also supports textual relational schema views [4]. Graphical EER design views are kept bi-directionally consistent with textual relational schema views. MViewsER has been used to model a variety of Information System problems, with the relational schema exported to relational database environments for Information System implementation.

6.2   The Integrated OOEER Environment

The conceptual data models used in the construction of SPE and MViewsER more or less equate to those defined in Section 4. We have integrated SPE and MViewsER into one integrated environment, OOEER, which supports integrated OOA/D and EER design and implementation. All of these views are kept consistent by the environment. As noted in section 3, some of these changes are (partially) automatically carried out by OOEER, while for others change descriptions are displayed to designers for manual implementation.

SPE and MViewsER were integrated by defining a repository based on an integrated conceptual data model (section 4). Mappings (section 5) were used to link the components and relationships in each notation's repository. The mappings also define translations for change descriptions generated by each environment's repository into updates on the integrated repository, then updates on the other notation's repository.

When an SPE view is edited (1), the modification is translated into SPE repository updates (2), generating change descriptions. The inter-repository relationships are sent change descriptions, and respond to these by updating the integrated repository (3). When the integrated repository components change, the inter-repository relationships to MViewsER's repository components translate the integrated repository components change descriptions into updates on MViewsER repository components (4). Indirect mapping changes are defaulted where possible and change descriptions displayed in views. Both SPE and MViewsER keep their multiple views consistent (5 and 6).

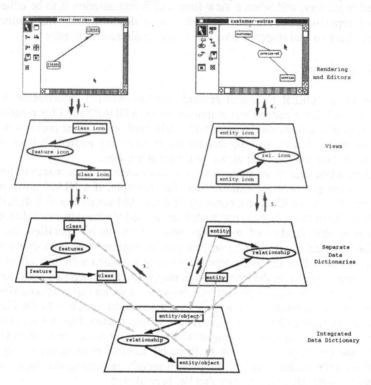

Fig. 8. Integrating SPE and MViewsER using the integrated data model.

Neither SPE nor MViewsER were modified in any way to support this integration process to produce OOEER. Change descriptions from another notation are displayed as special MViews "user updates" in the other notation's tools, requiring no special display mechanisms in the other tool. Any semantic errors detected during translation from the integrated repository are documented with "error" change descriptions.

6.3 Inter-repository Relationships

Inter-repository relationships are implemented as specialisations of MViews' generic many-to-many relationships. This allows one or more components from one repository to be connected to one or more components in another repository. When a change description from one component participating in the relationship is received, the relationship component determines the appropriate change to make to other participating components. This might be a simple update (automatic translation), a partial update (semi-automatic translation) or simply storing the change description against the affected component(s) (no automatic translation by OOEER possible). Using MViews' change description composition facilities [7], the inter-repository relationships can even wait for several change descriptions to be received and then translate them into changes on other related components.

We used MViews' lazy processing capabilities to minimise response time delay for users. Much of the update translation and view consistency management is done on-demand when a view is selected for editing. Change descriptions are cached in the integrated repository, and when a view from a different notation is to be edited, the integrated repository actions any cached change descriptions. This results in a minimum affect on tool response time when making discrete view edits.

6.4 Experience

We have used OOEER to model several small-to-medium Information System designs. As both direct and indirect mappings between OOA/D and EER notations are supported, both notations can be more effectively used on the same problem domain. When working with a view, designers are informed of any related changes in both other views for the notation and views for the other notation.

A major advantage of an integrated repository over a direct mapping between notations is for environment extensibility. For example, if a NIAM notation tool were to be added to OOEER, the concepts of the NIAM notation which directly and indirectly relate to those in the other models are related via the integrated data model. This reduces the number of mappings which have to be specified, as many translations, particularly the direct ones, are already implemented. Individual tools are also easier to extend, as the tool's repository can be extended with little affect on the integrated repository or on the inter-notation mappings. The integrated repository also provides a useful source for hypertext links between views for different notations.

Currently inter-repository relationships are automatically created by OOEER. We are currently extending OOEER to support user-defined relationships between different notation components, to allow a designer to relate one (or more) items in an OOA/D model to one (or more) items in an EER model. Limited consistency management across these relationships will be supported, mainly informing designers when a component on one side of the relationship has been altered.

In this work we have considered mappings between graphical icon-and-glue and textual OOA/D and EER notation components. Spatial constructs, such as Coad and Yourdon subjects [2] can be implemented, if desired. We are designing new tools to support NIAM diagrams, state transition diagrams and data flow diagrams, which will be integrated into OOEER. These different notations can be kept partially consistent with OOA/D and EER views using our technique. Some inter-notation consistency issues are more difficult to implement than others for these notations, and for some limited consistency can only be provided via user-defined relationships.

7 Conclusions

We have developed a new method for integrating different design notations within ISEEs. The conceptual data models of different design notations are defined and then an integrated data model derived, together with mappings of concepts and data changes between each data model. Tools supporting each notation are implemented based on this design by reusing the MViews framework. These separate tools are integrated by implementing an integrated repository based on the integrated conceptual data model. The concept and data change mappings are used to link related data from each notation's repository, and to keep these dynamically consistent as they change. We have developed OOEER, an ISEE which supports integrated OOA/D and EER notations using this approach. OOEER propagates direct changes between the OOA/D and EER notation views, such as entity, object and attribute creation, renaming, and deletion. It also propagates indirect changes, such as adding and renaming EER relationships and adding and changing OOA/D inheritance, aggregation and association relationships, not supported by most CASE tools.

We are extending OOEER to use data model mappings to support decision tracability between both analysis and design notations and different design notations. This will allow designers to trace analysis and design decisions through each notation's views and to implementation views. We are also extending OOEER to support version control for analysis and design views and Computer-Supported Co-operative Work facilities, as done for SPE [8]. Multiple designers will be able to collaborate on analysis and design using both multiple views and multiple notations. An issue is maintaining consistency between different notation views shared by designers. Our inter-notation mapping technique is being used to support intra-notation mapping in SPE i.e. mapping between analysis and design concepts and keeping these consistent under change. User-defined links between differently-named classes and entities, and their relationships, will allow designers to specify different EER and OOA/D structures, which can be manually linked and partially keep consistent by OOEER.

References

1. P.P. Chen: The Entity-Relationship Model - Toward a Unified View of Data. *ACM Transactions on Database Systems 1*, 1 (1976), 9-36.
2. P. Coad and E. Yourdon: *Object-Oriented Analysis,* Yourdon Press, Second Edition (1991).
3. J.C. Grundy, and J.G. Hosking: A framework for building visusal programming environments. In *Proceedings of the 1993 IEEE Symposium on Visual Languages,* IEEE Computer Society Press, 1993, pp. 220-224.
4. J.C. Grundy: *Multiple textual and graphical views for Interactive Software Development Environments*, Ph.D. dissertation, University of Auckland, Department of Computer Science, June 1993.
5. J.C. Grundy and J.G. Hosking: Constructing Integrated Software Development Environments with Dependency Graphs, Working Paper, Department of Computer Science, University of Waikato, 1994.
6. J.C. Grundy, J.G. Hosking, S. Fenwick, and W.B. Mugridge:*Visual Object-Oriented Programming,* Prentice-Hall (1994), Chapter 11.
7. J.C. Grundy, J.G. Hosking, and W.B. Mugridge, Supporting flexible consistency management via discrete change description propagation, Working Paper, Department of Computer Science, University of Waikato, 1995.
8. J.C. Grundy, W.B. Mugridge, J.G. Hosking, and R. Amor: Support for Collaborative, Integrated Software Development. accepted to the *7th Conference on Software Engineering Environments,* IEEE CS Press, April 1995.
9. B. Henderson-Sellersand J.M. Edwards: The Object-Oriented Systems Life Cycle. *Communications of the ACM 33*, 9 (1990), 142-159.
10. M. Heym and H. Österle: A Semantic Data Model for Methodology Engineering. In *Proceedings of the Fifth International Workshop on Computer-Aided Software Engineering,* IEEE CS Press, Washington, D.C., 1992, pp. 142-155.

11. B. Nuseibeh and A. Finkelstein: ViewPoints: A Vehicle for Method and Tool Integration. In *Proceedings of the Fifth International Workshop on Computer-Aided Software Engineering*, IEEE CS Press, Washington, D.C., 1992, pp. 50-61.

12. M. Ratcliffe, C. Wang, R.J. Gautier, and B.R. Whittle: Dora - a structure oriented environment generator. *IEE Software Engineering Journal* 7, 3 (1992), 184-190.

13. S.P. Reiss: Connecting Tools Using Message Passing in the Field Environment. *IEEE Software* 7, 7 (July 1990), 57-66.

14. X. Song, and L.J. Osterweil: A Process-Modeling Based Approach to Comparing and Integrating Software Design Methodologies. In *Proceedings of the Fifth International Workshop on Computer-Aided Software Engineering*, IEEE Computer Society Press, Washingon, D.C., 1992, pp. 225-229.

15. *TurboCASE Reference Manual*, StructSoft Inc, 5416 156th Ave. S.E. Bellevue, WA, 1992.

16. J.R. Venable:*CoCoA: A Conceptual Data Modelling Approach for Complex Problem Domains*, Ph.D. dissertation, State University of New York at Binghampton, 1993.

17. A.I. Wasserman, and P.A. Pircher: A Graphical, Extensible, Integrated Environment for Software Development. *SIGPLAN Notices* 22, 1 (January 1987), 131-142.

18. R.J. Wieringa: Combining static and dynamic modelling methods: a comparison of four methods. *to appear in Computer Journal* (1995).

A Federated Approach to Tool Integration

Malek Bounab and Claude Godart

CRIN/CNRS BP 239, 54506 Vandœuvre-lès-Nancy, France
E-mail: {bounab, godart}@loria.fr

Abstract. Due to enormous pressures from national and international marketplaces, Computer Integrated Manufacturing (CIM) has become a tremendously important area for both research and development. However, the current state of the art is still characterized by islands of automation. In order to connect these islands, appropriate frameworks have to be developed to integrate heterogeneous Computer Aided Design (CAD) tools. We present in this paper a federated approach to tool integration in distributed and heterogeneous environments making tools evolve in an autonomous way. We have experimented this approach by integrating PROPEL[1] and SPEX[2] CAD tools in the DMMS (Design Management and Manufacturing System) environment backed by a common PCTE[3] repository.

1 Introduction

CIM environments have known, these recent years, a tremendous expansion due to enormous pressures from national and international marketplaces. The purpose of CIM environments is to integrate all processes carried out within an enterprise. However, these environments are still characterized by heterogeneous islands of automation composed of monolithic CAD tools. Therefore, integrating tools becomes a key issue to offer homogeneous environments allowing (i) an uniform underlying communication system for events notification and messages interchanging between tools *(control integration)* (ii) an uniform repository in which all data are stored and shared *(data integration)* (iii) an uniform "look and fell" which enable users to swith between different tools easily *(presentation integration)* and (iv) an uniform and coordinated processing of activities with other tools *(process integration)*.

We focus in this paper on the data integration dimension. A standard approach consists in integrating all data into a large centralized database (like in GANDALF [1], CPS [2] and PECAN [3]). Though, tools involved in CIM environments are generally spread over different locations. On the other hand, a common representation doesn't always matches tools data modeling requirements

---

[1] PROPEL is a product of ITMI

[2] SPEX is a product of TNI, CRAN and SPIE-TRINDEL

[3] PCTE is an ISO standard providing an open repository for software development. We use in our experiment an implementation of PCTE 1.5 named Emeraude V12.5, product of GIE EMERAUDE

and it is often necessary to use different data models. Heterogeneous distributed databases (HDDB) seem to fulfill both previous requirements since they allow tools, scattered on different locations, to use data models which best fit their data modeling (eg: DATAPLEX [4] and IMDAS [5]). However, tools have to access a global schema, representing all data managed by HDDB, even for their own data, implying a loss of autonomy and performance.

This paper addresses the problem of tool integration in distributed and heterogeneous CIM environments where tool autonomy is an important requirement. We propose a federated approach built on the architecture of a federated database [6] preserving tools autonomy regarding the distribution and the heterogeneity of data. We present in section 2 the integration architecture and methodology followed to build *tool federations*. This methodology is experimented in the DMMS (Design Management and Manufacturing System) environment backed by a common PCTE repository. We focus in this paper particularly on data integration during the *design* step. Different integration steps leading to tool interoperability are described in section 3 and a production scenario showing tools cooperation for mechanical parts design concludes this section. The final section presents some lessons learned from our experiment and from the use of PCTE, initially designed for software engineering requirements, in a manufacturing environment.

2 Integration Architecture and Methodology

The DMMS environment, actually developed jointly by the Computer Science Research Center of Nancy (CRIN) and the Automation Research Center of Nancy (CRAN) [7, 8, 9] (figure 1), aims to establish a semantic link between different concurrent manufacturing functions.

DMMS intends to couple mechanical and automation working fields for designing and managing a product. It is composed of four working stations achieving (i) the design function, provided by automation and the mechanical working stations, which cooperate to design a product, (ii) the manufacturing function, provided by the flexible cell, which aims to execute the manufacturing of designed product, (iii) the maintenance function, provided by the maintenance working station, which insure the maintenance of a product during all its life cycle and (iv) the management of exchanged data between different working stations by the management working station. Each working station is composed of a set of tools integrated on top of a local repository. The different set of tools cooperate through a common PCTE repository.

The federated approach to tool integration is based on the reference architecture defined in [6] for database interoperability and consists in defining a set of schema levels which ensure, on the one hand, a tool autonomous access to its data and, on the other hand, a federated access to other tool's data via a canonical data model.

The data managed by tool and the relationships between them are defined by a *reverse engineering* process [10]. An abstract data representation is built using a conceptual data model which is, in our case, the ERA model [11].

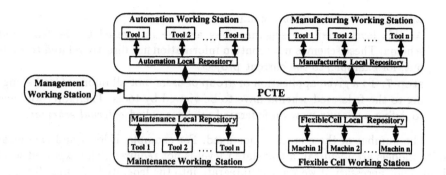

Fig. 1. DMMS ARCHITECTURE

Local accesses are done through local schemas expressed in the tool integration repository data model. This allows tools to access their own data locally and in an autonomous way without managing other data. We can then choose the most suitable local data model which best fit tools data modeling constraints and requirements.

Local schemas are then translated into a common data model which provides a coherent view of many distinct tools data. Different views, defined on these translated schemas, are integrated into a global federated schema representing all information which may be shared between tools. Finally, a view on these schemas allow tools interaction and cooperation. This view definition is visible to all federated tools in addition to their own local schemas.

To summarize, we give hereafter different steps of our methodology achieving tool integration in a heterogeneous and distributed environment.

- **step 1:** Define different tool federations by grouping tools according to a given criteria (eg: their application field).
- **step 2:** Define *conceptual schemas* by a reverse engineering process from tools managed data. The objective of this step is to define an abstract representation of tool data without considering any physical repository.
- **step 3:** Translate each conceptual schema to tool integration repository data model. The obtained schemas, expressed in the native data model of the database, are called *local schemas.*
- **step 4:** Translate each local schema to the canonical data model which unifies data representations through tool federation. The obtained schemas are called *translated schemas.*
- **step 5:** Build *exported schemas* by defining views on translated schemas. Exported schemas are requested because not all translated data have to be viewed by the federation. These views are defined for specific class of users and applications.
- **step 6:** Exported schemas are then integrated into *federated schemas.* The schema integration [12] provides data consistency between different exported schemas since common entities are merged into one unique entity after re-

solving name and structure conflicts.

At this level, auxiliary schemas may also be integrated to the federated schema. These schemas may contain information not directly related to tools but, for example, to the current project.

- **step 7:** To a given application or group of users, not all information belonging to the federated schema have to be viewed by tools. Therefore, we have to define a specific view on federated schemas called *external schemas*.

The number of these steps is not fixed. For example, if local and canonical data models are identical, a translated level is not required. The exported level is also not necessary if we want to integrate into the federated schema all translated schemas. In fact, the number of federation levels depends mainly on the federation components.

3 Experimenting the Tool Integration Methodology

We focus here on the design function which is mainly achieved by the mechanical and the automation working stations. This function deals with the relationship between the mechanical and automation skills which cooperate to design a product. It is a relatively long step since both two skills have to frequently reconsider their previous design. This is due to the set of physical requirements and constraints which must be considered during the manufacturing step.

The tool integration experiment involves the integration of PROPEL and SPEX CAD tools. These tools, respectively representative of mechanical and automation skills, have to cooperate widely to achieve mechanical and automation part design. MATISSE[4] database models mechanical local data while PCTE models those of the automation working station.

3.1 Reverse Engineering of the Tools

As we integrate only two tools belonging each to a different skill, each tool federation is reduced to only one tool. As a consequence, the first step of our methodology in not required. The second step consists in building conceptual schemas of the tools by reverse engineering from their data.

PROPEL Mechanical Design Tool

PROPEL [13] is an expert system generating process plans from part and workshop descriptions. The part is described by geometrical features (faces, slots...) and relationships between them (coaxiality, parallelism...). The workshop is described by a set of machines (lathes, milling machines ...), manufacturing tools present in the workshop (drills, face-cutters...) and the relationships between them. Part and manufacturing process plan descriptions are textual files which are either created by a tool or a user. In the following we present PROPEL and SPEX tools and the modeling of their data.

---

[4] MATISSE is an object oriented database produced by Intellitic International SNC.

Part and Manufacturing Process Plan Description and Modeling

The second step of the integration methodology consists in extracting data contained in the part and the process plan descriptions, by reverse engineering, in order to model data handled by PROPEL. The description of a part in PROPEL (figure 2.a) contains basic features composing it and the physical and geometrical characteristics of each feature. PROPEL being closed, we have considered only input and output data corresponding respectively to the part and the manufacturing process plan descriptions. The *part schema* (figure 2.b) includes all

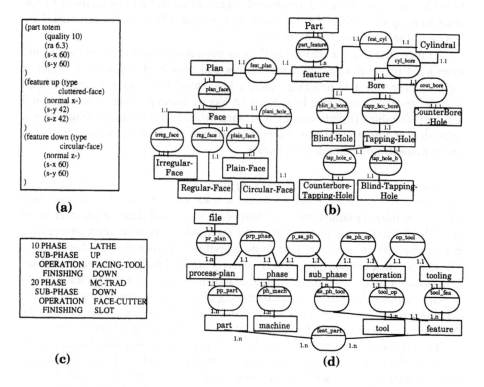

Fig. 2. Part and Process Plan Description and Modeling (step 2)

the features and parameters composing and describing a part. We have followed a *top-down* approach to break down a part into a set of features managed by PROPEL. Therefore, the schema describing a part contains all features which may occur in its description.

The manufacturing process plan generated by PROPEL (figure 2.c) represents operations to be processed in order to achieve a part manufacturing. These operations are structured in phases corresponding to machines involved in part manufacturing. From the process plan description generated by PROPEL, we build, by reverse engineering, the process plan schema depicted by figure 2.d. Each part (represented by the entity *part*) has one associated process plan (*process-plan* entity) linked to a *phase* entity. Each *phase* is linked to a set of *sub-phases* which are, in their turn, linked to *operations*. Each *operation* is composed of *toolings* processed on *features*. We associate, for each *phase*, a *machine* and, for each *sub-phase*, a *feature*.

SPEX Automation Design Tool

SPEX [14] is an environment allowing to specify, to design and to prototype automation systems. The objectives of SPEX are to allow designers to build reusable behaviors and to validate a functional organization during the analysis phase. SPEX manages two kind of automation components which are the *functional box* (FB) and the *functional diagram* (FD).

A functional box is a "behavioral" unity producing one or many output values from a set of input values and parameters and may be a graphcet, a ladder, a logical schema or a C program. Several behavioral boxes may be instantiated from a "generic" functional box. Each FB has its own identifier, a behavior and a set of variables (input, output and parameters). A functional diagram is a collection of FBs and/or FDs interconnected via their input/output interfaces and representing a composite behavior.

Building a SPEX Automation Design Application

We use a top down approach to define a SPEX application . That means that all FDs are initially empty and are completed by the automation engineer while needed information are received from the mechanical engineer. SPEX automation design application considers four basic activities occuring in a product design. These activities are the TRANSPORT activity which handles transport of products between machines during the manufacturing step, the TRANSFORM activity which considers the effective manufacturing of a product, the STORE/UNSTORE activities which ensure product storage and unstorage before its use and finally, the CONTROL activity which controls data flow between the above activities.

The information given by the mechanical engineer are considered in the transforming activity while the controling, transporting and storing/unstoring activities are defined by the automation engineer, the robotics engineer and the production manager. These activities are represented by CONTROL, TRANSPORT, STORE/UNSTORE and TRANSFORM FDs . The FD corresponding to TRANSFORM activity is built from information given by the process plan generation step. Each sub-phase of the process plan corresponds to a generic empty FD and to each of these FDs is associated a set of manufacturing tools used in this sub-phase. To each tool, is associated an empty FD which input/output variables and parameters are set by the automation engineer.

Automation Design Application Schema

The automation design application schema is deduced from the SPEX automation design application and is completed later by the automation engineer which has to define each FB behavior and connect different FBs and FDs making up the application. The schema built from this application comprises *Tool, Station,*

Control, Transform, Transport and *Store/Unstore* object types (figure 3). These object types are all linked to *I_Var*, *O_Var* and *Behavior* object types corresponding respectively to their input variables, output variables and behaviors.

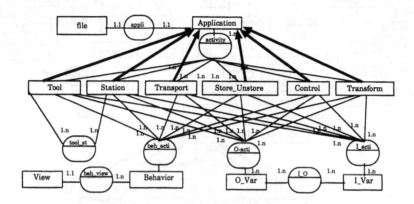

Fig. 3. The Automation Design Application Schema (step 2)

3.2 Tool Federation on top of PCTE

PCTE has been initially designed for software engineering needs. It is used in our architecture as a canonical data model in order to be experimented and evaluated for manufacturing requirements. It defines a repository in which data are stored and shared between tools. The choice of a standardized repository as a canonical data model is a key element of our architecture since it provides an open framework which homogenize different tool data representations making their integration and interoperation easier. Tools interoperability is achieved following the steps 3 to 7 of our integration methodology and is applied to the integration of SPEX and PROPEL tools by defining the five schema levels.

The Local Level

Data managed by SPEX and PROPEL were modeled, by a reverse engineering process, using an extended ERA data model independently from the tool integration repositories. We translate hereafter the conceptual schemas representing the data managed by the tools into their integration repository.

PROPEL integration repository is MATISSE. It is an object oriented database using an ERA like data model. Part and process plan conceptual schemas depicted respectively by figures 2.b and 2.d are translated to MATISSE data model. Each entity type is translated into an object class, each relationship into a link class and each attribute type into an attribute class. Cardinalities are kept unchanged. The resulting schemas are depicted by figures 4.a and 4.b.

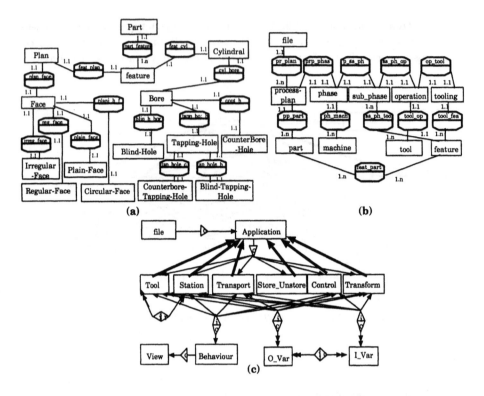

Fig. 4. PROPEL and SPEX local level (step 3)

SPEX automation design schema is translated into PCTE data model (figure 4.c). Each entity type is translated into an object type and each relationship type into a link type. The link category and attribute keys are defined by the designer. A formal definition of the mapping rules between the ERA and both MATISSE and PCTE data models is given in [8].

The Translated Level

We focus here on translating local schemas into the canonical data model corresponding to the fourth step of our integration approach. This translation is applied only to PROPEL schemas since the local schema (MATISSE) and the canonical data model (PCTE) are different. The correspondent translation rules transform each object class, link class and attribute class in MATISSE data model respectively into an object type, a link type and an attribute type in PCTE data model. Translated schemas of the part and the process plan are represented respectively by figures 5.a and 5.b. The cardinality of PCTE links doesn't traduce exactly the same semantics as MATISSE relationship cardinality since a cardinality *one* in PCTE represents a (0,1) or (1,1) relationship in MATISSE and a cardinality *many* in PCTE represents (0,n) or (1,n) in MATISSE. For a formal definition of the mapping rules between MATISSE and PCTE refer to [8].

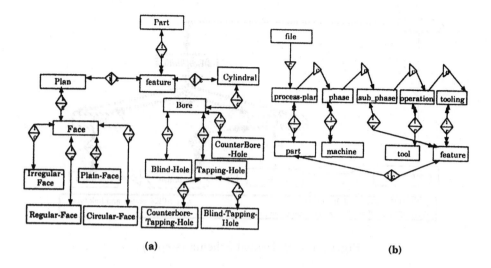

Fig. 5. Part and Process Plan Schemas in PCTE (step 4)

The Exported Level

The definition of the exported level from the translated level is carried out by defining a view on the translated schemas because not all translated schemas have to be seen and used by the federation. PCTE provides view definition thanks to the working schema (WS) mechanism. This mechanism stands for a filter since it allows to make visible only instances of object types it includes. The instances of object types which are not contained in the WS are not accessible and therefore invisible to the federated tools. Therefore, the exported schema should contain all tool schemas which have to be used by other tools of the federation. The inclusion of schemas and their order in the WS is managed by the user.

In our experiment, only the process plan and the automation design application schemas are included into the WS while the part schema remains local to PROPEL. The federation can therefore view instances of object types composing the process-plan and automation-design-application schemas.

The Federated Level

The sixth step consists in defining the federated level by integrating exported schemas into a federated schema. The integration process, as defined in [12], consists in solving, first, name and structure conflicts before defining common object type through which tools can cooperate. Finally, schema integration is processed by importing common object types and other related information which may be used by tools.

In PCTE, schema integration is achieved using importing mechanism provided by PCTE. From object and link types of exported schemas, we import object types common to schemas which have to be integrated. Importing these object types into the federated schemas allows tools to see, at the federated

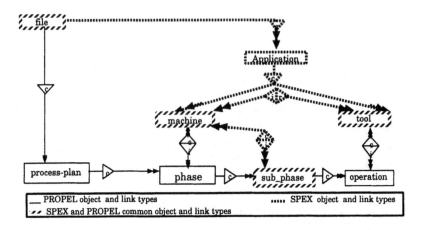

Fig. 6. The Federated Schema (step 6)

level, object instances created at the local level by other tools. In our case (figure 6), we integrate exported part and automation design application schemas. Object types *Process_plan*, *phase*, *sub_phase* and *operation* and their links are imported from the process plan schema. Object type *Application* is imported from automation design application schema. Therefore, the integrated schemas share object types *machine* (called *Station* in automation design application schema), *tool* and *sub_phase*.

The External Level

The external schema, representing the seventh step, is obtained by defining a view on the federated schema. This view may correspond to a given application or a class of users which do not need to view all the information represented by the federated schema. The external schema allows data exchange between SPEX and PROPEL tools through their common object and link types (Figure 8). We have integrated into the federated schema, in addition to the information of

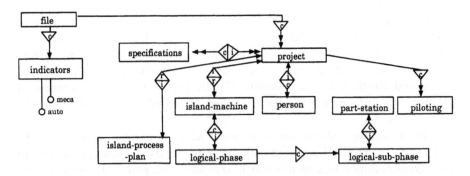

Fig. 7. The Auxiliary Management Schema

the process plan and automation design application schema, some management information related to the current project grouped in an auxiliary management schema (figure7). This schema represents the part, the manufacturing requirements (object type *requirements* containing a graphical representation of the currently manufactured part) and persons allowed to work on the project (object type *person*). We have also added to this schema a logical representation of the project which provides a link between logical and physical aspects of a project (object type *part_ station*), logical phase (object type *logical_ phase*) and sub-phase (object type *logical_ sub_ phase*). Object types *part* (called *project* in the management schema), *process-plan* (called *island-process-plan* in the management schema) and *application* (called *piloting* in the management schema) are common object types allowing the integration of the process plan, the automation design application and the management schemas.

External schema allows, thanks to the PCTE types importation mechanism to view object instances created at the local level. It is therefore possible, for any tool, to manipulate an object type instance of the external schema. Tools can access shared object type instances through which they can interoperate in an autonomous way by creating locally their instances and without any knowledge and management of other tool objects. The only information which should be known is the external schema. This one must always be included into tools ws to allow a local access to their objects and a federated access to other tool objects.

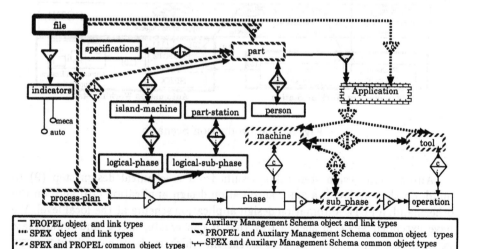

Fig. 8. The External Schema (step 7)

3.3 The Implemented Production Scenario

The objective of the production scenario depicted by figure 9 is to achieve parts design. The production scenario consists of two main steps which are the mechanical and the automation design steps managed by the management working station. This one allows the mechanical working station to begin its processing (1). From the information given by the part description file (2) (features and their physical and geometrical characteristics), we instantiate the MATISSE and PCTE part schemas (3) respectively at the local and the translated levels. PRO-PEL generates then, from the part description file and workshop machine and tool descriptions, the manufacturing process plan file (4). We process this file to extract information allowing the instantiation of MATISSE and PCTE process plan schemas (5) belonging respectively to the local and the translated levels. The end of the mechanical design step is notified to the management station through the external schema (6). This notification is considered by the management working station (7) which can now allow the automation station to start the automation design step (8).

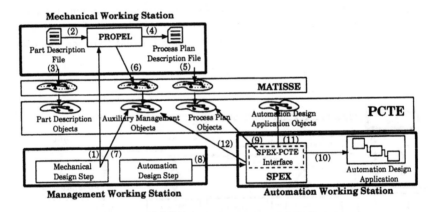

Fig. 9. The Production Scenario

Automation design step takes results from mechanical design step (9) to build, on the one hand, a SPEX automation design application (10) and, on the other hand, a PCTE automation design application schema at the local level. We have extended SPEX in such a way that it can create, access and manipulate PCTE object type instances. This extension, which we have named SPEX-PCTE interface, generates a SPEX automation design application by counting *sub-phase* object type instances belonging to the PCTE process-plan schema at the external level instantiated during the mechanical design step. Considering that each process plan sub-phase corresponds physically to a transformation site, SPEX-PCTE module creates as much FDs as sub-phases. Created FDs are linked to each other using their input/output variables. Finally, a schema representing a PCTE automation design application is generated at the local level. This schema is compiled to be instantiated (11). The end of this step is notified to the management working station (12). All notifications are done using *meca* and *auto* notification attributes belonging to *indicators* object type in the external schema. Thanks to the importation and the WS mechanisms of PCTE, object instances created at the translated level are visible at the external level since both the process plan and the application design application schemas are included into the WS.

4   Lessons Learned and Future Work

This paper presents a federated approach to integrate tools in an heterogeneous environment. We have experimented this approach by integrating two different, but complementary tools whose integration was never anticipated.

The federated approach presents some lacks mainly related to the incompatibility between the different data models. We have to choose, on the one hand, a local data model which models the best tool data and, on the other hand, a canonical data model which has to be semantically rich enough to support different product modeling. These choices must limit the semantic losts when translating schemas from local to canonical data model. For our experiment, we got a favorable situation since both PCTE and MATISSE data models are ERA like models and therefore relatively homogeneous. This has made easier the translation between the two models and has limited semantic losts. From this point of view, a first conclusion is that the PCTE data model, close to the ERA is an acceptable canonic model, even if little semantic constraint types are handled by PCTE (we proposed in [15] an extension of the PCTE, inspired from the NIAM data model to enhance semantic constraint management).

Our second conclusion is that PCTE, due to its schema integration mechanism, provides an active support to federated schema building and mutually to federated database access. It is generally accepted that tool interaction depends on the object type granularity considered in the exchange schema. A coarse granularity limits the number of managed object types but can penalize tools interactions due to a non enough detailed view of managed objects. On the other side, fine granularity allows an efficient interaction between tools by enhancing schema semantics but increases the set of object types we have to deal with. PCTE is better adapted to manage coarse grain objects. However, it was sufficient in the context of our experimentation. In fact, it seems us that it is more important to decrease the granularity of the services extracted from tools. The redesign of tools, in order to extract internal services, even if it is an expansive task, can take benefits of services provided by PCTE to allow a better visibility of tool intermediate results and as a consequence to increase interactions and positive synergetic effects.

As perspectives, we plan to extend PCTE data model, initially designed for software engineering requirements, to cover other CIM requirements such as fine granularity object management and type instance management while evolving schemas. In addition, PCTE manages concurrent accesses using locking mechanisms and transactions. These mechanisms are efficient for short time transactions but are particularly unsuitable for long term design processes which can take several hours and even several days. We plan to integrate to DMMS architecture long term transactions such as those implemented in COO [16].

References

1. D. Notkin. The GANDALF Project. *Journal of Systems and Software*, 5(2):91–106, May 1985.
2. T. Reps and T. Taitelbaum. The Synthesizer Generator. In P. Henderson, editor, *Proc. ACM SIGSOFT/SIGPLAN Software Engineering Symposium on Practical Software Development Environments*, pages 42–48, May 1984.
3. S.P Reiss. PECAN: Program Development System that Support Multiple Views. *IEEE Transactions on Software Engineering*, SE-11(2):276–285, Mar. 1985.
4. C.W. Chung. DATAPLEX: an access to heterogeneous distributed databases. *Communications of the ACM*, 33(1), Jan. 1990.
5. V. Krishnamurthy, S.Y.W. Su, H. Lam, M. Mitchell, and E. Barkmeyer. A distributed database architecture for an integrated manufacturing facility. In Computer Society of IEEE, editor, *Proceedings of the International Conference on Data and Knowledge Systems for Manufacturing and Engineering*, pages 4–13, 1987.
6. A.P. Sheth and J.A. Larson. Federated Database Systems for Managing Distributed, Heterogeneous and Autonomous Databases. *ACM CS*, 22(3), Sep. 1990.
7. G. Morel and P. Lhoste. *Prototyping a Concurrent Engineering Architecture*, volume 1 of *TSI Press Series*, pages 163–167, 1994.
8. M. Bounab. Tool Integration in Heterogeneous Environments: Experimentation in a Manufacturing Framework. Phd Thesis, National Polytechnical Institute of Lorraine, Oct. 1994. (in french).
9. M. Lombard-Gregori. Contribution to discrete part manufacturing engineering : prototyping a concurrent engineering architecture for manufacturing integrated systems. Phd Thesis, University of Nancy I, Feb. 1994. (in french).
10. E.J. Chikofsky and J.H. Cross II. Reverse Engineering and Design Recovery: A Taxonomy. *IEEE Software*, pages 13–17, Janvier 1990.
11. P.P. Chen. The Entity-Relationship model: Toward an Unified View of Data. *ACM Transactions on Database Systems*, 1(1):9–36, Mar. 1976.
12. C. Batini, M. Lenzerini, and S.B Navathe. A Comparative Analysis of Methodologies for Databases Schema Integration. *ACM Computer Survey*, 18(4), 1986.
13. J.P. Tsang. Planification par combinaison de plans: application à la génération de gammes. PhD Thesis, National Polytechnical Institute of Grenoble, 1987. (in french).
14. H. Panetto, P. Lhoste, G. Morel, and M. Roesch. SPEX : Du Génie Logiciel pour le Génie Automatique. In *4th Int. Workshop: Software Engineering & its Applications*, pages 211–221, Toulouse (France), Dec. 1991.
15. M. Bounab, J. C. Derniame, C. Godart, and G. Morel. DMMS: A PCTE Based Manufacturing Environment. In *Proc. PCTE'93 Int. Conference*, pages 431–449, Nov. 1993.
16. C. Godart. COO: A Transaction Model to Support COOperating Software Developers COOrdination. In I. Sommerville and M. Paul, editors, *Proceedings 4th European Software Engineering Conference*, pages 361–379, Garmisch (Austria), Sept. 1993. Springer Verlag. Lecture Notes in Computer Science, N° 717.

Domain Knowledge Reuse
During Requirements Engineering

Michael D. Gibson and Kevin Conheeney

School of Computing and Management Sciences,
Sheffield Hallam University,
100 Napier Street, Sheffield S11 8HD, United Kingdom.

Abstract. The accurate capture, understanding and representation of requirements is a critical step in the construction of effective and usable information systems. This activity is highly cognitive and is people and knowledge intensive; its success or failure is significantly influenced by the skills and especially the previous experience of the development staff involved. Many of the processes of requirements engineering are not well defined and remain difficult and problematic, significantly the initial investigation, elicitation and checking of requirements are poorly supported by current development tools and development methods. This paper describes research within the field of requirements engineering which draws upon AI/KBS research to adopt a knowledge based approach for requirements capture, modelling and validation and encourage the reuse of knowledge about typical information system applications and domains during such activities.

1. Introduction

The nature of modern information systems is changing, systems are becoming more complex and sophisticated; specialised information systems supporting decision making, systems which integrate organisational activities serving business processes rather than business areas and multiple organisation systems for new initiatives such as supply chain networks and virtual organisations. These developments increase the complexity and importance of accurately capturing and specifying the context and requirements of such systems. The incorrect specification of requirements remains one of the principle causes of inadequate information systems; poor requirement definition leading to systems which are ineffective, inefficient or do not satisfy user needs. There are numerous information systems development methodologies in existence, many supporting some aspect of requirements specification. These methodologies differ significantly in the development tasks which they address or the types of application for which they are suitable; the relative merits of such methods are widely documented [22, 9, 10]. A common feature of many of the commercially successful approaches is the increasing use of computer based tools to provide support for using the method or automate aspects of the development process. These development aids range from simple tools manipulating graphical structures associated with a method, to more sophisticated tools, integrating graphical input with a central development database, performing varying degrees of automated consistency and completeness checking. Recent work in this area has introduced "intelligent" tools which automate development activities or offer guidance to users about performing development tasks, or the heuristics of a particular development method.

The extent to which current development methods and tools are actually addressing the special challenges of the requirements engineering stage of development remains uncertain. Compared to other development stages, the requirements stage is especially difficult; many of the activities are cognitive and the information available to the developer is often unstructured, imprecise, incomplete, or may reflect fluctuating or conflicting user views of system requirements. A knowledge gap exists between user and developer: the developer lacks detailed application knowledge whilst the user lacks an understanding of the computer system development process and terminology. The existence of a knowledge gap can and does lead to communication difficulties between user and developer during the investigation of requirements and importantly during the validation of captured requirements. In an empirical study of how analysts work [12], significant amounts of informal fact gathering and elicitation activity took place unsupported by any sort of method, in a further study [11] over half of the problems cited by analysts were associated with user communication; validation activities were considered to be especially problematic. Another survey [21] observed that users found it difficult to understand and validate requirements and that the use of existing structured notations had little impact in this area. Recent work in the area continues to provide evidence that many development methods and tools do not adequately serve the requirement specification phase of development and reviews of current research indicate that there are many unfulfilled opportunities for further requirements engineering research [5].

This paper describes research which aims to represent knowledge about typical applications and domains and promote the reuse of this knowledge during requirement elicitation, modelling and validation activities. The research is an extension to an existing knowledge based requirements modelling language which was developed to model and validate information system requirements. The remaining sections of this paper review the foundations and aims of the research, introduce the requirement modelling language, explain how this is used to represent typical domain knowledge and how such knowledge might be used in conjunction with computer based tools. The final section of the paper reflects on initial research findings and outlines plans for further work in this area.

2. Research Background

A number of authors have proposed that the representation of many kinds of knowledge about the world is essential to requirements engineering [14, 1, 7]. These works suggest that a requirement specification should represent a wide range of knowledge: domain knowledge about the target system and its environment, development method knowledge and more general common sense or world knowledge. This view has generated interest in knowledge based representations such as semantic networks, frames and classical logic's as bases for rich modelling and inferencing mechanisms to represent and reason with various types of requirement knowledge.

A premise of our research is that much of the knowledge of interest to requirements specification can be identified, generalised and reused. Studies of how analysts actually work suggest that analysts extensively reuse knowledge about similar or previous applications they have worked on, using common or typical models as starting points and templates for considering the new situation under investigation [12]. It is common for analysts to use various forms of informal static models and animated examples both for their own benefit and during communication with end users. The use of analogy is also recognised by other works proposing the reuse of requirement knowledge in various forms [24, 16, 23, 24, 17, 19, 20]. The importance of analogy is reflected in range of studies of analysts productivity [3, 27] which confirm that previous experience significantly influences developer effectiveness and efficiency and the quality of the work they produce. Initial research in this area indicates that it is possible to identify types of information systems which share common properties and support similar problem domains and to classify these; an example of a partial type hierarchy is shown in Figure 1.

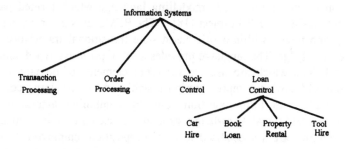

Figure 1. Partial classification of system types and uses

Within this hierarchy of system types there are characteristic objects, domain structure, and behaviour which typifies each type of application and are similar between supertype and subtype. Using the example of a loan control system it is possible to specify a generic description for such a domain, part of which might be:

" *a loan object exists, it is usual to lend the object to a hirer or borrower for a period of time and the object is returned at some time. At any point in time the object can be available for loan, can be on loan or under repair and so on.....* "

Even from this brief description it is possible to identify and classify domain concepts which typify this type of application:
-   common objects such as: *loan object, borrower, hirer, loan period.*

- common states such as: *object available, object on loan, object at repair.*
- common events such as: *lend object, return object.*

These characteristics apply in specialised forms to many types of loan control systems such as the ones shown in the Figure 1 and many others. An aim of this research is to represent such generic knowledge in greater detail, showing common objects, common behaviour, common domain constraints and the dependencies between all of these. Representing the essential structures and common behaviour of target domains will offer guidance to the developer during elicitation, support modelling by analogy and also facilitate further work into the automation of, or active support for requirement model development activities by suitable tools.

The following sections describe a language which is being used to model reusable domain knowledge and show examples of the range of domain knowledge that can be represented.

3. Requirement Knowledge Modelling

An existing Requirement Fact Modelling Language (RFML) [13] is being adapted to specifically represent appropriate aspects of reusable domain knowledge. The RFML was derived from a study of conceptual graph theory, a knowledge representation formalism developed and described comprehensively by Sowa [26] and from work on an earlier conceptual graph based modelling language which formed part of the Alvey Analyst Assist SE/IKBS project [18]. The RFML uses a constrained form of conceptual graph theory within a rule based state transitional framework to model requirement knowledge. The language provides a set of primitive typed concepts and conceptual relations which are used to represent elements of domain knowledge. More meaningful knowledge representation is achieved by combining concepts and conceptual relations to form assertions and by combining assertions to form propositions. An additional knowledge structure, a scenario is introduced by the language. Scenarios are a specialised form of proposition, employing a traditional antecedent consequent rule structure; rule pre-conditions and post-conditions are represented by combinations of concepts, assertions and propositions.

3.1 Language Overview

The basic components of the language are concepts and conceptual relations. A concept is some element of interest from a modelled domain. A conceptual relation represents a directed semantic link between concepts. An assertion is a collection of concepts and conceptual relations which exist between the concepts; forming a directed bipartite graph, representing some aspect of a modelled domain. The following is an example of a simple assertion, introducing the text based linear notation used throughout this paper:

```
[Person:*] -> (CHAR) -> [Name:*]
```
The linear notation represents:
* Concepts - as square brackets containing a concept label and referent value.

* Relations - as simple brackets containing a relation label.
* Arcs - shown as a dash and direction arrow.

Concepts are the items of interest from the modelled domain, the item can be real or abstract. Concepts are considered to be of certain types and these types may be classified in a concept type hierarchy. The RFML provides a set of primitive concept types from which domain specific concepts can be specified, some of these are shown in Figure 2.

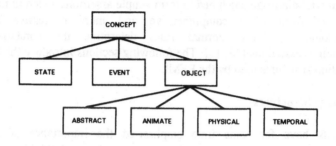

Figure 2. RFML Primitive Concepts

A concept is represented by a type label and an optional referent value. The label indicates the concept type class and the referent serves as a symbolic identifier or value for an instance or instances of the class. The following examples show some of the concept/referent combinations used by the RFML which appear in the examples given in this paper, a full treatment of referent identifiers is to be found in other work [13].

[Member] - represents the concept class, the highest level of the concept type Member, representing the set of all members known to the model.
[Member:(#)] - represents a specific set of instances of Member; the set is unique within a specific context; the size of the set may be specified or constrained as in:
[Member:(#)@integer]
[Member:*] - represents a specific instance of Member which can be symbolically identified and is unique within a specific context.
[Member:Jones] - represents a specific instance of Member which is symbolically identified and is unique within a specific context.
[Member:#] - represents an individual instance of Member which is unique within a specific context but is not necessarily identified; used to denote the indefinite article a Member or the Member.

The combination of type label and referent allows considerable freedom to specify domain knowledge at various levels of generality and detail, allowing the modelling of a domain at a number of resolution levels appropriate to the type of application and the nature of the domain.

Conceptual Relations are used to specify semantic relationships between concepts. In conceptual graph theory, the treatment of conceptual relations is derived from linguistic research into case roles and is based on Fillmore's case grammar [8]. The RFML follows this approach and provides a set of primitive relations each of which is defined by a formal definition showing the highest level concepts between which the relation may apply. Negated relations are supported and new relations can be defined by specialisation, all relations are classified in a type hierarchy in the same way as concepts.

Concepts and relations are combined to form simple assertions which in turn can are combined to form more comprehensive and more expressive knowledge representational structures. Formal rules determine the combination and manipulation of assertions [26, 13]. The following sections introduce the knowledge representation structures used by the RFML.

3.2 Language Structures

Psychologists have for some time emphasised the importance of chunks of knowledge as elementary patterns in human perception and thinking: a common approach which humans use to structure knowledge is in terms of set situation action rules [15]. The RFML uses assertions, propositions and rule based scenarios, to model elements of domain structure and domain behaviour.

Assertions are an association between at least one conceptual relation and two or more concepts. Assertions may describe knowledge relating to the behaviour or structure of a domain. The following are examples of a number of basic assertions from a domain:

```
[Book:*]->(CHAR)->[Title:*].  [MicroficheSystem:#]->(PART)->[FicheReader:{#}@4].
[Member:*]->(CHAR)->[UserNumber:*].    [ReadingDesk:{#}]->(LOC)->[ReadingRoom:#].
```

Propositions are packages of knowledge containing a number of related assertions or they may contain further nested propositions. Nested propositions may be connected to represent conjunctive, disjunctive or negated combinations of knowledge. A proposition is represented in the RFML as:

```
[[Proposition]] or alternatively as :  (PROPREL)->[[Proposition]].
```

The following example shows a propositional declaration for a Library domain:

```
[[[Member:*]->(CHAR)->[AccessLevel:Staff]]->(OR)->
[[Member:*]->(CHAR)->[AccessLevel:Student]]->(OR)->
[[Member:*]->(CHAR)->[AccessLevel:Limited]]->(OR)->
[[Member:*]->(CHAR)->[AccessLevel:Visiting]]].
```

Within the RFML, propositions may be specialised to form context, behaviour or constraint scenarios, as shown in Figure 3.

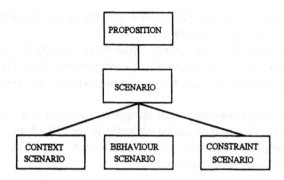

Figure 3. Proposition Subtypes

Scenarios are packages of knowledge linked to specific concept types. Scenarios are used to represent structural, contextual, behavioural and constraint declarations describing a modelled domain. A scenario is a specialised rule based form of proposition, where the proposition consists of two component propositions linked by a causal relation. A scenario rule structure consists of a left hand side antecedent proposition defining the necessary conditions which must exist before an instance of the concept type associated with the scenario can come into existence. The right hand side defines a consequent proposition showing the necessary conditions which must exist after the concept instance is introduced. Scenarios have the following representation:

```
[Concept]->(PROPREL)->
[[[Proposition]]
->(RESLT)->
[[Proposition]]].
```

4. Representing Domain Knowledge

The section on research aims gave an overview of the classification of common application domains and how concepts typical of these domains can be identified and typed. This sections gives examples of how it is possible to represent further knowledge about a domain, defining concepts, how concepts are usually related and to specifically represent knowledge about domain structure, behaviour, rules and the interaction between these.

4.1 Modelling Domain Contents

The typical structure and contents of a domain are represented by a number of assertions. These are used to specify typical domain concepts and common relationships between such concepts. They model the hierarchical ordering of concept types, relevant instances of types which may exist and the relations which may link concepts of various types at different levels of generality. For each concept typical of a domain, a cluster of assertions is specified for that concept showing all the important relations it may hold with other concepts in the same domain, some examples for a loan object might be:

```
[LoanObject:*]->(CHAR)->[Location:#].     [LoanObject:*]<-(OBJ)<-[ReturnObject:#].
[LoanObject:*]->(CHAR)-> [HireRate:#].    [LoanObject:*]<-(OBJ)<-[LendObject:#].
[LoanObject:*]->(STAT)->[OnLoan:#].       [LoanObject:*]->(STAT)->[Available:#].
```

Assertions represent knowledge about an application domain at a particular level of generality and resolution, they can be successively specialised, refined and extended to model appropriate examples of the application type. The following shows examples of assertion specialisation:

Inherent RFML model assertion:
```
[ANIMATE:*]<-(AGNT)<-[EVENT:#]->(OBJ)->[OBJECT:*].
```
Specialising the above to any loan domain:
```
[ANIMATE]->(SUB)->[Borrower].
[EVENT]->(SUB)->[LendObject].
[OBJECT]->(SUB)->[LoanObject].
[Borrower:*]<-(AGNT)<-[LendObject:#]->(OBJ)->[LoanObject:*].
```
and after further specialisation to a Library domain:
```
[Borrower]->(SUB)->[Member].
[LendObject]->(SUB)->[IssueBook].
[LoanObject]->(SUB)->[Book].
[Member:*]<-(AGNT)<-[IssueBook:#]->(OBJ)->[Book:*].
```

These simple assertions describe aspects of the structure of a domain and serve as building blocks from which more informative assertions and propositions describing the domain can be constructed. They also provide the material for the specification of scenarios to represent typical domain behaviour and important domain rules and constraints.

4.2 Modelling Domain Behaviour

Behaviour scenarios specify units of typical behaviour in a domain, constraints on when such behaviour may take place and the consequences of the behaviour. For each domain event a behaviour scenario models the concepts and relations between concepts which must exist prior to the event and the concepts and relations between concepts which must exist after the event has taken place. The following example shows a simple behaviour scenario for the event 'Lend Object' in a generic loan control domain:

```
[LendObject:#]->(BEHVR)->
[[[[Borrower:*]<-(AGNT)<-[LendObject:#]->(OBJ)-> [LoanObject:*]]->(AND)->
[[Borrower:*]->(STAT)->[ValidUser:#]]->(AND)->
[[LoanObject:*]->(STAT)->[Available:#]]]
->(RESLT)->
[[[LoanObject:*]->(ALLOC)->[Borrower:*]]->(AND)->
[[LoanObject:*]->(STAT)->[OnLoan:#]]].
```

Each behaviour scenario describes a unit of behaviour and sequences of behaviour scenarios may be used to describe threads of typical domain behaviour. The collection of all behaviour scenarios in the model represent the range of possible behaviour in a domain.

Context scenarios define the states which exist within a domain, further constraints on relationships between states and for each state the concepts and relations between concepts which must exist during that state. A state context scenario describes additional conditions which apply to those concepts related to the state whilst the state exists. The following shows an example of a context scenario associated with a loan control system state 'Available', note the use of negated relations:

```
[Available:#]->(CONTX)->
[[[LoanObject:*]->(STAT)->[Available:#]]
->(RESLT)->
[[[LoanObject:*]->(~STAT)->[OnLoan:#]]->(AND->
[[LoanObject:*]->(~STAT)->[AtRepair:#]]].
```

Context scenarios are useful to specify additional structural constraints relevant to a domain and further define the permissible consequences of domain behaviour.

4.3 Modelling Domain Constraints and Rules

In many domains there are application specific rules or general constraints or rules describing the structural aspects of a domain. Constraint scenarios are used to define restrictions on concept type populations, relations between concepts, operational properties of the domain such as integrity constraints, application specific rules and rules for deriving additional information from known information.

Constraint scenarios specify constraints on specific objects; expressed by relating an object to an appropriate constraint scenario. The scenario defines a pattern of concepts and relations showing conditions which must exist (or cannot exist) in the domain if an instance of the constrained object exists in the domain. The post-condition of the constraint scenario contains an assertion or assertions which indicate the possible effect on the domain if the constraint pre-condition is satisfied. The following scenario introduces the object 'Loan Duration' as relevant to a loan control domain and possible characteristics of the concept:

```
[LoanDuration:*]->(CONST)->
[[[Borrower:*]<-(AGNT)<-[LendObject:#]->(OBJ)->[LoanObject:*]]->(AND)->
[[LoanObject:*]->(STAT)->[OnLoan:#]]->(AND->
[[OnLoan:#]->(DURN)->[LoanPeriod:*]]->(AND)->
[[LoanDuration:*]->(GTR)->[LoanPeriod:*]]]
->(RESLT)->
[[LoanObject:*]->(STAT)->[Overdue:#]]->(AND)->
[[Borrower:*]->(STAT)->[OverdueBorrower:#]]].
```

The examples of domain knowledge presented in this section have been simplified and represent modelling at a very general level in the application type hierarchy. It is when these knowledge structures are specialised and extended to represent specific application domain examples that they become more meaningful and useful; the following section shows how such structures can be interpreted and used during requirement specification activities.

5. Using Domain Knowledge

An objective of this research is to model each level of a specified application type hierarchy by appropriate assertions, propositions and scenarios. Each of these declaratively describes an aspect of the application type and collectively they form a typical/generic model for that type of application and domain. Using declarations allows a modular approach to specifying domain knowledge and provides a number of useful abstraction levels to view the domain model from different perspectives.

Individually the declarations can serve as templates and prompts to the developer about aspects of an application type when considering a new development or they can be used as communication examples in user analyst dialogues for elicitation. For example, from the generic loan control event 'LendObject' described in a previous section:

```
[LendObject:#]->(BEHVR)->
[[[[Borrower:*]<-(AGNT)<-[LendObject:#]->(OBJ)->[LoanObject:*]]->(AND)->
[[Borrower:*]->(STAT)->[ValidUser:#]]->(AND)->
[[LoanObject:*]->(STAT)->[Available:#]]]
->(RESLT)->
[[[LoanObject:*]->(ALLOC)->[Borrower:*]]->(AND)->
[[LoanObject:*]->(STAT)->[OnLoan:#]]].
```

To specialise this to a library domain generates a number of possible questions which may need to be addressed, examples are: *what is the loan object involved? what is the borrower called? when is a loan object considered available? what is a valid user in the domain? how is the allocation of object to borrower recorded?*

Addressing such questions can guide elicitation activities and the further study of existing domain descriptions and documentation or they can provide a framework for developer-user communication. The following example shows an interpretation of the original scenario specialised for the event 'IssueBook' in a library domain:

```
[IssueBook:#]->(BEHVR)->
[[[[Member:*]->(AGNT)->[BorrowBook:#]->(OBJ)-> [Book:*]]>(AND)->
[[Member:*]->(CHAR)->[Loans:{#}@<6]]->(AND)->
[[Book:*]->(STAT)->[BookAvailable:#]]->(AND)->
[[Book:*]->(~STAT)->[BookReserved:#]]]
->(RESLT)->
[[[Book:*]->(STAT)->[BookOnLoan:#]]->(AND)->
[[Member:*]->(CHAR)->[Loans:{#}]<-(INCL)<[Book:*]]]].
```

A central theme of our approach is that a new requirement model is developed by specialising, refining or adapting selected parts of the relevant domain model if this is appropriate. Additionally, the existing knowledge representation structures can be used by developers as patterns for modelling their own interpretation of the new domain. Currently these activities are analyst directed, an aim of future research is to provide intelligent tool support to guide and monitor domain knowledge reuse activities. The ability of the RFML to represent many of the domain declarations in a rule based format provides the basis for the operational interpretation of the language by suitable tools. This allows tool support for assisting with completeness and consistency checking and for executing the model to assist in the understanding and validation of modelled knowledge. By selecting and executing behaviour scenarios, the developer can experiment with domain models and the evolving requirement model. Typical or alternative patterns of domain behaviour can be tested; examining the ordering and dependencies of domain events and states and the validity of resulting behaviour on modelled domain rules and constraints.

6. Tool Support for the Approach

At present, tool support for the approach is based on an existing RFML workbench which was implemented to demonstrate the use of the language for building a requirement model. The RFML workbench is implemented using an extended version of Smalltalk/V Windows Release 2.0 [6] on a 486 PC. The Smalltalk environment has been modified to include an extended Prolog interpreter which provides a partial implementation of the Prolog language [2]. The Prolog facilities provide a foundation for implementing the workbench knowledge bases and appropriate knowledge inference mechanisms. Figure 4 provides an overview of the workbench architecture and functionality.

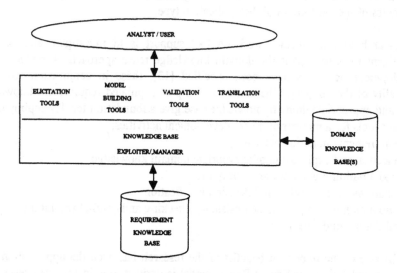

Figure 4. The Architecture of the RFML Workbench

The common representation of domain knowledge and requirement knowledge allows exploitation by common tools, the developer is able to browse a populated domain knowledge model alongside the building and population of a new requirement model. This encourages modelling by analogy, allowing the study of typical domain concepts, domain behaviour and structure and experimenting with this; providing templates of domain knowledge from which to specify application specific models. Work is ongoing to specify how to browse generic models to guide elicitation and model building activities and guidance on execution and experimentation with behaviour scenarios.

7. Conclusions and Further Work

The research described here is in its early stages, but has already given useful insight into the potential of domain knowledge reuse, especially for initial fact gathering and elicitation activities which at present are poorly supported.

One of the first and important steps in requirements engineering is bridging the gap between informally stated requirements and a model containing structured and formalised requirements. The reuse of domain knowledge and development by analogy appear to be a useful and supportable way of making this step. There are significant similarities between common types of business information systems, our research to date indicates it is possible to classify and define these types. By providing generic models of application types, and appropriate support tools, direct support can be given to requirement elicitation and modelling by refinement and adaptation rather than reinvention. Further work is required to establish the extent to which information systems can actually be classified and generalised and the appropriate formats of effective generic models. The approach also needs to be tested to evaluate the usefulness or limitations of generic models when applied to real life examples of specialisation's of the application type.

A research aim for further work on tool support is to investigate and develop intelligent tools to exploit the domain knowledge reuse approach. A set of RFML development heuristics have been specified [13]; these in conjunction with the formality of the language, the contents of a part populated requirement knowledge base and appropriate domain knowledge base give a foundation for developing active support tools for a number of model development activities:
- requirement elicitation activities,
- selection and explanation of appropriate domain knowledge
- model building guidance and critiquing
- requirement traceability and decision justification
- automation of completeness/consistency checking and conflict resolution.
- validation guidance tools

Finally one of the important benefits of the research has been the appreciation that once a populated and validated RFML model is derived, this in turn can serve as a long term knowledge base of user requirements and application domain knowledge, providing a foundation for later stages of development and a reference point for revision and maintenance of the system after implementation. This also introduces the possibility of reusing such a model at a future date for system updates or as an additional source of domain knowledge to support the development of similar applications or other applications in the same domain.

References

1. A. T. Borgida, J. Mylopoulos: "Knowledge Representation as the basis of Requirements Specification". *COMPUTER*, Vol. 18, No 4, April 1985.
2. W. F. Clocksin, C. S. Mellish: *"Programming in Prolog"*. Springer-Verlag, Berlin, 1984.
3. B. Curtis, H. Krasner, N. Iscoe: "A Field Study of the Software Design Process for Large Systems". *Communications of the ACM*, Vol. 31, No 11, pp 1268-1287, November 1988
4. A. J. Czuchry: "Where's the Intelligence in the Intelligent Assistant for Requirements Analysis". *Proceedings Second Annual Knowledge-Based Software Assistant Conference*, Published by Rome Air Development Center, NY 13441-5700, January 1988.
5. A. M. Davis, P. A. Freeman: "Guest Editors Introduction: Requirements Engineering". *IEEE Transactions on Software Engineering*, Vol. 17, No 3, pp 210-211, March 1992.
6. DIGITALK Inc. "Smalltalk/V *Object-Oriented Programming System (OOPS) Tutorial and Programming Handbook - Windows Series"*, Digitalk, California, USA, 1992.
7. E. D. Falkenberg, H. Van Kempen, N. Mimpen: "Knowledge-Based Information Analysis Support". in *Proceedings of IFIP TC2/TC8/WG 2.6/WG 8.1 Artificial Intelligence in Databases and Information Systems*, Guangzhou, China, 1990.
8. C. J. Fillmore: "The Case for Case". in *Universals in Linguistic Theory*, E. Bach, R. T. Harms (Eds.), Holt Rhinehart and Winston Inc, 1968.
9. G. Fitzgerald, N. Stokes, J.R.G. Wood: "Feature Analysis of Contemporary Information Systems Methodologies". *The Computer Journal*, Vol. 28, No 3, pp 223-230, 1985.
10. C. Floyd: "A Comparative Evaluation Of System Development Methods", in [Olle et al 86], 1986.
11. D. J. Flynn, R.Warhurst, M. D. Gibson, D. Browne, R. Summersgill: "An Empirical Study into the Process of Validating a Specification". *Proceedings 2nd International Conference on Information Systems Development Workbenches*, Gdansk, Poland, pp 401-420, September 1990.
12. M. D. Gibson, C. Harthhoorn: *"The use of JSD"*. Analyst Assist Project Research Report AA-U0010, UMIST, Manchester, UK, 1987.
13. M. D. Gibson: "RFML: An Executable Requirement Specification Language for Information System Development", PhD Thesis, Faculty of Technology, UMIST, Manchester, England, 1992.

14. S. J. Greenspan, J. Mylopoulos, A. Borgida: "Capturing More World Knowledge in the Requirements Specification". *Proceedings of 6th International Conference on Software Engineering*, England, UK, pp 225-234, September 1982.

15. F. Hayes-Roth: "RULE-BASED SYSTEMS". *Communications of the ACM*, Vol. 28, No 29, pp 921-932, September 1985.

16. D. R. Harris: "An Overview of the Knowledge-Based Requirements Assistant". *Proceedings Second Annual Knowledge-Based Software Assistant Conference*, Published by Rome Air Development Center, NY 13441-5700, USA, January 1988.

17. M. Lloyd-Williams: "Knowledge-based CASE tools: improving performance using domain specific knowledge". *Software Engineering Journal*, pp167-173 July 1994.

18. P. Loucopoulos, P. J. Layzell, R. E. M. Champion, M. D. Gibson: "A Knowledge-Based Requirements Engineering Support Environment". *Proceedings of the 3rd Annual Knowledge-Based Software Assistant Conference*, Utica, NY, USA, pp 139-154. 1989.

19. N. A. M. Maiden: "Analogical Specification Reuse During Requirements Analysis", PhD Thesis, Department of Business Computing, City University, London, July 1992.

20. N. A. M. Maiden, A. G. Sutcliffe: "Requirements engineering by example: An empirical study", Proceedings of IEEE symposium on Requirements Engineering, IEEE Computer Society Press, pp 104-112, 1993

21. J. T. Nosek, R. B. Schwartz: "User Validation of Information System Requirements: Some Empirical Results". *IEEE Transactions on Software Engineering*, Vol. 14 ,No 9, pp 1372-1375, September 1988.

22. T. W. Olle, H. G. Sol, A.A. Verrijn-Stuart (Eds.): "*Information Systems Design Methodologies: improving the practice*". North-Holland Publishing Company, IFIP, 1986.

23. P. P. Puncello, F. Pietri, P. Torrigiani: "ASPIS: A KNOWLEDGE-BASED ENVIRONMENT FOR SOFTWARE DEVELOPMENT". *ESPRIT Achievements and Impact*, North-Holland, pp 375-391, 1987.

24. C. Rich, R. C. Waters, H. B. Rubenstein: "Towards a Requirements Apprentice". *Proceedings of the 4th International Workshop on Software Specification and Design*, London, 1987.

25. H. B. Rubenstein, R. C. Waters: "The Requirements Apprentice: Automated Assistance for Requirements Acquisition". *IEEE Transactions on Software Engineering*, Vol. 17, No 3, pp 226-240, March 1991.

26. J. F. Sowa: "*Conceptual Structures: Information Processing in Mind and Machine*". Addison-Wesley, Reading, MA, USA, 1984.

27. G. M. Wijers, H. Heijes: "Automated Support for the Modelling Process". in *Advanced Information Systems Engineering Second Nordic Conference CAiSE 90*, Sweden May 90, Springer Verlag, New York, pp 88-108, 1991.

Strategies and Techniques: Reusable Artifacts for the Construction of Database Management Systems

Andreas Geppert, Klaus R. Dittrich

Computer Science Department
University of Zurich
Winterthurerstr. 190, CH-8057 Zurich, Switzerland
Email: {geppert|dittrich}@ifi.unizh.ch

Abstract

Abstraction, selection, and integration of reusable artifacts are still open problems in reuse-based software construction. We investigate how these problems can be solved for one sample domain of system software: database management systems. We propose *dimensions* for functional subdomains where different design choices are to be made. *Strategies* are the design choices for dimensions; their application leads to refined architectures and designs. Moreover, they are used to control the integrity of designs. *Techniques* are classes in the sense of object-oriented programming and implement combinations of strategies; they are reused during subsystem implementation. Through the various levels of abstraction, a designer/implementor of a database management system is guided towards reusable artifacts in all phases of a construction process.

Keywords: software reuse, DBMS-construction, system design and specification

1 Introduction and Motivation

Software reuse [11] has been proposed as a means for the systematical construction of software systems in a less costly way than is possible by starting implementations from scratch. Reuse is not restricted to code fragments only, but is also applicable to specifications, designs, etc.. We therefore prefer to talk about (reusable) *software artifacts*. In order to make reuse work, several problems must be solved [11]:

- *abstraction*: software designers need to understand *what* they are going to reuse. In order to be understandable, artifacts must be represented at the appropriate level of abstraction.
- *selection*: especially for large collections of reusable artifacts, it is a problem to find the "right" artifact to reuse for a given problem. Software designers therefore need help for selecting candidate artifacts for reuse.
- *integration*: even if reusable artifacts have been found for each component, those still need to be integrated into a coherent, consistent software system.

Depending on the domain of interest, these problems are aggravated by the following reasons. If for a domain (of software systems to be constructed) standard solutions are not known and many (semantically) different implementation approaches are known, then a reuse-based approach has to support the classification of these variants (the abstraction problem). Consequently, it is then harder to find the appropriate variant in the large collection of reusable artifacts (the selection problem). Furthermore, if standard interfaces do not exist and implementations are not interchangeable, the problem is to achieve a consistent design and to make compatible choices of artifacts to be reused (the integration problem).

In this paper, we propose *strategies* and *techniques* as concepts that address the problems of abstraction, selection, and integration in reuse-based software construction. Specifically, we assume that the domain of interest is characterized by large sets of variants for certain functionalities, and that standard solutions do not exist for most functionalities. In our approach,

- *dimensions* represent properties that are used for classification and represent design decisions to be made,
- *strategies* distinguish among variant design decisions on a high level of abstraction,
- *techniques* are reusable components implementing combinations of strategies.

Throughout the paper we assume that object-oriented technology is applied.

We show that dimensions, strategies, and techniques can be used to solve the aforementioned problems in the reuse-based construction of database management systems (DBMSs). A DBMS is software that provides for the persistent management of databases, including modelling and storage of data, declarative retrieval and manipulation, recovery, multi-user access, integrity enforcement, and so forth. A large variety of data models, transaction models, integrity maintenance concepts, authorization models, and so on exists, and many different implementations for each of these models exist. All the problems mentioned above therefore occur in reuse-based DBMS-construction. However, since these problems are present in other domains as well, we feel that our results can be helpful in other fields of software construction, too.

Subsequently, we describe the underlying architecture model of this approach and then introduce the three concepts. We show how they are used during the construction process. Throughout the paper, we present examples from the concurrency control field.

2 The Architecture Model

Reusability of analysis and design information is much more promising than code reuse [3, 13]. Hence, the DBMS-constructor[1] has to be guided through all the construction phases towards reusable artifacts, and —moreover— concepts must be provided that allow the representation of analysis and design information. Second, recall the integration problem: reused artifacts still need to be integrated into a coherent entirety. We thus propose an architecture model for DBMSs that is able to

1. represent reusable architectures and designs,
2. integrate reused components into a coherent DBMS.

Apart from these features, the architecture model is intended to meet a variety of requirements:

- structural decomposition and information hiding,
- modeling of activities and behavioral decomposition,
- support for architectural constraints, and
- transparency and integration.

---

1. Synonymously, DBMS-Implementor (DBI)

These requirements are all met by the so-called *broker/services architecture model*. The prime concepts of this model are brokers, services, and responsibilities.

A *service* is a specific functionality provided by the DBMS[2] or a part thereof. A service has a *signature*, which in turn consists of a name and a list of typed formal parameters. Services can be requested by DBMS-components through the raising of *events*. In raising such an event, a requestor has to supply actual parameters according to the service definition. Each service defines (a set of) possible *replies*. Whenever a service can be provided successfully, one of the replies is raised. That is, replies are raised like request events, and can have parameters as well.

Brokers are active entities and implement subsystems. They are able to request services and to satisfy requests for services. Brokers have a state, which can be composed out of further (sub)brokers or passive objects.

Responsibilities are relationships between services and brokers, they define which broker provides a specific service. Whenever a request is made, the responsible broker "catches" the event and reacts by executing the service implementation. Services are implemented through sets of production rules. Each production rule defines an event (the triggering event, i.e., the request), a condition, and an action. Actions of production rules in turn are sequences of messages sent to the passive components of the broker, or generic operations such as replies.

In the case that multiple production rules are defined for the same event (i.e., within the same activity), their execution order can be constrained if necessary. The execution order is defined through a partial ordering of production rules.

Based on these concepts, a DBMS-architecture is defined as follows.

Definition 1 (DBMS-Architecture)

A *DBMS-architecture* is a collection of brokers, services, and responsibilities.

A DBMS presents itself to its clients via a special broker called the *globe*[3]. The globe is responsible for those services that the DBMS-clients can request as well as for coordinating the brokers for the various subsystems. In Figure 1 an example of the brokers/ services architecture model is illustrated. Apart from the globe, the architecture contains three brokers on the top level: the object management subsystem (OMS), the transaction management subsystem (TMS), and the integrity management subsystem (IMS). Arrows represent service requests, and the white rectangle represents an "event bus" which is required for exchanging requests and replies.

3   Strategies and Techniques

Feasible reuse techniques must be developed for each aspect of a DBMS. Generation is one possibility (e.g., for query optimizers [8]). For other aspects a large variety of design and implementation alternatives exist that cannot be handled by generators. For these aspects, we propose the use of configuration/composition. Obviously, a reuse-based construction method must support the representation, classification, and selection of reusable artifacts whenever such a variety exists. Second, it is a characteristic

---

2. Henceforth, we refer to a DBMS under construction simply as "DBMS".

3. **global broker**, also a sign of power and authority (Webster's dictionary).

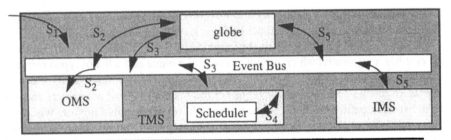

Figure 1. Brokers and Service Requests

of DBMSs (and presumably of other system software, too), that standard interfaces do not exist. Moreover, the correctness of the choice of a specific approach for some DBMS-functionality may depend on the choices already made for other DBMS-components. Hence, the construction approach must enforce consistency of reused artifacts [14]. In this section, we introduce strategies and techniques as the major concepts for consistent reuse of artifacts for large component domains. We first give an overview of the different levels of abstractions used in our approach, and then describe the concepts of strategy and technique in detail.

3.1 Levels of Abstraction of DBMS-Software Artifacts

Selection, abstraction, and integration are the very problems for any reuse-based method. In the DBMS-construction context, these problems are handled by introducing different levels of abstraction. At least for those subsystems that have to be composed, the use of the various abstractions guides the DBI from partial and abstract designs towards reusable classes.

In the sequel, let us consider an arbitrary but fixed (part of an) aspect that has to be realized by means of composition/configuration, such as *database concurrency control*. Concurrency control is the DBMS-task of preventing inconsistencies caused by interleaved, concurrent transaction executions. Strict two-phase locking (s2PL) is the concurrency control mechanism used most often, but many others have been proposed and used as well. Subsequently, we assume that the reader has a basic knowledge on database transaction concepts.

One result of domain analysis is a number of *dimensions* (or categories of strategies) for the aspect in question. For the DBI, a dimension is a set of alternative design decisions, each of which extends the design and/or a broker in a specific way.

As an example, one dimension for concurrency control is *validation time*, and the required services for this dimension are `validate` and `register` (the former checks whether a database access on behalf of a transaction is allowed w.r.t. to the actual schedule, while the latter records this access).

Each possible design decision is termed a *strategy*. Thus, a category of strategies determines a design dimension, and each strategy represents a specific design alternative. Strategies are defined as constraints on the (DBMS- or subsystem) design.

In the example (*validation time*), the following strategies can be identified: *pre-claiming* (request `validate` at the begin of the transaction execution), *pessimistic* (perform validation before the actual database access), and *optimistic* (request `validate` after the database access, but before the transaction is allowed to commit).

In this way, a strategy refines (or constrains) the design of brokers and subsystems. Whenever multiple dimensions refer to the same service, it is necessary to consider the selected strategies in their combination in order to determine a realization of the service. *Techniques* specify how combinations of strategies are realized. In special cases, where a strategy is orthogonal to others, a technique specifies the realization of the single strategy. Combinations of strategies can also be realized by various distinct techniques —this is actually the motivation for distinguishing strategies from techniques.

Techniques are components and specify how the combination of strategies is realized in terms of classes. Therefore, each technique specifies a state and a set of method signatures, along with pre-and postconditions for each method as well as invariants to be fulfilled by the state. In addition, a technique determines how it conforms to the strategy combination, e.g., which method realizes which service.

As an example, consider concurrency control again. In this case, let *validation time* and *validation reaction* be two dimensions, where *pessimistic validation* and *blocking* are two strategies, respectively. Then, strict two-phase locking is a technique that realizes the combination of both, `getLock` is a method of the technique, and this method conforms to validation (i.e., has to be called upon the `validate` request within the activity for `validate`).

A technique will be composed out of classes that perform specific tasks of the technique. These classes in turn are called *primitives*, and may be used in an arbitrary number of techniques (e.g., consider a `lockTable` class for the management of locks).

In the sequel, the four levels of abstraction will be defined in more detail.

3.2 Strategies

3.2.1 Formal Specification of Strategies
The definition of strategies specifies their meaning in terms of logic and can be used to reason about strategies and designs.

3.2.1.1 The Domain
The domain models the entities to reason about during broker design and strategy selection. Namely, these entities are brokers, services, service implementations, replies, and strategies as well as techniques themselves.

Let B, D, PC, PN, R, SE, ST, T be finite sets of identifiers, where
- B is the set of broker names,
- D is the set of strategy dimension names,
- PC is a set of parameter class names,
- PN is a set of parameter names,
- R is the set of reply names (events),
- SE is the set of service names,
- ST is the set of strategy names,
- T is the set of technique names.

3.2.1.2 Formulas

Table 1 shows the built-in predicates for the specification of brokers and strategies..

name	domain	meaning
has_component (b_1,b_2)	broker × broker	b1 is a component of b2
supports (b, s)	broker × service	b is responsible for s
applies(b, s)	broker × strategy	b applies s
has_parameter (s, pn, pt)	service × parameter name × parameter class	s has a parameter named pn and pn is of type pt
requests (s_1, s_2)	service × service	s1 requests s2
before (s_1, s_2, s_3)	service × service × service	within s1, s2 is executed before s3
within (s_1, s_2)	service × service	s2 is executed within s1
replies (s, r)	service × reply	s replies with r
raises (s, e)	service × exception	s possibly raises e
incompatible (s_1, s_2)	strategy × strategy	s1 and s2 are incompatible
realizes (t, s)	technique × strategy	t realizes s

Table 1 Predicates and Corresponding Domains

Structural decomposition of brokers is expressed by the predicate has_component. This predicate evaluates to true whenever the second broker is a direct component of the first one.

The second predicate for brokers expresses responsibilities. Namely, supports is true for a broker b and a service s if b is responsible for a service named s. The application of strategies by a broker is reflected by the predicate applies; this predicate is evaluated to true for a broker b and a strategy named s whenever b is defined to use s.

The fact that a service (realization) requires another service is expressed with the predicate requests. Note that the second service does not necessarily have to be requested within the realization of the first one. This is specified by the predicate within, which evaluates to true for services s1 and s2 if within the realization of s1 a request is raised for the service named s2. The condition that a specific service has to be requested before another one is modeled by the predicate before.

Furthermore the predicate has_parameter(s,n,p) requires the signature of a service named s to have a parameter named n, which in turn has to be of type (or class) p. The reply of a service definition is constrained by means of the predicate replies, which evaluates to true whenever the reply name is a possible reply event for the service in question.

The knowledge on strategies and techniques is modeled by two predicates for incompatibilities and realization of strategies. The predicate incompatible is defined for pairs of strategies, it specifies that the two strategies must not be chosen in combination. Second, `realizes(st,t)` evaluates to `true` if the technique named t is a realization of the strategy st.

Formulas can be constructed by means of the usual logical connectors and quantifiers. Strategies are then defined as formulas over a set of brokers.

Definition 2 (Strategy)
Let s be the name of a strategy, b the name of a broker, and f a formula with b as a free variable. A definition for the strategy named s is `strategy(s,b) :⇔ f`.

3.2.1.3 Properties of Brokers and Designs

The notion of strategy as defined above supports capturing the meaning of a specific strategy. Second, it can also be used in order to reason about brokers and designs.

Assume a rulebase of strategy definitions and predicates (facts) reflecting strategy incompatibilities. Furthermore, consider a design as a collection of facts in terms of the predicates introduced above. Then, a broker (or an entire design) is considered to be *strategically correct* if the design does not yield a contradiction to the rulebase.

Definition 3
Let b1, ..., bn be the set of names of brokers under design, let F be a conjunction of formulas over b1, ..., bn, and let fs be the definition for strategy s. Then, the design is strategically correct if the following implications are true:

- $\forall$ i: {1..n} F $\land$ applies(bi, s) $\Rightarrow$ fs
- $\forall$ i: {1..n} $\forall$ s: ST $\forall$ s': ST F $\land$ applies(bi,s) $\land$ applies(bi,s') $\Rightarrow$ ¬ incompatible(s,s').

These two conditions specify that a design does not apply contradicting decisions w.r.t. the strategy repository. Therefore, we will refer to strategies synonymously as "refinements of brokers and designs" and "constraints on brokers and designs".

3.2.2 Sample Strategies

The concept of strategies has been used to classify approaches in the field of database concurrency control. Due to space restrictions, we cannot describe the entire performed domain analysis, but only give a summary and an example (for details, see [7]). 25 database concurrency control approaches proposed in the literature have been analyzed. On the top level, we obtained seven dimensions:

- *validation time*: when is a database access validated?
- *validation basis*: is a conflict-based, read/write schema used, or are transaction structure or transaction semantics taken into account?
- *validation reaction*: what happens when access cannot be granted immediately (e.g., transaction abort)?
- *granularity*: what is the granularity of validation (e.g., single objects)?
- *versioning*: are different versions of data items used?
- *data dependency*: does validation take the value of data items into account?
- *type dependency*: are the semantics of data types taken into account?

Most dimensions have two or three different strategies defined. As an example, consider the definition of the strategies for the validation time dimension in Example 1.

---

validationTime := {pre-claiming, pessimistic, optimistic}

strategy(pre-claiming, scheduler) :⟺
     within(begin, validate) ∧ has_parameter(validate, access, list(DBRequest))
strategy(pessimistic, scheduler) :⟺
   ∀ s: SE ∀ db-op: DB-Operation
     (within (s, db-op) ∧ supports (OMS, s)) ⟹
        (within(s, validate) ∧ before (s, validate, db-op) ∧ within (validate, register))
strategy(optimistic, scheduler) :⟺
   ∀ s: SE ∀ db-op: DB-Operation
     (within (s, db-op) ∧ supports (OMS, s))
       ⟹ (within(s, register) ∧ within(commit, validate)

incompatible(optimistic, updateInPlace)

Example 1. Validation Time Strategies

The `optimistic` strategy is a typical participant in an incompatibility: this strategy must not be chosen when OMS performs update-in-place for objects.

3.3 Specification of Techniques and Primitives

The first step in designing a broker is the selection of strategies. The ultimate goal, however, is to identify components that can be reused for the implementation of the broker and its subcomponents. How can one bridge the gap between strategies/brokers and components to be reused? Essentially, the following is required:

1. The design and implementation phases (see below) have to support the determination of candidates for reuse. Typically, a class repository will be quite large, such that it is an urgent task to restrict the selection space as far as possible.
2. Candidates can be correctly reused only under specific conditions (i.e., constraints concerning their usage). Hence, supporting *semantic integrity* for combinations of reused components [14] is required. In fact, instead of selecting a number of components and later on checking for consistency, it is preferred to propose only those candidates that can be reused while preserving consistency.
3. An underlying formalism for selection and representation of reusable components is required due to several reasons:
   - to support reasoning about semantic integrity of reused components,
   - to unambiguously describe semantics of components,
   - to support the precise definition of new components and techniques.

Subsequently, we show how techniques and primitives are specified.

3.3.1 Specification of Techniques

The role of a technique is to specialize the description of (a combination of) strategies and to bridge the gap between strategies and primitives (classes). The following properties characterize a technique:

- a unique name,
- the strategies it realizes,
- the primitives or techniques it uses, and
- conditions under which the use of this technique or its components is correct.

Techniques are akin to *contracts* [9], but we conceive techniques as formal specifications of *classes* as well (unlike the contract approach). A technique is specified by means of the following features:

- an enumeration of the participants,
- the signatures of the methods it provides,
- the signatures of the methods it requires from the participants,
- preconditions and postconditions for methods,
- invariants,
- conformances to the definition of strategies it realizes.

Techniques are implemented in terms of their component objects (the participants). The knowledge about participants is reflected in the technique specification.

Most important for ensuring the semantically correct specification of techniques are conditions and invariants. Preconditions and postconditions are always attached to single method signatures. A precondition states constraints on parameters to be obeyed by each client of the method. In other words, a precondition defines under which condition the method can be legally applied. A postcondition defines how any object executing the method is obliged to behave, i.e., it is a constraint on the server side. This principle is termed "programming by contract" [12], since pre- and postconditions are conceived as obligations for clients (preconditions) and servers (postconditions).

Invariants are another kind of constraint and specify conditions to be preserved by the technique implementation and its participants. Especially, invariants can refer to the state of instances and do not have to be attached to single methods.

Conformances specify how the technique implements specific strategies. Conformances are mappings from services defined for strategies to methods of a technique.

Consider the strict lock management technique in Example 2. Note that this specification is incomplete for the sake of brevity. The formal syntax of the technique specification language is not given, but the meaning of the various clauses is described subsequently. The INCLUDES clause specifies the participant techniques or primitives. Some participants are still generic and need to be instantiated (or specialized) for a concrete application of this technique (e.g., Modes for the concrete set of lock modes). In this case, the "<" sign specifies that the type before the sign has to be a subtype of the type after the "<". In other words, these participants are comparable to framework objects, i.e., abstract classes. The STATE clause specifies instance variables specific to the technique. The METHOD clauses specify the methods the technique provides to its clients. A method can be constrained by pre- and postconditions. The optional ACTION clause specifies messages that a component instance can send to other objects. Finally, the CONFORMANCES clause specifies *how* the technique implements specific strategies or services. In the example, getLock is an implementation of the validate service.

```
COMPONENT                              // Refer to the text for explanations.
      StrictLockManager
INCLUDES                               // Participating techniques, primitives
      TAID
      Modes < LockModes      // Modes is a subclass of the generic class LockModes
      Compat< Compat_Table
```

```
          DeadlockMgr
          LockRequest < DBRequest
          LockReqReply < ValidationReply
STATE                                                    // instance variables
          locktable: LockTable
          compat: Compat
          deadlockMan: DeadlockMgr
METHOD                                       // methods provided by the technique
          getLock (req: LockRequest): LockReqReply
          PRECONDITIONS
             req->ta->state = RUNNING
          POSTCONDITION
             LockReqReply = GRANT
                ⇒ locktable' = locktable->insert(req->ta, req->oid, req->mode)
             LockReqReply = BLOCKED
                ⇒ deadlockMan->add_edge(req->ta, lockTable->lockholder(req->oid))
METHOD
          release_locks (ta: TAID)
             ...
ACTION
          resume (DBRequest)
CONFORMANCES                             // how the technique implements strategies
       getLock CONFORMS TO (validate, register)
       ...
END StrictLockManager
```

Example 2. Technique StrictLockManager

3.3.2 Specification of Primitives

A primitive is a class and is described by the following properties:

- a unique name,
- a formal specification, and
- a documented implementation.

Therefore, for the sake of uniformity, the same formalism as for techniques is used for their specification. See Example 3 for an example.

```
COMPONENT
          LockTable
INCLUDES
          HashTab
          LockEntry < HashEntry
          TAID
          OID
STATE
          locks:HashTab [Key::OID,HashEntry:: LockEntry]
          taLocks: HashTab [Key::TAID, HashEntry::LockEntry]
METHOD
          setLock(ta: TAID, object: OID, entry: LockEntry)
             ...
METHOD
          deleteLocks(ta: TAID)
             ...
METHOD
```

```
getLock(object: OID) : list(LockEntry)
...
```

Example 3. Primitive LockTable

---

4 The Role of Strategies and Techniques in the Construction Process

In this section, we describe the role of strategies and techniques in the DBMS-construction process and discuss their usefulness with respect to reusability.

4.1 Outline of the Construction Process

In this section we outline the construction process model as far as necessary for understanding the role of strategies and techniques; details can be found in [7].

The first phase covered by a construction process for a DBMS is analysis. This phase determines the functionality required from the DBMS. One major outcome of this phase is the determination of *relevant aspects*. In the second phase, an architecture skeleton is selected for reuse (e.g., the one represented in Figure 1). In a subsequent phase, *subsystem design* is performed. In this phase, strategies are selected for the relevant aspects and dimensions and are applied to brokers. In other words, each strategy selection refines the corresponding broker design. Subsequently, during subsystem implementation techniques are determined that realize selected strategies.

The knowledge on strategies and techniques is stored in repositories. These repositories are used during subsystem design and implementation in a possibly iterative process (Figure 2). Given certain combinations of strategies, the DBI queries the repository for techniques realizing the strategies. If techniques are found ("full match"), he/she can decide simply to reuse the technique. Otherwise, he/she has two possibili-

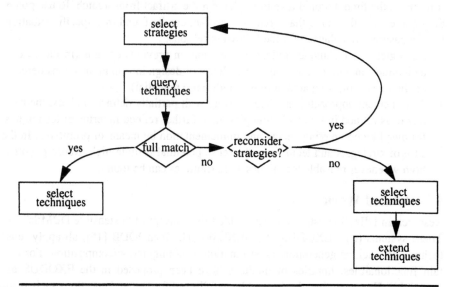

Figure 2. Iterative Selection of Strategies and Techniques

ties: he/she can revoke one or more strategy selections, or develop a new technique. In the second case, she/he can select the "best" technique (the one that realizes most of the strategies) as a starting point, extend this technique, and finally update the repository with the new technique.

4.2 Strategies, Techniques, and Reusability

Concrete dimensions, strategies, and techniques are the results of a domain analysis perfomed before DBMSs are actually constructed. Such a domain analysis can be successively refined and extended as more experience on the domain becomes available. Dimensions, strategies, and techniques are also intended to help the DBI understand the universe of discourse (here, the design and implementation approaches of an domain and their respective relationships with and implications on other aspects).

During the specific phases of the actual construction process, concepts of strategies and techniques are used to assist the DBI in various respects:

- for a given component to be realized, the set of categories represents knowledge on decisions to be made,
- decisions concerning strategies affecting "many" other components and heavily restricting further decisions can be made first, such that backtracking is decreased and the search space is "pruned" early,
- conflicting decisions can be recognized early based on information on incompatible strategies,
- the gap between design and implementation is bridged in that suggestions concerning reusable techniques are made,
- implementation of techniques is supported by reusable primitives.

The proposed approach balances important facets of reuse: *reuse potential* and *reuse payoff*. Reuse payoff denotes the efforts that have been saved through reusing artifacts. It refers to the time it would take to implement the artifact from scratch. Reuse potential denotes the likelihood that a reusable artifact can be found in a specific situation. Both measures are balanced for the following reasons:

- Strategies and techniques reflect information on previous designs (in the case of techniques on a more concrete level). Reuse of design information is considered to be the most promising area of reuse (high reuse potential).
- A refinement approach is applied: starting with partially defined brokers, their behavior is refined in terms of strategies, then further refined in terms of techniques, followed by completing design and implementation by means of primitives. In the case of strategies and techniques the reuse potential is quite high. Reuse payoff is high whenever reusable techniques and primitives can be found.

5 Related Work

Research in DBMS-construction has yielded the concept of "extensible DBMSs" [5]. These systems (e.g., EXODUS [4], GENESIS [1], OpenOODB [15]) all apply reuse techniques, such as generation/transformation or configuration/composition. For certain functionalities, libraries of modules have been proposed in the EXODUS approach [4]. However, this idea has not been followed further, and questions such as the representation and selection of alternatives during a construction have not been answered in EXODUS.

The GENESIS approach has been extended for hierarchical software systems in general [2]. The central notion of this approach is the *component*, where each component is an element of a *realm*. All the elements of a realm have the same interface, but possibly different implementations. Then, a software system is described as a kind of algebraic expression. In this approach, the selection problem is still not solved.

The *Open OODB* approach [15] attempts to support the construction of object-oriented DBMSs. Open OODB distinguishes a meta-architecture and an extensible collection of modules implementing specific functionalities (*policies*). The meta-architecture defines a set of kernel modules, mechanisms to define the system architecture (boundaries between components), and so forth. For some specific functional tasks, various policies can be applied (and can even be exchanged dynamically). Each domain for which multiple policies can be used is controlled by a policy manager, and all the policies of a specific domain are required to guarantee the same invariants (which ensures that they are interchangeable). The notion of policy is similar to our concept of strategy, however in the Open OODB it is still unclear how alternative strategies can be represented and how selection can be supported.

Frameworks [10] and contracts [9] have been proposed as means of design reusability. However, both allow for less abstraction than our concepts of strategies, and the multiple levels of abstraction in our approach are better suited to solve the selection problem.

Ultimately, software reuse has also been a major issue in the ITHACA project [6]. In ITHACA, generic application frames are engineered and reused, resulting in specialized application frames. Specification is supported through the RECAST tool, and composition of components is supported by the VISTA visual scripting tool. Both tools use the software information base (SIB) and its selection tool for retrieving and storing reusable artifacts. The SIB would be a well-suited platform for storing and retrieving information on strategies and techniques. However, when compared to the RECAST/VISTA approaches, dimensions, strategies, and techniques better support the classification, representation, and selection of components whenever a large variety of such alternatives exists for a given domain.

6   Conclusion and Future Work

In this paper, we have introduced the notions of dimension, strategy, technique, and primitive. These concepts are helpful in a construction approach for DBMSs that is based on large-scale reuse. Especially, the concepts foster reuse during the subsystem design and subsystem implementation phases.

Though not stressed in this paper, dimensions, strategies, and techniques are helpful for understanding the universe of discourse (such as concurrency control). As such, a domain analysis results in definitions of dimensions and strategies.

The current state of this work is as follows. An implementation of a strategy information system has been performed on top of an object-oriented database system. A domain analysis has been done for the field of transaction management, and the concepts of strategies and techniques have been used intensively for the concurrency control domain. Authorization, query processing, and access paths are further sample domains where these concepts appear as necessary, since in these domains a large variety of alternative approaches exists, too. Currently, we intend to build a large technique repository, again for the concurrency control domain in the first phase.

We have developed the notion of strategy and technique in the context of DBMS-construction, since this is the area of software engineering we are especially interested in. An interesting question will be whether the concepts can be helpful for the reuse-based construction of other kinds of software systems. Actually, we feel that our proposal is valuable at least for other kinds of *system software*, whenever they are characterized by a large set of alternative implementations for the same functionality. On the other hand, the concepts are possibly less necessary in areas where standard designs and implementations are known (e.g., certain kinds of application systems).

7 References

1. D.S. Batory: *GENESIS: An Extensible Database Management System*. IEEE Trans. on Software Engineering, 1988.
2. D. Batory, S. O'Malley: *The Design and Implementation of Hierarchical Software Systems with Reusable Components*. ACM ToSEM 1:4, 1992.
3. T.J. Biggerstaff, C. Richter: *Reusability Framework, Assessment, and Directions*. IEEE Software, July 1987.
4. M.J. Carey, D.J. DeWitt, D. Frank, G. Graefe, M. Muralikrishna, J.E. Richardson: *The Architecture of the EXODUS Extensible DBMS*. In K.R. Dittrich, U. Dayal (eds): Proc. Intl. Workshop on Object-Oriented Database Systems, IEEE Computer Science Press, 1986.
5. M. Carey, L. Haas: *Extensible Database Management Systems*. SIGMOD Record 19:4, 1990.
6. M.G. Fugini, O. Nierstrasz, B. Pernici: *Application Development Through Reuse: The ITHACA Tools Environment*. ACM SIGOIS Bulletin 13:2, August 1992.
7. A. Geppert: *Methodical Construction of Database Management Systems*. Doctoral Dissertation, University of Zuerich, Switzerland, 1994.
8. G. Graefe, D.J. DeWitt: *The EXODUS Optimizer Generator*. Proc. of the ACM SIGMOD Intl. Conf. on Management of Data, San Francisco, CA, May 1987.
9. R. Helm, I.M. Holland, D. Gangopadhyay: *Contracts: Specifying Behavioral Compositions in Object-Oriented Systems*. Proc. ECOOP 90.
10. R.E. Johnson, B. Foote: *Designing Reusable Classes*. Journal of Object-Oriented Programming 1:2, 1988.
11. C.W. Krueger: *Software Reuse*. ACM Computing Surveys 24:2, 1992.
12. B. Meyer: *Object-Oriented Software Construction*. Prentice Hall, 1988.
13. J.M. Neighbors: *Draco: A Method for Engineering Reusable Software Systems*. In T.J. Biggerstaff, A.J. Perlis (eds): *Software Reusability*. Volume I: Concepts and Models. ACM Press, 1989.
14. W. Stacy, R. Helm, G.E. Kaiser, B. Meyer: *Ensuring Semantic Integrity of Reusable Objects* (Panel Discussion). Proc. OOPSLA, Vancouver, Canada, October 1992.
15. D.L. Wells, J.A. Blakeley, C.W. Thompson: *Architecture of an Open Object-Oriented Database Management System*. IEEE Computer 25:10.

The Impact of New Information Architectures on Industry and Government Transformation

Giampio Bracchi

Dipartimento di Elettronica e Informazione
Politecnico di Milano
Italy

Information and communication technologies (ICT) enable re-engineering business and government organizations and mirror flexible, fast, focused and friendly organizational structures.

Meeting appropriate standards of service is today key to effectiveness of organizations. ICT architectures should be designed accordingly to achieve competitive levels of flexibility and responsiveness, moving away from outdated conceptions of information systems. They constitute an enabler of the overall business strategy, an agent of the transition from mechanical to organic models of organizations, and a catalyst of productivity. In this framework, ICT infrastructures are thehub of different design dimensions, including people, technology, business activities, and information.

New distributed information infrastructures can empower integration of activities across departments, functions, suppliers and customers, give access to information and knowledge, connect knowledge workers.Telecommunications-based transactions offer immediate links between the firm and its external context, overcoming physical boundaries, and offering the basis for the development of models of "network companies".

By separating storage from processing, distributed architectures offer new design dimensions through the distinction between the accumulation of information value (storage) and its delivery (processing).

The integration of the information industry offers in a near perspective multimedia technologies and broadband network services capable to support innovative designs for organizational processes and human resources.

Architectures have to be planned and created for guiding and facilitating the migration from today fragmented and sub-optimized information systems to the target platforms; insufficient definition of business objectives and of tranformation needs and lack of experience with the new diversified information technologies are the main problems in managing the migration process.Information service resources must restructure their organization, processes, skills and performance measurements accordingly, in order to meet their new strategic and operational role.

The significant investments for the new information infrastructures should be economically justified. The influence of ICT investments on productivity is traditionally analyzed correlating a single investment with a benefit index. The problem is the difficulty of isolating benefits delivered by ICT from other factors contributing to a firm's business performance. Moreover, benefits of today ICT are often linked to differentiation and flexibility more than to cost reduction.

Consequently, the impact of ICT investments have to be measured on global indexes of firm performance, and quantative cost-benefit analysis criteria have to be combined with more qualitative ones.

Benchmarking approaches could be usefully applied in the evaluation of ICT architectures. Existing benchmarking methods focus on specific problems and do not address the whole information integrating infrastructure, its adherence to business requirements, and its performance: new models and metrics are needed for assessing the value of ICT solutions against business process requirements.

Standard Transformations for the Normalization of ER Schemata

Otto Rauh[1] and Eberhard Stickel[2]

[1] Fachhochschule Heilbronn, Daimlerstr. 35, D-74653 Künzelsau
[2] Europa-Universität Viadrina, Große Scharrnstr. 59, D-15230 Frankfurt (Oder)

Abstract: Normalization, which makes up the core of the design theory for relational databases, is also considered an important technique to improve the quality of ER schemata. We first present a framework for describing ER schema transformations. Then a normal form, ER-BCNF^{null}, is defined which corresponds to BCNF but takes null values into account. Finally, a set of transformations is suggested which might be used to achieve this normal form.

1 Introduction

Normalization has been accepted as an important property of Entity-Relationship (ER) schemata improving the clarity of these schemata and avoiding both data inconsistencies and costly data manipulations in the databases derived from them (cf. e.g. Batini 1992). There is an elaborate normalization theory for relational databases that may also be utilized for ER modelling. Unfortunately, relational normalization algorithms do not go very well with ER modeling, at least if we want to preserve the stepwise and intuitive design process which is typical for the ER approach. In contrast, a method based on standard transformations is far better suited. Standard transformations rely on a classification of unfavourable constellations. For certain patterns of such situations, transformations are described in an abstract manner. The designer who is faced with an unfavourable situation identifies this situation with one of these patterns and then takes the action suggested.

There has been valuable preliminary work on the subject, going into two directions. Kobayashi (1986), Rosenthal (1988) and Hainaut (1991, 1993) contributed to the elaboration of the basic principles. Chung (1981), Ling (1985a, 1985b) and Batini (1992) suggested standard transformations for different purposes. Nevertheless, until now the subject has not gained the attention it deserves and needs more working out.

We shall first present a general framework for describing ER schema transformations. Then normal forms for ER schemata will be defined and a set of standard transformations will be presented to achieve them. Finally, we shall give an outlook on further work on the subject which is necessary.

2 A Framework for Describing ER Schema Transformations

2.1 Schema Description

Exact description of ER schemata is a prerequisite for describing schema transformations. Our schema descriptions will consist of two parts: (i) a description of schema structure, written in a simple language, (ii) a set of constraints. We shall make use of ER diagrams as well, but only for the purpose of illustration. The following example describes the structure of a schema S_1:

S_1 :   EntitySet *Employee* (Attributes *EmpID*, *EmpName* not null; Identifier *EmpID*);
EntitySet *Department* (Attributes *DeptID*, *DeptName*; Identifier *DeptID*);
RelationshipSet *MemberOf* (Participants (*Employee, Employee*, (1,1)),
(*Department, Department*, (0,n)));

There is an entry for each *construct*, i.e. each entity set and each relationship set, of the schema. A relationship set entry contains a three-tuple for every participating entity set (*participant*), consisting of its name, its role within the relationship set, and its cardinality. If the entity set in question participates only once in the relationship set the role name may be the same as the entity name. Sometimes there are attributes too in a relationship set entry, but not in this example. Domain declarations for attributes, which would be necessary in a practical schema declaration, are omitted to keep the description simple.

There are basically two types of constraints that influence the values of a database. *Implicit constraints* are consequences of structure and its semantics. Attributes, for instance, must always be functionally dependent on the identifier, and identifier attributes have only definite values. *Explicit constraints* are not implied by structure and thus have to be declared separately. We use a descriptive language, called ERC (Entity-Relationship Calculus) to express arbitrary constraints for ER schemata (cf. Rauh 1994). ERC is mainly based on relational tuple calculus (TRC) which has already been proposed by Codd (1972).

Constraints in ERC are always *closed* formulas in the sense that every variable is bound by a quantifier. Thus a truth value can be assigned to such a rule with respect to a certain database instance. Let us assume one such rule, stating that department names have to be unique:

$$(\forall d_1, d_2)(Department(d_1) \land Department(d_2) \land \neg(d_1 == d_2)$$
$$\rightarrow d_1[DeptName] \neq d_2[DeptName])$$

The double equality sign '==' is used to denote identity of entity sets or relationship sets. The familiar equality sign '=' is applied only to express equality of attribute values.

For some kinds of constraints, e.g. functional dependencies (FD), where there are special notations, these notations will be used if they are more convenient. In particular for the schemata used in this paper, these special notations will suffice.

2.2 Basic Concepts of Schema Transformations

Let S be an ER schema. Then with $s(S)$ we denote a database instance that is structured according to S and meets its constraints. A *schema transformation* T is a pair $((S_1, S_2), t)$, where S_1 is the source schema, S_2 denotes the target schema, and t is a list of assignments converting a database instance $s_1(S_1)$ into a database instance $s_2(S_2)$. According to Hainaut (1993), the first element of T, i.e. (S_1, S_2), is called the *structural mapping*, whereas t is the *instance mapping*. Formulating an instance mapping for a certain structural mapping (S_1, S_2) assigns a meaning to the components of the target schema S_2 which are fed with data from $s_1(S_1)$ by t. Thus we may call t the *semantics* of the transformation (Hainaut 1993). There might be many instance mappings for a certain structural mapping.

Not necessarily, an instance mapping has to provide an assignment for every component of the target schema, neither is it necessary that the whole source database is transferred to the target database. We are, however, especially interested in transformations which convert data without loss of information. In order to be able to describe such transformations, we introduce the concept of reversible transformation.

A schema transformation $T = ((S_1, S_2), t)$ is *reversible* if there exists a transformation $W = ((S_2, S_1), w)$ such that an arbitrary database instance $s_1(S_1)$ may be converted into an instance $s_2(S_2)$ by using T, and s_2 may be re-converted into s_1 by using W afterwards. W is called an *inverse* transformation to T (cf. Hainaut 1993).

Apart from those special cases when a schema containing too much information is reduced, we should demand reversibility for any transformation a schema is undertaken to improve its quality.

2.3 Instance Mappings

An instance mapping consists of a set of assignments which have the general form

$$< \text{schema component} > := < \text{query} >,$$

where < schema component > is an entity or relationship set of the target schema, and < query > is a database query referring to the components of the source schema. In this paper, we shall use ERC to formulate such queries. There are two basic forms of assignments to entity sets:

$$< \text{entity set name} > := \text{'\{' } < \text{entity variable} > \text{'|' } < \text{condition} > \text{'\}'}$$
$$< \text{entity set name} > := \text{'\{' } < \text{value list} > \text{'|' } < \text{condition} > \text{'\}'}$$

The first one is really a short form. It may be used if an entity set is not changed during the transformation, except perhaps for its name. We have to use the second form if this condition does not hold, maybe because the entity set in the target schema has another set of attributes than that in the source schema or because it is composed of several constructs of the source schema. In this case the attribute values which are the elements of < value list > must match the list of attributes in the declaration of the entity set. For each value of the identifier of this entity set, a new entity is supposed to be constructed on the basis of the assignment.

There are also two basic forms for relationship set assignments, depending on whether the relationship set in question has attributes or not:

< relationship set name >   :=   '{' < participant list > '|' < condition > '}'
< relationship set name >   :=   '{' < participant list >; < value list >   '|'
                                 < condition > '}'.

Therein < participant list > is a list of entity variables which take a special form if the entity set in question is not taken over unchanged from the source schema. Then < entity variable > consists of an *entity designator*, which is a function assigning an entity to a list of attribute values that are interpreted as its identifier values. An entity designator has the general form < entity set name > (< attribute variable list >), where < attribute variable list > takes the values of the identifier's attributes. If the relationship set in question has any attributes the second of the two forms has to be taken, and the attributes have to be listed in < value list >.

We continue our example and define a second schema S_2:

S_2:   EntitySet *Employee* (Attributes *EmpID, EmpName, EmpDept not null*; Identifier *EmpID*).

For a transformation $U = ((S_2, S_1), u)$, a suitable instance mapping u is

$Employee := \{e[EmpID], e[EmpName] \mid Employee(e)\}$

$Department := \{e[EmpDept], null \mid Employee(e)\}$

$MemberOf := \{Employee(e[EmpID]), Department(e[EmpDept]) \mid Employee(e)\}$.

In line three, entity designators are used to denote the entities of types *Employee* and *Department* which participate in *MemberOf* relationships. A transformation in the other direction is $V = ((S_1, S_2), v)$, where v is

$Employee := \{e[EmpID], e[EmpName], d[DeptID] \mid Employee(e) \land$

$Department(d) \land (\exists m)(MemberOf(m) \land$

$m: Employee == e \land m: Department == d)\}$.

In this assignment, a *participant function* like *m:Department* represents the participant in a relationship which plays the role denoted behind the colon.

For such small examples reversibility is easy to assess. $U = ((S_2,S_1), u)$ is a reversible transformation as $V = ((S_1,S_2), v)$ is a transformation inverse to U. In contrast to U, V is not reversible. Attribute *DeptName* of entity set *Department* in S_1 is not contained in the result part of the query in the only assignment v consists of. Moreover, there is also no other reversible transformation since there is no attribute in S_2 that could take the values of *DeptName*.

3 Standard Transformations for Normalization

3.1 Normal Forms for ER constructs

In relational database design, third normal form (3NF) is generally considered a sufficient condition for a table if functional dependencies (FD) are the only dependencies to be taken into account. Among the different forms of 3NF, Boyce-Codd normal form (BCNF) is probably the most popular and plausible. Surely, not every possible BCNF database has the property of preserving all functional dependencies (cf. Ullman 1988, p. 404). But as this is only a theoretical possibility and hardly a practical one, there is no reason why we should not choose BCNF as the desired structure for ER constructs. We use a definition given by Gardarin (1989, p. 164) to characterize BCNF: A relation scheme R is said to be in *Boyce-Codd normal form* (*BCNF*) if, for all disjoint nonempty sets X and Y in R, if $X \to Y$ then X is a superkey for R.

Unfortunately, null values are ignored in this definition and other definitions of BCNF. Let $R(\underline{A}, B, C)$ be a relation scheme and $F = \{A \to B, B \to C\}$ a set of FD's in R. Then normalization algorithms demand decomposition into $(\underline{A}, B)$ and $(\underline{B}, C)$, tacitly assuming that if B is null then C is null as well. If this was not the case B could not serve as a primary key in the second scheme. Rather than using decomposition $\{(\underline{A}, B), (\underline{A}, C)\}$ instead, which has other shortcomings, we shall use a weaker form of BCNF, called BCNF^{null}, that tolerates such situations:

> A relation scheme R is said to be in BCNF^{null} if whenever $X \to Y$, $X \cap Y = \emptyset$, holds in R, and Y is always *null* if X is *null*, then X is a superkey for R.

It is easy to see that a relation scheme in BCNF is in BCNF^{null} as well.

To be able to apply BCNF and BCNF^{null} (and arbitrary normal forms) to ER constructs, we use the concept of construct relation scheme (CRS). Let K be a construct of an ER scheme and all attributes of K be atomic. The *construct relation scheme* for K, written $CRS(K)$, is formed according to the following rules:

- If K is an entity set then $CRS(K)$ contains all the attributes of K. The identifier of K becomes the primary key of $CRS(K)$.

- If K is a relationship set then $CRS(K)$ has the following set of attributes: the attributes of K, if there are any, plus the union of the identifiers of all the participants of K. All these identifiers are declared as foreign keys, and all foreign keys are declared "not null". The primary key of $CRS(K)$ consists of the union of the identifiers of the identifying participants.

Normal forms for ER databases are based on construct relation schemes: Let K be an ER construct. Then K is in ER-BCNF (ER-BCNF^{null}) if $CRS(K)$ is in BCNF (BCNF^{null}). Similar definitions may be formulated for all normal forms of relational database theory.

We shall use both ER-BCNF and ER-BCNF^{null} to judge whether a certain construct requires normalization or not. Which of both forms applies depends on the situation.

In general, we may say that, in a completely normalized schema, every construct meets at least ER-BCNF^{null}.

3.2 The Basic Conception for ER Normalization

Our approach to ER modelling is strongly influenced by the analysis approach to BCNF normalization (cf. Ullman 1988, p. 403). Just like in relational normalization, unfavourable constructs are decomposed, the major difference being that the connections between the parts are not maintained by foreign keys but in a manner which is adequate for ER. If the violation of ER-BCNF or ER-BCNF^{null} was caused by only one functional dependency one transformation suffices, otherwise transformations have to be applied repeatedly until no harmful dependency is left. As every transformation removes one of the harmful dependencies and does not add new ones the process terminates. In the end, no harmful dependency is left.

Transformations to achieve ER-BCNF^{null} or ER-BCNF have a common property which normalization transformations striving for higher normal forms do not possess. Suppose K is a construct violating ER-BCNF or ER-BCNF^{null}. Then one of the constructs created during the transformation, we call it normally K', has the same identifier as K. More precisely, $CRS(K')$ has the same primary key as $CRS(K)$. We shall call such transformations *detachments*, in contrast to *splitting* transformations, where this property does not hold.

Despite some common features, there are also significant differences between our approach and relational normalization:

- When decomposing an entity set we always preserve the identifier of the original construct K when it is changed to K', at the most it might be renamed. This is because, unlike a key of a relation, an identifier of an entity set is explicitly defined by the designer; it is not just one of the candidate keys.

- In contrast to relational normalization, ER normalization *alone* cannot guarantee a nonredundant and reasonably structured schema. Whereas relational normalization takes the whole of the schema as input, the application of normal forms within ER modeling is only local (cf. Rauh 1993). We can, for instance, convert every entity set into constructs meeting ER-BCNF or ER-BCNF^{null}, but there might still be double entity sets in the schema, perhaps under different names. This is why an ER schema should have the porperty of *minimality* in addition to the property of *normality* (see Batini 1992, Rauh 1993 for details).

3.3 Transformation of Entity Sets (Transformation N1)

For the sake of simplicity, we take the same name for a construct and for the set of its attributes during the following treatment of standard transformations. Similarly, the name of a CRS is also used for its set of attributes. The meaning should always be clear from the context. We shall use stars (*) for lower or upper bounds of cardinalities if their values are of no importance in the special context. Throughout the discussion, we will assume that all attributes of a CRS are functionally dependent on the primary key. Thus only additional functional dependencies will be mentioned explicitly. Furthermore, we shall follow a constant pattern in our discussion of transformations. First, a description of the (unfavourable) initial situation is given, and the transformation is portrayed in an informal manner. We thereby address structural and instance mappings at the same time by discussing how the attributes of the source schema are to be shifted to the target schema. Then a formal description of the source and target schemata is provided to define the structural mapping, and the instance mapping is given as a set of ERC assignments.

Before we describe how an unfavourable entity set may be transformed into more favourable constructs, let us first state in which situations normalization is necessary: In general, an entity set *requires normalization* if it violates ER-BCNF^{null}.

Initial situation: Let K be an entity set with the set of attributes K and the identifier S, $S \subset K$. K is not in ER-BCNF^{null} as there is a FD $X \rightarrow Y$, with $X \subset K$, $Y \subset K$ and $X \cap Y = \emptyset$, where X is not a superkey for $CRS(K)$, and Y is *null* if X is *null*. K is linked to an entity set L with identifier C by a relationship set KL. We have to consider two variants

a) C is functionally dependent on X, and if X is *null* then C is *null* as well.
b)   The condition assumed for a) does not hold.

There is an important implication following from this description: in variant a) the upper bound of KL's cardinality on the side of K must be 1 as C is functionally dependent on X, and X, being a subset of K, is dependent on the identifier S.

Please notice that there is no loss of generality in assuming that, in the initial situation, K is connected with only one other entity set. If there are other relationship sets they are treated accordingly.

Fig. 1: Source schemata for N1, variant a) left, variant b) right

Informal Description of Transformation: An new entity set N with the set of attributes $N = \{X, Y\}$ and the identifier X is created. Entity set K is changed to K' by removing those attributes of X and Y that are not contained in the identifier of K. Consequently, K' has the set of attributes $K' = (K \setminus (Y \setminus S)) \setminus (X \setminus S) = (K \setminus (X \cup Y)) \cup S$, with S being the identifier. K' and N are connected by a new relationship set $K'N$, the cardinalities of which are determined by the following rules: If X has been declared *not null* within K, the cardinality on the side of K' is $(1,1)$, otherwise it is $(0,1)$. The cardinality on the side of N is set to $(0,n)$ provided that there are no further constraints suggesting another choice. How L is to be connected with the other entity sets of the target schema depends on the variant. If variant b) applies the former connection with K is retained under the new name $K'L$, with K' as participant instead of K. In case of variant a) KL is dropped, and a new relationship set NL

between N and L is created. Its cardinality on the side of N is the same as the cardinality on the side of K in the former relationship set KL, i.e. $(0,1)$ or $(1,1)$. For the side of L, $(0,n)$ must be taken unless additional constraints suggest another choice.

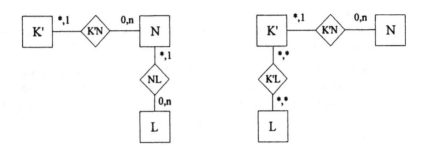

Fig. 2: Target schemata for N1, variant a) left, variant b) right

Structural Mapping: The source schemata are nearly identical for variants a) and b). We begin with a). To avoid confusion, we shall write $A \rightarrow B$, if B is functionally dependent on A, and $A \Rightarrow B$ for $\neg A \vee B$:

EntitySet K $(K;$ Identifier $S)$; $S, X, Y \subset K$; $X \rightarrow Y$, $\neg(X \rightarrow K)$; $X = null \Rightarrow Y = null$
EntitySet L $(L;$ Identifier $C)$; $C \subseteq L, X \rightarrow C$; $X = null \Rightarrow C = null$
RelationshipSet KL $((K, K, (*,1)), (L, L, (*,*)))$.

For variant b), we get

EntitySet K $(K;$ Identifier $S)$; $S, X, Y \subset K$; $X \rightarrow Y$, $\neg(X \rightarrow K)$; $X = null \Rightarrow Y = null$
EntitySet L $(L;$ Identifier $C)$; $C \subseteq L$
RelationshipSet KL $((K, K, (*,*)), (L, L, (*,*)))$.

The target schema for a) is

EntitySet K' $(K';$ Identifier $S)$; $S \subseteq K'$
EntitySet N $(X, Y;$ Identifier $X)$
EntitySet L $(L;$ Identifier $C)$; $C \subseteq L$
RelationshipSet $K'N$ $((K', K', (*,1)), (N, N, (0,n)))$
RelationshipSet NL $((N, N, (*,1)), (L, L, (0,n)))$.

For b), we drop the declaration for NL and add the following declaration instead:

RelationshipSet $K'L$ $((K', K', (*,*)), (L, L, (*,*)))$.

Instance Mapping: For variant a), we get:

$$K' := \{k[(K \setminus (X \cup Y)) \cup S] \mid K(k)\}$$
$$N := \{k[X], k[Y] \mid K(k) \wedge k.X \neq null\}$$
$$L := \{l \mid L(l)\}$$
$$K'N := \{K'(k[S]), N(k[X]) \mid K(k) \wedge k.X \neq null\}$$
$$NL := \{N(k[X]), l \mid K(k) \wedge L(l) \wedge (\exists kl)(KL(kl) \wedge kl \colon K == k \wedge kl \colon L == l)\}$$

Instead of NL, $K'L$ is needed for variant b):

$$K'L := \{K'(k[S]), l \mid K(k) \wedge L(l) \wedge (\exists kl)(KL(kl) \wedge kl \colon K == k \wedge kl \colon L == l)\}.$$

3.4 Transformation of Relationship Sets (Transformation N2)

A relationship set K *requires normalization* if one of the following conditions holds

1. K violates ER-BCNF^{null},

2. K violates ER-BCNF because of a harmful dependency $X \rightarrow Y$ in $CRS(K)$, and X is functionally dependent on a proper subset of the set of participant identifiers of K.

Initial Situation: A relationship set K with the set of attributes K, $K \neq \varnothing$, and the participants P_1, P_2, ..., P_n which may be all or in part identifying for K. K is not in ER-BCNF as there is a FD $X \rightarrow Y$, $Y \subset K$ and $X \cap Y = \varnothing$, in $CRS(K)$ where X is not a superkey for $CRS(K)$. For simplicity, we write RK for both $CRS(K)$ and its attributes. Suppose S_1, S_2, ..., S_n are the identifiers of the participants. Then the set of attributes is $RK = K \cup S_1 \cup S_2 \cup ... \cup S_n$. X and Y must be proper subsets of RK. There are three variants which have to be considered. The first two of them correspond with condition 2 mentioned above:

a) X is, either trivially or nontrivially, functionally dependent on exactly one of the participant identifiers S_1, S_2, ..., S_n in RK.

b) K has an arity greater than two and there is a full FD of X on the union of at least two of the identifiers S_1, S_2, ..., S_n.

c) Neither a) nor b) apply, but if X is *null* then Y is *null*.

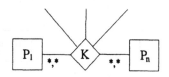

Fig. 3: Source schema for N2

Remark: For variants a) and b), already a violation of ER-BCNF is seen as a reason for transforming K as there are entity sets that can absorb $\{X, Y\}$, so that X is not needed as an identifier. This is not the case for c), where only a violation of weaker ER-BCNF^{null} causes a transformation, and an infringement of ER-BCNF must be tolerated. The additional condition $X = null \Rightarrow Y = null$ is set to mark the violation of weaker ER-BCNF^{null}.

Informal Description of transformation, variant a): Let us assume that X is dependent on the identifier S_m of participant P_m. We change the name of K into K' and remove Y and the subset of X that has been contained in it. Thus K' has attributes $K' = K \setminus (X \cup Y)$. P_m is changed to P_m' and enriched by the additional attributes X and Y, as far as they are not already there. Consequently, P_m' has the attributes P_m, $A = X \setminus P_m$, and $B = Y \setminus P_m$.

Structural Mapping, variant a): In the source schema declaration, there is an entry for every entity set P_i, $i = 1, 2, ..., n$. Similarly, the declaration for K contains every P_i as a participant.

EntitySet P_i (P_i, Identifier S_i); $S_i \subseteq P_i$
RelationshipSet K ((P_i, P_i, (*,*)); K);.

In addition, the following constraints are valid in the source schema: $S_m \to X; X \to Y; Y \subset K; X \subset (K \cup P_m)$. In the target schema, P_m becomes P_m' and gets a separate declaration. For all other P_i, $i = 1, 2, ..., m - 1, m + 1, ..., n$, the declaration remains the same:

EntitySet P_i (P_i; Identifier S_i); $S_i \subseteq P_i$
EntitySet P_m' (P_m, A, B; Identifier S_m); $S_m \subseteq P_m'$
RelationshipSet K' ((P_1, P_1, (*,*)), ..., (P_{m-1}, P_{m-1}, (*,*)), (P_m', P_m', (*,*)),
   (P_{m+1}, P_{m+1}, (*,*)), ..., (P_n, P_n, (*,*)); K')

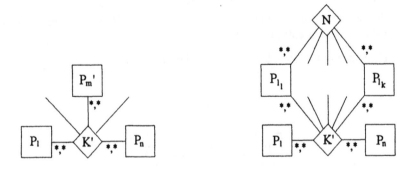

Fig. 4: Target Schemata for N2, variant a) left, variant b) right

Instance Mapping for variant a): As in the description of the target schema, P_m' is treated separately:

$$P_i := \{p \mid P_i(p)\}, \qquad i = 1,2,\ldots,m-1,m+1,\ldots,n$$
$$P_m' := \{p[P_m], k[X \setminus P_m], k[Y \setminus P_m] \mid P_m(p) \wedge K(k) \wedge k: P_m == p\}$$
$$K' := \{p_1, p_2, \ldots, p_n; k[K \setminus (X \cup Y)] \mid P_1(p_1) \wedge P_2(p_2) \wedge \ldots \wedge P_n(p_n)$$
$$\wedge k: P_1 == p_1 \wedge k: P_2 == p_2 \wedge \ldots \wedge k: P_n == p_n\}$$

Notice that, if X is not contained in K, then $k[X]$ refers to an empty set of attributes, and so does $k[X \setminus P_m]$.

Informal Description of Transformation, variant b): Suppose that X is fully functionally dependent on $S_{l_1} \cup S_{l_2} \cup .. \cup S_{l_k}$ where S_{l_i} is the identifier of participant $P_{l_i}, i = 1,2,\ldots,k$. Then a new relationship set N is created between $P_{l_1}, P_{l_2}, \ldots, P_{l_k}$. N gets those subsets of X and Y as attributes that have been contained in K, and consequently has attributes $N = (X \cap K) \cup Y$. The cardinalities of N are the same as those of K in the same position unless there are additional constraints suggesting another choice. X and Y are removed from K as far as they have been there. K becomes K', now having the set of attributes $K' = K \setminus (X \cup Y)$.

Structural Mapping, variant b): Apart from explicit constraints, the source schema is the same as for a):

EntitySet P_i (P_i, Identifier S_i); $S_i \subseteq P_i$
RelationshipSet K ((P_i, P_i, (*,*)); K);.

Constraints to consider are: $\{P_{l_1}, P_{l_2}, \ldots, P_{l_k}\} \rightarrow X$; $X \rightarrow Y$; $Y \subset K$; $X \subset (K \cup S_{l_1} \cup S_{l_2} \cup .. \cup S_{l_k})$. Compared to variant a), the target schema is enlarged by the declaration for relationship set N:

EntitySet P_i (P_i; Identifier S_i); $i = 1, 2, \ldots, n$; $S_i \subseteq P_i$
RelationshipSet K' ((P_i, P_i, (*,*)); K'); $i = 1, 2, \ldots, n$;
RelationshipSet N (($P_{l_i}, P_{l_i}, (*,*)); N$); $i = 1, 2, \ldots, k$

Instance Mapping, variant b):

$$P_i := \{p \mid P_i(p)\}, \qquad i = 1,2,\ldots,n$$
$$K' := \{p_1, p_2, \ldots, p_n; k[K \setminus (X \cup Y)] \mid P_1(p_1) \wedge P_2(p_2) \wedge \ldots \wedge P_n(p_n)$$
$$\wedge k: P_1 == p_1 \wedge k: P_2 == p_2 \wedge \ldots \wedge k: P_n == p_n\}$$
$$N := \{p_1, p_2, \ldots, p_k; k[(X \cap K) \cup Y] \mid P_{l_1}(p_1) \wedge P_{l_2}(p_2) \wedge \ldots \wedge P_{l_k}(p_k)$$
$$\wedge K(k) \wedge k: P_{l_1} == p_1 \wedge k: P_{l_2} == p_2 \wedge \ldots \wedge k: P_{l_k} == p_k\}$$

Informal Description of Transformation, variant c): Let $P_{j_1}, P_{j_2}, \ldots, P_{j_u}$ be the identifying partipicants of K and $S_{j_1}, S_{j_2}, \ldots, S_{j_u}$ be their identifiers. K is changed into an entity set K' with attributes $\{D_1 = S_{j_1}, D_2 = S_{j_2}, ..., D_u = S_{j_u}, E = K \setminus X, F = K \setminus Y\}$ and identifier $\{D_1, D_2, ..., D_u\}$. K' is connected with the former participants of K by n binary relationship sets. Their cardinalities on the side of K' are all (1,1). On the side of the former participants the cardinalities of K in the same positions are taken. A new entity set N is created with attributes $\{X, Y\}$, X being the identifier. In the source schema, X may have been overlapping with one or more identifiers of the participants. Let us assume that $P_{x_1}, P_{x_2}, ..., P_{x_r}$ are those participants, and $A_1 \subseteq S_{x_1}$, $A_2 \subseteq S_{x_2}, ..., A_r \subseteq S_{x_r}$ are the attributes overlapping with X. Then $X = A_1 \cup A_2 \cup ... \cup A_r \cup (X \setminus (S_{x_1} \cup S_{x_2} \cup ... \cup S_{x_r}))$. As we want N to consist of the attributes $\{X, Y\}$, we set $N = \{A_1, A_2, ..., A_r, B = X \setminus (S_{x_1} \cup S_{x_2} \cup ... \cup S_{x_r}), Y\}$. N is connected with K' by a binary relationship set $K'N$ which has no attributes. With respect to the cardinalities of $K'N$ the following rules are applied: The upper bound on the side of K' is 1 since there is at most one X-value for a certain K'-entity. For the lower bounds, we take 0 if nulls have been allowed for X within K, 1 if not. On the side of N, the cardinality is $(1,n)$ since X and Y were originally defined within K and could not exist without an instance of K and, on the other hand, certain values of X may well occur together with different instances of K'.

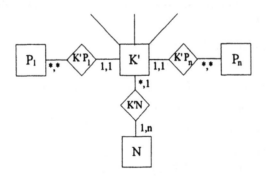

Fig. 5: Target schema for N2, variant c)

Structural Mapping for variant c): The source schema is the same as for a) and b), except for the constraints, which are: $X \to Y$; $Y \subset K$, $X \subset (K \cup P_1 \cup ... \cup P_n)$. Now the target schema contains two new entity sets K' and N, n binary relationship sets $K'P_i$ and a new relationship set $K'N$:

EntitySet $P_i (P_i;$ Identifier $_{si})$; $i = 1, 2, ..., n$; $S_i \subseteq P_i$
EntitySet $N (A_1, A_2, ..., A_r, B, Y$; Identifier $A_1, A_2, ..., A_r, B)$
EntitySet K' $(D_1, D_2, ..., D_u, E, F$; Identifier $D_1, D_2, ..., D_u)$
RelationshipSet $K'P_i$ $((K', K', (1,1)), (P_i, P_i, (*,*))$; $i = 1, 2, ..., n$
RelationshipSet $K'N$ $((K', K', (1,1)), (N, N, (1, n))$.

Instance Mapping for variant c):

$$P_i := \{p \mid P_i(p)\}, \qquad i = 1, 2, \ldots, n$$

$$N := \{p_1[S_{x_1} \cap X], p_2[S_{x_2} \cap X], \ldots, p_r[S_{x_r} \cap X], k[X \setminus ((S_{x_1} \cap X) \cup (S_{x_2} \cap X) \cup$$

$$\ldots \cup (S_{x_r} \cap X))], k[Y] \mid K(k) \wedge P_{x_1}(p_1) \wedge P_{x_2}(p_2) \wedge \ldots \wedge P_{x_r}(p_r) \wedge k : P_{x_1} == p_1 \wedge$$

$$k : P_{x_2} == p_2 \wedge \ldots \wedge k : P_{x_r} == p_r\}$$

$$K' := \{p_1[S_{j_1}], p_2[S_{j_2}], \ldots, p_u[S_{j_u}], k[K \setminus X], k[K \setminus Y)] \mid P_{j_1}(p_1) \wedge P_{j_2}(p_2) \wedge \ldots \wedge$$

$$P_{j_u}(p_u) \wedge K(k) \wedge k : P_{j_1} == p_1 \wedge k : P_{j_2} == p_2 \wedge \ldots \wedge k : P_{j_u} == p_u\}$$

$$K' P_i := \{K'(p_1[S_{j_1}], p_2[S_{j_2}], \ldots, p_u[S_{j_u}]), p \mid P_{j_1}(p_1) \wedge P_{j_2}(p_2) \wedge \ldots \wedge P_{j_u}(p_u) \wedge$$

$$P_i(p) \wedge (\exists k)(K(k) \wedge k : P_{j_1} == p_1 \wedge k : P_{j_2} == p_2 \wedge \ldots \wedge k : P_{j_u} == p_u)\}$$

$$K' N := \{K'(p_1[S_{j_1}], p_2[S_{j_2}], \ldots, p_u[S_{j_u}]), N(p_1[S_{x_1} \cap X], p_2[S_{x_2} \cap X], \ldots, p_r[S_{x_r} \cap X],$$

$$k[X \setminus (S_{x_1} \cup S_{x_2} \cup \ldots \cup S_{x_r})]) \mid P_{x_1}(p_1) \wedge P_{x_2}(p_2) \wedge \ldots \wedge P_{x_r}(p_r) \wedge K(k)\}$$

4   Summary and Outlook

A general framework for the description of ER schema transformations has been introduced and then been applied to describe a set of standard transformation to achieve an ER normal form derived from BCNF, but taking null values into account.

The results presented mark only the first step within a greater project to develop standard transformations to improve the quality of ER designs. Much work has still to be done. For instance, normalization up to fifth normal form, which is not covered by this paper, will be dealt with in a future publication. In addition, there are many interesting but unsolved questions concerning the properties of schema transformations. A significant problem is, for example, how reversibility can be assessed for arbitrary transformations. An approach presented by Makowsky (1986) in another context may be used for this purpose: The basic principle is to translate an ER schema into a relational database scheme, called *ER-compatible relational database scheme (ERS)*, that reflects its structure so closely that both schemata might be used as substitutes for each other. The ERS of an ER schema consists of the CRS of all its constructs. Hence there is a one to one correspondence between relation schemes and ER constructs. We can then show how the ERS of the target schema is produced from the ERS of the source schema using a series of lossless database operations. The concept of lossless decomposition, which is closely related to the concept of reversibility, can be used as an aid. Unfortunately, relational database theory provides only a limited basis for judging upon losslessness if null values are not neglected (cf. Maier 1983, Ullman 1988, Atzeni 1993). Thus some basic work has to be done previously.

References

Atzeni, P., De Antonellis, V. (1993). Relational Database Theory, Redwood City, California: Benjamin/Cummings

Batini, C., Ceri, S., Navathe, S. (1992). Conceptual Database Design: An Entity-Relationship Approach, Redwood City, California: Benjamin/Cummings

Chung, I., Nakamura, F., Chen, P. (1983). A Decomposition of Relations Using the Entity-Relationship Approach. Proc. of the 2nd International Conference on Entity-Relationship Approach, Washington, D.C. 1981, North-Holland, 1983

Codd, E, (1972). Relational Completeness of Data Base Sublanguages. In: R. Rustin (ed.), Data Base Systems, Englewood Cliffs, New Jersey: Prentice-Hall

Gardarin, G. and Valduriez, P. (1989). Relational Databases and Knowledge Bases, Reading, Mass.: Addison-Wesley

Hainaut, J.-L. (1990). Entity-Relationship Models: Formal Specification and Comparison. In H. Kangassalo (ed.), Proceedings of the 9th International Conference on the Entity-Relationship Approach, Lausanne, Switzerland, 1990

Hainaut, J.-L., Tonneau, C., Joris, M., Chandelon, M. (1993). Schema Transformation Techniques for Database Reverse Engineering. In: Proceedings of the 12th International Conference on Entity-Relationship Approach, Arlington, Texas, Dec 15-17, 1993

Jajodia, S., Ng, P.A. (1983). The Problem of Equivalence for Entity-Relationship Diagrams. IEEE Transactions on Software Engineering 9 (1983), No. 5, pp. 617-630

Kobayashi, I. (1986). Losslessness and Semantic Correctness of Database Schema Transformations: Another Look of Schema Equivalence. Information Systems, Vol. 11, No. 1, pp.41-59, 1986

Ling, T.W. (1985a). A Normal Form for Entity-Relationship Diagrams. Proc. of the 4th International Conference on Entity-Relationship Approach, Chicago 1985, North-Holland

Ling, T.W. (1985b). An Analysis of Multivalued and Join Dependencies Based on the Entity- Relationship Approach. Data & Knowledge Engineering 1 (1985), pp. 253-271

Maier, D. (1983). The Theory of Relational Databases, Rockville, Md: Computer Science Press

Makowsky, J., Markowitz, V., Rotics, N. (1986). Entity Relationship Consistency for Relational Schemas. In G. Ausiello and P.Atzeni (eds.), ICDT '86, Springer-Verlag

Rauh, O. and Stickel, E. (1993), Searching for Compositions in ER Schemes. In R. Elmasri, V. Kouramajian (eds.), Proceedings of the 12th Int' Conference on Entity-Relationship Approach, Arlington, TX, 1993

Rosenthal, A., Reiner, D. (1988). Theoretically Sound Transformations for Practical Database Design. Proc. of the 6th International Conference on Entity-Relationship Approach, New York 1987, pp. 115-132, North-Holland

Ullman, J. (1988). Principles of Database and Knowledge-Base Systems, Volume I, Rockville, Maryland: Computer Science Press

The Rapid Application and Database Development (RADD) Workbench — A Comfortable Database Design Tool *

Meike Albrecht[2], Margita Altus[1], Edith Buchholz[2],
Antje Düsterhöft[2], Bernhard Thalheim[2]

[1] University of Rostock, Department of Computer Science
[2] Brandenburgian Technical University of Cottbus, Institute of Computer Science
meike | buch | duest @ informatik.uni-rostock.de
altus | thalheim @ informatik.tu-cottbus.de

Abstract. We present a workbench for database design which supports designers efficiently and informally to achieve correct and efficient databases.

1 Introduction

The performance of a database (especially efficiency and consistency) heavily depends on design decisions. In order to achieve an effective behaviour of the database, database designers are requested to find the best structure and the simplest basic database operations. The result of the database design process depends on the professionality of the designer and the quality of the support by a database design system. Therefore development of a comfortable database design system is an important task.

In this paper we present a database design system which is adaptable to a designer. It contains components which enable even novice or unskilled users the design of correct databases. An extensive support of database designers in choosing design strategies and checking correctness of design steps is contained in the approach. These components also use natural language to acquire information about databases and discuss design decisions by means of examples.

The different components in the workbench work closely together. The designer does not need to enter an information twice, all components communicate via a DataDictionary. Therefore, the designer can decide which support he/she wants to use for every design task.

In the system we use a special extension of the entity-relationship model, the *Higher-order Entity-Relationship Model* (HERM), which is used for representing structural, semantic and behavioural information. The workbench is currently implemented in a joint project of different groups [BOT90] in Cottbus, Dresden, Münster and Rostock. In the following sections we explain main parts of the workbench.

---

* This work is supported by DFG Th465/2.

2 Why Another Tool Box

During the last decade several dozens of computer-aided database engineering tools
(CASE) have been developed and used in practice (e.g. [1]). At present, we can distinguish three generations of database design systems ([BCN92, RoR89]).

- The *first generation tools* were based on the classical "waterfall" model of software development: requirement analysis, conceptual design, logical design, testing and maintenance. Most of them were platforms for a design from scratch.
  These tools did not support changes during the life-cycle of the database.
- *Second generation tools* which become available now are designed as complete
  workbenches for the design support over the complete life-cycle of a database.
  Such tools use graphic subsystems and support consistency of the design. Some of
  them help the user to find out which information is entered several times and/or
  which is inconsistent. Further, some systems generate design documentations for
  the complete design process. Most of the workbenches are adaptable to different
  platforms and can generate different translations for a given design.
- Although second generation tools are now put into practice, *third generation
  tools* are already under development. There are proposals in which manner tools
  can be customized. Third generation tools will be more user-friendly and user-
  adaptable (using, for instance, user-driven strategies which are influenced by
  special organizational approaches in enterprizes). Designers can use strategies
  which are model-dependent and have a support for reasoning in natural language.
  They provide a tuning support. Users can apply object-oriented development
  strategies.

The progress of design tools is based on software, hardware and methodology development. AI techniques contributed to design approaches appending methodological
support, knowledge engineering approaches and customizability. Novel technologies
like object orientation and hypertext are affecting database design systems. Databases are evolving. Therefore, design systems need to support evolution and re-
engineering. New and more complex applications require better design systems. Sum-
marizing, advanced design tools should satisfy the following requirements [BCN92].

1. The tool needs an *advanced* and *powerful user interface*. The presentation on the
   screen should be consistent. Further, the user interface supports recognition of
   past design decisions and uses a graphical language.

---

[1] Accell, AD/VANCE, Aris, Axiant, Bachmann/Database Administrator,
CA-ADS/Online, CA-Ideal, CASE Designer, CASE Generator, case/4/0, Colonel, CO-
MIC, DatAid, DataView, (DB)², DBleaf, DBMOD, DDB CASE, DDEW, EasyCASE,
Enter Case, ErDesigner, ERWin/SQL, ERWin/DBF, ERWin/ERX, Excelerator, Focus,
Front & Center, GainMomentum, Gambit, Hypersript Tools, Ideo, IDEF, IEF, IEW,
Informix-4GL Rapid Development System, InfoPump, Ingres/Windows4GL, Innovator,
JAM, Maestro II, Magic, MTS, Natural, Ossy, PackRat, Paradigm Plus, PFXplus, Pose,
PowerHouse, ProdMod-Plus, Progress 4GL, RIDL*, QBEVision, ROSI-SQL, S-Designor,
SECSI, SIT, SQL Forms, StP/IM, Superbase Developer Edition, SuperNOVA, System
Architect, TAXIS, TeamWork, Uniface, VCS, XPlain, and ZIM.

2. *Flexibility* and *broad coverage* are important features of design systems. The tool supports the complete design process. Editors for schema and dataflow design, analyzers, synthesizers and transformers are well integrated. Different design strategies are supported. There are interfaces to external tools and different platforms. The methodology support can be adapted to the user and can be enforced in different degrees.

3. The tool set is *robust, well integrated* and has an efficient *theory support*. The tool is efficiently supporting the acquisition of semantics, not just graphics. The performance implications of design decisions can be discussed with the designer. Alternatives can be generated. The system has the ability to cope with missing information, an aid for recovering from wrong results. Further, the tool can display different versions of the same schema and cope with bad schemas as well as good.

4. A database design tool set should be *extensible* in multiple directions.

The current development of technology enables the development of components for a third generation database design system. But at present, there is no tool which supports a complete design methodology. Most tools currently available support only a part of the design process in a restrictive manner. There are tools which do not support integrity and/or are mainly graphical interfaces. Further, there are only very few tools which can claim to be a third generation design tool. Many design tools are restricted to certain DBMS.

Therefore, development of a database design tool is still a big challenge.

Based on an analysis of systems supporting database design the database design system (DB)^2 has been developed [Tha92]. It is supporting a high-level efficient database design. The system is based on an extension of the entity-relationship model for structural design and on a graphical interface. Further, a high-level language for specification of integrity constraints and operations has been developed. Five years of extensive utilization of (DB)^2 in more than 100 different user groups gave us a deeper insight into the design process and the needs of database designers.

Based on the experiences with (DB)^2 we are developing a new design system RADD (*R*apid *A*pplication and *D*atabase *D*evelopment). The aim of this paper is to demonstrate that the requirements on database design systems can be met by current technology. First, we represent an Overview of the new design system RADD. Then we illustrate different tools of this system in more detail.

3 Overview of RADD

The RADD (*R*apid *A*pplication and *D*atabase *D*evelopment) does not require the user to understand the theory, the implementational restrictions and the programming problems in order to design a database scheme. A novice designer can create a database design successfully using the system. These tools are based on the extended entity-relationship model (HERM) whereby structural constructs are added and integrity constraints and operations are used.

Basically, the system in Figure 1 consists of three major components:

– **Design Tools:** Since designers require different kinds of representation the design tools support graphical, procedural and logical techniques for application specification.

- **Graphical Editor:** The system is based on an extended entity-relationship model which allows the user to specify graphically the structure of an application, the integrity constraints which are valid in the given application and the processes, operations and transactions which are necessary for the given application. This extension requires an easy-to-handle and advanced support for graphics. Further, the editor enables the designer to represent the complete design information. The designer develops the structure, static and dynamic semantics, and the operations of the application. Several components support the specific design tasks, e.g. semantics can be developed using an abstract approach, using an approach based on examples or refining the meaning of natural language sentences.

- **Customizer/Strategy support:** The user interface is adapted to skills, abilities and intentions of the database designer. This tool allows customization of the user interface. The designer is supported in choosing an appropriate database design strategy. Based on the chosen design strategy this tool controls and verifies design steps.

- **Acquisition support:** Acquisition of specifications can be supported by different strategies. This tool uses learning approaches for acquisition of structure, semantics and operations. The user interface of this tool is an example discussion.

- **Natural language support:** The designer who is able to express properties of his application based on natural language can be supported by moderated dialogues. During such dialogues the designer refines his/her current design. The system validates whether the specification meets certain completeness requirements. The system RADD supports German language in a specific manner. The structure and semantics of German sentences are used for the extraction of structural, semantical, operational and behavioural specification.

- **Version manager and reverse/reengineering tool:** The design system stores versions of current, previous and sample specifications. These specifications can be partially or completely included into current specifications or can be used for replacing parts of current specifications.

– **Optimization:** In the tool there is a component which tries to find for a drafted database an equivalent and more efficient database.

- **Behavior estimation:** Based on frequency, priority and semantics of operations the complexity of the current database can be estimated in dependence of implementational techniques used by a chosen class of DBMS.

- **Behavior optimization:** Based on the results of behaviour estimation this tool discusses with a designer various possibilities for redesign and improvement of database behaviour. Improvement includes modification and optimization of database schemata, their corresponding integrity constraints and operations.

– Translator: This component translates the result of the design process into the language of a specific database management system that is used in the given application. This tool is developed on the University at Münster (Germany) and therefore not described in this paper. It embodies gates to different (relational, object-oriented, hierarchical and Network) DBMS and can be used also as an input for the design process.

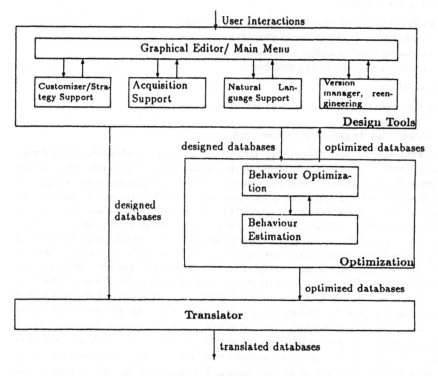

Figure 1: Overview of the RADD workbench

In the next sections we present some main parts of the workbench in detail. In *section 4* we show how designers can be supported in the design steps individually. *Section 5* describes the semantic acquisition as a part of the acquisition support. In *section 6* we demonstrate the natural language support. *Section 7* discusses the utilization of the workbench. In *section 8* we give a conclusion of the paper and consider future work.

4 User Guidance

There is a variety of database design strategies proposed in the literature (e.g. [Ris88, FIH89, BCN92, FuN86, Leo92]). Most approaches propose that the designer is mainly using one strategy. However, observations on database designers show that they use different strategies depending on the application properties, their skills and abilities and the chosen platform for implementation. This change in strategy necessitates a support for database designers. Further, database designers change their strategy according to the reached stage of the scheme. Any change in strategy makes the design task more complex. Since database designers normally delay some of the design decisions, any change in strategy requires deliberate adaptation. For this reason, experienced database designers need a strategy support as well. Therefore, a *user guidance tool* is currently developed and included into RADD. This tool supports the designer

- in developing and applying his/her own strategy,
- in discussing decisions in designer teams,
- in tracing delayed design decisions, and
- in customizing the design workbench.

It is based on

- a framework for deriving design strategies,
- a user model, and
- a customizable graphical environment.

The Framework for Adaptable Database Design Strategies. Each design strategy needs to support a designer during a consistent development of database schemes. Thus, a strategy should be content preserving, constraint preserving, minimality preserving and update simplicity preserving [Yao85]. Analysing known design strategies, primitive steps can be extracted. These *primitives* are the basis for the strategy support in RADD. The designer can choose his/her own strategy and compose the strategy from primitives. The system RADD supports this choice based on the user model, user preferences, and characteristics of the application. On this basis, the designer can switch among bottom-up, top-down, modular, inside-out and other strategies. The *controller* derives graph grammar rules for the maintenance of consistency and for the specific support of designers. The variety of different strategies is based on the dimensions of database design which are *design directions* like the top-down or bottom-up approach or mixed strategies, *control mechanism* of design strategies and the *modularity concept* [Tha94]. Strategy consultancy and error control are included in the user guidance tool. Besides the primitives each design strategy is related with a set of checkpoints. The design of the unit 'borrow' in our library example involves a rough specification on the interface. The checkpoint after this step examines the interface description and the skeleton of the library example.

The User Modelling Component. The strategy support is based on a model of the user. The behavior of a user depends on this model, on the application area and on the team support. The user model is *explicitly* represented by a set of *profiles* in the workbench. For instance, designers experienced in entity-relationship models develop their applications differently than those designers which are used to relational database design. The customizer uses this information and generates an optimal environment for the designer. This *adaptable* environment can be enabled or disabled. Further, the RADD component guard the actions of users. If the profile of the user changes then the system generates a proposal for a change of the RADD environment. This *dynamic* user model also represents changes in knowledge, skills and capabilities.

The Information in our User Model. The *user* of the database design environment is classified regarding his properties, his capabilities, his preferences (kinds of

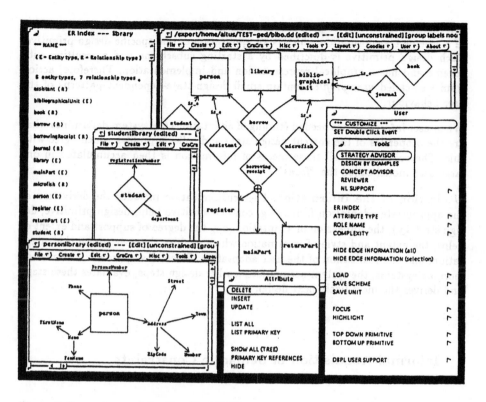

Figure 2: Screendump of the Graphical Editor

input, output and dialog) and his system knowledge, his application knowledge and his knowledge about design concepts and design strategies, and he will be supported with respect to this *classification*.

Acquisition of the User Information. The users knowledge and actions are analysed with the aim to propose the most appropriate design strategy before the scheme transformation process starts and the most likely next design step after each user design action. The user analysis is divided into two parts: the direct analysis (user's answers in an interrogation) and the indirect analysis (user's actions in the design environment, e.g. selection of types in the diagram, or selection of commands/ design primitives). In this way, the analysis contains both *explicit* and *implicit acquisition* of user model information.

Representation of User Characteristics. Individual users are represented by a collection of frames. General frames store user-specific information which is long-term static information with respect to the user classification. Action frames store information on the use of particular actions. A user action results in the execution of a scheme transformation which is an application of one specific design primitive. Each design primitive is described by a starting subscheme and a resulting sub-scheme and has a graphical representation and implementation. Therefore, action frames so-called *user profiles* contain small design-state-dependent patterns of the user behaviour.

When user information is needed ('timing of adaptation) the system determines what are the properties of the current design state and collects profiles which agree with this. The collection of all these pieces of information is then accumulated in one large user model called the *"focus"*.

Utilization of the Information. User customization includes the derivation of the appropriate adaptation forms (e.g. context-sensitive help, design primitive, design strategy), the dimension of adaptation (e.g. the degree of support and extent of help), the extent and style of information which enables the user to use this adaptation, and the realization of the user adaptation. Since this approach is similar to learning systems, the system accumulates earlier design steps, evaluates these steps and derives the most likely next design step.

5 Informal Acquisition of Semantic Constraints

Correct and complete determination of semantic constraints is one of the most difficult tasks in database design because semantic constraints are formally defined and therefore designers often misunderstand them. But semantic constraints are necessary to ensure that restructuring operations can proceed correctly. Therefore a support of acquisition of correct and (as far as possible) complete sets of semantic constraints by a tool is important.

Most database designers know the context of the application but they cannot express knowledge about the application in semantic constraints. Our tool shall help designers in specifying constraints by using an informal approach basing on example relations.

Analysis of Example Relations. In the approach we first need some real-world data for the database. From these data it is derivable that some constraints cannot be valid. We want to show it by a sample relation 'Persons'.

PersonsNumber	Name		Address				Phone
	FamName	FirstName	Town	ZipCode	Street	Number	
218263	Meier	Paula	Berlin	10249	Mollstr	30	3293238
948547	Mueller	Karl	Berlin	12621	Mittelweg	281	3743654
323983	Schmidt	Anna	Rostock	18055	Gerberstr	30	8834736
239283	Weber	Peter	Rostock	18055	Gerberstr	15	9329392

The following keys cannot be valid:

- Adress.Number   - Adress.City Adress.ZIP Adress.Street

Further, it is derivable from the instance that the following functional dependencies are not valid:

- Address.Number ⟶ PersonsNumber   - Address.Number ⟶ Name.FamName
- Address.Number ⟶ Name.FirstName   - Address.Number ⟶ Address.Town
- Address.Number ⟶ Address.ZipCode   - Address.Number ⟶ Address.Street
- Address.Number ⟶ Phone
- Address.Town Address.ZipCode Address.Street ⟶ PersonsNumber
- Address.Town Address.ZipCode Address.Street ⟶ Name.FamName
- Address.Town Address.ZipCode Address.Street ⟶ Name.FirstName
- Address.Town Address.ZipCode Address.Street ⟶ Address.Number
- Address.Town Address.ZipCode Address.Street ⟶ Phone

Invalid keys and invalid functional dependencies can be derived from one relation. Invalid exclusion dependencies between two relations and non-possible cardinalities can be found from sample relations. These invalid semantic constraints restrict search space which must be checked for semantic constraints.

Explicit Determining Semantic Constraints. Often database designers can determine some semantic constraints, for instance a key of a relation. Therefore, explicit determination of semantic constraints is also supported in the tool, because designers who know semantic constraints do not want to search for them in examples.

Search for Further Constraints. If a designer cannot enter semantic constraints or if he/she cannot determine all constraints then the tool supports the search for further constraints. All semantic constraints which are still not yet analysed (not violated by the example and not explicitly entered) could be valid and therefore they must be checked. It is possible to inquire those semantic constraints with examples. We want to show it for an inclusion dependency, only:

	PersonsNumber	FamName	FirstName	City	ZIP	Street	Number
Persons:		Meier Schulz Lehmann					

	StudentsNumber	FamName	FirstName	Department
Students:		Schmidt		

Is it possible that — Students.FamName — contains values which are not in — Persons.FamName — (y/n) ?

Keys, functional dependencies, exclusion dependencies and cardinality constraints can also be inquired by an example discussion.

Efficient Acquisition of Unknown Semantic Constraints. The set of unknown constraints which must be checked can be very large. The number of independent functional dependencies and keys of a relation can reach $O(2^n)$ where n is the number of attributes of a relation. The maximal number of unary inclusion and exclusion dependencies is $O(n^2)$ where n is the number of attributes of the whole database.

Therefore, not all unknown constraints can be checked one after the other. *Heuristic rules* are necessary which estimate the plausibility of the validity of unknown constraints. These heuristics can use much vague information about the database which reflects *background knowledge of the designer* that is already implicitly contained in the database. Structural information, already known semantic information, sample relations and sample transactions (if they are known) are utilized in the heuristic rules.

We want to show only some heuristics.

From *attribute names* sometimes keys are derivable if the substrings -name-, -number-, -id-, -#- occur in the names. Similar attribute names can indicate existing inclusion or exclusion dependencies or foreign keys. *The same values in the instances* also point to inclusion and exclusion dependencies or foreign keys. From *transactions* specified on the databases we can conclude which attributes are probably keys, and which functional and inclusion dependencies must hold.

First, those constraints which seem to be valid are inquired with the example discussion.

In that way unknown semantic constraints are inquired in an informal and efficient way. The designer needs not to be able to enter formal semantic constraints, but with this tool he can determine valid constraints by an example discussion, only. These semantic constraints are necessary for the translation and optimization of databases.

6   The Natural Language Interface (NLI)

Motivation and Aims of the Linguistic Approach. A database designer has to use a high level of abstraction for mapping his real-world application onto an entity relationship model. In fact, most users are able to describe in their native language the entities that will form the basic elements of the prospective database, how to administer them and the processes they will have to undergo. For that reason we decided to choose the natural language German for supporting the database design process.

In this section we illustrate how natural language in a dialogue system can be used for gathering the knowledge of the designer and how it can be transfered into an extended entity-relationship model. The dialogue together with the knowledge base will be used for drawing to the designers attention special facts resulting from the syntactic, the semantic and the pragmatic analyses of the natural language input. The system makes suggestions for completing the design applying the knowledge base.

The specification and formalisation of semantic constraints and behaviour is one of the most complex problems for the designer. Within natural language sentences the designer uses semantic and behaviour constraints intuitively. For that reason within the natural language design process we focus on extracting comprehensive information about the domain from natural language utterances. The results of the dialogue are available in the internal DataDictionary for the other tools (graphical interface, integrity checker, strategy adviser,...) of the system. The NLI is described in more detail in [BDT94].

The Structure of the NLI. The natural language interface consists of a dialogue component, a component for the computational linguistic analysis and a pragmatic component. Each component will be described in the next sections.

Moderated Dialogue. For the acquisition of designer knowledge we decided to choose a moderated dialogue system. A moderated dialogue can be seen as a question-answer-system. The system asks for input or additional questions considering the acquisition of database design information. These questions are frames which will be updated in the dialogue process. The designer can formulate the answer in natural language sentences. Within the dialogue the results of the syntactic, semantic and pragmatic analyses will be used for controlling the dialogue.

Computational Linguistic Analysis. The computational linguistic analysis consists of a syntactic and a semantic check of the natural language sentences.

- The designer input into the dialogue tool is first submitted to a *syntax analyser*. In order to check the syntax of a sentence we have implemented an ID/LP parser (Immediate Dependence/ Linear Precedence) which belongs to the family of Unification Grammars. The parser works on the basis of a lexikon of German words and a restricted area of German sentences.
- Interpreting the *semantics* of the designer input we are using the two-step model that contains the word semantics and the semantics of the sentence. Verbs form the backbone of the sentences. We have tried to find a classification of verb semantics that can be applied to all verbs in the German language. This classification is, at this stage, independent of the domain to be analysed. To identify the meaning of sentences we have used the model of semantic roles. The units in a sentence are seen to fulfil certain functional roles corresponding to the verb classification.

Pragmatic Interpretation. The aim of the pragmatic interpretation is the mapping of the natural language input onto HERM model structures using the results of the syntactic and semantic analyses. We handle this transformation as a compiler process. An attribute grammar with common rules and heuristics as semantic functions form the basis of the transformation. Common rules will be used for analysing the syntax tree structures of the syntactic analysis. The heuristics are expressed in contextfree and contextsensitive rules and represent assumption needed for the transformation of natural language phrases into HERM structures. The advantage of this strategy is the possibility to connect not only word classes (e.g. nouns, verbs, adjectives) with HERM structures but also phrases of the sentence (e.g. genitive phrase) and IIERM structures.

Procedures for extracting *semantic information* are also started from the transformation grammar if special words are identified. Within the knowledge base these words will be marked. The acquisition of the semantic information will be instantiated using the attribute grammar within the process of capturing structural information. *Information on behaviour* can be best gained from a knowledge base. Special words indicate the occurence of processes. If such words are recognized a process classification will be applied in order to capture the according post, main and preprocesses.

7 Using the Workbench

Practical Applications. The workbench is supporting large and complex design tasks and assists in team work. Currently, RADD is used in two large projects in Cottbus Technical University.

- The environmental system project intends to evaluate the potentiality of the southern Brandenburgian landscape after and during extensive coal mining. It is the largest ongoing project at Cottbus Tech. The size of the databases to be used in an integrated manner is estimated by tens of TB. The databases represent the industrial, mining, geological, hydrological, biological, chemical and (fertile) soil information of the area. They are used for simulation of different development scenarios. Re-engineering existing databases is a part of this project. The environmental system integrates existing soil, geographic, geologic and hydrographical DBMS. Sometimes, the documentation of the systems is missing. The user profiles of developers of these databases are diverse. Users of RADD are all kinds of environmental engineers, chemist and geologists. Most of them do not have a database background.
- The Campus Information System will replace the management information system. It includes library, mail and other services on a www basis. RADD is used for the development of databases and workflow management.

Further, a number of smaller student projects uses RADD as well.

A demo of RADD can be found in a public telnet directory of our institutes. RADD will be demonstrated during the German computer exhibition CeBit 95.

Generating Design Strategies, User Support and Consistent Database Design. A typical application of RADD would be the following. After modeling of users, project groups and application areas the system supports mixed, modular design of a complex application by a team. The natural language interface is used for the development and refinement of a skeleton of the application which is the basis for modular design and for the distribution of design tasks among the team members. Using their own design strategies the team members model their part of the application in a toggle mode (consistent structural design, semantics acquisition, design of operations and transactions, and evaluation of operational bottlenecks). Since the graph grammar supports only step-by-step transformations misconceptions can be detected early. Checkpoints are used to enforce completion of design steps before other design steps can be initiated. At the end of the design, the transformation of the complete design into the logical and physical language of the chosen implementation platform is performed.

8 Conclusion

The workbench RADD currently under development is intended to become a third generation design system. Convenient design is supported by an advanced and powerful user interface. RADD allows the specification of structure, semantics and behaviour in consistent manner. The database designer can use different design strategies and is supported even if the chosen strategy is to be changed. Since users prefer expressing their application on the basis of natural languages the design system RADD is able to extract structural, semantical and operational specification of an application from sentences stated in natural languages. The natural language interface provides an efficient support for this facility. Another important advantage of the workbench is that the database designer gets estimations on operational behaviour during conceptual database design and is supported during optimization of conceptual schemes. The optimizer computes operational bottlenecks in the design and proposes partial changes in the design.

Future work will concentrate on repository support and complete systems design. Further RADD will support object-oriented DBMS and open integrated systems. In parallel we develop an approach for reusing database designs and for integrating existing designs into other applications.

References

[ABDT95] M.Albrecht, E.Buchholz, A. Düsterhöft, B.Thalheim: An Informal and Efficient Approach for Obtaining Semantic Constraints using Sample Data and Natural Language. Workshop "Semantics in Databases", 1 - 11, Prague, 1995.

[AlT92] M.Altus, B.Thalheim. Design by Units and its Graphical Implementation. In: Kurzfassungen des 4. GI-Workshops "Grundlagen von Datenbanken", Technical Report ECRC-92-13, Barsinghausen, 1992.

[Alt94] M.Altus. A User-Centered Database Design Environment. In: The Next Genaration of Case Tools, Proceedings of the Fifth Workshop on NGCT, Utrecht, The Netherlands. 1994.

[BCN92] C. Batini, S. Ceri, and S. Navathe, Conceptual database design, An entity-relationship approach. Benjamin Cummings, Redwood, 1992.

[BDT94] Edith Buchholz, Antje Düsterhöft, Bernhard Thalheim, Exploiting Knowledge Gained from Natural Language for EER Database Design. Technical Report I - 10 - 1994, Computer Science Institute, Cottbus Technical University, 1994.

[BOT90] P. Bachmann, W. Oberschelp, B. Thalheim, and G. Vossen. The design of RAD: Towards an interactive toolbox for database design. RWTH Aachen, Fachgruppe Informatik, Aachener Informatik-Berichte, 90-28, 1990.

[CoG93] P. Corrigan and M. Gurry, ORACLE Performance Performance. O'Reilly & Associates, Inc., 1993.

[FlH89] C.C. Fleming and B. von Halle, Handbook of relational database design. Addison-Wesley, Reading, 1989.

[FuN86] A.L. Furtado and E.J. Neuhold, Formal techniques for database design. Springer, Heidelberg, 1986.

[Kok90] A.J.Kok. User Modelling for Data Retrieval Applications. Vrije Universiteit Amsterdam, Faculteit Wiskunde en Informatica, 1990.

[KoS91] H.F. Korth and A. Silberschatz, Database System Concepts. McGraw-Hill, 1991.

[Leo92] M. Leonard, Database design theory. Macmillan, Houndsmills, 1992.

[MaR92] Heikki Mannila, Kari-Jouko Räihä, The Design of Relational Databases. Addison-Wesley, 1992.

[Ris88] N. Rishe, Database Design Fundamentals. Prentice-Hall, Englewood-Cliffs, 1988.

[RoR89] A. Rosenthal and D. Reiner, Database design tools: Combining theory, guesswork, and user interaction. Proc. 8th ER-Conference, 1989

[RoS87] L.A. Rowe and M.R. Stonebreaker. The POSTGRES Data Model. In Proceedings of the Thirteenth International Conference on Very Large Data Bases, 83 – 96, Brighton, UK, September 1987.

[ScT93] K.-D. Schewe and B. Thalheim, Fundamental Concepts of Object Oriented Concepts. Acta Cybernetica, 11, 4, 1993, 49 – 81.

[ScT94] K.D. Schewe and B. Thalheim, Achieving Consistence in Active Databases. Proc. Ride-ADS, 1994

[Sha92] D.E. Shasha, Database Tuning – A Principle Approach. Prentice Hall, 1992.

[SiM 81] A.M. Silva, M.A. Melkanoff, A method for helping discover the dependencies of a relation, In Advance in Database Theory, eds H. Gallaire, J. Hinker, J.-M. Nicolas, Plenum Publ. 1981, S 115-133

[SST94] K.-D. Schewe, D. Stemple and B. Thalheim, Higher-level genericity in object-oriented databases. Proc. COMAD (eds. S. Chakravarthy and P. Sadanandan), Bangalore, 1994

[StG 88] Veda C. Storey, Robert C. Goldstein, Methodology for Creating User Views in Database Design, ACM Transactions on Database Systems, Sept. 1988, pp 305-338

[StS90] D. Stemple and T. Sheard, Construction and calculus of types for database systems. Advances in Database Programming Languages (eds. F. Bancilhon, P. Buneman), Addison-Wesley, 3 - 22, 1990.

[StS91] D. Stemple and T. Sheard, A recursive base for database programming primitives. Next Generation Information System Technology (eds. J.W. Schmidt, A.A. Stognij), LNCS 504, 311 - 332, 1991.

[StT94] M. Steeg and B. Thalheim. Detecting Bottlenecks and Computing better Operational Behavior on Conceptual Data Schemes, October 1994, submitted.

[Su85] S.S. Su, Processing-Requirement Modeling and Its Application in Logical Database Design. In Principles of Database Design (ed. S.B. Yao), 1: Logical Organization, 151 -173, 1985.

[TAA94] B.Thalheim, M.Albrecht, M.Altus, E.Buchholz, A.Düsterhöft, K.-D.Schewe. The Intelligent Toolbox for Database Design RAD (in German). GI-Tagung, Kassel, Datenbankrundbrief, Ausgabe 13, Mai 1994, p.28-30.

[Tha92] B. Thalheim, The database design system $(DB)^2$. Database - 92. Proc. Third Australian Database Conference, Research and Practical Issues in Databases, (eds. B. Srinivasan, J. Zeleznikow), World Scientific, 279–292, 1992.

[Tha94] B.Thalheim. Database Design Strategies. Technical Report I - 02 - 94, Computer Science Institute, Cottbus Technical University, 1994.

[Ull82] J. D. Ullman Principals of Database Systems. Computer Science Press, Rockville, MD, 1982.

[Wie87] G. Wiederhold, File Organization for Database Design. McGraw-Hill, 1987.

[Yao85] S.B. Yao (ed.) Principles of database design, Volume I: Logical organizations. Prentice-Hall, 1985.

A Psychological Study on the Use of Relationship Concept -- Some Preliminary Findings

Keng Siau, Yair Wand, Izak Benbasat

Faculty of Commerce and Business Administration
University of British Columbia
2053 Main Mall, Vancouver BC
Canada V6T 1Z2

Abstract. Conceptual models are central to information systems analysis and design. One of the main constructs in information modelling is the concept of relationship which is popularized by the entity-relationship model. Despite the prominence of relationship concept in information modelling for the last two decades, little or no empirical research has been conducted to understand its usage by users. Several recent studies found that the relationship concept is problematic in information modelling, particularly the degree and connectivity (i.e., structural constraints) of the relationship. In our research, we investigate the importance of relationship concept for information modelling through a series of psychological experiments. This paper will present one of the studies that was conducted to investigate the use of relationship concept by expert users.

1   Introduction

Conceptual models can be considered as the cornerstone of information systems analysis and design. Not only do conceptual models provide the abstraction required for thinking about data-intensive applications [30], they also provide a formal basis for tools and techniques used in developing and using information systems [25]. In addition, conceptual models facilitate the communication between designers and end users [24] by providing them with a conceptual representation of the enterprise that does not include many of the details of how the data is physically stored.

One of the most popular and prominent conceptual models is the entity-relationship (ER) model introduced by Chen [8]. The ER model differs from the earlier models in that it adopts the view that the real world consists of entities and relationships, and that it makes a clear distinction between them. Brodie [5] states that "*the popularity of the ER model for high level database design is due to its economy of concepts and the widespread belief in entities and relationships as natural modelling concepts.*" Chen [8] claims that the incorporation of relationships among entities makes the ER model easier to use than previously proposed models. The results of several empirical studies [1, 2, 7, 10, 18, 19, 27] generally indicate that ER model, compared to earlier models, is easier to understand by end users and that designers and end-users perform better when using the ER model.

During the last few years, the object-oriented (OO) approach has become increasingly important and popular; and it undoubtedly will be (if it is not already) the new paradigm in information modelling. Kim [21] defines the core OO modelling concepts as consisting of object, object identifier, attributes, methods, encapsulation, message passing, class, class hierarchy, and inheritance. One of the main distinctions between OO and ER models, as noted by some researchers [11, 17], is that the abstraction of association (represented by relationship in ER models) is not directly supported in OO models but is instead achieved indirectly by allowing interobject references. Graham [17] indicates that *"(one) problem (with OO models) is the difficulty of modelling relationship types in an object-oriented database."* Elmasri and Navathe [11] conclude that *"this is an inherent weakness of the OO approach and is due to the fact that this approach treats each object as a self-contained unit of information."* Kim [21] also mentions that *"the core (OO) model, though powerful, simply does not capture some of the semantic-integrity constraints and semantic relationships that are important to many types of application."*

Even though the relationship concept is downplayed or ignored by some of the earlier OO models, it has resurfaced in some of the recently proposed OO models [4, 6, 13, 17, 20, 23, 26] -- sometimes under different names such as link or association. The reason is nicely summarized by Booch [4] -- *"an object by itself is intensely uninteresting. Objects contribute to the behavior of a system by collaborating with one another."* Similarly, Embley *et al.* [13] state that *"objects... are often meaningless unless we understand some relationship among them."* This leads to their proposal of object-relationship model. The OO models by Champeaux *et al.* [6] and Rumbaugh *et al.* [26] even include the notion of object relationships which is almost identical to the one proposed by Chen [8]. Martin and Odell [22] also introduce the concept of object-relationship diagram.

The revival of relationship concept in information modelling is important. A good conceptual model should allow one to build a description of the subject matter that is consistent to the way humans conceptualize the same subject matter [24]. If relationship is one of the main concepts that humans use to view the world, then the notion of relationship should exist in a conceptual model.

1.1 Problems with Relationships

Although the relationship concept has been utilized heavily in information modelling, it is also one of the most problematic concepts. Goldstein and Storey [16] found that users of an automated database design tool had difficulty distinguishing between relationships and attributes. Elmasri and Navathe [11] mention that *"it is sometimes convenient to think of a relationship type in terms of attributes."* Similarly, Codd [9] states that *"one person's entity is another person's relationship."* A recent empirical study by Batra *et al.* [2], which compares the relational and ER representations, discovered that *"the most notable error found in the solutions prepared by the subjects was the incorrect representation of connectivity of relationships."*

The main reason for this unfortunate state is the lack of understanding on the use of relationship concept by users. Although many researchers have accepted, or once accepted, that relationship is natural in modelling the real world [8, 11, 29], this belief is based mainly on common sense and intuition rather than systematic and empirical evaluation. However, our common sense can be false and radically misleading at times. As researchers, we need to approach the problem scientifically and provide, at least, an explanation of why certain concepts are important or why not. Common sense can never serve as a substitute for empirical research [15]. Our research, therefore, will attempt to fill this gap by empirically investigating the usage of relationship concept through a series of psychological experiments. This paper presents one of the studies that was conducted to understand the use of relationship concept by expert users.

2   Mandatory versus Optional Relationship

A structural constraint (sometimes known as cardinality constraint) can be considered as a constraint on the number of objects that must participate in a mapping. The structural constraint is usually specified using a pair of integer numbers (min, max). The minimum number indicates the least number of objects to which a given object must map. The maximum number indicates the greatest number of objects to which a given object must map. This gives rise to two types of relationship -- optional and mandatory.

For example, consider the following two diagrams. The first diagram indicates that a person entity can work for zero, one, or many employers. The second diagram, on the other hand, depicts that an employee must work for at least one employer.

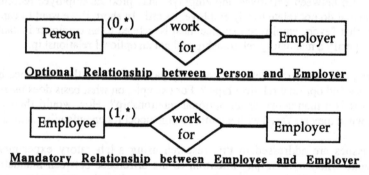

Optional Relationship between Person and Employer

Mandatory Relationship between Employee and Employer

The optional relationship, thus, corresponds to the structural constraint (0, *), which indicates that there may be zero, one or many interactions. The mandatory relationship, on the other hand, corresponds to the structural constraints $(x, *)$, $x \geq 1$, which indicates that there must be at least one interaction.

2.1   Importance of Distinction Between Mandatory and Optional Relationship

The proper use of mandatory and optional relationships in information modelling is important as it ensures that the semantics of the domain is correctly captured. Although the distinction between mandatory and optional relationships is rather straight-forward and clear-cut, it is not difficult to discover that mandatory relationship is actually a "subset" of optional relationship. Rather than specifying a relationship as (1, *) (i.e., a mandatory relationship), the designers or users could easily specify it as (0, *). Though the second specification is "not wrong", it is not "correct" either. By changing the minimum participation from 1 to 0 (i.e., mandatory to optional), the underlying semantics of the relationship is changed. For example, by changing the minimum cardinality from 1 to 0 in the second diagram (as shown below), we have changed the meaning of the relationship. In this case, the structural constraint indicates that an employee need not work for any employer which is literally incorrect because a person is not an employee unless s/he works for an employer. Thus, there is a contradiction between the structural constraint and the underlying semantics in the diagram.

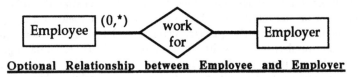

Optional Relationship between Employee and Employer

The incorrect use of structural constraint also directly affects the accuracy and integrity of the database. A mandatory relationship indicates that the existence of an entity depends on its being related to another entity via the relationship type. The use of an optional relationship when a mandatory relationship is warranted will result in an inconsistent database state. For example, the use of optional instead of mandatory relationship between employee and employer may produce employee records in the database that do not relate to any employer record. In short, if we want to capture the concept that "every employee instance must be related to an employer instance," we have to specify a mandatory relationship and not an optional relationship.

However, one wonders whether users really pay attention to the difference between mandatory and optional relationships ? For example, on what basis does users decide whether it is a mandatory or an optional relationship? How would their decision change when they are faced with an information model for an unfamiliar domain ?

These issues are addressed in this research using a laboratory experiment. To investigate whether users pay attention to the difference between mandatory and optional relationships, we asked the subjects to select the appropriate structural constraints (i.e., mandatory or optional) for a set of ER diagrams. To analyze how they will react when given models from unfamiliar domains, we provided them with two types of diagrams -- one type from familiar domains and the other from unfamiliar domains. Their selection of structural constraints for these two types of domains will also provide us some cues on their selection procedures.

We chose laboratory experiment in this study because of its superiority in controlling extraneous variables [3]. Another important factor is the ability to manipulate the independent variable [14]. Although field study will provide us with a more realistic background, it is very difficult, if not impossible, for us to manipulate the independent variable in this experiment using field study. The following section discusses the experimental design.

3 Experiment Design

3.1 Independent Variables

The independent variable for this study is domain characteristics which consists of two levels -- familiar group and unfamiliar group. The familiar group consists of questions that are taken from common real-life examples that are well-understood by the subjects in our study -- such as university course selection and enrollment. For unfamiliar group, we used very specific concepts from areas such as neurocognition and psychophysics, which are alien to this group of subjects. With these unfamiliar cases, the subjects have to guess the structural constraints for the ER diagrams. For example, the first diagram below is from a familiar domain whereas the second is from an unfamiliar domain.

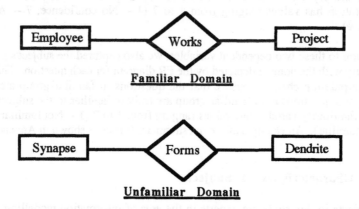

All the subjects are presented with the same set of questions from both familiar and unfamiliar domains. This repeated measure design is chosen so that each subject can act as his/her own control. The entire set of questions (i.e., familiar and unfamiliar groups) is randomly ordered in each questionnaire. In other words, every questionnaire is unique in order. This ensures that order effect is controlled by randomization. All the diagrams are presented without structural constraints.

The specific context of the diagrams are not given to the subjects because we wanted to analyze how the subjects will response with incomplete information. This is consistent with real-world scenarios as designers typically do not have a very detailed understanding of the application environment. Most of the time, designers rely on common sense and experience to help them construct and understand information models. Giving the subjects full knowledge of the contexts would also defeat the purpose of the study as the subjects would rely on the case descriptions rather than the information models to decide on the answers. Moreover, diagrams with unfamiliar domains would have become familiar with detailed descriptions.

3.2   Dependent Variables

The dependent variables in this study are the choice of interpretation (i.e., mandatory or optional relationship), and the confidence level of the interpretation. The choice of interpretation is a multiple-choice question. Subjects are presented with a choice of Must or May to describe the relationship. Must corresponds to mandatory relationship whereas May corresponds to optional relationship. We decided to use Must and May instead of (1, *) and (0,*) because the former is more intuitive and understandable. This ease of understanding is important because we intend to replicate this study using naive subjects.

To counter order bias, half of the questions present Must as the first choice and the other half list May as the first choice. This is to control for order effect in case the subjects simply circle the first choice for each question. The confidence of interpretation has values ranging from 1 to 7 (1 -- No confidence, 7 -- Absolute confidence).

In addition to these two dependent variables, we also captured the subject's perceived familiarity with the domain depicted by the ER diagram for each question. This serves as a manipulation check to ensure that the questions in familiar group are indeed familiar and questions in unfamiliar group are truly unfamiliar to the subjects. This domain familiarity variable has values ranging from 1 to 7 (1 -- Not familiar at all, 7 -- Very familiar). An example of the questionnaire format is shown in Appendix A.

3.3   Characteristics of Subjects

The subjects in this study are experts in the area of information modelling. In this paper, we will define experts as users who have substantial training and experience in data modelling. This group of subjects consists of MIS graduate students and professors from a well-known west coast university in North America. The experiment was conducted at the beginning of one of the weekly MIS workshops.

A demographic information sheet was completed by each subject prior to the experiment. A total of 24 subjects participated in this experiment. The subjects' expertise with the entity-relationship model and some of its concepts were also captured in the demographic information sheet and summarized in the table below. The expertise is measured using a scale of 1 to 5 (1 -- Totally unfamiliar, 5 -- Very familiar).

Variable	Mean	Std. Dev.
ER Model	4.17	0.92
Entity	4.33	0.70
Relationship	4.21	0.72
Cardinality	3.67	1.31

As can be seen from the table, the subjects were comfortable with the ER model and its constructs (the average is 4 on a 5-point scale). Cardinality, as expected, has the lowest score and is the only one with a mean score of less than 4. This is consistent with the findings in other studies (e.g., the study by Batra *et al.* [2] which found that cardinality is one of the most difficult concepts to master).

3.4   Test Characteristics

Test characteristics refer to the method employed for data collection. A paper and pencil test was used in this study. For the choice of structural constraint, two choices were provided to the subjects -- Must or May (i.e., mandatory or optional). An open-ended interpretation test was not chosen because of the difficulties involved in interpreting the subjects' answers. A total of 12 questions consisting of 6 familiar and 6 unfamiliar domains were given to each subject. An instruction set that explains the basic modelling concepts in ER model (e.g., entity, relationship, structural constraints) and gives examples of different structural constraints was attached to the front of the questionnaire. No training or discussion was provided as the instruction set was designed to be self-contained and self-explanatory. Extra care was taken to ensure that the instruction set was not biased. The subjects could refer to the instruction set as and when necessary.

3.5   Hypotheses

The null hypotheses for the study is listed below.

Hypothesis H1:   There is no difference in the choice of interpretation between familiar and unfamiliar groups.

Hypothesis H2:   There is no difference in the confidence of interpretation between familiar and unfamiliar groups.

The alternative hypotheses to the null hypotheses are that the two groups will be different. A two-tailed test is used since we do not have strong theoretical prediction about the outcomes.

4   Experimental Results

The number of subjects for each group and the number of observations are summarized below. The number of observations for the unfamiliar group is less than 144 (i.e., 24 subjects X 6 questions) because some unfamiliar questions were left blank by the subjects.

Groups	No. of Subjects	No. of Questions Per Subject	No. of Observations
Familiar	24	6	144
Unfamiliar	24	6	131

The first hypothesis regarding the choice of structural constraints for the two groups is analyzed using the nonparametric x^2 test. The results show x^2 (1,275) = 0.018 with p < 0.893. Thus, the null hypothesis is not rejected which means that there is no significant difference between the choices for the two groups. The following table summarizes the result of x^2 test.

Frequency	Must Choice	May Choice	Total
Familiar Group	15	129	144
Unfamiliar Group	13	118	131
Total	28	247	275

<u>Table of Group By Choice of Interpretation</u>

As can be seen, the number of May is overwhelmingly greater than the number of Must for both groups. There is almost no difference between the two groups in the choice of structural constraints. Indeed, the percentage difference between the two groups is less than 1% for both choices, as shown in the diagram below.

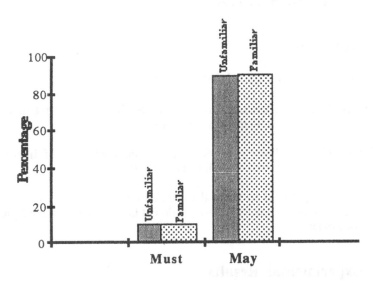

The hypothesis regarding confidence level between the two groups is analyzed using General Linear Models. The results show that the confidence level of the familiar group is significantly higher than that of the unfamiliar group (p < 0.0001). Similarly, the perceived domain familiarity level for familiar group is significantly higher than that of the unfamiliar group (p < 0.0001).

Measure	DF	SS	MS	F	Pr > F
Confidence Level	1	346.90	346.90	148.06	0.0001
Domain Familiarity	1	750.75	750.75	340.00	0.0001

The means and standard deviations for the confidence level and perceived domain familiarity are depicted below. The average confidence level for the familiar group is almost twice that of unfamiliar group. As for domain familiarity, the score for familiar group is more than twice the score for unfamiliar group. This is important as it shows that the subjects perceived a great difference between the familiar and unfamiliar groups. In other words, the results of perceived domain familiarity show that the manipulation of familiarity and unfamiliarity domains has been very successful.

	Confidence Level Mean (Std. Dev.)	Domain Familiarity Mean (Std. Dev.)
Familiar Group	4.86 (2.10)	5.68 (1.49)
Unfamiliar Group	2.53 (1.88)	2.26 (1.71)

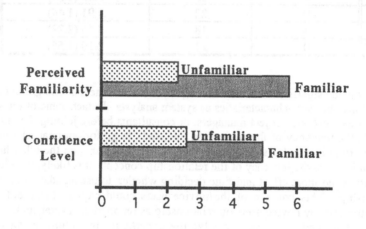

5   Discussion of Experimental Results

The aim of this experimental study is to investigate how the mandatory and optional relationships will be used by experts. The results show an overwhelming number of May versus Must, even for unfamiliar group. The popularity of May over Must is evident in all the questions (as shown below).

We believe the main reason for the popularity of May is that these subjects realize that May can be considered a 'superset' (as discussed in section 2.1). The use of Must precludes May whereas the reverse is not necessarily true. The choice of Must means that a relationship must exist between the two entities. However, May does not mean that the relationship does not exist. It simply means that the relationship can either exist or not exist. Hence, when faced with uncertainty, it is highly likely that the subjects simply chose the optional relationship -- just to be on the safe side.

	Familiar	Group	
	No. of Must Choices	No. of May Choices	Confidence Level Mean (Std. Dev.)
Q1	1	23	4.71 (1.97)
Q2	2	22	4.29 (2.26)
Q3	6	18	5.00 (2.15)
Q4	2	22	4.25 (1.94)
Q5	4	20	5.42 (2.02)
Q6	0	24	5.50 (2.15)
	Unfamiliar	Group	
Q7	1	21	3.14 (1.91)
Q8	4	18	2.05 (1.68)
Q9	4	18	2.55 (1.99)
Q10	0	22	1.91 (1.44)
Q11	4	18	3.45 (2.22)
Q12	0	21	2.10 (1.55)

So, what is the significance of this finding? We can assume that this group of expert subjects has the same characteristics as system analysts. In fact, some of the subjects were system analysts, project managers, or consultants before joining the university. As such, the tendency of the subjects in this study to go for optional relationship is expected to hold true for system analysts as well. End users, on the other hand, are not familiar with the intricacy of the relationship concept. It is likely, therefore, that they will spend more effort and time deciding whether to use mandatory or optional relationship. This concern of the novice users could explain the problems and difficulties face by novice users on relationship as reported in several studies [2, 16]. On the other hand, the experts resolve the uncertainty by simply using optional relationships. This difference in attitude might be a potential communication problem or conflict between end users and designers.

Another observation is that the highest confidence level (i.e., 3.45 for Q11) in unfamiliar group is still lower than the lowest confidence level in familiar group (i.e., 4.25 for Q4). It appears that the perceived familiarity of the domain gives the subjects higher confidence in their results. One question that is of particular interest is Q11. For this particular question, the entities are Floor and Button, and the relationship connecting them is Associates. This is the only question in the unfamiliar group that uses common words such as Floor and Button, though the subjects might not know the domain is lift operation. The rest of the questions in that group uses terminology from neurocognition and psychophysics that are unfamiliar to the subjects. Although this question (i.e., Q11) has a substantially lower confidence level than those questions in the familiar group, it has the highest confidence level (3.45) in its group. It thus appears that the use of common words also has a positive effect on the confidence of the subjects.

6 Conclusion and Future Research

The aim of this research is to perform an in-depth analysis of the relationship concept through a series of experiments. This paper describes one of the studies conducted to investigate the use of mandatory and optional relationships by expert users. The results of the study indicate a predominant use of optional over mandatory relationships by experts subjects, even for domains that are totally unfamiliar to them. This indicates that expert users generally go for optional relationships when faced with uncertainty (irrespective of familiar or unfamiliar domain). The results also show that familiar domains cause subjects to feel more confident (more accurately -- overconfident) in their answers.

Another of our studies extends this study by deliberately creating a conflict between the information depicted by the structural constraints and the underlying semantics. The aim of the study is to investigate whether the subjects will focus on the structural constraints or the underlying semantics of the ER diagrams. The results show that expert subjects exhibit *semantic negligence* and *attentional bias*. In other words, expert subjects tend to focus on the information represented by the structural constraints and ignore the underlying semantics depicted by the ER diagrams [28].

Our subsequent studies will investigate the difference between experts and novices on the use of relationship concept. This will allow us to gain a better understanding of the communication problem between end users and designers. As for the contribution, this research is likely to be the first that rigorously analyze a modelling construct using psychological experiments. Thus, this research promises to make significant contribution to information systems modelling. In addition, the methodology and technique used in this research can serve as a framework for future research endeavor in this area.

Acknowledgments. The authors would like to thank the anonymous reviewers for their insightful and valuable comments. This research was supported in part by the Natural Sciences and Engineering, and Humanities and Social Sciences Research Councils of Canada.

References

1. Batra, D. and Srinivasan, A., A Review and Analysis of the Usability of Data Management Environments, International Journal of Man-Machine Studies, 36, 1992, pp. 395-417.

2. Batra. D., Hoffer J.A., and Bostrom, R.P., Comparing Representations with Relational and EER Models, Communication of ACM, Vol. 33, No. 2, February 1990, pp. 126-139.

3. Benbasat, I., Laboratory Experiments in Information Systems Studies with a Focus on Individuals: A Critical Appraisal, in: The Information Systems Research Challenge: Experimental Research Methods (Volume 2), Benbasat, I. (Ed.), Harvard Business School, 1989.

4. Booch, G., Object Oriented Design with Applications, The Benjamin/Cummings Publishing Company, 1991.

5. Brodie, M.L., On the Development of Data Models, in : On Conceptual Modelling, Brodie, M.L., Mylopoulos, J. and Schmidt, J.W. (eds.), Springer-Verlag, 1984.

6. Champeaux, D.D., Lea D., Faure, P., Object-Oriented System Development, Addison-Wesley Publishing Company, 1993.

7. Chan, H.C., Wei, K.K. and Siau, K.L., User-Database Interface: The Effect of Abstraction Levels on Query Performance, Management Information Systems Quarterly (MISQ), Vol. 17, No. 4, December 1993, pp. 441-464.

8. Chen, P.P., The Entity-Relationship Model: Toward a Unified View of Data, ACM Transactions on Database Systems Vol. 1, No. 1, 1976, pp. 166-192.

9. Codd, E.F., The Relational Model for Database Management : Version 2, Addison-Wesley, 1990.

10. Davis, J.S., Experimental Investigation of the Utility of Data Structure and ER Diagrams in Database Query, International Journal of Man-Machine Studies, 1990, 32, pp. 449-459.

11. Elmasri, R. and Navathe, S.B., Fundamentals of Database Systems, Addison Wesley, 1989.

12. Elmasri, R., Hevner, A. and Weeldreyer, J., The Category Concept: An Extension to the Entity-Relationship Model, Data Knowledge Engineering, Vol. 1, No. 1, 1985, pp. 75-116.

13. Embley, D.W., Kurtz, and Woodfield, S.N., Object-Oriented System Analysis -- A Model-Driven Approach, Yourdon Press, Englewood Cliffs, New Jersey, 1992.

14. Emory, C.W., and Cooper, D.R., Business Research Methods, Fourth Edition, Irwin, 1991.

15. Flanagan, M., and Dipboye, R., Research Settings in Industrial and Organizational Psychology: Facts, Fallacies and The Future, Personnel Psychology, 34, 1981, pp. 37-47.

16. Goldstein, R.C. and Storey, V., Some Findings on the Intuitiveness of Entity-Relationship Constructs, Entity-Relationship Approach to Database Design and Querying, Lochovsky F H (ed.), 1989, pp. 9-23.

17. Graham, I., Object Oriented Methods, Addison-Wesley, 1991.

18. Jarvenpaa, S.L., and Machesky, J.J., Data Analysis and Learning: An Experimental Study of Data Modeling Tools, International Journal of Man-Machine Studies, 1989, 31, pp. 367-391.

19. Jih, K. W.J., Bradbard, D.A., Snyder, C.A., and Thompson G.A., The Effects of Relational and Entity-Relationship Data Models on Query Performance of End Users, International Journal of Man-Machine Studies, Vol. 31, 1989, pp. 257-267.

20. Khoshafian, S. Object-Oriented Databases, John Wiley & Sons, 1993.

21. Kim, Won, Introduction to Object-Oriented Databases, The MIT Press, 1990.

22. Martin , J., and Odell, J.J., Object-Oriented Analysis and Design, Prentice Hall, 1992.

23. McGregor J.D., and Sykes, D.A., Object-Oriented Software Development: Engineering Software for Reuse, Van Nostrand Reinhold, 1992.

24. Mylopoulos, J., Conceptual Modeling and Telos, In: Conceptual Modeling, Databases and CASE, John Wiley & Sons, New York, 1992.

25. Rolland, C., and Cauvet, C., Trends and Perspectives in Conceptual Modeling, In: Conceptual Modeling, Databases, and CASE, John Wiley & Sons, New York, 1992.

26. Rumbaugh, J., Blaha, M., Premerlani, W., Eddy, F., and Lorensen, W., Object-Oriented Modeling and Design, Prentice Hall, Englewood Cliffs, NJ, 1991.

27. Siau, K.L., Chan, H.C. and Wei, K.K., User-Database Interaction : Experimental Comparisons of Conceptual and Logical Abstraction Levels, working paper, National University of Singapore, 1993.

28. Siau, K.L., Wand, Y., and Benbasat, I., The Use of Relationship Concept in Information Modelling, University of British Columbia, Working paper, 1995.

29. Teorey, T.J., Database Modeling and Design -- The Entity-Relationship Approach, Morgan Kaufmann Publishers, 1990.

30. Willumsen, G., Conceptual Modeling in IS Engineering, In: Executable Conceptual Models in Information Systems Engineering, Trondheim, Nov. 1993, pp. 11-21.

Appendix A

Circle one of the following two options that more correctly reflects the participation of the Employee entity type in the Assigns relationship type:

1.   must assign

2.   may assign

What is the confidence level of your above choice?

       1   2   3   4   5   6   7
No confidence   Absolute confidence

What is your familiarity with the domain depicted in the diagram?

       1   2   3   4   5   6   7
Not familiar at all   Very familiar

Alignment of Software Quality and Service Quality

Priit Parmakson

Institute of Informatics
Tallinn Technical University, Estonia

Abstract. Software is today an integral or even main component of various service systems. Therefore it is of interest to analyze how software quality is related to service quality. Due to somewhat different nature of services and software, but also due to historical reasons, software quality models and service quality models differ a lot at first look. In an example of widespread quality models in service management and software areas, it will be shown that substantial level of alignment can be reached between these models. However, these models use different languages and also contain quality attributes which can not be translated easily into language of other model. That gives reason for further elaboration of both quality models.

1 Introduction

Software is often a component (and frequently a main one) in a service system, though it is not common to view usage of software as service. When looking at existing models of software quality and service quality, we notice that these models differ remarkably. We will explore if a common ground can be found between quality models developed in two completely different research areas - software engineering and service management.

It would be good if software engineers could relate quality concepts they know well from software engineering to service aspects of their work. Indeed, the work of information system (IS) professionals is even more seen as service. At the same time, feedback from industry indicates that IS graduates are often weak in customer service skills. Insufficient service orientation of IS departments has been also frequently discussed (see, for example [21, 28]). Modern practice of IS development requires more experts who will be proficient in both developing a service (business) concept and building an information system.

2 Concept of Service

Meaning of the word 'service' has enlarged in recent times. Traditionally the service is understood as a process between human server(s) and human customer(s), where customer requires some transformation to be done by server. Though machines and software can be used as tools in traditional service, human-human interaction is dominant in this definition. A broader meaning of service does not assume that server is human. Instead, server can be a machine or software system (e.g. ATMs, electronic shopping systems, Internet services). According to this meaning, use of software is also use of service. Still broader meaning of the word `service' does not even assume that customer is human. Instead, customer can also be a machine or technical system. That meaning is used in several ways in IS domain. For example, a telecommunications network provides services to applications, server offers services to client applications (client-server approach), an object has services (in object-oriented approach).

Due to some couple of dozen different sub-meanings of the word 'service', any widely applicable definition of service would have unavoidably an abstract nature. Some of the general definitions have been provided by Berry [1]: "Service is a deed, a performance, or an effort which is rendered by one party for another"; and Grön-roos (cited in [12]): "A service is an activity or series of activities of more or less intangible nature that normally, but not necessarily, take place in interactions between the customer and the service employees and/or physical resources or goods and/or systems of the service provider, which are provided as solutions to customer problems."

3 Software Systems are also Service Systems

Pure service systems in a traditional sense (with dominating human-human communication) are becoming less common. The difference between manufacturing systems and service systems is also eroding. The product is more than a good, it is also the service package which delivers and maintains that good for the customer. Service becomes an integral part of the product. Pure service system, as well as pure information systems are abstractions - there are flows of material, information and humans in almost any process.

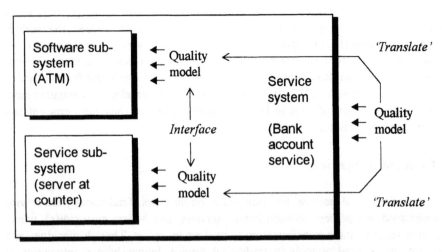

Fig 1. Aligning and interfacing quality models

Software is commonly an element in a larger (computer-based) system, which includes also hardware, people, documentation, machines, procedures etc. (Fig. 1). The larger system can be a part of still larger system. Software requirements derive from system requirements. Purpose of quality of the software is to ensure quality of the encompassing service system. It is often said that system requirements must be translated (mapped) to requirements to system components (among these, to software). Quality Function Deployment is one of the methods which can be used to do this translation. Ideally, the business model of the company and the requirements model for the IS must be seamless [17]. However, if the language used to describe requirements at business level (quality of service system) and language used to describe requirements at system-component level (for example, quality of software component) differ principally, then the translation may be complicated and error-prone. Therefore it is desirable to align languages (models) of quality used for service systems and software systems.

Frequently a traditional human-human service system and a software-dominated service system work in parallel. For example, a bank customer can invoke transactions at ATM or at counter (served by human). Again, if the models used to analyze quality of automated service and non-automated service are radically different, then interfacing the two systems may be complicated.

4 Structure of Quality Models

Both in service quality and software quality, no better representations than attribute-based have been devised for modeling quality. The general concept of quality is decomposed into number of quality attributes. Quality attributes are usually grouped into hierarchical structure, but more complex relationships between quality attributes have been used as well, mostly to represent synergy or conflict effects. Also, relative importance of attributes can be estimated.

Opinions differ about how to find appropriate quality attributes. Some researchers advocate a stable, general set of quality attributes while others emphasize tailoring the set of quality attributes to concrete situation. For example, the Critical Incident Technique [3] uses systematic elicitation of quality attributes hierarchy from a set of empirical service incident descriptions (both satisfactory and unsatisfactory incidents). Usefulness of the generic quality models is the underlying point here. Several authors tend to deny usefulness of generic service quality models, either explicitly or implicitly, by suggesting to elicitate customer requirements in each separate case. That means building the quality model from the scratch. According to this view, service systems are too different to get much help from a generic quality model. IEEE Standard for a Software Quality Metrics Methodology [14] also provides a list of quality attributes with reservation that the list is only an illustrative one. However, generic quality models could be useful to provide more elaborated frameworks than broad motivational guidelines of type `customer is a king` [15]. Certainly the customer research provides important data, but it can not be assumed that all significant quality attributes can be extracted on the basis of customer input only. Customer research can also be expensive and require experienced analysts.

5 Software Quality Models

Software quality can be defined as "the degree to which software possesses a desired combination of attributes" [14]. Several well-known software quality models (Boehm, McCall) consist of sets of quality attributes, which are structured into hierarchy. The model developed by ISO [16] uses three-level quality evaluation hierarchy: factors, criteria, metrics. On the highest level, the quality factors represent aggregate concepts. On the lowest level, the quality metrics can be given quantitative or qualitative values. Criteria are refinements of factors. The model proposed in IEEE standard [14] has six upper-level quality attributes (factors):

- Functionality
- Reliability (Does the system behave accurately all the time?)
- Usability (Is the system easy to learn and use?)
- Efficiency (The amount of resources required by the system to perform its function)
- Maintainability (Is it easy to find and fix an error in a system? Is is easy to enhance the system?)
- Portability (Is it easy to transfer the system from one environment to another?).

Though each of the software quality models proposed up to now has a somewhat different set of quality attributes, the differences are not large and the models follow well a common, established ideology.

6 Service Quality Models

Service quality has been a widely discussed concept. Four mainstream definitions of quality have been: quality as an excellence, value to customer, conformance to specifications, meeting and exceeding customer expectations [23]. Nevertheless, more extended and deeper definitions of quality have seen sought for recently: "Quality isn't something you lay on top of subjects and objects like tinsel on a Christmas tree" [22]. We will build our discussion on the following understanding of service quality (Fig. 2): *Service quality is a fit between service provider's process and customer's process, but also between other, related processes.*

This definition is in accord with several recently developed viewpoints to service quality:

- *Process view of the customer relationship* [27] - the relationship consists of interactions which may have different content, frequency, duration etc. Interactions between server and customer are analyzed from a long-term point of view. Both parties of the relationship are engaged in their own processes as well (the provider's process and the customer's process).
- *Extension of the concept of quality to cover all stakeholders of the firm.* Achieving customer satisfaction is an admirable goal, but a firm is also responsible to multiple sets of stakeholders (owners, personnel, customers, suppliers,

authorities etc), each of whose evaluates the firm on different criteria [10, 13, 18].

- *Partnership.* The claim "Customer is always right" is a too strong abstraction, because: (a) limitless adaptation to customer expectations drives costs (a satisfied customer is not inevitably a profitable customer); (b) customers may simply not know what is possible (R.Normann cited in [27]). Therefore, adaptation must occur from both service provider's and customer's side. Note that Figure 2 is symmetric. Indeed, customers may depend on service provider as well (for example, due to high switching costs). It makes sense to talk also about requirements to customer.

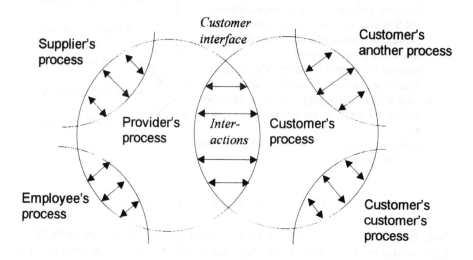

Fig 2. Processes involved in service

Direct consequences from the definition above are: (a) it is not enough to ask customer to state his needs - both customer and server processes must be understood and modelled at appropriate level of detail; (b) one must also look how provider's process and customer's process are fitted to other processes. Output from the service process is really only the input to customer's other processes.

Some of the most well-known generic service quality models are SERVQUAL [29] and Grönroos' model [8]. Based on empirical data, Zeithaml et al have identified ten general criteria most used by customers in judging service quality (Fig. 3). While in software quality domain the set of quality attributes is quite stable, service quality models vary considerably more. For example, Figure 3 depicts some relationships between SERVQUAL and a service quality model proposed by Gilmore and Carson [7].

SERVQUAL [29]   Gilmore and Carson [7]

- Tangibles (appearance of physical facilities,   • Physical facilities
  equipment, personnel and communication ma-
  terials)   • Choice/range of product
- Reliability (ability to perform the promised
  service dependably and accurately)   • Promotional materials
- Responsiveness (willingness to help customers
  and provide prompt service)   • Presentation of product
- Competence (possession of the required skills
  and knowledge to perform the service)   • Price/value for money
- Courtesy (politeness, respect, consideration,
  and friendliness of contact personnel)   • Information advice
- Credibility (trustworthiness, believability, hon-
  esty of the service provider)   • Proactive communication
- Security (freedom from danger, risk or doubt)
- Access (approachability and ease of contact)   • Willingness to help
- Communication (keeping customers informed
  in language they can understand and listening to   • Accessibility to customers
  them)
- Understanding the Customer (making the effort
  to know customers and their needs)

Fig 3. Two general service quality models

Note that the quality attributes in these general quality models are quite different from attributes used in software quality models. However, if the service system contains software then the software quality requirements must be derived from service quality requirements.

7 Aligning Software Quality Model with Service Quality Model

Next we try to relate service quality attributes to software quality attributes (Fig. 4). Quality attributes of the SERVQUAL model appear on the left, while the right column provides a list of software quality attributes, which is compiled on basis of the documents [14] and [16]. SERVQUAL is a representative service quality model - despite of some recent criticism, it has had most influence during the last decade. Note that only two quality attributes bear exactly the same names in both models (Reliability and Security). Five service quality attributes (Responsiveness, Credibility, Access, Communication, Understanding the Customer) can be partly translated into one or more software quality attributes. Both models contain also attributes for which there are no analogies in other model. Thus the alignment between two models is not complete.

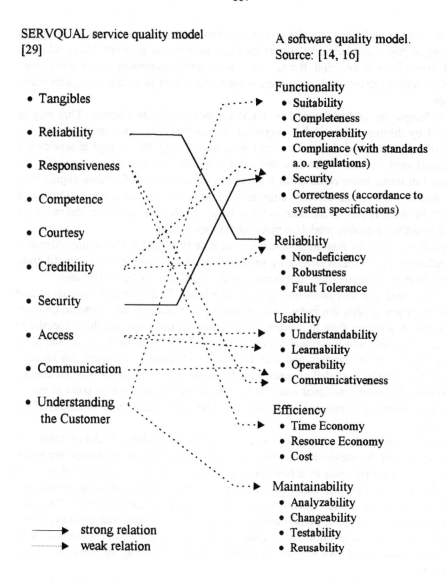

SERVQUAL service quality model [29]

A software quality model.
Source: [14, 16]

Functionality
• Tangibles
• Reliability
• Responsiveness
• Competence
• Courtesy
• Credibility
• Security
• Access
• Communication
• Understanding the Customer

• Suitability
• Completeness
• Interoperability
• Compliance (with standards a.o. regulations)
• Security
• Correctness (accordance to system specifications)

Reliability
• Non-deficiency
• Robustness
• Fault Tolerance

Usability
• Understandability
• Learnability
• Operability
• Communicativeness

Efficiency
• Time Economy
• Resource Economy
• Cost

Maintainability
• Analyzability
• Changeability
• Testability
• Reusability

⟶ strong relation
⋯▶ weak relation

Fig 4. Relations between attributes of service quality and software quality

8 Reasons for non-alignment

The most interesting observation from the comparison above is that in software quality models there are no analogies to Courtesy. In principle, Courtesy may be related to Security, Communicativeness and Cost (courtesy gives the customer a feeling of security and helps to make communication more open; also, customers are not willing to pay a psychological cost related due to arrogant servers). These relations look however quite artificial. Reason may lay in social dimension that is much more explicit and important in human-human interaction than in human-computer interaction.

The languages used in the models compared above are quite different. That may be caused by different historical backgrounds of the fields. Service management has traditionally dealt with human-human interaction, though the concept of service has enlarged continuously. Therefore the service quality attributes are frequently expressed in terms more common to human-human interaction. Software engineering has technical roots and service concepts have been only slowly gained influence in this field. As it is still uncommon to view usage of software as service, the language used in software quality models is more technology-related.

Another reason for non-alignment seems to hide in mixed use of quality attributes of different types in service quality models. The discussion here will benefit from distinction of functional/non-functional, 'what'/'how' and core/cue attributes.

Functional and non-functional quality attributes. Distinction of functional and non-functional quality attributes (and accordingly - requirements) seems to be more common in software than in services. Functional requirements are those specific to the system, while non-functional requirements are 'additional' in the sense that these are common for all systems and may be usually assumed. Non-functional requirements may also be regarded as constraints to the functional requirements. Of course, distinction between functional and non-functional criteria depends on point of view - non-functional requirements (e.g. security) can be dealt explicitly as functions of the system.

Courtesy seems to be a non-functional service quality attribute. Social dimension is present in any human-human interaction, and indirectly also in human-computer interaction. Courtesy may be a functional quality attribute if the customer is ready to pay for additional psycho-social benefits acquired due to higher than usual courtesy. Should a software service system show respect towards customer and how? Respect to user is not an issue in home-made small software programs, but certainly it is a problem in many large information systems. An intelligent software system must be able to be courteous. We suggest to consider adding Courtesy to software quality models.

'What' and 'how' quality attributes. It is a good practice in IS requirements engineering to separate 'what' and 'how' requirements. An analogous thinking is useful for quality attributes in general. Some attributes are part of the problem while other attributes are part of the solution. Differences in quality models may be explained partly by the fact that one model can include solution-oriented attributes while another model can emphasize underlying, basic attributes. SERVQUAL seems to contain three 'how' attributes: Tangibles, Competence and Understanding the Customer. Indeed, customers are rarely interested in tangibles and competence per se.

Core and cue attributes. Customers are judging service frequently on service cues ('little things' or supplemental services). That is because: (a) customers may assume that the core offering will be of high quality; (b) typically there is little variability in the core offerings; (c) core quality attributes of the service may be hard to judge [13]. Quality cues are what the customer observes (price, brand name, country of origin, store name), and core quality attributes are what the consumer wants. Often the true state of a quality attribute cannot be observed by the individual, but must be inferred through the cues [26]. SERVQUAL also seems to contain one cue attribute - Credibility. The core/cue distinction looks new to software quality.

9 Service management and software engineering: exchange of knowledge and methods

Manufacturing quality management seems to be more deeply developed than service quality management [5, 11]. Indeed, several quality tools and methods which have originated in manufacturing, have been recently applied or proposed to be applied to service processes (for example, application of robustness concept to service processes [25]; application of poka-yoke, or fail-safe methods in services [6]). As for opposite example, O'Hara and Frodey [10] transferred a model developed for evaluating service success to manufacturing. Similarly, we expect to see a transfer of methods and concepts from IS/software engineering field to services as well.

Concept of service has enlarged and complexity of service systems has grown. Despite that, public discussion about service quality relies largely on psychological and cultural points of view. Services can and should be analyzed from different points of view: cultural, psychological, economic, management, organization theory, information systems theory, social etc. Customer service can be viewed even as a performing art [30]. Service systems should be analyzed also both in macro-level (in context of business environment) and micro-level (single service transaction). Models and methods which pretend to comprehensive treatment of services should be therefore multi-disciplinary. Service management is seen as not yet a coherent research area [9]. Therefore it is natural that different disciplines impact the service management perspective. IS development methodologies which seek to integrate service analysis and IS design are still rare, for example a SPITS methodology (Strategic Planning of IT Services) [19]. As more system thinking approaches to service quality are being called for [2, 24], we expect more ideas and concepts to be transferred from IS/software engineering field to service management. Recent developments in business modelling [17] and enterprise modelling [4] are examples of how system analysis methods diffuse into business management domain. It seems also probable that some convergence will occur between IS usability analysis and service usability analysis.

Though services are becoming more knowledge- and information-intensive [20], IS developers often treat service quality as not being within their range of competence. The result will be poor match between service quality models specified by service management specialists and software quality models developed by system analysts.

10 Conclusion

Although this exploratory study has found the correspondence between widespread models of service quality and software quality to be incomplete, both service management and software engineering can benefit by widening and re-interpreting their quality languages.

References

1. Berry L.L. (1984) Services Marketing is Different. In: Lovelock (ed.), Services Marketing. Prentice-Hall.
2. Bitran G., Lojo M. (1993) A Framework for Analyzing the Quality of the Customer Interface. European Management Journal, 11, 4, 385-396.
3. Bitner M.J., Booms B.H., Tetreault M.S. (1990) The Service Encounter: Diagnosing Favorable and Unfavorable Incidents. Journal of Marketing, 54, 1, 71-84.
4. Bubenko J.A. et al (1992) Computer Support for Enterprise Modelling and Requirements Acquisition. Esprit III Project 6612: Deliverable 3-1-3-R 1 Part B.
5. Cavaness J.P., Manoochehri G.H. (1993) Building Quality into Services. SAM Advanced Management Journal, 1, 4-8.
6. Chase R.B., Stewart D.M. (1994) Make Your Service Fail-Safe. Sloan Management Review, 2, 35- 44.
7. Gilmore A., Carson D. (1993) Quality Improvement in a Services Marketing Context. Journal of Services Marketing, 7, 3, 59-71.
8. Grönroos C. (1984) A Service Quality Model and Its Marketing Implications. European Journal of Marketing, 18, 4, 36-44.
9. Grönroos C. (1994) From Scientific Management to Service Management. International Journal of Service Industry Management, 5, 1, 5-20.
10. O'Hara J., Frodey C.A. (1993) A Service Quality Model for Manufacturing. Management Decision, 31, 8, 46-51.
11. Henkoff R. (1994) Service is Everybody's Business. Fortune, June 27.
12. Holmlund M., Kock S. (1992) Quality-based Service as an Establishing Strategy in Business Networks. Working Paper No. 249, Swedish School of Economics and Business Administration, Helsinki.
13. Iacobucci D., Grayson K., Ostrom A. (1994) Customer Satisfaction Fables. Sloan Management Review, 2, 93-96.
14. IEEE (1992) Standard for a Software Quality Metrics Methodology. IEEE Std 1061-1992. Institute of Electrical and Electronics Engineers.
15. Iivari J., Koskela E. (1987) The PIOCO Model for Information Systems Design. MIS Quarterly, 401-419.
16. ISO (1988). ISO/IEC JTC1/SC7/WG3. Software Quality Evaluation. Software Quality Metrics. Working document. International Standardization Organization.
17. Jacobson I., Ericsson M., Jacobson A. (1995) The Object Advantage. Addison-Wesley.

18. Kankkunen K. (1993) Broadening the Concept of Quality: a Systems Model of Quality and Stakeholder Satisfaction. PhD Diss. Tampere University of Techology, Finland.

19. Leppanen M., Lyytinen K., Halttunen V. (1992) Tietojenkasittelystrategian maarittely. Strateginen tietohallintopalveluiden kehittamismenetelma (SPITS). University of Jyvaskyla, Finland.

20. Mattsson J. (1994) Improving Service Quality in Person-to-Person Encounters: Integrating Findings from a Multi-disciplinary Review. The Service Industries Journal, 14, 1, 45-61.

21. Ouellette L.P. (1994) A Formula for IS Service. Journal of Systems Management. 1, 34-35.

22. Pflaum P.E. (1994) Personal communication.

23. Reeves C.A., Bednar D.A. (1994) Defining Quality: Alternatives and Implications. Academy of Management Review, 19, 3, 419-445.

24. Ronkko, M. (1994) Palvelujen tunnusluvut. Hallinnon tutkimus, 1, 67-71.

25. Snee R.D. (1993) Creating Robust Work Processes. Quality Progress, 2, 37-41.

26. Steenkamp J-B.E. (1990) Conceptual Model of the Quality Perception Process. Journal of Business Research, 21, 309-333.

27. Storbacka K. (1993) Customer Relationship Profitability in Retail Banking. Swedish School of Economics and Business Administration, Helsinki.

28. Watson R.T. et al. (1993) User Satisfaction and Service Quality of the IS Department: Closing the Gaps. Journal of Information Technology, 8, 257-265.

29. Zeithaml V.A., Parasuraman A., Berry L.L. (1990) Delivering Quality Service. Balancing Customer Perceptions and Expectations. The Free Press.

30. Zemke R. (1993) Customer Service as a Performing Art. Training, 3, 40-44.

A Guide for Software Maintenance Evaluation: Experience Report.

Véronique Narat, Arthur Vila

Electricité de France,Direction des Etudes et Recherches
Service Informatique et Mathématiques Appliquées
1, avenue du Général de Gaulle, 92141 Clamart, France.

Abstract. This paper presents an experience report carried out at Electricité de France, the French electrical power company. It shows how applied research activities on the software maintenance problems are set up within a quality and software engineering division. It then particularly focuses on an experience aiming at assisting software maintenance managers to evaluate their maintenance organisation. This experience is based on a guide that provides questions to ask a software maintenance team, and the way to evaluate the answers and conclude about first steps towards maintenance improvement.

1 The Software Engineering Context at Electricité de France

1.1 Activities and people

Electricité de France (EDF) is the French national company that produces, distributes and provides electricity to the whole country. As such, the EDF has to deal with an extensible amount of varied computerized applications: from data processing applications written in Cobol to scientific applications written in Fortran.

The Research and Development Directorate of Electricité de France (EDF-DER) is in charge of numerous software products used to carry out studies in many technical fields, like mechanics, hydraulics, electric transmissions, or other fields of application. The 1500 Research Engineers in charge of these domains are people of great knowledge in their application field, but are scarcely software engineers first. For them, computers and software are tools, and algorithms are firstly translations of equations. Nevertheless, software production is an increasing part of their activity, because of the continuous improvement of mathematical models and because of the moving computer technology.

Most of the codes are long life software, constantly modified to incorporate improved models of the domain they describe. They are usually written in FORTRAN, even if more and more parts of codes are now written in C or C++ programming languages (especially pre-processors and post-processors). These options are consistent with the computers we have, which are mainly CRAY and IBM mainframes, reached through over 1000 Unix workstations interconnected by FDDI and LAN networks.

1.2 Overview of the Quality and Software Engineering Team

Software Engineering has been a concern for many years at EDF-DER, and a specific team (the Quality and Software Engineering Team) of 13 is in charge of theoritical and practical software engineering related problems. Their role is not to impose software engineering techniques, ideas or tools but rather to assist, give advice and propose solutions to software engineering problems. EDF engineers may ask assistance to the QSE team but they may also ask to other experts inside or outside the company.

In order to be competitive in front of these other experts, QSE has divided its main activities in two parts:
• assistance on projects, either on methodological or on technical aspects,
• theoritical studies based on state-of-the-art issues that have to be adapted to EDF's specific problems.

The four domains in which the Quality and Software Engineering Team is currently working are the following:
• Quality Assurance domain, where the QA manual of EDF-DER is produced as well as guides for the assistance on QA problems and lectures on the subject; and where software code and projects audits are done on request, on the QA point of view.
• Software Development domain, where a CASE tool dedicated to Fortran projects and supporting a methodological approach is provided to projects under development. Lectures on software engineering subjects are also given.
• Information System domain, where a strong support on project organisation and on the analysis and design phases is given and theoritical studies on object-oriented analysis methods are in progress.
• Software maintenance domain, where the problems related to software evolutions are studied, especially on a methodological point of view, in close relationship with the QA and software development domains.

2. The software maintenance group setting-up

Within the QSE team, the software maintenance group is the youngest; it started four years ago, this means that software maintenance has been recently considered as an issue to be studied on its own at EDF-DER. Due to the large number of problems the subject covers and the limited resources we have to carry out these problems, we decided first to analyse the main requirements of EDF-DER in software maintenance of scientific applications, in order to decide the priority domains to work on.

2.1 Requirement analysis phase

Two different ways of working on the requirement analysis phase have been investigated: prototype design and interviews or questionnaires campaign.

We built small tool prototypes with the help of colleagues who agreed to be more involved, in order to highlight specific needs that were not met by market tools and also to demonstrate feasability or difficulty of some of the requirements. This experience showed first the difficulty to provide tools which meet specific needs, but also the necessity to provide such tools in order to establish a dialog between software maintainers and QSE. Talking about a tool is more attractive than just talking in theory and it gives a basis to understand each other.

In parallel, we also sent questionnaires to a large number of project maintainers. These questionnaires covered several aspects of software maintenance: organisation (definition of the roles within the project), method (which method was used during the development, is it still in use), tool (which tools are used), programming rules (do they exist, are they described formally), documentation (which documentation is maintained and how). After a first questionnaire analysis step, we refined this analysis by interviews when necessary, with people who agreed to spend half a day to answer specific questions.

2.2 The software maintenance domains studied

These two ways of defining the software maintenance requirements in a scientific domain led to the exhibition of four main domains to investigate in priority:
1• software maintenance tools,
2• software maintenance documentation,
3• maintenance of software developement methods and tools used,
4• software maintenance organisation.
    Following these results, four studies began, each of which dealing with one of those points.
• The first study aims at knowing software maintenance tools, from debuggers to configuration management tools, with a particular attention put on code comprehension tools.
• The second point we are working on concerns the identification of the useful software maintenance documentation.
• The third point is strongly connected to the work done by the software development group into QSE and consists in showing how a CASE tool used during development evolves in maintenance.
• The last point comes from the observation that many software maintenance projects suffer from a lack of organisation. It is usually rather easy to come to this conclusion but more difficult to find the way to cure the situation. Our first work is then to provide ways to find where to put efforts on first improvements. Our approach is described in chapter 3.

3. An approach for software maintenance organisation evaluation

3.1. What are the kind of problems within a software maintenance organisation?

Often time, when all the actors of a project agree to blame its maintenance, no one points out the same responsible cause. If customers tend to claim for quicker fixing and constant evolutions, maintainers incriminate both their managers who seem not to realise the actual technical problems, and the customers who never know what they want, or always want more. Managers who have to balance between customers complaints and detailed technical argumentations from their team must become a referee without always knowing the rules of the game they are all playing. In order to clarify this kind of situation, our approach is supposed to help the project manager analyse the situation by giving him an overview of everyone's point of view.

3.2. The approach

General description: The approach we took is based on the idea that during the software maintenance phase of a project, problems encountered can generally be divided into three classes:
• communication problems,
• techniques problems,
• strategic problems.

Communication problems occur when the role of each actor is not clearly identified. Our approach gives a framework to show the information flow between all the actors.

Techniques problems are due to shortcomings in the maintenance structure. The approach helps settle technical answers to these problems.

Finally, having a better idea of how strategic the project is will assist the decision making on the project maintenance.

The process: Our approach aims at analysing the main class of problems on a project, in order to find what to improve first. It is based on a three-steps process, composed of a questionnaire and a guide to analyse the answers, as described in figure1.

The analysis is supposed to be carried out by the manager of the project currently being maintained. In the first step, the manager sends the questionnaire to all the actors of the maintenance. In the second step, all the answers are collected and analysed with the help of our guide. Finally, a diagnosis is made on the first way where efforts should be put to improve the maintenance.

• *The questionnaire*
The questionnaire (see appendix A) is deliberately short, to be quickly answered. It is divided into three parts of five questions each, corresponding to the three topics (communication, techniques, strategy) we address. It is sent to all the actors of the maintenance in order to be able to evaluate whether the information circulates correctly between them. In some specific cases, let to the evaluation leader's appreciation, interviews can be made rather than a questionnaire mailing.

• *The answers analysis*
The answers are then analysed with the help of our guide. The first action consists in considering whether all the roles of the maintenance are clearly identified. For this purpose the information flow of the project is drawn with the given answers of the first five questions. The information flow is then compared to the "correct" (in theory) information flow as shown figure 2. In this theoritical model, all the roles played in a maintenance process are exhibited. Several roles can be played by a single actor but the roles must be clearly identified. Comparing the model of the project and the theoritical model allows to exhibit missing role identification, and then correct communication problems.

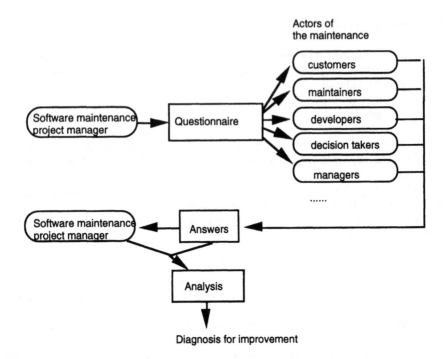

Fig. 1. The process set up in the approach

This first step allows to display a taxonomy of all the maintenance actors. Every actor can be put in a certain class corresponding to a role, and then answers can be gathered by roles, to facilitate their evaluation.

The second step of the analysis is made with an evaluation grid (see example on appendix B), which allows to sort the answers. At the end of this step, the main tendancy of the problems encountered is given and a diagnosis and solutions can be considered.

• *Diagnosis and solutions for improvement*

For each class of problems (communication, techniques, strategy) general solutions for improvement are given. Roughly, three types of solutions are given:
- If a communication problem has been detected, an organisation identifying clearly each one's role must be set up formally. It is important to point up at this step that all the roles identified in figure 2 must be clearly fulfilled by a person. Even though an actor may have several roles, this person must realise that he/she plays several roles and must behave in accordance with his/her role.
- For technical problems, tools must be used, documentation written, and the organisation formally described, by following software engineering rules.
- If the analysis showed up that the software is not strategic for the company, efforts must be put on organisation and in finding replacement solutions. Moreover, it is devoted to the maintenance manager in that case, to find ways of motivation for the maintenance team. Motivation can obviously come from a deep involvement but also

by a new expertise acquisition. Choosing to use a new tool at this stage may be an efficient mean of remotivating people.

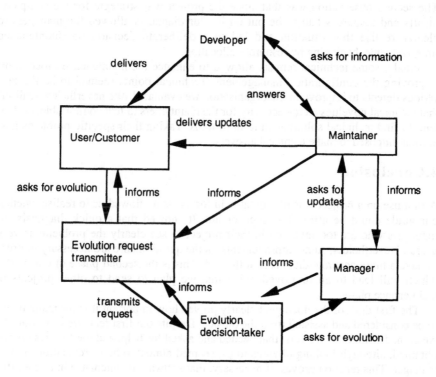

Fig.2. Information flow between maintenance roles

Application on a project

This guide has been experimented on a project currently being maintained by a team of 7, for 15 years and which will not be replaced by the year 2000.

As it was the first experiment, the evaluation has been carried out by the maintenance group of the QSE team and not by the maintenance project manager.

We asked the manager a list of the people involved in the maintenance process. He provided us with a list of 25, composed of developers, customers (including evolution request transmitter and evolution decision-taker) and maintainers. We first sent the questionnaires but we also decided to go interview the maintainers, who wished to have opportunity to talk about their job. On a total amount of 25 questionnaires, we collected 15 answers.

The first observation that was made concerned the communication within the project. The evaluation pointed out that some roles were not clearly identified. It did not mean that the first questions were answered by "I don't know", but it emphasized differences between the answers. In fact, decision-taking roles were sometimes given to different people and this situation led to conflicts. A first way of improvements consisted then to formally describe the organisation to put in place. Once described, the organisation had to be supported by making everyone aware of roles and people within the project. The main success factor for this first improvement is a strong involvement of hierarchical management, who must formally define everyone's task.

The second observation was that since the project was strategic for the company, efforts and resources had to be put on it. Our diagnosis allowed the managers to clearly realise this situation and led to a deliberate decision on maintenance improvements, beginning by resources allocation.

Finaly, some technical remaks allowed to enhance the maintenance process, by improving the configuration management. Technical points seemed to be the less serious defects to improve in the organisation we evaluated. We nevertheless realised that technical novelties were necessary for the maintainers to feel comfortable, as they tend to find technical solutions in term of tools. Taking their specific problems into account imposed to make technical answers.

4.Conclusion

A first use on a project was of a great help for us, as it allowed us to realise whether our guide could be utilised as such or not. It showed that a quick diagnosis for managers who are too involved in their project to see clearly the problems is very useful. Nevertheless, some improvements on the questionnaire are necessary in order to have a more accurate diagnosis at the end. This is the second phase of our work , which will lead to an improved guide that we plan to send to other projects in maintenance phase.

The first draft of the document clearly proved how important it is for maintainers to be considered and assisted from the outside. Despite our first fear, we were warmly welcomed within the projects, that needed and asked for help, and the first results we obtained, although looking obvious to us, seemed almost to be a "revelation" to the manager. This reaction proves, if necessary, that software maintenance in a scientific domain, is more than ever a subject to work on, with a need of concrete help to provide to projects.

Appendix A : the questionnaire

Maintenance of the project:	Date: .. / .. / ..
Name Role in the project	
C1: Who did develop the code?	
C2: Who does use the code?	
C3: Who does ask for evolution?	
C4: Who does make it evolve?	
C5: Who does decide for evolution?	
T1: Where is the code located?	
T2: Where is the documentation located?	
T3: How is the project history managed?	
T4: How are the correction requests managed?	
T5: Does it exist a culture (programming rules...) within the project?	
S1: Is the code strategic for the company?	
S2: What is the life expectancy of the code?	
S3: Where is the "know-how" in the code?	
S4: Who must control this "know-how"?	
S5: Is there any marketing plan for this code?	

Appendix B: Examples of evaluation grid

General observation on the answers

Evaluation criterion	Is there a general agreement on the answers?
Observation	Yes
Possible interpretations	A general agreement may mean that the maintenance organisation is satisfactory with a good information flow It may also mean that the project is small enough for th eproject to be managed only by one or two people with no problems. A common and strong culture within the project can also lead to identical answers. Finally, giving the questionnaire to too few people with the same kind of roles may lead to an identity in the answers.
Observation	No
Possible interpretations	There are answers but they are different or there is sometimes no answers. Sometimes, an absence of answer may be admitted. In such case, see the evaluation grid for each specific question. Differences in the answers may be a problem because it could come from "incorrect" knowledge of some of the actors. It could also point out a lack of communication between the different classes of actors.

Particular observation on question T4 asked to a user/customer

Evaluation criterion	Is there an answer?
Observation	No
Possible interpretations	There is no formal process for problem report, evolution request,...
Observation	Yes
Possible interpretations	Answers should be compared to answers from other classes of actors in order to see if the process is the same for everyone.

Natural Naming in Software Development: Feedback from Practitioners

Kari Laitinen

VTT Electronics / Embedded Software
P.O. Box 1100, 90571 Oulu, Finland

Abstract. During a five-year period several groups of software developers have been educated on using natural naming in software development. Generally, natural naming means avoiding abbreviations. In programming it means that program elements such as variables, tables, constants, and functions should be named using whole natural words and grammatical rules of a natural language. To assess the usefulness of natural naming and the importance of naming in general, we have requested the opinions of 52 software developers who have participated in naming courses or to whom a naming handbook has been introduced. The subjects had to judge the relevancy of 25 statements related to naming. The results of the inquiry indicate that most software developers, and especially the experienced ones, consider that natural naming facilitates their work.

1 Introduction

People need to write, read, and understand different kinds of documents in software development work. Documents are equally important in the development of information systems as well as in the development of less-traditional software systems, such as telecommunications systems and embedded computer systems. Software development can, in fact, be regarded as a documentation process during which more and more elaborate documents emerge as the work proceeds [11]. Typically, some sorts of requirements descriptions are produced first. They are followed by design documents and implementation documents from which an executable software system can be generated. Some software documents may be written according to some development methods (e.g. [1, 20]). Implementation documents can be source programs or other descriptions which can be processed with computer tools (e.g. compilers or application generators).

Software development is partly a learning and communication process [3]. Documents are important in communication and thereby the understandability of software documents affects the efficiency of software development work. Usually, the least understandable software documents are the implementation documents which need to describe all the details of the system being developed and which are, in most cases, source programs.

The use of different kinds of abbreviations (e.g. acronyms and shortened words) is common in software documentation and in the world of computers in general. The use of abbreviations has been, and still is, especially popular in source programs as names for different program elements such as variables, constants, and procedures. One reason for this is that, unlike modern tools, early software development tools allowed only short names. Our concern is, however, that the overuse of abbreviations makes source programs and other documents difficult to understand, which is harmful in software development and maintenance.

As source programs are the most contaminated with abbreviations and they are developed and maintained in many software development organizations, we will study the problems related to abbreviations in the context of source programs. To avoid abbreviations, a principle called natural naming has been proposed [8, 9, 10]. Natural naming means that all names in source programs should be constructed using, preferably several, natural words of a natural language while respecting the grammatical rules of the natural language. The natural names should also describe the functionality of the program. By using natural names it is possible to bring source programs symbolically closer to other types of software documents which contain written words of a natural language. Because natural naming can be applied to many types of software documents, the idea is an important issue in software documentation.

Intuitively, a natural name like "customer_number" is more understandable than an abbreviated name like "cnumbr" or "cn". Also, naturally named programs seem to be much more understandable than the same programs written with abbreviated names (see Fig. 1). It has not, however, been fully proven that natural naming is always an appropriate principle in software documentation. We need more experience and evidence about natural naming. In this paper we will present and analyze practitioners' opinions about natural naming. During the last five years we have given several courses on natural naming and also delivered naming handbooks in software development organizations. The practitioners' opinions have been collected by asking them to answer a questionnaire about natural naming.

We believe that asking software developers' opinions on the use of natural naming is a relevant research method. We will justify this belief in the second section in which we discuss related work which deals with naming. In the third section we will explain what we have taught to software developers and how they were questioned. In the fourth section we analyze the feedback received from the people involved.

2 Related Work

Empirical understandability tests have been carried out to find out how people understand source programs. Tests related to naming are reported in [2, 15, 16, 17, 18]. The effect of naming has usually been tested by presenting a badly named source program to a group of students and the same program with more informative names to another group of students. The performance of the student groups has been measured by asking questions about the programs or by asking the students to modify the programs. The reported understandability tests have not, however, always produced

```
#define    C0001      13
#define    C0002      0
#define    C0003      1
/*-------------------------------------*/

f0001 ( char  s0001 [],
        int   *i0001 )

/*-------------------------------------*/
{
    int  i0002,  i0003 ;

    *i0001 = C0002 ;

    i0003 = strlen ( s0001 ) ;

    if ( i0003 > C0001 )
    {
        *i0001 = C0003 ;
    }
    else
    {
        for (i0002=0; i0002<i0003; i0002++)
        {
            if(( s0001[ i0002] < '0') ||
               ( s0001[ i0002] > '9') )
            {
                *i0001 = C0003 ;
            }
        }
    }
}
```

Version (a): Numerical names

```
#define    CNUMMAX    13
#define    VALID      0
#define    NVALID     1
/*-------------------------------------*/

isvalid ( char  cnumbr [],
          int   *rcode )

/*-------------------------------------*/
{
    int  i,  len ;

    *rcode = VALID ;

    len = strlen ( cnumbr ) ;

    if ( len > CNUMMAX )
    {
        *rcode = NVALID ;
    }
    else
    {
        for ( i=0 ; i<len ; i++ )
        {
            if (( cnumbr[ i] < '0') ||
               ( cnumbr[ i] > '9') )
            {
                *rcode = NVALID ;
            }
        }
    }
}
```

Version (b): Abbreviated names

```
#define    MAXIMUM_CUSTOMER_NUMBER_LENGTH      13
#define    CUSTOMER_NUMBER_IS_VALID            0
#define    CUSTOMER_NUMBER_IS_NOT_VALID        1

/*----------------------------------------------------------------------*/

check_customer_number_validity ( char  possibly_valid_customer_number [],

                                 int  *success_code )

/*----------------------------------------------------------------------*/
{
    int   customer_number_index,   customer_number_length ;

    *success_code = CUSTOMER_NUMBER_IS_VALID ;

    customer_number_length = strlen ( possibly_valid_customer_number ) ;

    if ( customer_number_length > MAXIMUM_CUSTOMER_NUMBER_LENGTH )
    {
        *success_code = CUSTOMER_NUMBER_IS_NOT_VALID ;
    }
    else
    {
        for (  customer_number_index  =  0  ;
               customer_number_index  <  customer_number_length ;
               customer_number_index  ++    )
        {
            if(( possibly_valid_customer_number[ customer_number_index] < '0') ||
               ( possibly_valid_customer_number[ customer_number_index] > '9') )
            {
                *success_code = CUSTOMER_NUMBER_IS_NOT_VALID ;
            }
        }
    }
}
```

Version (c): Natural Names

Fig. 1. Differently written versions of the same source program

statistically significant results, although the performance of the subjects has usually been better with source programs containing clearer names.

It is hard to test how names affect understandability, because it is difficult to judge how much meaning there is in a name. Different people may interpret the same names in a different manner [13]. In the context of the mentioned understandability tests the term "mnemonic name" is used, whereas we speak about natural names. Weissman [18] has used one to three words long natural names in his tests, but Curtis et al. [2], for instance, have used mnemonic names in Fortran programs. Because Fortran has traditionally had the six-character restriction in name lengths, Curtis et al. could not use very long natural names. That may be one reason why they did not find any differences in performance when different kinds of names were used. We would also like to point out that the term "mnemonic" is not very accurate. It has been used to denote instructions of assembler languages (e.g. [6]). In these cases, "mnemonic" means abbreviations such as MOV, STA, and LDA. To make a distinction between mnemonic names and natural names, let us study the following names which could all represent the same variable:

(1)   n
(2)   nbytes
(3)   bytes
(4)   byte_count
(5)   number_of_bytes
(6)   number_of_bytes_in_buffer

Since we recommend that a natural name should contain more than one word, only names (4), (5), and (6) above can be considered natural, whereas all of them excluding name (1), could be considered mnemonic. By studying the examples above, we can also notice that natural names can usually be constructed in many ways.

Because understandability tests have not produced statistically significant data, we can say that the effect of naming is difficult to measure. We can find support to this statement in other scientific fields. Natural naming is using a natural language to describe how programs work. Therefore, studying naming in software documentation is related to linguistics. Linguists admit that natural languages are complex and they are not yet fully understood [4]. The complexity of natural languages can thus be one reason why the effects of natural naming are so hard to measure in the context of software documentation. Because natural languages change all the time, even the concept "natural word" is vague. Thereby the definition for natural naming is vague. New words emerge in natural languages and even some abbreviations can be considered belonging to natural languages. Philosophers have also studied meanings of natural words and other symbols. Famous philosophical studies related to languages have been done by Wittgenstein. He was, however, dissatisfied with his work, possibly because he did not find any clear and conclusive theories to explain languages and how they relate to the real world [19].

Despite the fact that naming seems to be a hard research subject the following facts appear to support the use of natural naming in software documentation:

- The use of abbreviations has been criticized in other contexts of technical documentation [5, 12].
- Natural names are generally used in graphic-textual descriptions of software development methods (e.g. [1, 20]). We can assume that natural naming is one reason why graphic-textual descriptions are considered useful in software development.
- Some software development methods (e.g. [14, 20]) recommend the use of so-called pseudo coding which means describing programs with a language that is somewhere in between a natural language and a programming language. The use of natural naming brings source programs closer to natural language.

To summarize the discussion above, we can say that we already have evidence about the usefulness of natural naming, but more evidence is needed. For this reason, we have surveyed the opinions of people who are engaged in practical software development work. Our research approach can be justified by taking into account the fact that practical software development differs a great deal from studying short examples of programs in a classroom. The source programs of practical software systems may, for example, contain about one thousand different names, whereas the number of names in the program examples used in understandability tests can be counted in a few tens. Supposing that the mentioned understandability tests had produced statistically significant data in support of natural naming, we could still not be completely sure that natural naming would be useful in practical software development work, because the experiments were done during a short period of time and with students. Supposing also that experiments in a classroom would never produce any significant data, it could still be possible that natural naming would be useful in practical work [17]. Because it is hard to do controlled experiments in which we could compare two different groups building the same real software system using different naming styles, we have to rely on the opinions and intuitions of people.

3 Practical Arrangements

3.1 Introduction of a Handbook for Natural Naming

All software developers who participated in this study had been given a naming handbook. The main ideas of the naming handbook are published in [9]. The first version of the naming handbook was introduced about five years ago, and new versions have emerged afterwards. All versions of the handbook include the following:

- a definition for the principle of natural naming;
- a high-level classification of names needed in programs: function names, constant names, and data names;
- rules for constructing different types of names (e.g. function names should have at least two words, and an imperative verb should be used at the beginning of a function name);

- instructions to use so-called name refining words to separate related names;
- name tables that provide low-level classifications of different types of names, suggest certain words to be used, and give some examples of appropriate names; and
- examples of naturally named programs.

3.2 Preparation of Courses on Natural Naming

A typical course on natural naming is a half day session, combined with other instructions on programming style. The courses given to the respondents of our survey involved the introduction of the ideas presented in the naming handbook. The following additional issues were highlighted on every course:

- The use of natural naming was justified by explaining its potential benefits and disadvantages.
- The use of abbreviations was strongly discouraged. Programs were compared with other types of writings in which abbreviations are less common (see Fig. 2).
- Natural naming was considered the easiest way to establish standard naming practices, since, compared to maintaining a list of acceptable abbreviations, nothing needs to be maintained when a pure form of natural naming is applied.

A typical naming course also involved public discussion on specific naming problems in the organization where the participants worked.

In newspapers we use whole English words and very few abbreviations. If newspapers were written like programs they would look like the text below.

In n_paper we use whl Engl wrd and very few abbr. If n_paper were writ like progr they wld lk like this txt.

Fig. 2. A slide used on a naming course

3.3 Naming Questionnaires

The naming-related inquiries were arranged so that all the responding subjects had at least one year to get accustomed to using the natural naming approach. All subjects were familiar with a naming handbook, and some of them had attended a naming course. It should be noted that we did not arrange the courses or develop the naming handbook in order to be able to arrange the inquiries afterwards.

The primary hypothesis for the naming inquiries can be formulated as "Natural naming facilitates the work of software developers". The inquiry form contained 25 statements which were either for or against this primary hypothesis. Each individual statement on the form can be considered an elementary hypothesis for this study (see Table 1). The subjects had to judge the relevancy of each statement by answering "completely disagree", "partially disagree", "no opinion", "partially agree", or "completely agree".

Fifty two software developers filled in and returned the inquiry form. Twelve persons to whom the inquiry form had been sent did not return it. One subject reported being too busy, and perhaps some of the non-reacting respondents did not consider the subject important. The missing responses have not been noted in the statistical calculations in the appendices, although it could have been possible to count them as having "no opinion" on all the statements.

3.4 The Responding Groups

Nearly all of the subjects who responded to the inquiries were using the C programming language in their work, and all had tools that allowed the use of long natural names in programs. All respondents spoke Finnish, but most of them used English to document their programs. At least half of the respondents had a master's level degree from a university. 27 of the respondents work in two telecommunications companies, and the remaining 25 respondents work in a research institute. The experience of the subjects ranges from 2 to 20 years. The subjects represent several application domains: telecommunications systems, real-time embedded systems, various PC and workstation-based software engineering and testing tools, and systems involving artificial intelligence.

4 Analysis of the Responses

Table 1 lists the statements and summarizes the responses. The statements are in the same order as they were presented to the subjects. The third column shows the distribution of the answers in percentages We have used the numeric scale of one to five in order to make a statistical analysis of the responses. According to the scale, 1 means "completely disagree", 2 means "partially disagree", 3 means "no opinion", 4 means "partially agree", and 5 means "completely agree". Some of the statements of the questionnaire are against the use of natural naming. These are marked with a minus (-) sign in Table 1. Correspondingly, plus (+) signs denote those statements which support natural naming.

The rightmost column of Table 1 contains statistical data which has been calculated using the numeric scale. The t-test was used to find out whether the responses can be considered statistically significant. The t-values have been calculated by comparing the responses given to each statement with the responses of an equally large imaginary group which was normally distributed. The respondents of the imaginary comparison group had no opinion on any statement. In this invented comparison group, the distribution over the alternatives from 1 to 5 was 10%, 20%, 40%, 20%, and 10%, respectively. The t-values which are marked with an asterisk (*) indicate statistical significance. When the t-value is more than 2, the likelihood that the mean response does not correspond with reality is less than 5%.

Table 1. Summary of the responses given to the naming questionnaire

	STATEMENT	RESPONSES (%)					+/-	Mean response, standard deviation, and t-value.		
		1	2	3	4	5				
1	The time required to write long names slows down software development.	38	40	3	17	0	-	2.0	1.1	4.65*
2	More and more often, I find myself thinking about appropriate wording for a name needed in a program.	9	9	25	42	13	+	3.4	1.1	1.81
3	In practice, there emerge difficulties when natural names are used.	17	21	17	37	5	-	2.9	1.2	0.33
4	The use of naming guidelines limits the freedom of software development work.	42	40	3	9	3	-	1.9	1.1	4.93*
5	Discussion related to choosing suitable names has increased among my colleagues.	17	21	30	23	7	+	2.8	1.2	0.76
6	Natural naming does not contribute to how easily we can locate the place in a program that we are searching for.	29	35	13	11	9	-	2.4	1.3	2.61*
7	The understandability of the programs written by my colleagues has not improved after the introduction of the naming guidelines.	12	16	52	14	4	-	2.8	1.0	0.89
8	One needs several months to get accustomed to using natural naming in programming.	26	32	17	15	7	-	2.4	1.3	2.37*
9	Because there is such a hurry in projects there is no time to think the understandability of names.	34	40	5	15	3	-	2.1	1.2	3.83*
10	It is difficult to change a naming style one has once adopted.	28	32	9	23	5	-	2.4	1.3	2.34*
11	Commonly used abbreviations, such as i, j, ptr, tbl, and msg should be accepted without exception.	2	15	13	44	25	-	3.8	1.1	3.49*
12	Generally, too little attention is paid on naming.	0	11	11	47	29	+	3.9	0.9	4.60*
13	The natural naming course / the naming handbook really changed my attitudes towards naming.	7	13	30	42	5	+	3.3	1.0	1.18
14	Other programming style factors, such as indentation, uniform use of braces, and uniform order of function arguments, contribute more to the understandability of programs than naming.	0	41	33	25	0	-	2.8	0.8	0.85
15	Nowadays, I always try to use natural naming.	2	13	11	49	23	+	3.8	1.0	3.69*
16	Clearly, during the past couple of years, the names in my colleagues' programs have become longer.	4	4	60	14	16	+	3.4	1.0	1.69
17	Compared to the use of abbreviations or single letters, the use of natural names makes the thinking process of software developers easier.	5	2	9	55	26	+	4.0	1.0	4.63*

Table 1 (continued). Summary of the responses given to the naming questionnaire

	STATEMENT	RESPONSES (%)					+/-	Mean response, standard deviation, and t-value.
		1	2	3	4	5		
18	Trying to invent suitable names is a means for analysing the problem at hand.	2	23	15	32	26	+	3.6 1.2 2.63*
19	It is useful if one can remember the names in programs.	0	4	16	37	41	+	4.2 0.9 5.81*
20	Abbreviated names are easier to remember than natural names.	37	35	16	6	4	–	2.0 1.1 4.32*
21	I am satisfied with my work when I am able to invent descriptive names when writing a program.	6	6	31	45	10	+	3.5 1.0 2.26*
22	It is necessary to pronounce the names in practical work. Natural naming has facilitated the oral communication.	2	9	41	41	5	+	3.4 0.8 2.02*
23	It would be easier to learn information technology and programming, if the program examples used in teaching and literature were naturally named.	3	7	25	36	26	+	3.8 1.1 3.49*
24	With how many fingers do you use the keyboard of your terminal (1 = 2 fingers, 2 = 4 fingers, 3 = 6 fingers, 4 = 8 fingers, and 5 = 10 fingers).	0	25	21	28	25	o	3.5 1.1
25	Being able to type with 10 fingers speeds up software development.	7	11	21	28	30	o	3.6 1.3 2.71*

4.1 General Observations

All the statistically significant responses, excluding statement 11, indicate some kind of positive attitude towards the use of natural naming. Considering all the responses given, we could not find any indication that the use of natural naming was somehow harmful, which would have subsequently made us wary about recommending this naming approach.

Because of the fact that many public names (e.g. library functions and operating system calls) in large software systems are abbreviated, it is unlikely that someone working in a software development group could always use purely natural names. Therefore, instead of asking whether the subjects *use* natural naming, we asked whether they *try* to use natural naming. All the respondents who reported their agreement with the natural naming approach also gave the most positive responses to all the statements.

Clearly, the majority of the respondents agree that too little attention is paid to naming (S12)[1]. This supports the notion that literature provides too little advice on naming. Textbooks on programming and software engineering usually state that descriptive names should be used. However, no instructions are given on how the names can be made descriptive and informative [10].

---

[1]These markings refer to the statements in Table 1.

Although the respondents seem to favor the natural naming approach, they also want to use the traditional and most common abbreviations (S11). Using purely natural names and accepting the commonly used abbreviated variable names, such as i, j, tbl, ptr, and msg, is contradictory. Natural names seem to be favored as global and public names.

4.2 Observations Related to Understanding, Communication, and Thinking

The distribution over the five alternatives is the highest in responses to the statements related to the understandability of programs (S7, S14, and S16) and to communication among software developers (S5 and S22). This shows that the respondents had no clear opinion on these matters. It may also indicate that they do not pay attention on how they communicate with their colleagues or whether programs are understandable. We had anticipated that natural naming would facilitate oral communication. However, there is only minimal evidence that favors this anticipation (S22).

The responses do not clearly indicate whether naming, indentation, or some other programming style factor contributes the most to the understandability of programs (S14). This may mean that it is difficult to make a clear distinction between programming style factors, or that programs are always considered rather hard to understand and, therefore, improvements in understandability are difficult to perceive. Only a minority of the respondents had found that the names in their colleagues' programs have clearly become longer, whereas most of the respondents had no opinion (S16).

Although the communicability of programs was found difficult to judge, most of the respondents agreed that if program examples used in teaching and textbooks were naturally named, learning information technology and programming would be easier (S23). Indeed, programs must be complex reading to those who see them for the first time. If we lessen the complexity by using commonly known words instead of abbreviations, it is obvious that a person unfamiliar with programs is able to perceive something familiar when he or she tries to find out what a program does.

Laitinen and Mukari [10] show that judging the relevancy of names is a means for analyzing the problems of an application domain. It is thus relevant to presume that software developers, at least unconsciously, use naming as a thinking tool. The responses support this presumption (S18). Considering the thinking process during programming, the respondents gave answers that support the use of natural naming (S17, S18, S19, and S20). Generally, abbreviated names were considered more difficult to remember than natural names (S20).

4.3 Observations on Practical Matters

The majority of the respondents see no difficulty in using naming guidelines in their work (S4). In practice, however, the use of natural naming can cause some difficulties. For example, long natural names do not fit so easily on a screen or on a piece of paper, and some software development tools are not able to interpret long names. The respondents had to judge whether the benefits of natural naming exceed the practical inconveniences. Unfortunately, we did not find any significant data about this matter.

Software developers often need to find a certain piece of code in a program module or related pieces of code in several program modules. These kinds of search activities are often carried out during software maintenance. The majority of the respondents consider that the use of natural naming makes the search activities easier (S6). It is rather obvious that searching for natural words is easier than searching for something that symbolically represents a concept of the real world. For example, if a maintenance task is to change the definition and processing of a customer number in a system, it is easier to start searching the names which contain the natural words "customer" or "number," rather than trying to guess what name might represent the customer number.

A complaint sometimes expressed by a participant on a naming course is that natural names are long and too much time is therefore wasted in writing them. However, these are the opinions of a minority, since most of the respondents disagreed with this kind of a statement (S1). The respondents thus seem to consider that the physical writing process is not the activity that takes most of the time needed in implementing a computer program, or they think that the time that is required to write longer names is paid back as the resulting programs can be understood more readily. Although the speed of the physical writing process would not directly affect how quickly programs can be created, software developers do spend a considerable amount of their time operating their computers. Therefore, we also asked how well the respondents are able to type. Although there is great variation in opinions, most of the respondents agree that being able to type with ten fingers indeed speeds up software development (S25).

4.4 Comparing Different Groups of Respondents

As the respondents consisted of different types of people, we made some comparisons between different respondent groups. In the case of individual statements, we did not find very many statistically significant differences between different groups, However, when we compared all the responses of the groups we found some important differences. To compare the general attitude towards natural naming, we first reversed the numeric scale of those statements in Table 1 which are against natural naming, and then compared all the responses of one group to all the responses of another group. Statements 24 and 25 were excluded in these comparisons.

We found out that people with more than 3 years of experience are more enthusiastic about natural naming than less experienced software developers in the same company. In this comparison, the mean response for the less experienced people was 3.4 while the mean for the more experienced people was 3.7. These figures are significantly different with t-value 2.56. When we compared people working in a research institute to those working in commercial companies we found out that people working in companies (mean response 3.6) have a more positive attitude towards natural naming than people working in a research institute (mean response 3.4). The mean responses were significantly different with t-value 3.36.

The fact that the experienced people in companies have especially positive attitudes towards natural naming is an indication of the usefulness of this approach. The respondents represent typical people in the software industry. They work in large projects, need to co-operate intensively, and also carry out software maintenance. The comparison group, software developers in a research institute, do not usually work in large development groups. Some of them develop software only for scientific purposes or occasionally. Maintenance does not usually belong to their duties.

We also made artificial respondent groups by comparing people who completely agreed or disagreed with some statement to the other people who had a different attitude. Generally, people who agree with statements like 15 tend to be more enthusiastic about natural naming than others. We had presumed that skillful typists, the people who responded with 5 to statement 24, would have a more positive attitude towards natural naming than others, but we did not get statistically significant data that would support this presumption.

5 Concluding Discussion

We summarize the most important findings of this study as follows:
- The natural naming approach can be considered useful in software development. We could not find anything that would prevent us from recommending the use of natural naming in practical work.
- Compared to using abbreviations, the respondents believe that using natural names facilitates their thinking process. Trying to invent descriptive names is obviously an important means for problem analysis in software development.
- Experienced software developers in industrial organizations were more enthusiastic about the natural naming approach than less experienced developers or the software developers in a research institute.
- The understandability of programs is hard to assess since the respondents did not give clear opinions whether natural naming facilitates communication or had improved the understandability of source programs.

On the basis of these findings we can say that software development organizations in particular, but also the research community, should focus more attention on naming and on the use of natural languages in software documentation. Although more or less official naming rules exist in many industrial software development organizations, naming is still often a matter of a programmer's personal taste and style. Organizations should, however, strive to establish naming rules, as accurate as possible, in order to standardize their programming practices. We recommend that natural naming principles be favored in the creation of these rules. Naming rules, among other kinds of programming rules, can be conveniently adopted as part of a quality system for software development [7]. When naming rules belong to a quality system, they can be adjusted according to the standard practices of the quality system.

Software development usually involves writing other types of software documents than source programs. All software documents that describe the same system should be understandable and they should not be contradictory. Therefore, it is important that the names used in programs correspond with the textual expressions in other types of software documents. Considering their software documentation practices, software development organizations should try to ensure that they use the same terminology in requirements descriptions, design documents, and source programs. One solution is to maintain standard vocabularies for the application domains in which the organization is involved.

Those engaged in research should, in our opinion, pay more attention to naming as well. Practically every software development method and tool involves the use of a natural language in some form or another. It is possible that naming is a difficult research subject because natural languages are hard subjects. However, we feel that naming and the use of natural languages should be taken into account in research related to information systems and other software systems. It is well known that software development is a difficult process to manage. One reason for this may be that natural languages are used too carelessly in the development process.

Acknowledgments

This work has been funded by the Technical Research Centre of Finland (VTT). The author wishes to thank the people who responded to the naming questionnaires and who helped in delivering and collecting the forms. The anonymous referees of the two versions of this paper have also helped with their comments. Special thanks are due to Mr. Douglas Foxvog, Prof. Pentti Kerola, Ms. Minna Mäkäräinen, Dr. Veikko Seppänen, Ms. Eija Tervonen, and Dr. Matti Weckström.

References

1. P. Coad, E. Yourdon: Object-oriented analysis. Englewood Cliffs, New Jersey: Prentice-Hall 1990

2. B. Curtis, S. B. Sheppard, P. Milliman, M. A. Borst, T. Love: Measuring the psychological complexity of software maintenance tasks with the Halstead and McCabe metrics. IEEE Transactions on Software Engineering 5, 96-104 (1979)

3. B. Curtis, H. Krasner, N. Iscoe: A field study of software design process for large systems. Communications of the ACM 31, 1268-1287 (1988)

4. V. Fromkin, R. Rodman: An introduction to language, fourth edition. New York: Holt, Rinehart, and Winston 1988

5. A. M. Ibrahim: Acronyms observed. IEEE Transactions on Professional Communication 32, 27-28 (1989)

6. Intel: MCS-80/85 family user's manual. Santa Clara, California: Intel 1979

7. ISO 9000-3: Quality management and quality assurance standards - part 3: Guidelines for the application of ISO 9001 to the development, supply, and maintenance of software. Geneva, Switzerland: International Organization for Standardization 1991

8. D. A. Keller: A guide to natural naming. ACM SIGPLAN Notices 25, 5, 95-102 (1990)

9. K. Laitinen, V. Seppänen: Principles for naming program elements, a practical approach to raise informativity of programming. In: Proceedings of InfoJapan'90 international conference, part I. Tokyo: Information Processing Society of Japan 1990, pp. 79-86

10. K. Laitinen, T. Mukari: DNN-Disciplined natural naming, a method for systematic name creation in software development. In: Proceedings of 25th Hawaii international conference on system sciences, Vol. II. Los Alamitos, California: IEEE Computer Society Press 1992, pp. 91-100

11. K. Laitinen: Document classification for software quality systems. ACM SIGSOFT Software Engineering Notes 17, 4, 32-39 (1992)

12. D. Logsdon, T. Logsdon: The curse of the acronym. In: Proceedings of the international professional communications conference. New York: IEEE 1986, pp. 145-152

13. P. R. Newsted: Flowchart-free approach to documentation. Journal of Systems Management 30, 4, 18-21 (1979)

14. M. Page-Jones: The practical guide to structured systems design, second edition. Englewood Cliffs, New Jersey: Prentice Hall 1988

15. S. B. Sheppard, B. Curtis, P. Milliman, T. Love: Modern coding practices and programmer performance. Computer 12, 12, 41-49 (1979)

16. B. Shneiderman: Software psychology, human factors in computer and information systems. Cambridge, Massachusetts: Winthrop Publishers 1980

17. B. E. Teasley: The effects of naming style and expertise on program comprehension. International Journal of Human-Computer Studies 40, 757-770 (1994)

18. L. M. Weissman: A methodology for studying the psychological complexity of computer programs. Ph.D. Thesis. Toronto, Canada: Department of Computer Science, University of Toronto 1974

19. L. Wittgenstein: Philosophical investigations. Oxford, England: Basil Blackwell 1953

20. E. Yourdon: Modern structured analysis. Englewood Cliffs, New Jersey: Prentice-Hall 1989

Springer-Verlag
and the Environment

We at Springer-Verlag firmly believe that an international science publisher has a special obligation to the environment, and our corporate policies consistently reflect this conviction.

We also expect our business partners – paper mills, printers, packaging manufacturers, etc. – to commit themselves to using environmentally friendly materials and production processes.

The paper in this book is made from low- or no-chlorine pulp and is acid free, in conformance with international standards for paper permanency.

Lecture Notes in Computer Science

For information about Vols. 1–857
please contact your bookseller or Springer-Verlag

Vol. 858: E. Bertino, S. Urban (Eds.), Object-Oriented Methodologies and Systems. Proceedings, 1994. X, 386 pages. 1994.

Vol. 859: T. F. Melham, J. Camilleri (Eds.), Higher Order Logic Theorem Proving and Its Applications. Proceedings, 1994. IX, 470 pages. 1994.

Vol. 860: W. L. Zagler, G. Busby, R. R. Wagner (Eds.), Computers for Handicapped Persons. Proceedings, 1994. XX, 625 pages. 1994.

Vol: 861: B. Nebel, L. Dreschler-Fischer (Eds.), KI-94: Advances in Artificial Intelligence. Proceedings, 1994. IX, 401 pages. 1994. (Subseries LNAI).

Vol. 862: R. C. Carrasco, J. Oncina (Eds.), Grammatical Inference and Applications. Proceedings, 1994. VIII, 290 pages. 1994. (Subseries LNAI).

Vol. 863: H. Langmaack, W.-P. de Roever, J. Vytopil (Eds.), Formal Techniques in Real-Time and Fault-Tolerant Systems. Proceedings, 1994. XIV, 787 pages. 1994.

Vol. 864: B. Le Charlier (Ed.), Static Analysis. Proceedings, 1994. XII, 465 pages. 1994.

Vol. 865: T. C. Fogarty (Ed.), Evolutionary Computing. Proceedings, 1994. XII, 332 pages. 1994.

Vol. 866: Y. Davidor, H.-P. Schwefel, R. Männer (Eds.), Parallel Problem Solving from Nature - PPSN III. Proceedings, 1994. XV, 642 pages. 1994.

Vol 867: L. Steels, G. Schreiber, W. Van de Velde (Eds.), A Future for Knowledge Acquisition. Proceedings, 1994. XII, 414 pages. 1994. (Subseries LNAI).

Vol. 868: R. Steinmetz (Ed.), Multimedia: Advanced Teleservices and High-Speed Communication Architectures. Proceedings, 1994. IX, 451 pages. 1994.

Vol. 869: Z. W. Raś, Zemankova (Eds.), Methodologies for Intelligent Systems. Proceedings, 1994. X, 613 pages. 1994. (Subseries LNAI).

Vol. 870: J. S. Greenfield, Distributed Programming Paradigms with Cryptography Applications. XI, 182 pages. 1994.

Vol. 871: J. P. Lee, G. G. Grinstein (Eds.), Database Issues for Data Visualization. Proceedings, 1993. XIV, 229 pages. 1994.

Vol. 872: S Arikawa, K. P. Jantke (Eds.), Algorithmic Learning Theory. Proceedings, 1994. XIV, 575 pages. 1994.

Vol. 873: M. Naftalin, T. Denvir, M. Bertran (Eds.), FME '94: Industrial Benefit of Formal Methods. Proceedings, 1994. XI, 723 pages. 1994.

Vol. 874: A. Borning (Ed.), Principles and Practice of Constraint Programming. Proceedings, 1994. IX, 361 pages. 1994.

Vol. 875: D. Gollmann (Ed.), Computer Security – ESORICS 94. Proceedings, 1994. XI, 469 pages. 1994.

Vol. 876: B. Blumenthal, J. Gornostaev, C. Unger (Eds.), Human-Computer Interaction. Proceedings, 1994. IX, 239 pages. 1994.

Vol. 877: L. M. Adleman, M.-D. Huang (Eds.), Algorithmic Number Theory. Proceedings, 1994. IX, 323 pages. 1994.

Vol. 878: T. Ishida; Parallel, Distributed and Multiagent Production Systems. XVII, 166 pages. 1994. (Subseries LNAI).

Vol. 879: J. Dongarra, J. Waśniewski (Eds.), Parallel Scientific Computing. Proceedings, 1994. XI, 566 pages. 1994.

Vol. 880: P. S. Thiagarajan (Ed.), Foundations of Software Technology and Theoretical Computer Science. Proceedings, 1994. XI, 451 pages. 1994.

Vol. 881: P. Loucopoulos (Ed.), Entity-Relationship Approach – ER'94. Proceedings, 1994. XIII, 579 pages. 1994.

Vol. 882: D. Hutchison, A. Danthine, H. Leopold, G. Coulson (Eds.), Multimedia Transport and Teleservices. Proceedings, 1994. XI, 380 pages. 1994.

Vol. 883: L. Fribourg, F. Turini (Eds.), Logic Program Synthesis and Transformation – Meta-Programming in Logic. Proceedings, 1994. IX, 451 pages. 1994.

Vol. 884: J. Nievergelt, T. Roos, H.-J. Schek, P. Widmayer (Eds.), IGIS '94: Geographic Information Systems. Proceedings, 1994. VIII, 292 pages. 19944.

Vol. 885: R. C. Veltkamp, Closed Objects Boundaries from Scattered Points. VIII, 144 pages. 1994.

Vol. 886: M. M. Veloso, Planning and Learning by Analogical Reasoning. XIII, 181 pages. 1994. (Subseries LNAI).

Vol. 887: M. Toussaint (Ed.), Ada in Europe. Proceedings, 1994. XII, 521 pages. 1994.

Vol. 888: S. A. Andersson (Ed.), Analysis of Dynamical and Cognitive Systems. Proceedings, 1993. VII, 260 pages. 1995.

Vol. 889: H. P. Lubich, Towards a CSCW Framework for Scientific Cooperation in Europe. X, 268 pages. 1995.

Vol. 890: M. J. Wooldridge, N. R. Jennings (Eds.), Intelligent Agents. Proceedings, 1994. VIII, 407 pages. 1995. (Subseries LNAI).

Vol. 891: C. Lewerentz, T. Lindner (Eds.), Formal Development of Reactive Systems. XI, 394 pages. 1995.

Vol. 892: K. Pingali, U. Banerjee, D. Gelernter, A. Nicolau, D. Padua (Eds.), Languages and Compilers for Parallel Computing. Proceedings, 1994. XI, 496 pages. 1995.

Vol. 893: G. Gottlob, M. Y. Vardi (Eds.), Database Theory – ICDT '95. Proceedings, 1995. XI, 454 pages. 1995.

Vol. 894: R. Tamassia, I. G. Tollis (Eds.), Graph Drawing. Proceedings, 1994. X, 471 pages. 1995.

Vol. 895: R. L. Ibrahim (Ed.), Software Engineering Education. Proceedings, 1995. XII, 449 pages. 1995.

Vol. 896: R. N. Taylor, J. Coutaz (Eds.), Software Engineering and Human-Computer Interaction. Proceedings, 1994. X, 281 pages. 1995.

Vol. 897: M. Fisher, R. Owens (Eds.), Executable Modal and Temporal Logics. Proceedings, 1993. VII, 180 pages. 1995. (Subseries LNAI).

Vol. 898: P. Steffens (Ed.), Machine Translation and the Lexicon. Proceedings, 1993. X, 251 pages. 1995. (Subseries LNAI).

Vol. 899: W. Banzhaf, F. H. Eeckman (Eds.), Evolution and Biocomputation. VII, 277 pages. 1995.

Vol. 900: E. W. Mayr, C. Puech (Eds.), STACS 95. Proceedings, 1995. XIII, 654 pages. 1995.

Vol. 901: R. Kumar, T. Kropf (Eds.), Theorem Provers in Circuit Design. Proceedings, 1994. VIII, 303 pages. 1995.

Vol. 902: M. Dezani-Ciancaglini, G. Plotkin (Eds.), Typed Lambda Calculi and Applications. Proceedings, 1995. VIII, 443 pages. 1995.

Vol. 903: E. W. Mayr, G. Schmidt, G. Tinhofer (Eds.), Graph-Theoretic Concepts in Computer Science. Proceedings, 1994. IX, 414 pages. 1995.

Vol. 904: P. Vitányi (Ed.), Computational Learning Theory. EuroCOLT'95. Proceedings, 1995. XVII, 415 pages. 1995. (Subseries LNAI).

Vol. 905: N. Ayache (Ed.), Computer Vision, Virtual Reality and Robotics in Medicine. Proceedings, 1995. XIV, 567 pages. 1995.

Vol. 906: E. Astesiano, G. Reggio, A. Tarlecki (Eds.), Recent Trends in Data Type Specification. Proceedings, 1995. VIII, 523 pages. 1995.

Vol. 907: T. Ito, A. Yonezawa (Eds.), Theory and Practice of Parallel Programming. Proceedings, 1995. VIII, 485 pages. 1995.

Vol. 908: J. R. Rao Extensions of the UNITY Methodology: Compositionality, Fairness and Probability in Parallelism. XI, 178 pages. 1995.

Vol. 909: H. Comon, J.-P. Jouannaud (Eds.), Term Rewriting. Proceedings, 1993. VIII, 221 pages. 1995.

Vol. 910: A. Podelski (Ed.), Constraint Programming: Basics and Trends. Proceedings, 1995. XI, 315 pages. 1995.

Vol. 911: R. Baeza-Yates, E. Goles, P. V. Poblete (Eds.), LATIN '95: Theoretical Informatics. Proceedings, 1995. IX, 525 pages. 1995.

Vol. 912: N. Lavrac, S. Wrobel (Eds.), Machine Learning: ECML – 95. Proceedings, 1995. XI, 370 pages. 1995. (Subseries LNAI).

Vol. 913: W. Schäfer (Ed.), Software Process Technology. Proceedings, 1995. IX, 261 pages. 1995.

Vol. 914: J. Hsiang (Ed.), Rewriting Techniques and Applications. Proceedings, 1995. XII, 473 pages. 1995.

Vol. 915: P. D. Mosses, M. Nielsen, M. I. Schwartzbach (Eds.), TAPSOFT '95: Theory and Practice of Software Development. Proceedings, 1995. XV, 810 pages. 1995.

Vol. 916: N. R. Adam, B. K. Bhargava, Y. Yesha (Eds.), Digital Libraries. Proceedings, 1994. XIII, 321 pages. 1995.

Vol. 917: J. Pieprzyk, R. Safavi-Naini (Eds.), Advances in Cryptology - ASIACRYPT '94. Proceedings, 1994. XII, 431 pages. 1995.

Vol. 918: P. Baumgartner, R. Hähnle, J. Posegga (Eds.), Theorem Proving with Analytic Tableaux and Related Methods. Proceedings, 1995. X, 352 pages. 1995. (Subseries LNAI).

Vol. 919: B. Hertzberger, G. Serazzi (Eds.), High-Performance Computing and Networking. Proceedings, 1995. XXIV, 957 pages. 1995.

Vol. 920: E. Balas, J. Clausen (Eds.), Integer Programming and Combinatorial Optimization. Proceedings, 1995. IX, 436 pages. 1995.

Vol. 921: L. C. Guillou, J.-J. Quisquater (Eds.), Advances in Cryptology – EUROCRYPT '95. Proceedings, 1995. XIV, 417 pages. 1995.

Vol. 923: M. Meyer (Ed.), Constraint Processing. IV, 289 pages. 1995.

Vol. 924: P. Ciancarini, O. Nierstrasz, A. Yonezawa (Eds.), Object-Based Models and Languages for Concurrent Systems. Proceedings, 1994. VII, 193 pages. 1995.

Vol. 925: J. Jeuring, E. Meijer (Eds.), Advanced Functional Programming. Proceedings, 1995. VII, 331 pages. 1995.

Vol. 926: P. Nesi (Ed.), Objective Software Quality. Proceedings, 1995. VIII, 249 pages. 1995.

Vol. 927: J. Dix, L. Moniz Pereira, T. C. Przymusinski (Eds.), Non-Monotonic Extensions of Logic Programming. Proceedings, 1994. IX, 229 pages. 1995. (Subseries LNAI).

Vol. 928: V.W. Marek, A. Nerode, M. Truszczynski (Eds.), Logic Programming and Nonmonotonic Reasoning. Proceedings, 1995. VIII, 417 pages. 1995. (Subseries LNAI).

Vol. 929: F. Morán, A. Moreno, J.J. Merelo, P. Chacón (Eds.), Advances in Artificial Life. Proceedings, 1995. XIII, 960 pages. 1995 (Subseries LNAI).

Vol. 930: J. Mira, F. Sandoval (Eds.), From Natural to Artificial Neural Computation. Proceedings, 1995. XVIII, 1150 pages. 1995.

Vol. 931: P.J. Braspenning, F. Thuijsman, A.J.M.M. Weijters (Eds.), Artificial Neural Networks. IX, 295 pages. 1995.

Vol. 932: J. Iivari, K. Lyytinen, M. Rossi (Eds.), Advanced Information Systems Engineering. Proceedings, 1995. XI, 388 pages. 1995.

Vol. 933: L. Pacholski, J. Tiuryn (Eds.), Computer Science Logic. Proceedings, 1994. IX, 543 pages. 1995.

Vol. 934: P. Barahona, M. Stefanelli, J. Wyatt (Eds.), Artificial Intelligence in Medicine. Proceedings, 1995. XI, 449 pages. 1995. (Subseries LNAI).

Vol. 935: G. De Michelis, M. Diaz (Eds.), Application and Theory of Petri Nets 1995. Proceedings, 1995. VIII, 511 pages. 1995.